ASSASSINATION CLASSROOM

YUSEI MATSUI

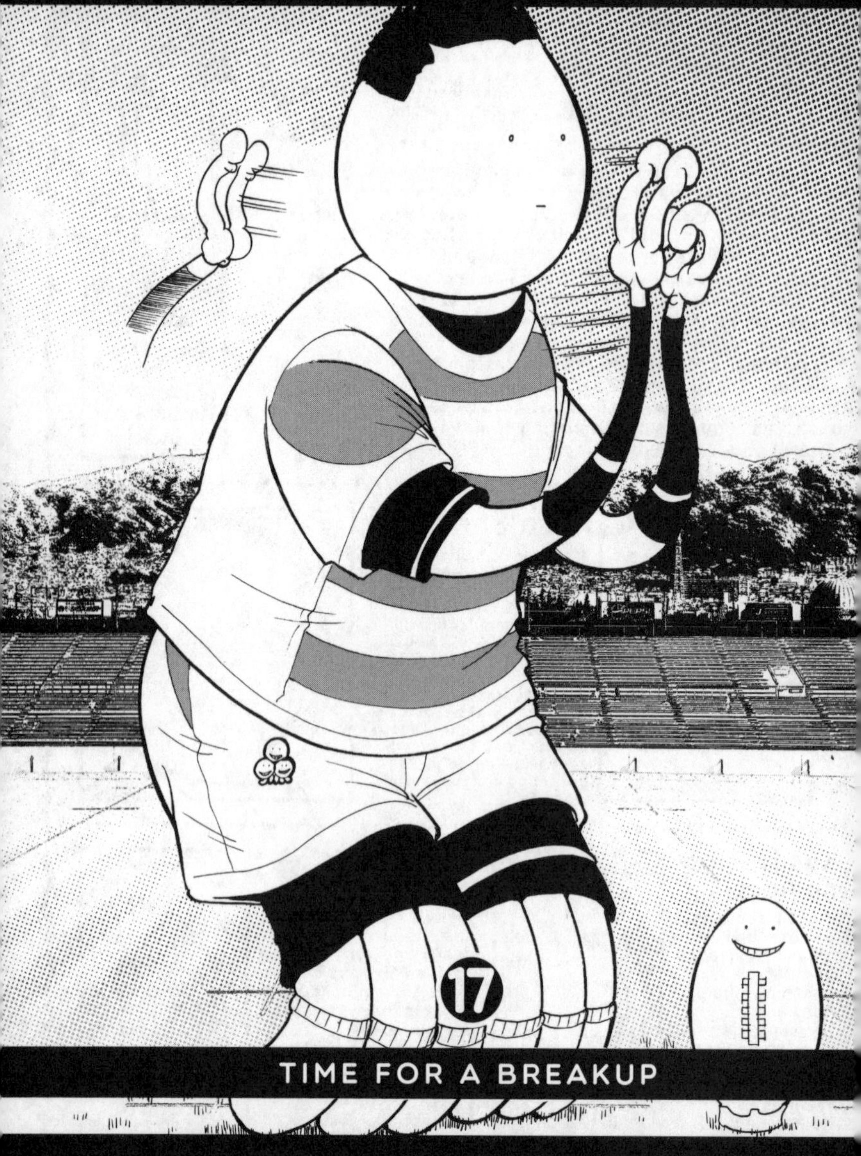

17

TIME FOR A BREAKUP

Koro Tribune

January Issue

Published by: Class 3-E Newspaper Staff

Now that we've learned about Koro Sensei's past, will we still be able to kill him...?!

AFTER GIVING IT A GREAT DEAL OF THOUGHT, THE ANSWER I ARRIVED AT WAS...
...THAT I MUST STAKE MY LIFE ON TEACHING THE ASSASSINATION CLASSROOM.

Story Thus Far

Kunugigaoka Junior High Class 3-E is taught by a monster who even the armies of the world with all their state-of-the-art technology can't kill. That monster, Koro Sensei, is fated to self-destruct and take the planet Earth with him, so...

...a bounty has been placed on his head. It comes down to his students in 3-E, the so-called "End Class." Once looked down upon by the rest of the school, this class of misfits is now respected for the athleticism and focus they have developed thanks to the dedicated instruction of Koro Sensei and Mr. Karasuma of the Ministry of Defense. A strong bond has formed between the students and Koro Sensei, transcending their relationship as assassins and targets, and now that they've learned the truth about Koro Sensei's past, the students are beginning to have doubts about assassinating him...

WITH THESE...
...I'M SURE YOU'LL BECOME...

Who imagined he would have such a bizarre back-story...?

Koro Sensei

A mysterious, man-made, octopus-like creature whose name is a play on the words "koro senai," which means "can't kill." He is capable of flying at Mach 20 and his versatile tentacles protect him from attacks and aid him in everyday activities. He followed in the footsteps of Aguri, the woman who saved his humanity, by becoming the teacher of Class 3-E.

Kaede Kayano

Class E student. She enrolled in Class E to avenge her sister's death by killing Koro Sensei. Her tentacles have since been removed. Does she have special feelings for Nagisa now...?!

Nagisa Shiota

Class E student. He has a hidden talent for assassinations and has decided to hone those skills to help others. He's a good kisser too.

I WANT TO SEARCH FOR A WAY...
...TO SAVE KORO SENSEI'S LIFE.

How did the others react to Nagisa's proposal...?!

pick up!

Kaede Kayano

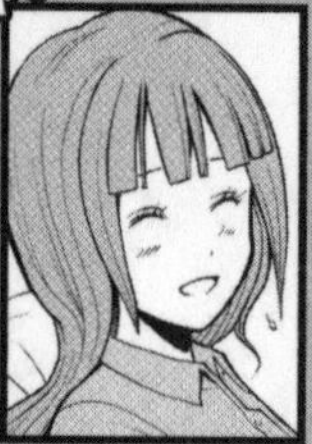

She feels responsible for the doubts her fellow students are having about the assassination. How will all this affect Koro Sensei's fate?

Akabane

Class E student. He learned to take his studies a bit more seriously after some initial failures and earned first place in the overall school scores on the second semester midterm.

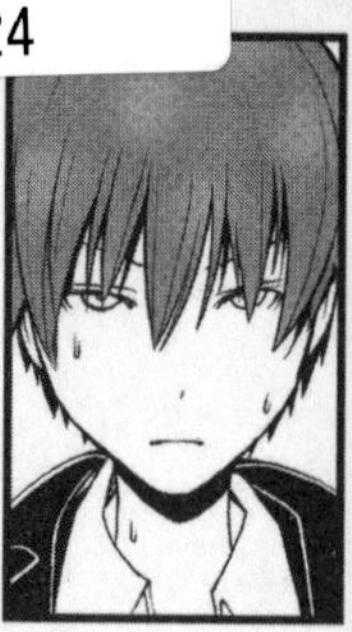

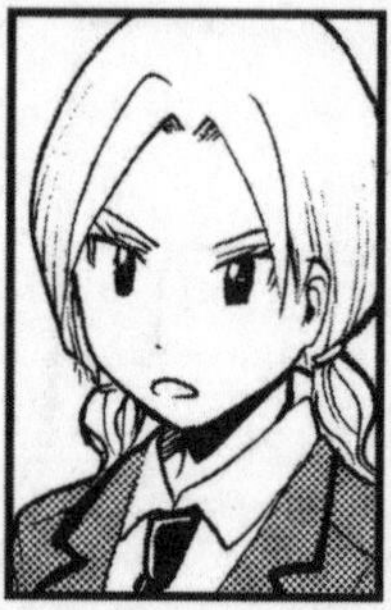

Rinka Hayami

Class E student. She and Chiba are the top snipers of Class E. She has good motion perception and is skilled at shooting moving targets, as well as shooting while in motion herself.

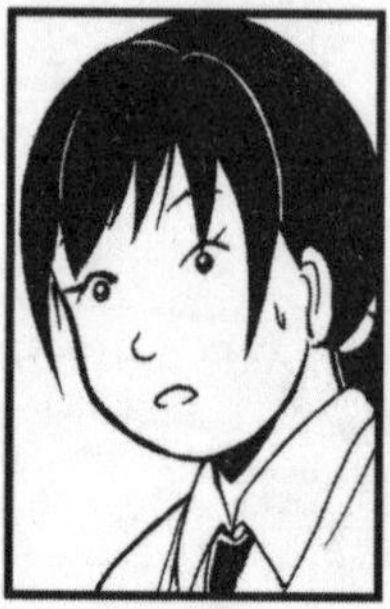

Sumire Hara

Class E student. A maternal figure in Class E, she is skilled at cooking and sewing. Her assassination skills employing bait and traps are the best in the class.

Karma ignored all of our messages over winter break!!

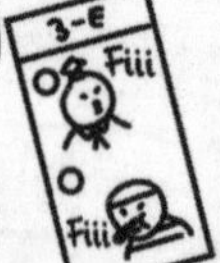
3-E
Fiii
Fiii

Given his personality, he must have been thinking things over on his own. But we were still annoyed, so we texted him a lot of LINE stickers.

Tadaomi Karasuma

Member of the Ministry of Defense and the Class E students' P.E. teacher. Though serious about his duties, he has successfully built good relationships with his students.

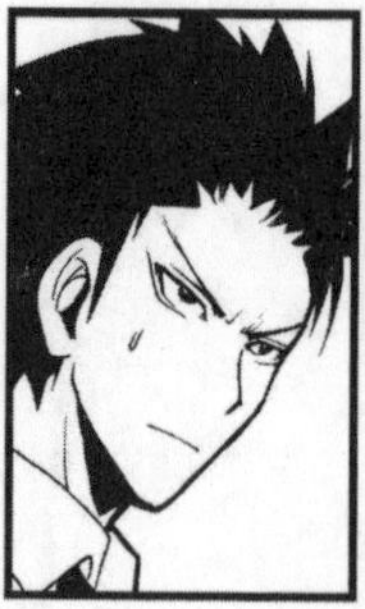

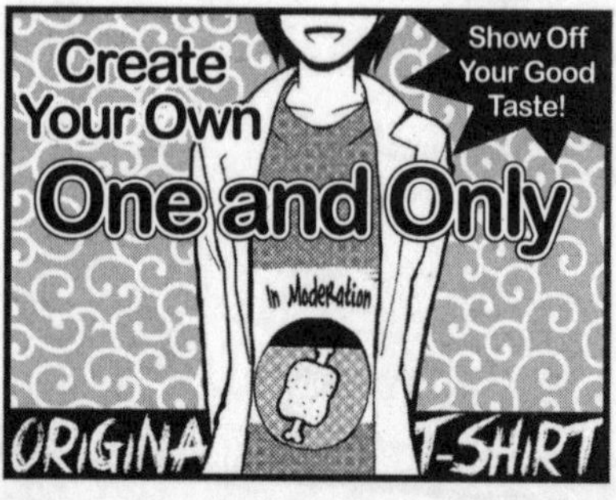
Create Your Own
One and Only
Show Off Your Good Taste!
In Moderation
ORIGINA
T-SHIRT

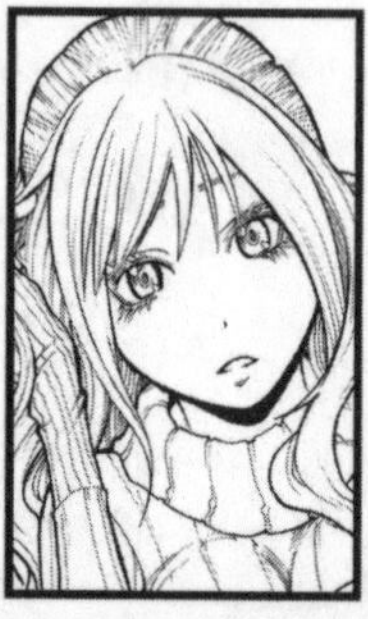

Irina Jelavich

A sexy assassin hired as an English teacher. She's known for using her "womanly charms" to get close to a target, but she's totally hopeless when it comes to flirting with Karasuma.

ASSASSINATION CLASSROOM ⑰ CONTENTS

English Test

(Question 1):
Q1: Choose the most appropriate word from options
(1) through (5) for each question

(1) Nagisa : What's wrong, Hayami?

Hayami : I lost my gun, so I can't sho—

1 badly   2 e—

(2) The—

very—

1 driv—

(3) This m—

1 invite—

(4) Terasal—

he got (—

1 rich

(5) Isogai : H—

Karaoke .—

1 far   2—

Question 2):

2: Translate—

to English (1)—

カルマと知り合—

①Karma   ②—

I ☐—

1 ⑥-①   2 ①—

あなた達はできる—

①your assassina—

You need ☐—

③-⑤   2 ④-

| Grade | 3 | Class | E | Name | CONTENTS | Score | |

CLASS 143 TIME FOR A BREAKUP

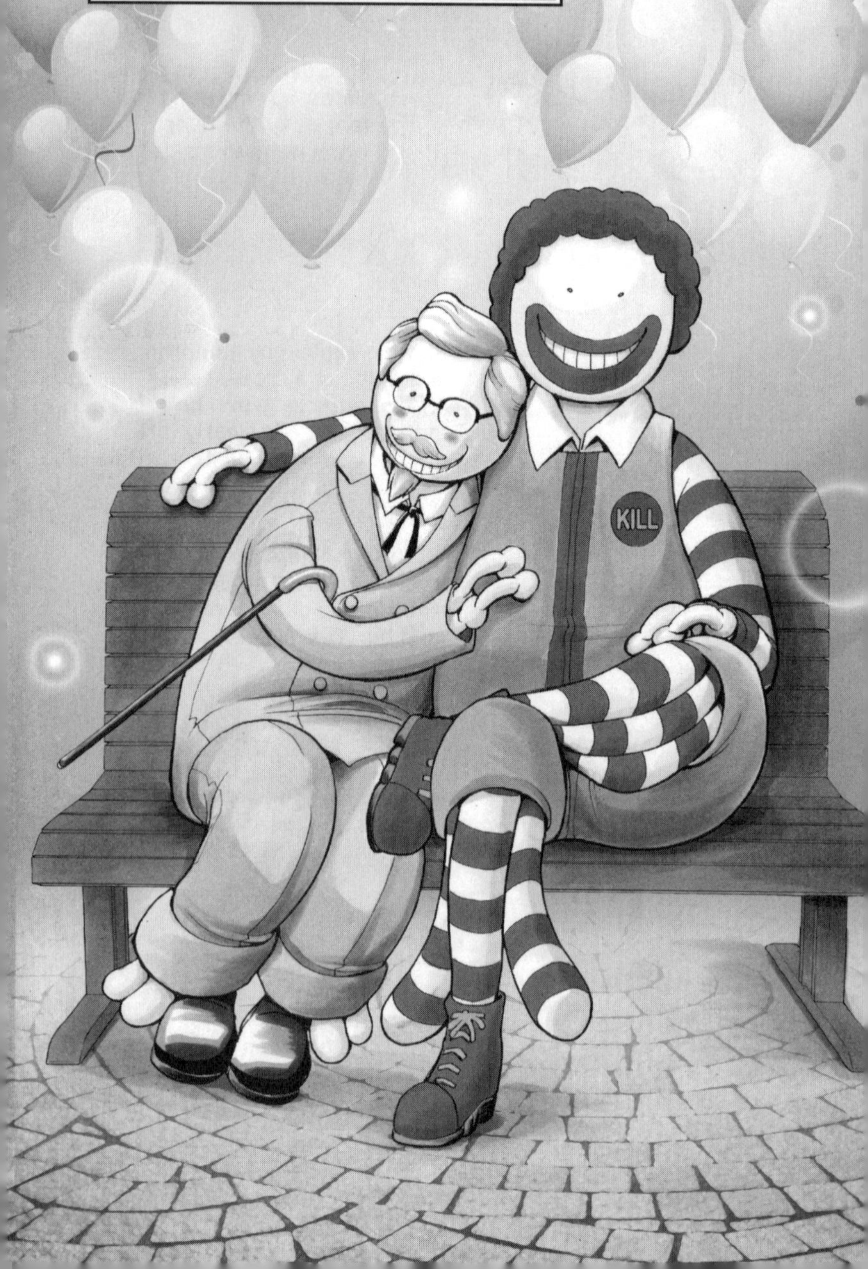
KILL

Koro Sensei's Secrets, Encyclopedia Entry②
−Bare-Tentacled−

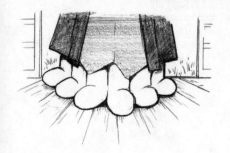

Koro Sensei doesn't wear shoes, so why don't his feet dirty the floor when he goes inside?

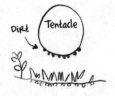

Let me explain by exhibiting a graphic of a cross-section of his tentacle. When he's outside, there is clearly dirt on the bottom of his tentacles.

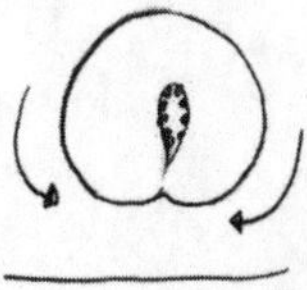

But the moment he enters a room, he folds the dirt into the surface of his tentacle and buries it inside!

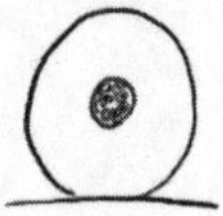

It's just like using a kneaded eraser! The dirt either melts away or gets burned up inside Koro Sensei's body.

And that's how Koro Sensei keeps the surface of his tentacles all clean and slimy!

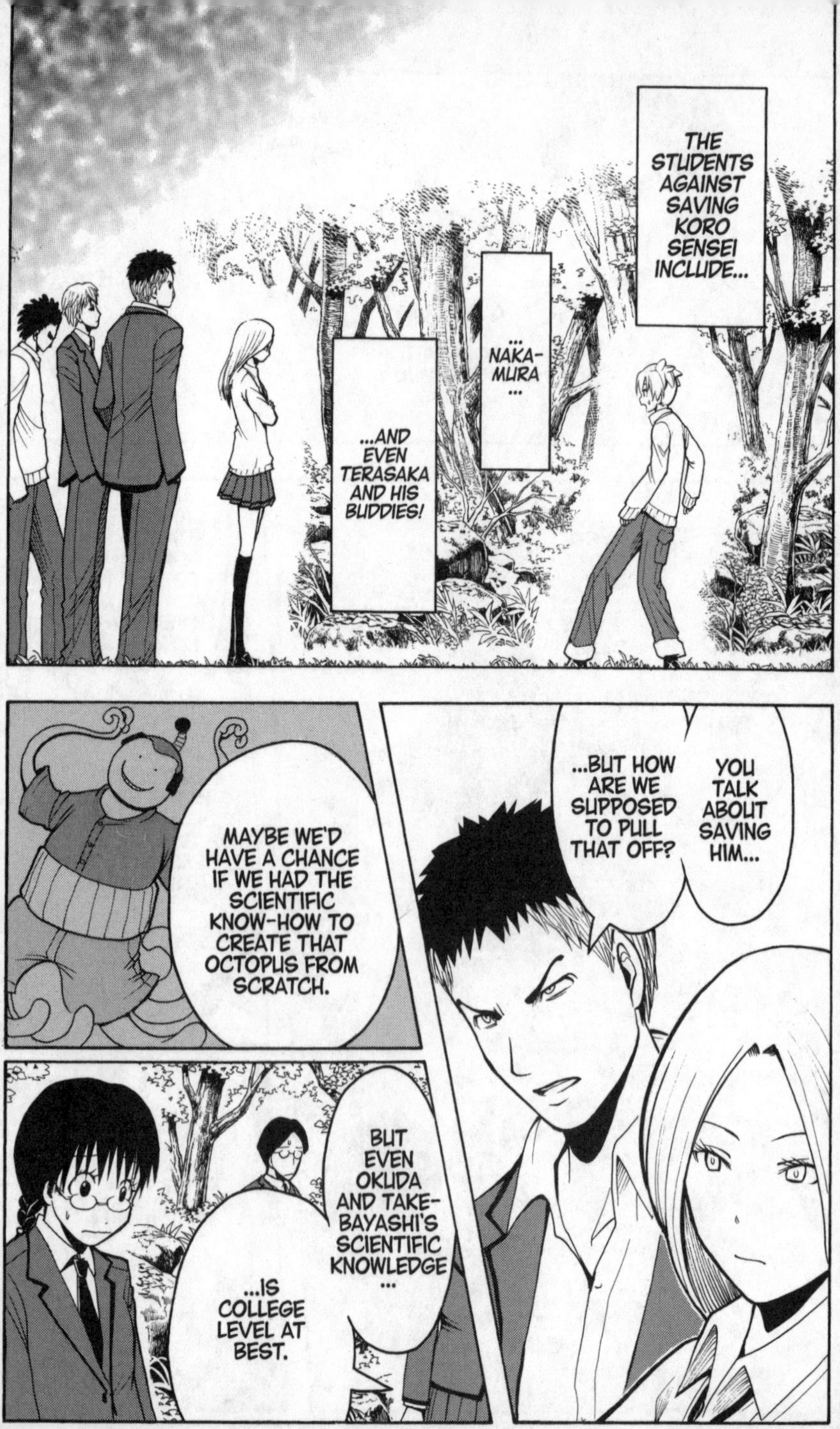
THE STUDENTS AGAINST SAVING KORO SENSEI INCLUDE...
...NAKAMURA...
...AND EVEN TERASAKA AND HIS BUDDIES!
YOU TALK ABOUT SAVING HIM...
...BUT HOW ARE WE SUPPOSED TO PULL THAT OFF?
MAYBE WE'D HAVE A CHANCE IF WE HAD THE SCIENTIFIC KNOW-HOW TO CREATE THAT OCTOPUS FROM SCRATCH.
BUT EVEN OKUDA AND TAKE-BAYASHI'S SCIENTIFIC KNOWLEDGE...
...IS COLLEGE LEVEL AT BEST.

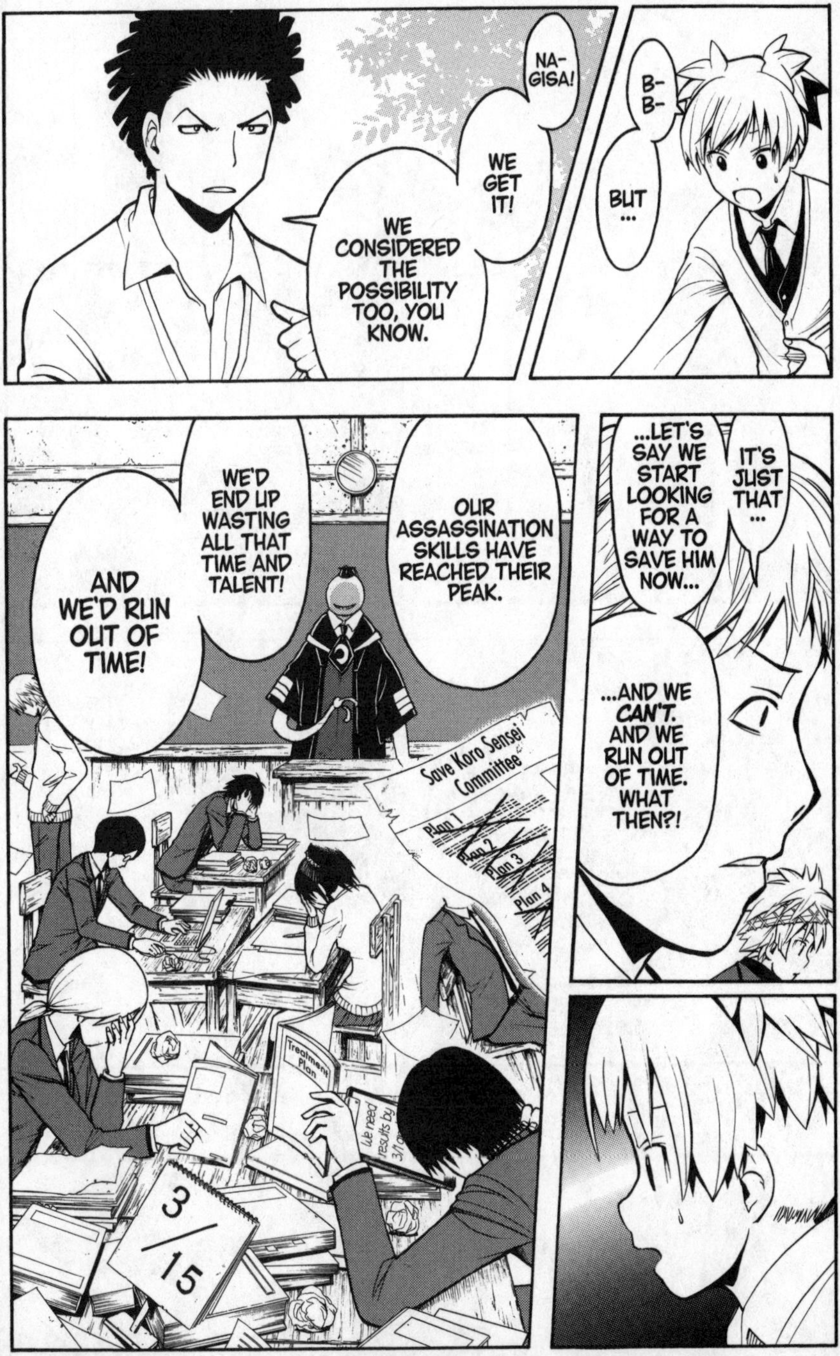
B- B-
BUT ...
NA-GISA!
WE GET IT!
WE CONSIDERED THE POSSIBILITY TOO, YOU KNOW.
IT'S JUST THAT ...
...LET'S SAY WE START LOOKING FOR A WAY TO SAVE HIM NOW...
...AND WE CAN'T. AND WE RUN OUT OF TIME. WHAT THEN?!
OUR ASSASSINATION SKILLS HAVE REACHED THEIR PEAK.
WE'D END UP WASTING ALL THAT TIME AND TALENT!
AND WE'D RUN OUT OF TIME!
Save Koro Sensei Committee
Plan 1
Plan 2
Plan 3
Plan 4
Treatment Plan
We need results by 3/1
3/15

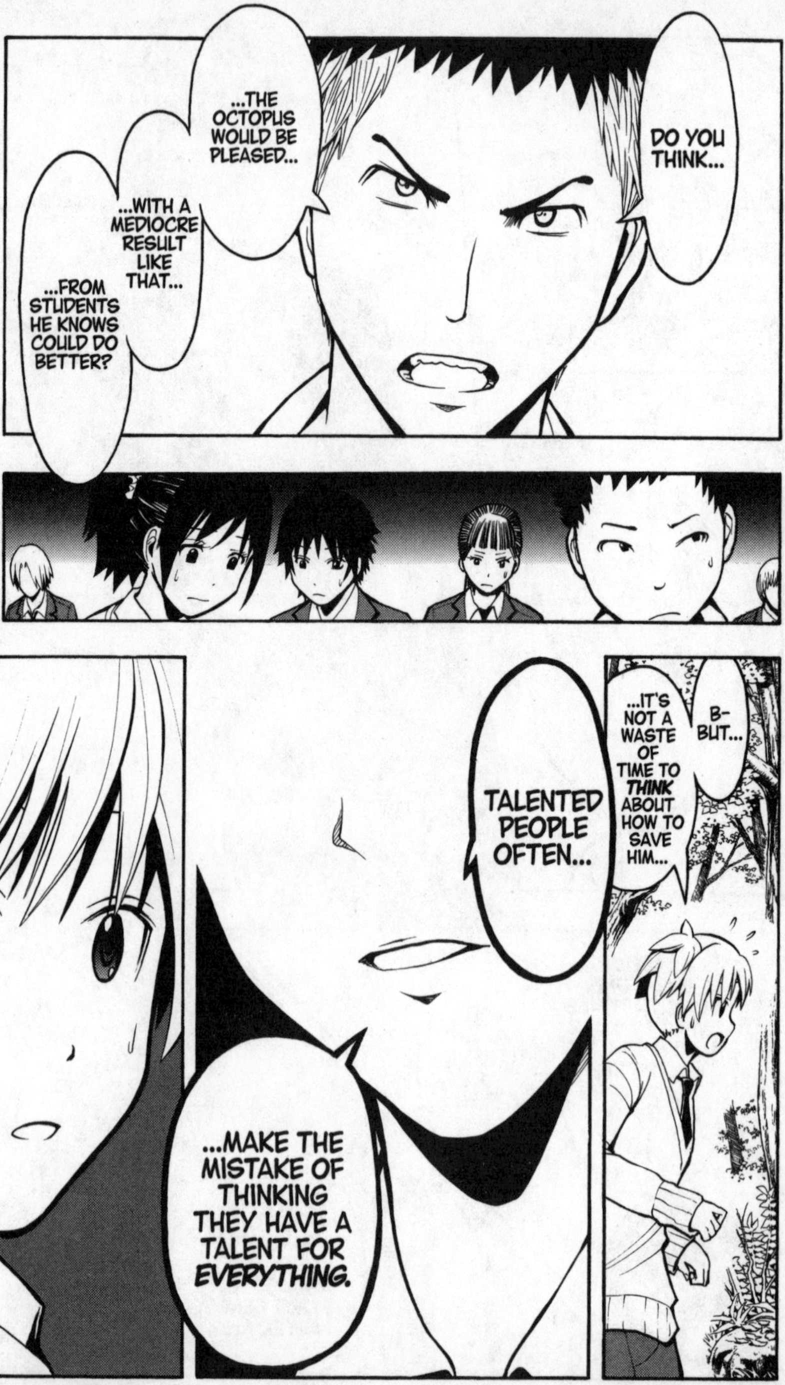
DO YOU THINK...
...THE OCTOPUS WOULD BE PLEASED...
...WITH A MEDIOCRE RESULT LIKE THAT...
...FROM STUDENTS HE KNOWS COULD DO BETTER?
B-BUT...
...IT'S NOT A WASTE OF TIME TO *THINK* ABOUT HOW TO SAVE HIM...
TALENTED PEOPLE OFTEN...
...MAKE THE MISTAKE OF THINKING THEY HAVE A TALENT FOR *EVERYTHING.*

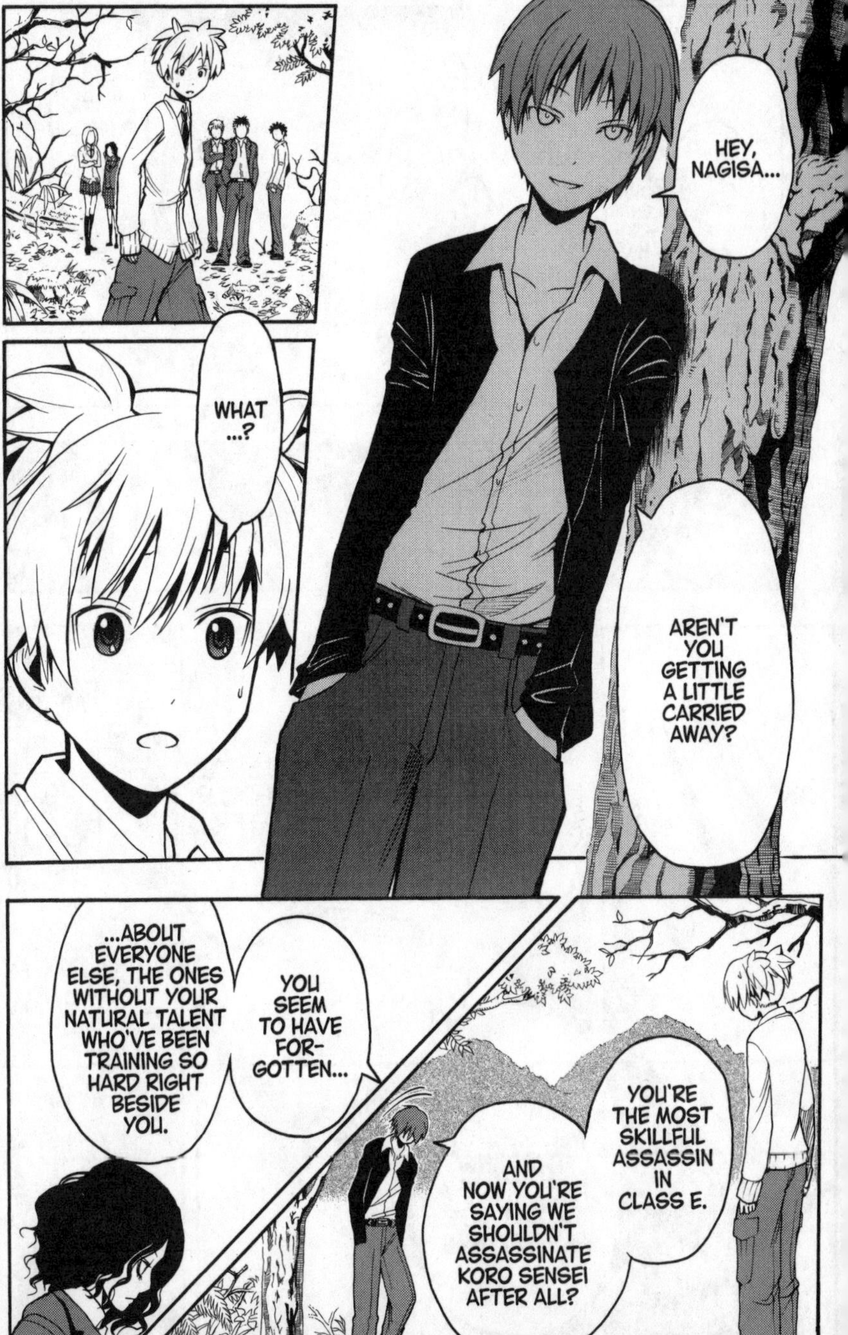
HEY, NAGISA...
AREN'T YOU GETTING A LITTLE CARRIED AWAY?
WHAT ...?
YOU'RE THE MOST SKILLFUL ASSASSIN IN CLASS E.
AND NOW YOU'RE SAYING WE SHOULDN'T ASSASSINATE KORO SENSEI AFTER ALL?
YOU SEEM TO HAVE FOR-GOTTEN...
...ABOUT EVERYONE ELSE, THE ONES WITHOUT YOUR NATURAL TALENT WHO'VE BEEN TRAINING SO HARD RIGHT BESIDE YOU.

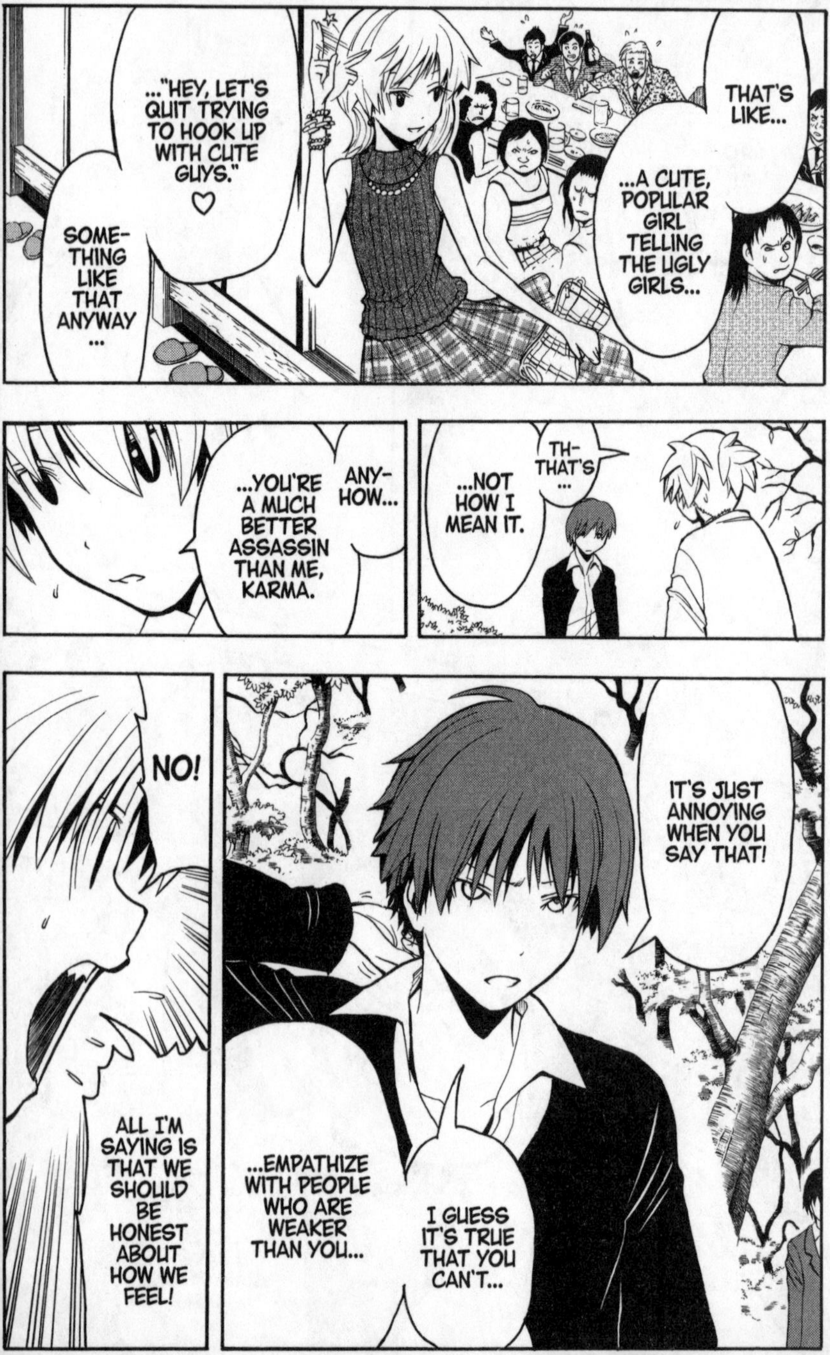
THAT'S LIKE...
...A CUTE, POPULAR GIRL TELLING THE UGLY GIRLS...
..."HEY, LET'S QUIT TRYING TO HOOK UP WITH CUTE GUYS." ♡
SOME-THING LIKE THAT ANYWAY...
TH-THAT'S...
...NOT HOW I MEAN IT.
ANY-HOW...
...YOU'RE A MUCH BETTER ASSASSIN THAN ME, KARMA.
IT'S JUST ANNOYING WHEN YOU SAY THAT!
I GUESS IT'S TRUE THAT YOU CAN'T...
...EMPATHIZE WITH PEOPLE WHO ARE WEAKER THAN YOU...
NO!
ALL I'M SAYING IS THAT WE SHOULD BE HONEST ABOUT HOW WE FEEL!

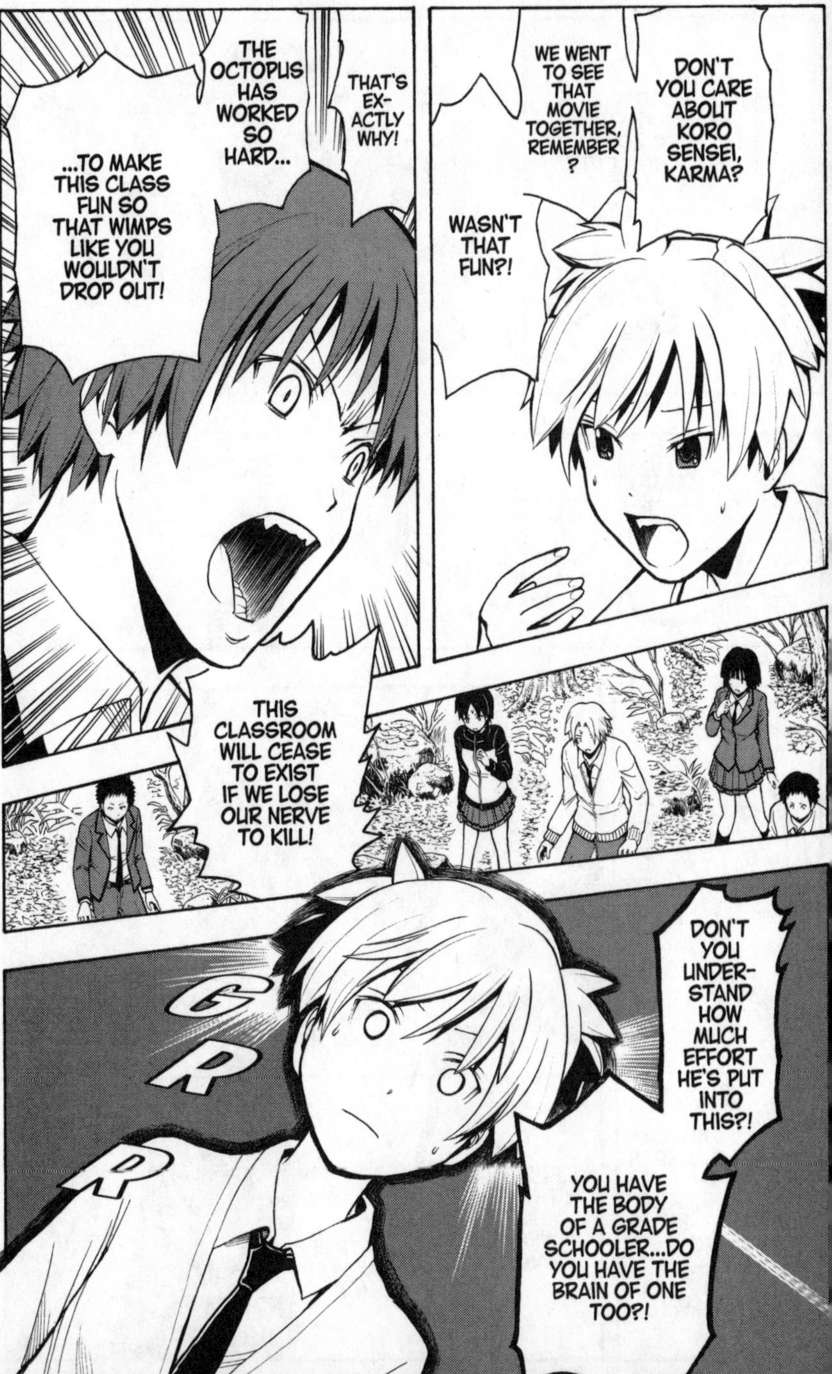
DON'T YOU CARE ABOUT KORO SENSEI, KARMA?
WE WENT TO SEE THAT MOVIE TOGETHER, REMEMBER?
WASN'T THAT FUN?!
THAT'S EX-ACTLY WHY!
THE OCTOPUS HAS WORKED SO HARD...
...TO MAKE THIS CLASS FUN SO THAT WIMPS LIKE YOU WOULDN'T DROP OUT!
THIS CLASSROOM WILL CEASE TO EXIST IF WE LOSE OUR NERVE TO KILL!
DON'T YOU UNDER-STAND HOW MUCH EFFORT HE'S PUT INTO THIS?!
YOU HAVE THE BODY OF A GRADE SCHOOLER...DO YOU HAVE THE BRAIN OF ONE TOO?!
GRR

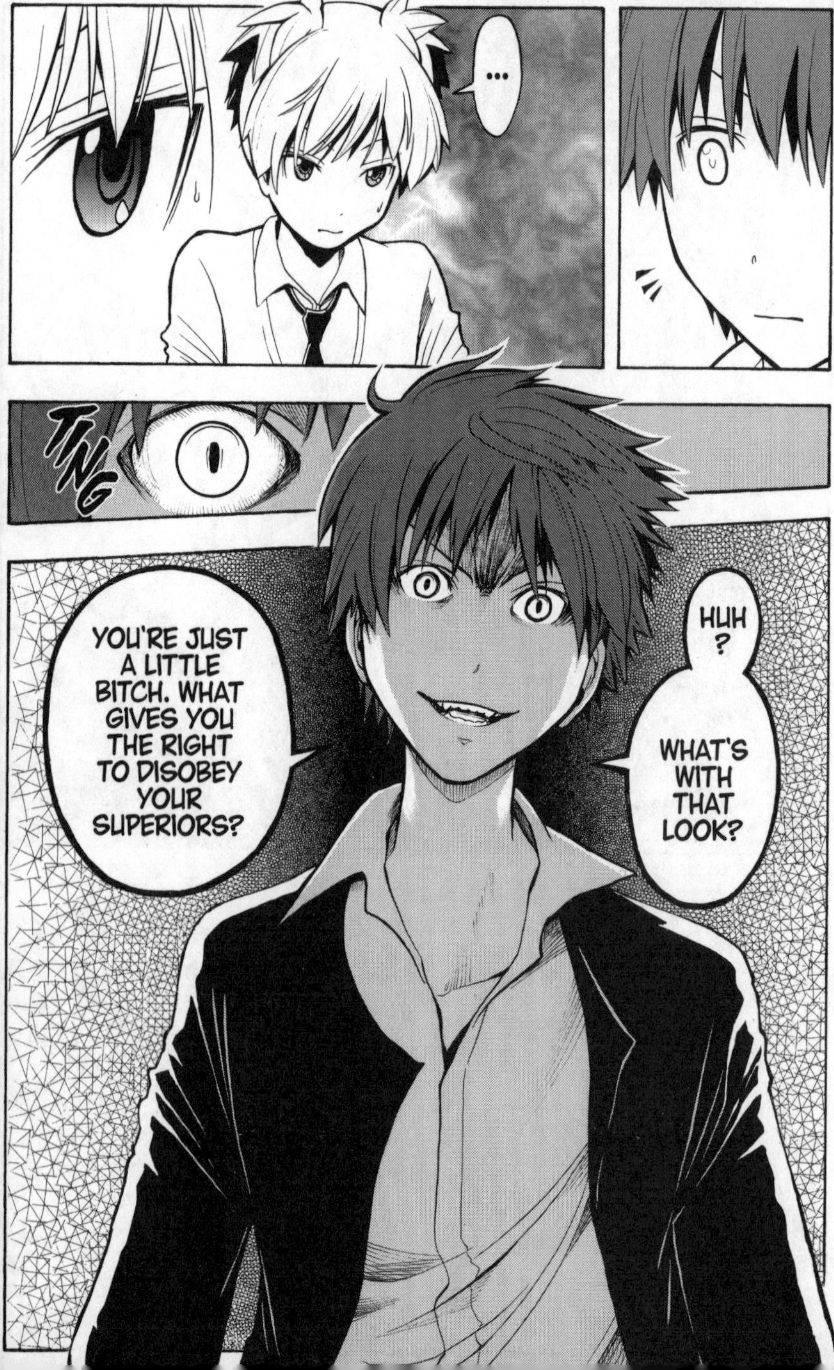
...
TING
HUH ?
WHAT'S WITH THAT LOOK?
YOU'RE JUST A LITTLE BITCH. WHAT GIVES YOU THE RIGHT TO DISOBEY YOUR SUPERIORS?

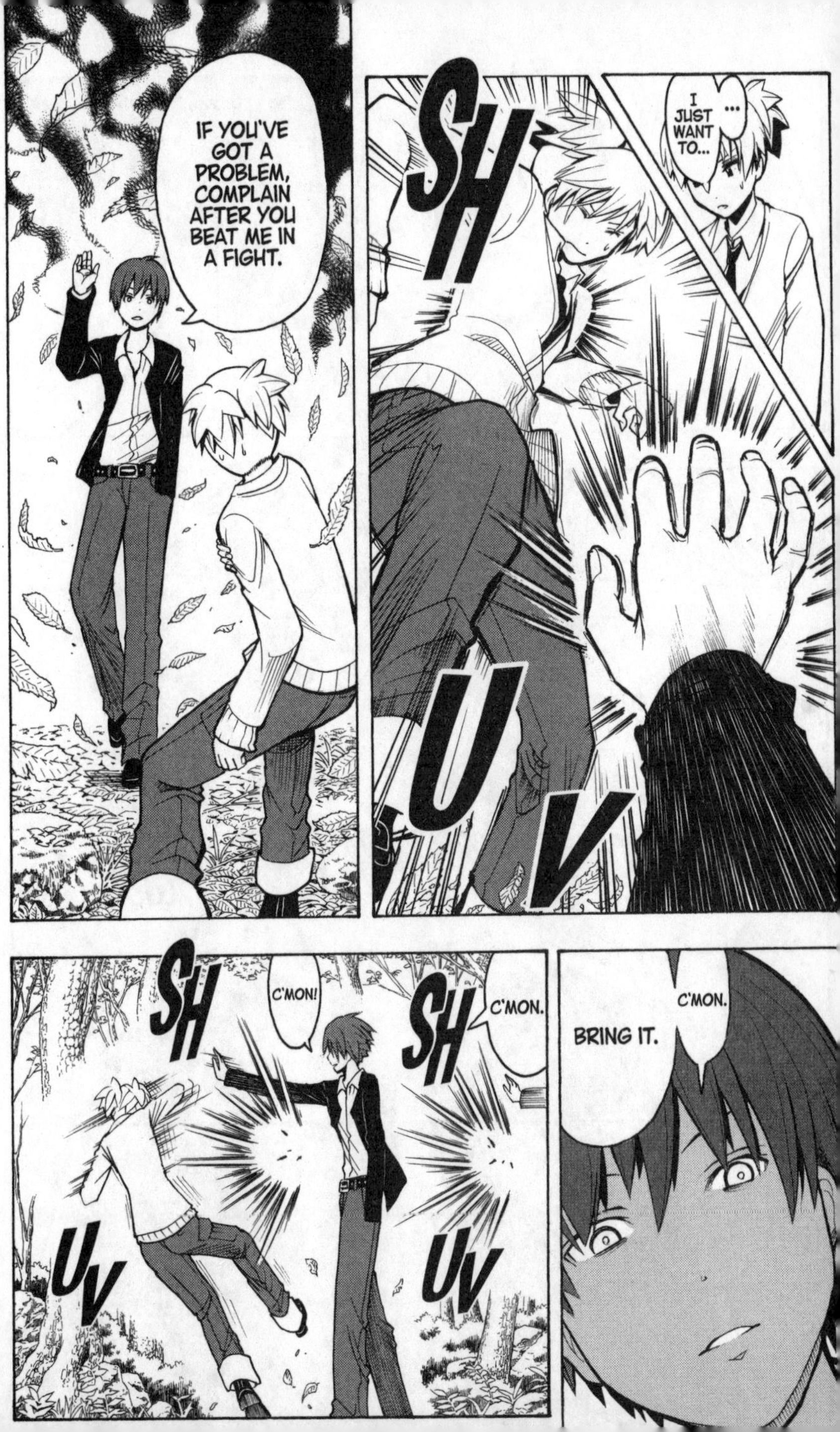
...
I JUST WANT TO...
SH
UV
IF YOU'VE GOT A PROBLEM, COMPLAIN AFTER YOU BEAT ME IN A FIGHT.
C'MON.
BRING IT.
SH
C'MON.
UV
SH
C'MON!
UV

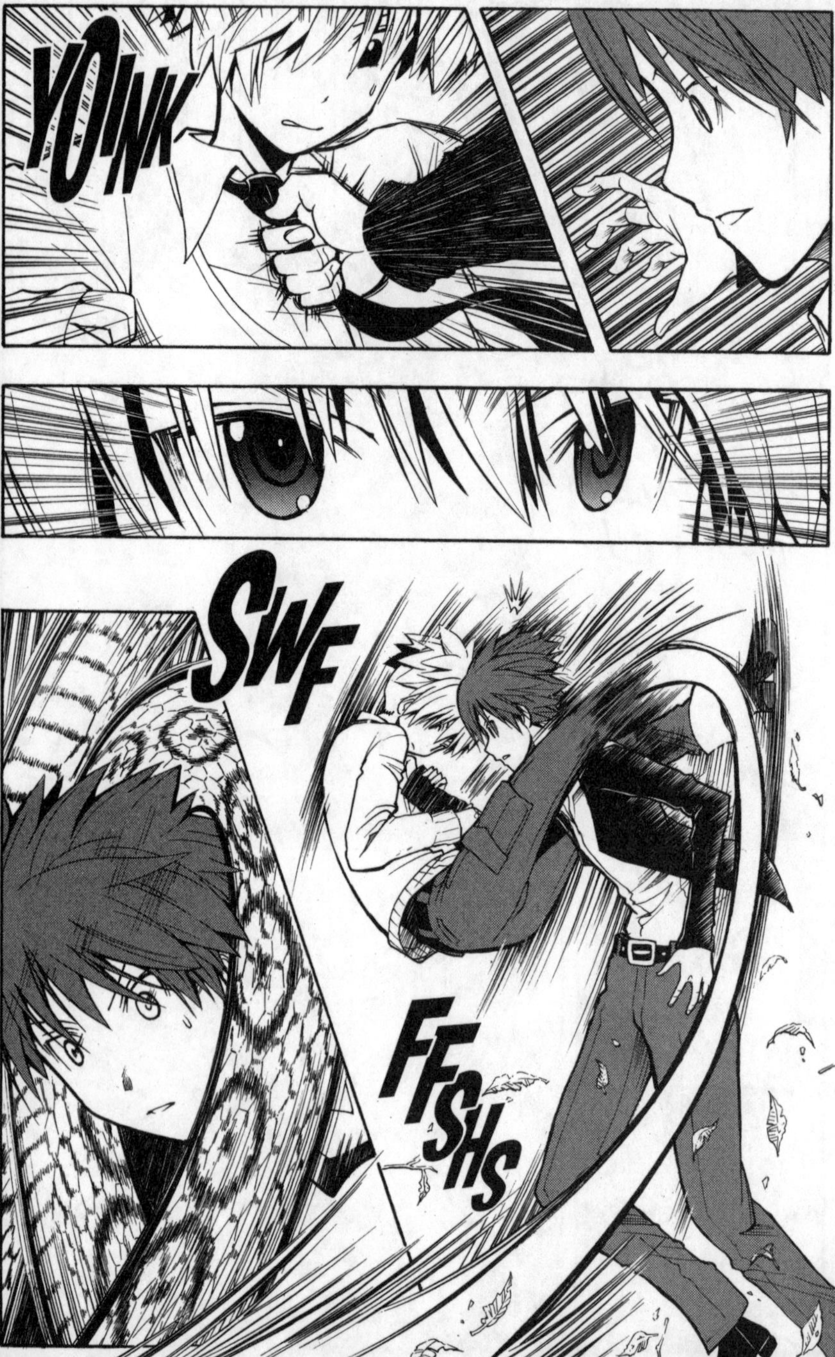
YOINK
SWF
FFSHS

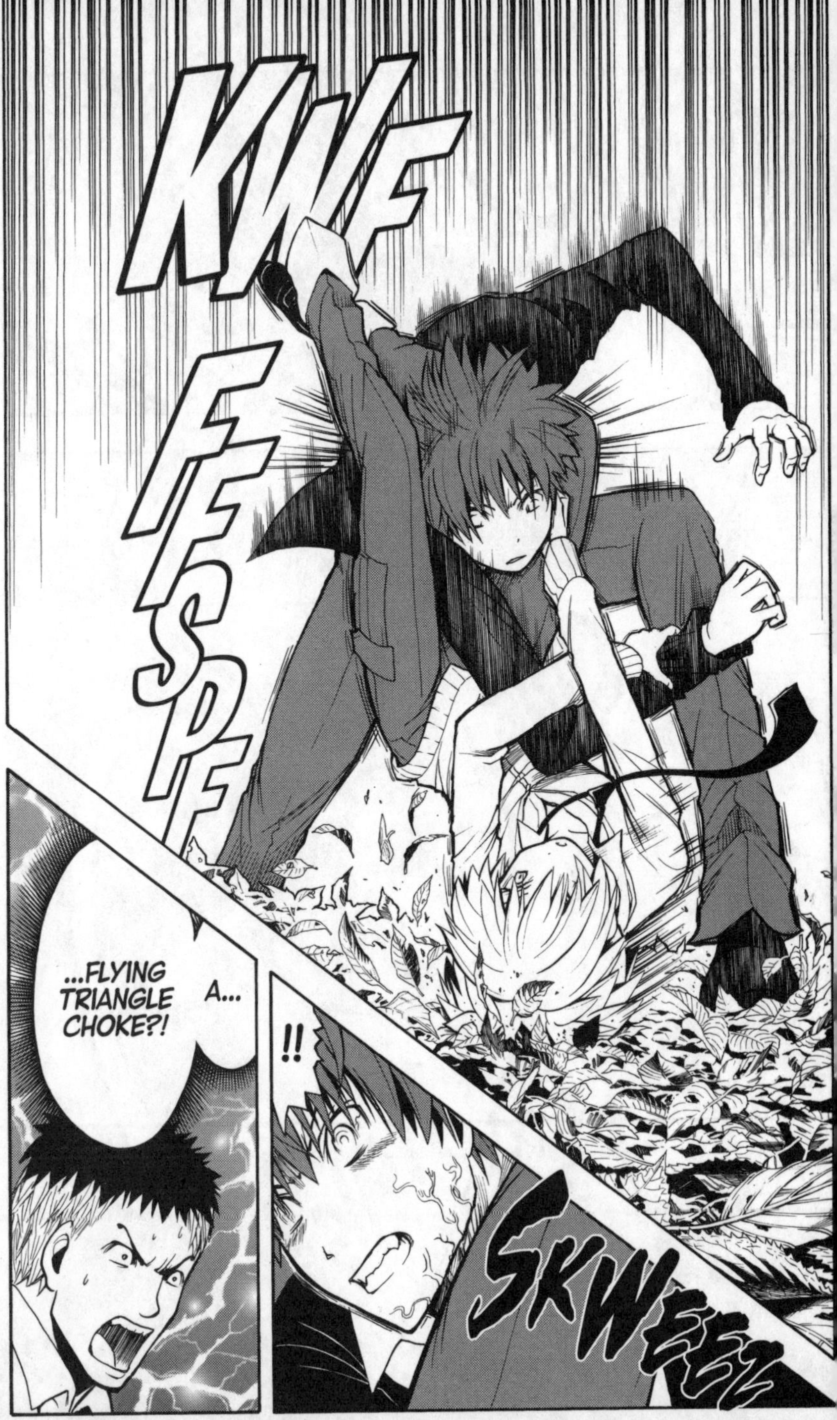
KWF
FFSPF
!!
SKWEEZ
A...
...FLYING TRIANGLE CHOKE?!

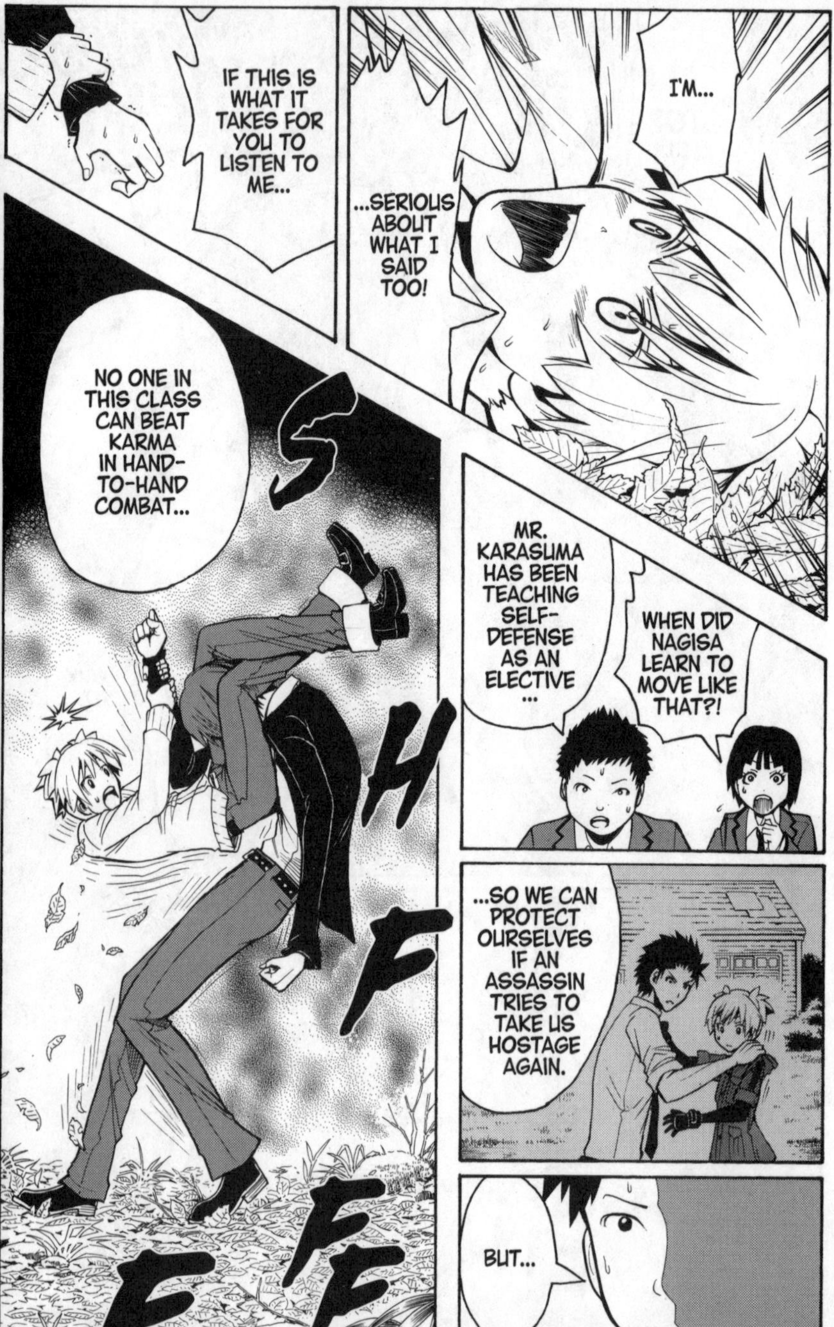
I'M...
...SERIOUS ABOUT WHAT I SAID TOO!
IF THIS IS WHAT IT TAKES FOR YOU TO LISTEN TO ME...
WHEN DID NAGISA LEARN TO MOVE LIKE THAT?!
MR. KARASUMA HAS BEEN TEACHING SELF-DEFENSE AS AN ELECTIVE...
...SO WE CAN PROTECT OURSELVES IF AN ASSASSIN TRIES TO TAKE US HOSTAGE AGAIN.
BUT...
NO ONE IN THIS CLASS CAN BEAT KARMA IN HAND-TO-HAND COMBAT...
SHFFFF

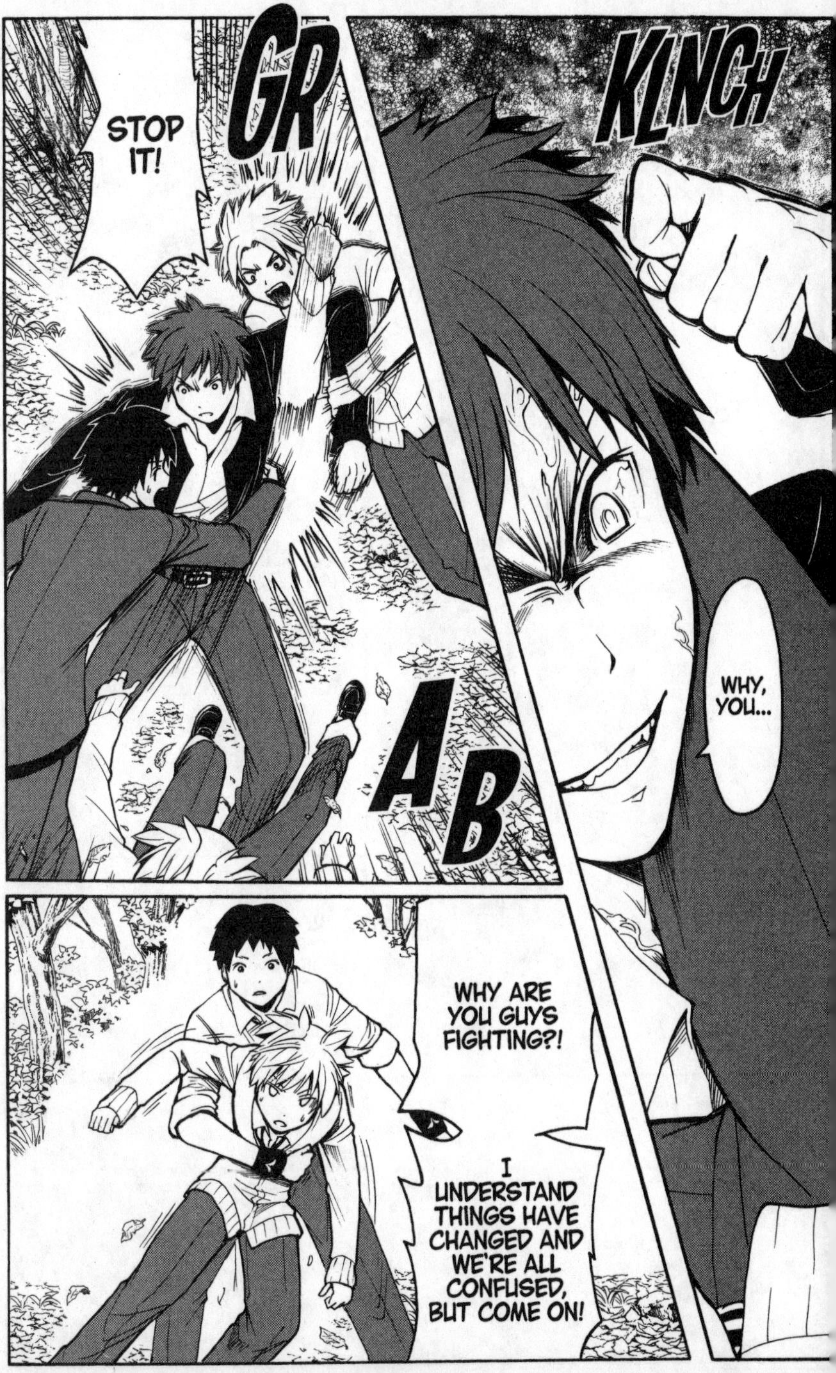
KLNCH
WHY, YOU...
STOP IT!
GR
AB
WHY ARE YOU GUYS FIGHTING?!
I UNDERSTAND THINGS HAVE CHANGED AND WE'RE ALL CONFUSED, BUT COME ON!

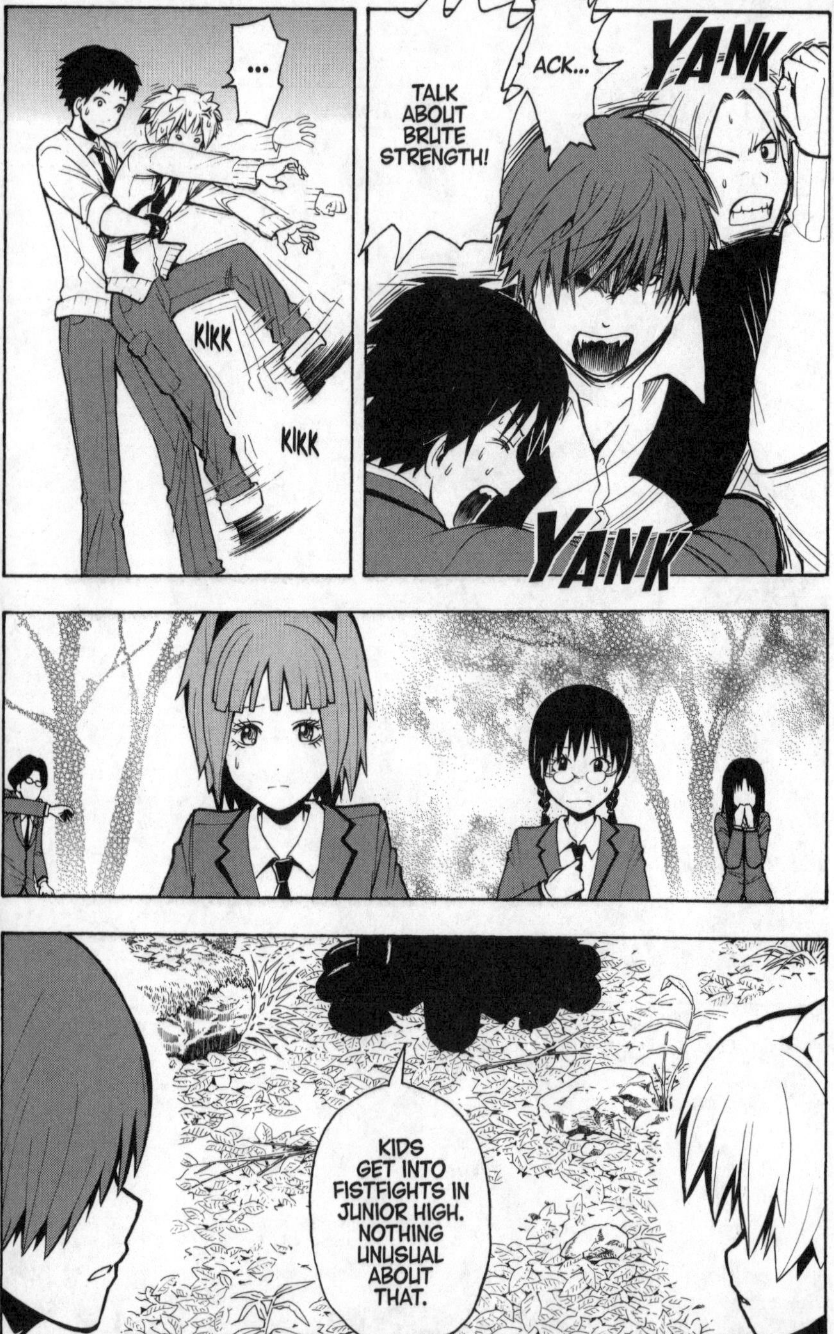
YANK
ACK...
TALK ABOUT BRUTE STRENGTH!
YANK
...
KIKK
KIKK
KIDS GET INTO FISTFIGHTS IN JUNIOR HIGH. NOTHING UNUSUAL ABOUT THAT.

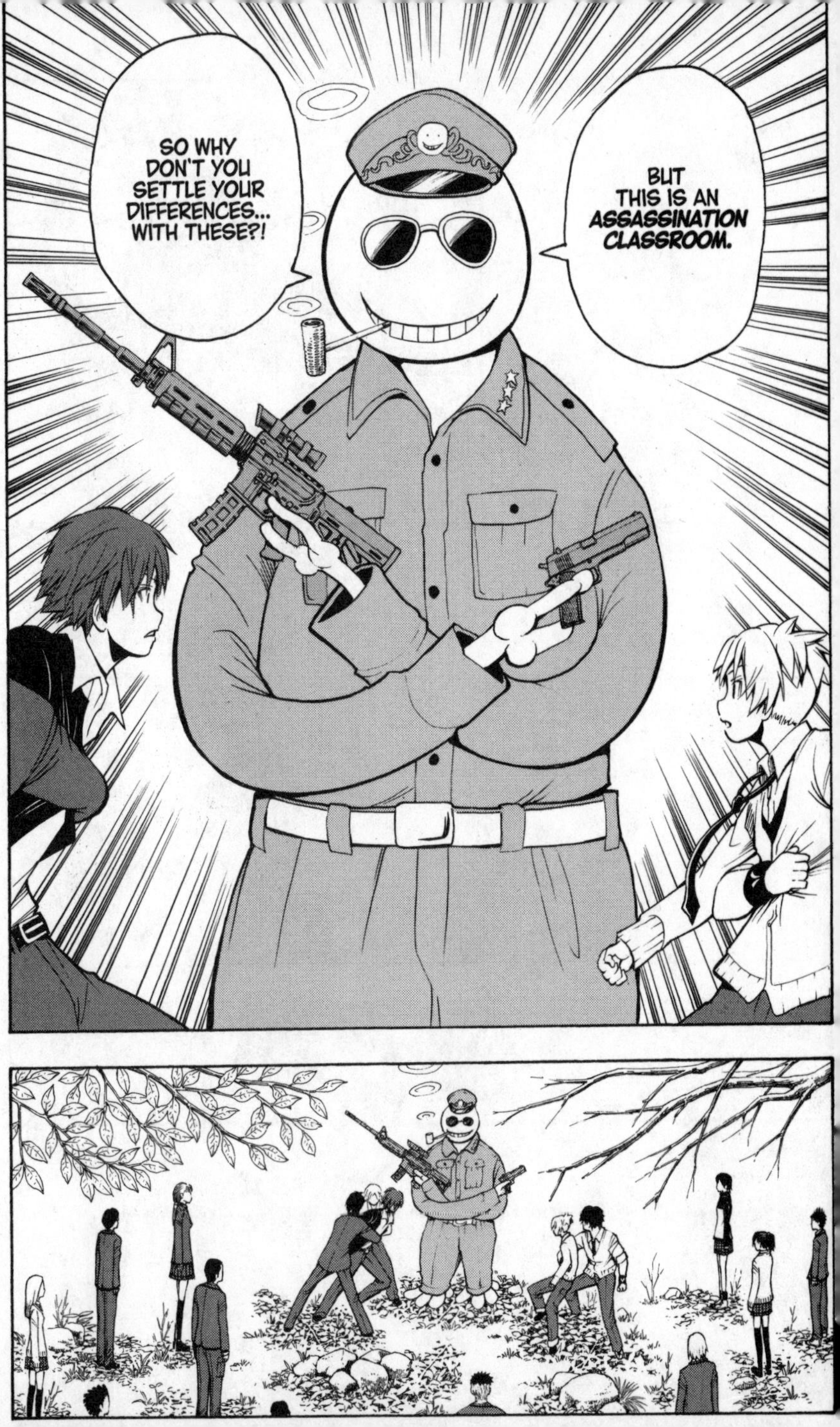
BUT THIS IS AN ASSASSINATION CLASSROOM.
SO WHY DON'T YOU SETTLE YOUR DIFFERENCES... WITH THESE?!

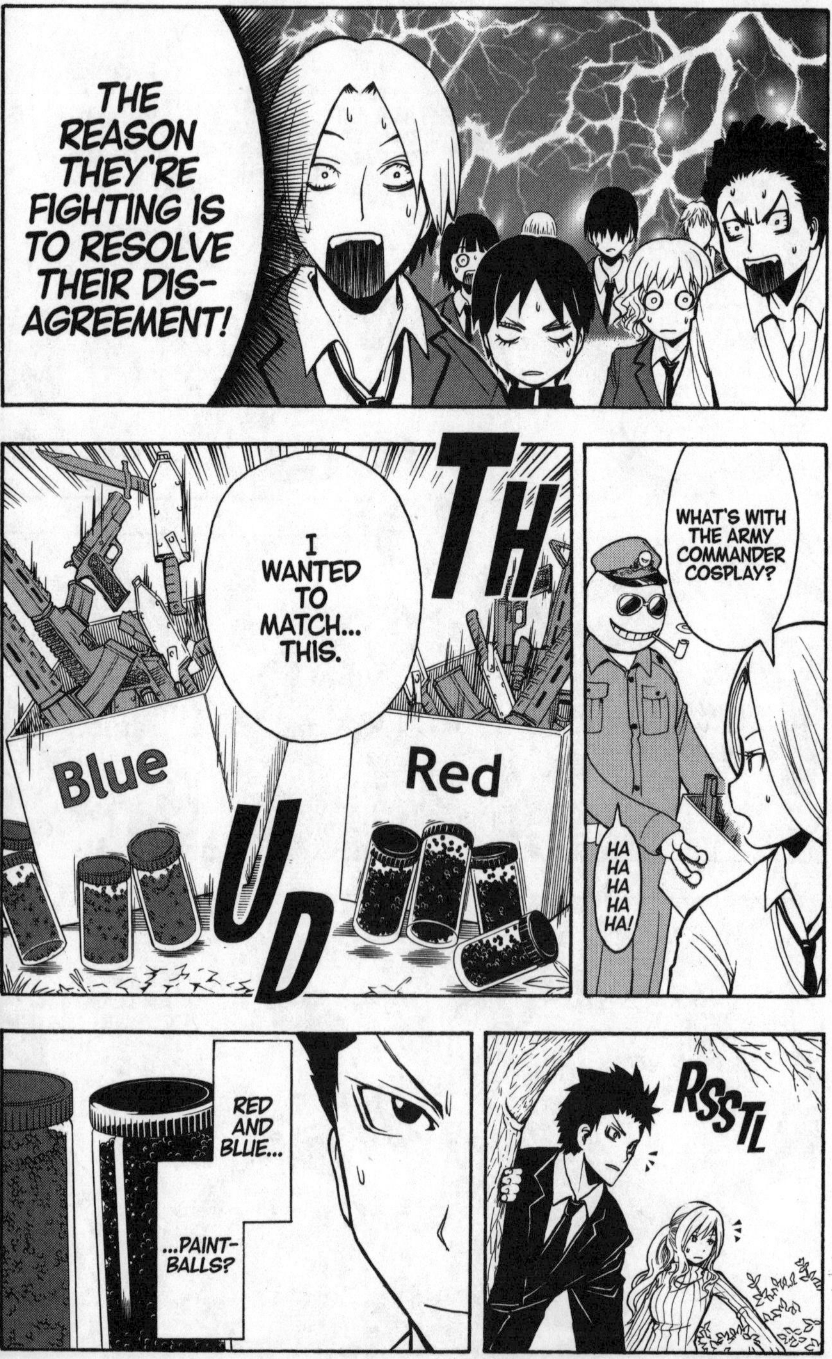
THE REASON THEY'RE FIGHTING IS TO RESOLVE THEIR DIS-AGREEMENT!
WHAT'S WITH THE ARMY COMMANDER COSPLAY?
HA HA HA HA HA!
I WANTED TO MATCH... THIS.
THUD
Blue
Red
RSSTL
RED AND BLUE...
...PAINT-BALLS?

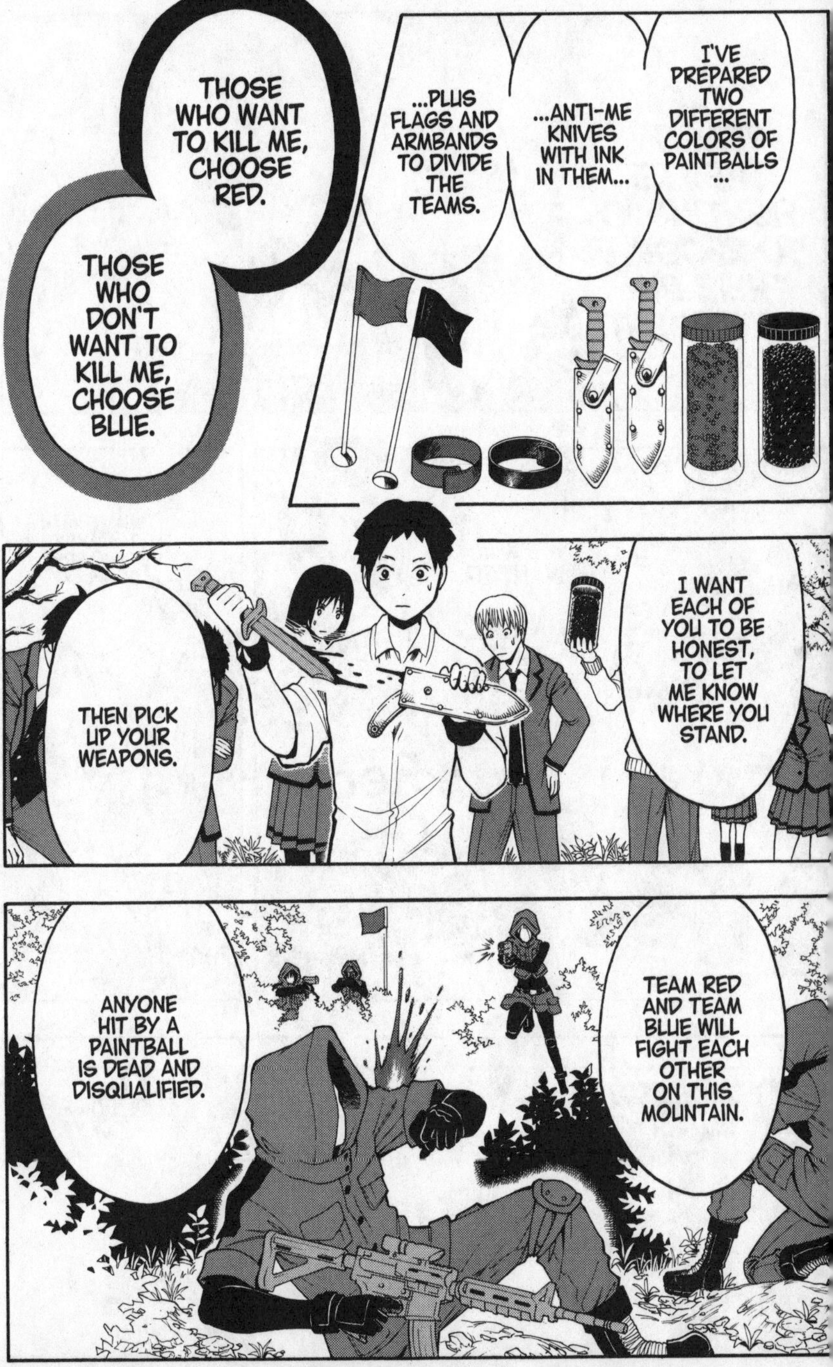
I'VE PREPARED TWO DIFFERENT COLORS OF PAINTBALLS...
...ANTI-ME KNIVES WITH INK IN THEM...
...PLUS FLAGS AND ARMBANDS TO DIVIDE THE TEAMS.
THOSE WHO WANT TO KILL ME, CHOOSE RED.
THOSE WHO DON'T WANT TO KILL ME, CHOOSE BLUE.
I WANT EACH OF YOU TO BE HONEST, TO LET ME KNOW WHERE YOU STAND.
THEN PICK UP YOUR WEAPONS.
TEAM RED AND TEAM BLUE WILL FIGHT EACH OTHER ON THIS MOUNTAIN.
ANYONE HIT BY A PAINTBALL IS DEAD AND DISQUALIFIED.

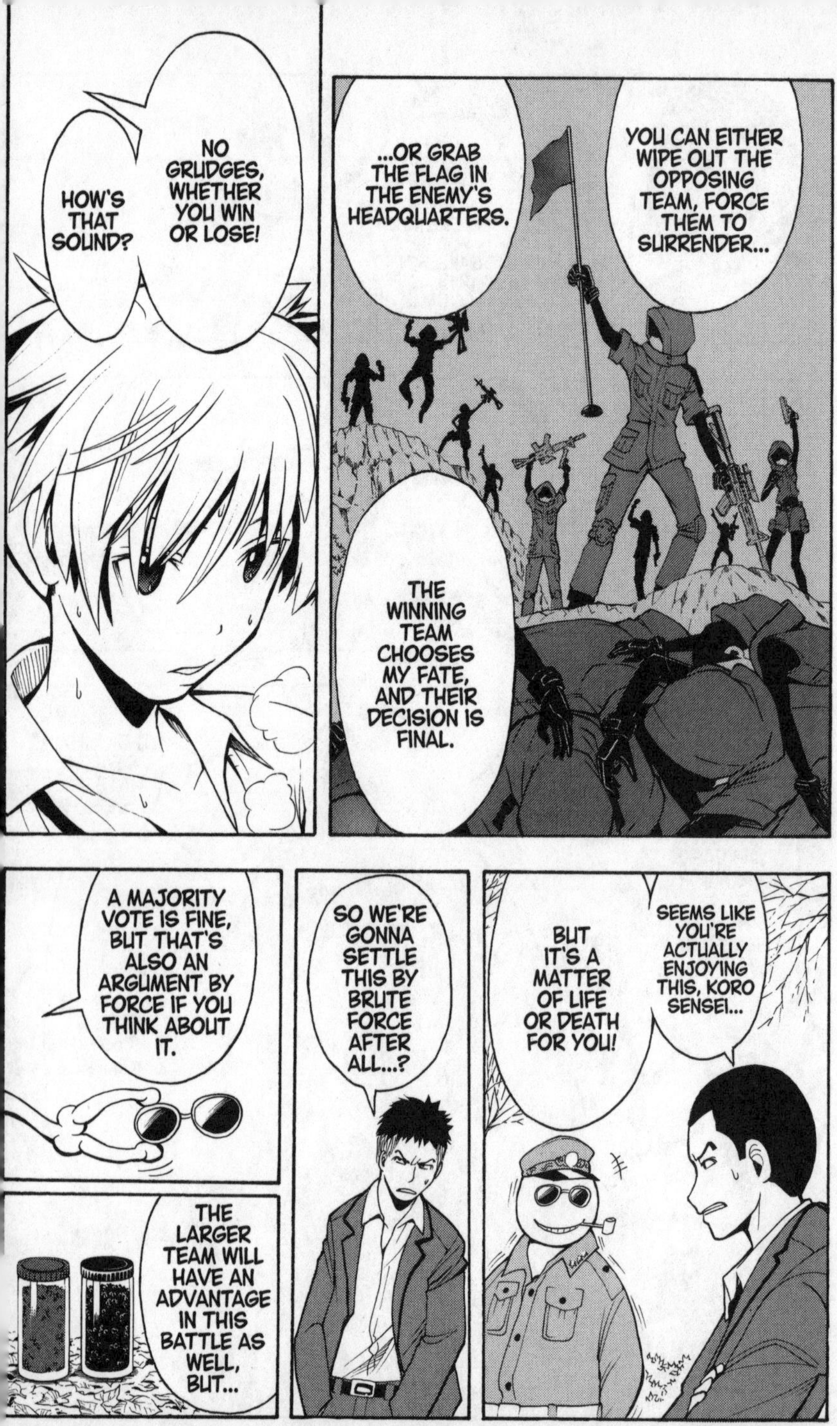
YOU CAN EITHER WIPE OUT THE OPPOSING TEAM, FORCE THEM TO SURRENDER...
...OR GRAB THE FLAG IN THE ENEMY'S HEADQUARTERS.
THE WINNING TEAM CHOOSES MY FATE, AND THEIR DECISION IS FINAL.
NO GRUDGES, WHETHER YOU WIN OR LOSE!
HOW'S THAT SOUND?
SEEMS LIKE YOU'RE ACTUALLY ENJOYING THIS, KORO SENSEI...
BUT IT'S A MATTER OF LIFE OR DEATH FOR YOU!
SO WE'RE GONNA SETTLE THIS BY BRUTE FORCE AFTER ALL...?
A MAJORITY VOTE IS FINE, BUT THAT'S ALSO AN ARGUMENT BY FORCE IF YOU THINK ABOUT IT.
THE LARGER TEAM WILL HAVE AN ADVANTAGE IN THIS BATTLE AS WELL, BUT...

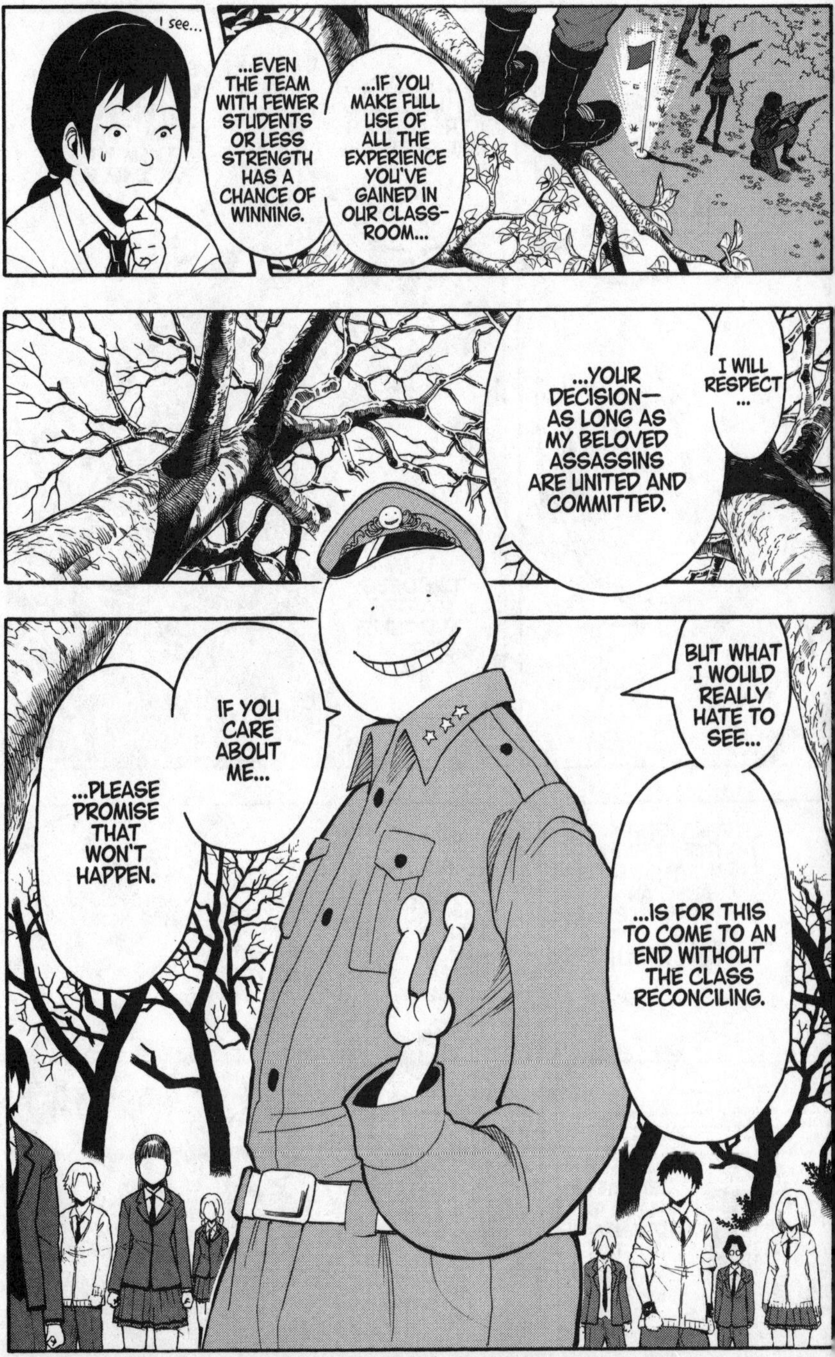
...IF YOU MAKE FULL USE OF ALL THE EXPERIENCE YOU'VE GAINED IN OUR CLASS-ROOM...
...EVEN THE TEAM WITH FEWER STUDENTS OR LESS STRENGTH HAS A CHANCE OF WINNING.
I see...
I WILL RESPECT...
...YOUR DECISION—AS LONG AS MY BELOVED ASSASSINS ARE UNITED AND COMMITTED.
BUT WHAT I WOULD REALLY HATE TO SEE...
...IS FOR THIS TO COME TO AN END WITHOUT THE CLASS RECONCILING.
IF YOU CARE ABOUT ME...
...PLEASE PROMISE THAT WON'T HAPPEN.

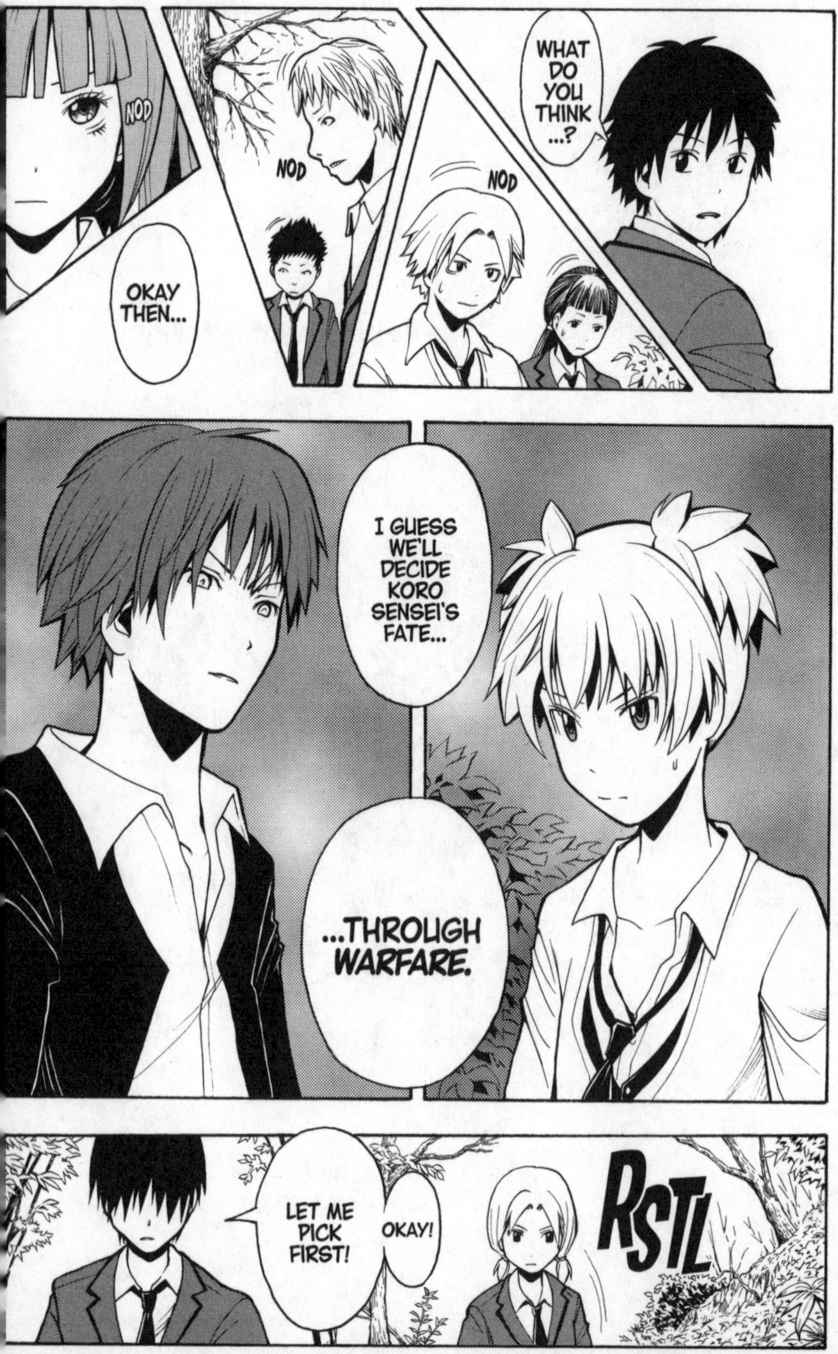
WHAT DO YOU THINK ...?
NOD
NOD
NOD
OKAY THEN...
I GUESS WE'LL DECIDE KORO SENSEI'S FATE...
...THROUGH WARFARE.
RSTL
OKAY!
LET ME PICK FIRST!

Nagisa's Fighting Ability, Checkup①

Power

Hngh... Hngh...

He can be fully restrained by two girls.

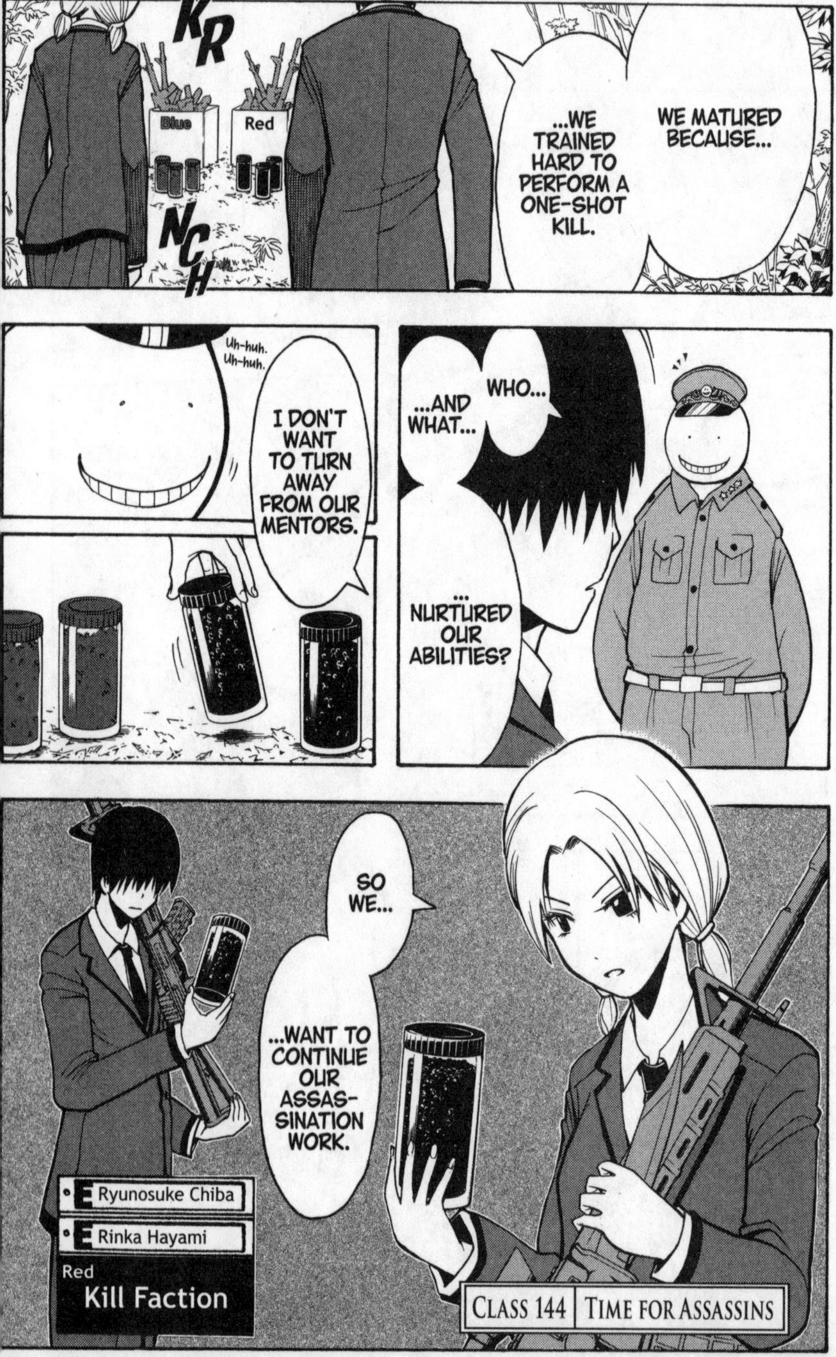
WE MATURED BECAUSE...
...WE TRAINED HARD TO PERFORM A ONE-SHOT KILL.
Red
Blue
KRNCH
WHO...
...AND WHAT...
...NURTURED OUR ABILITIES?
Uh-huh. Uh-huh.
I DON'T WANT TO TURN AWAY FROM OUR MENTORS.
SO WE...
...WANT TO CONTINUE OUR ASSASSINATION WORK.
E Ryunosuke Chiba
E Rinka Hayami
Red
Kill Faction
CLASS 144 TIME FOR ASSASSINS

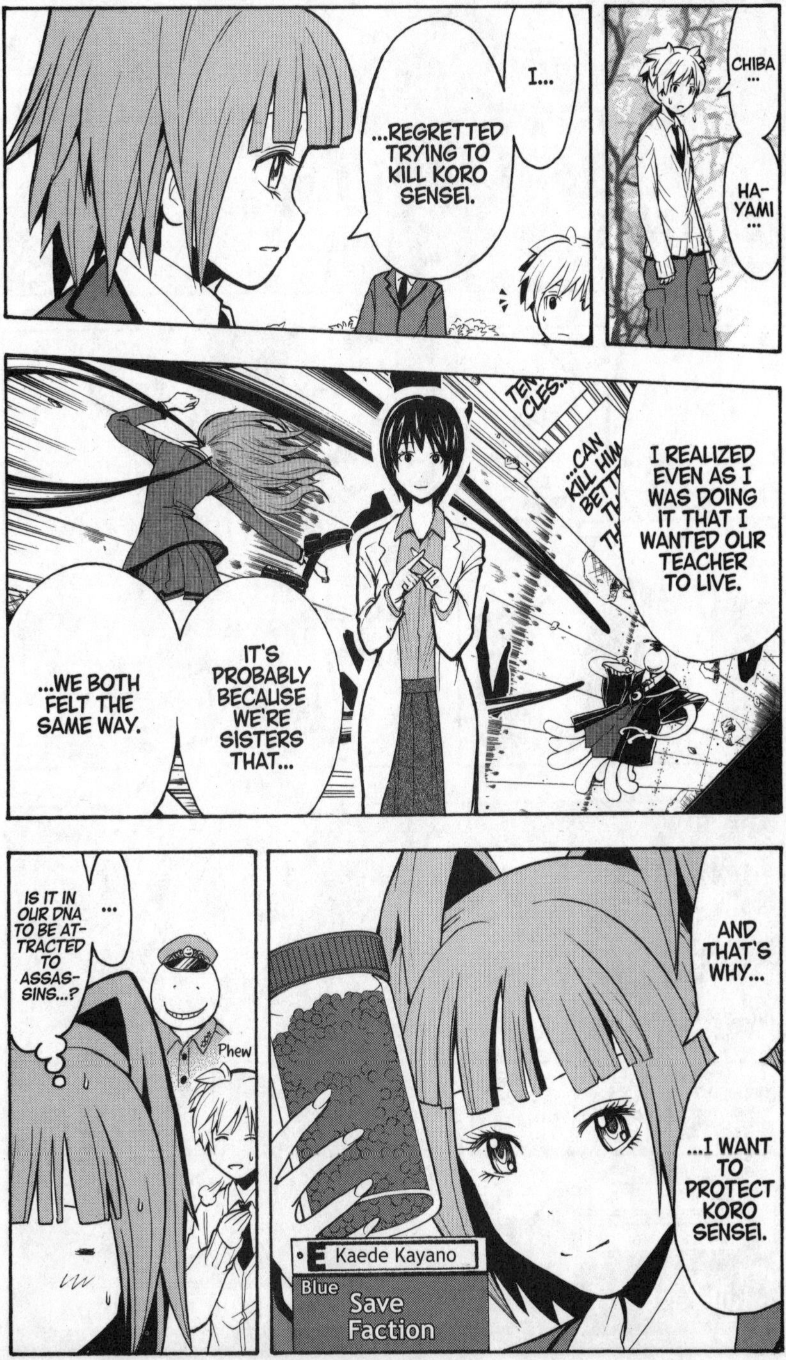
CHIBA...
HAYAMI...
I...
...REGRETTED TRYING TO KILL KORO SENSEI.
I REALIZED EVEN AS I WAS DOING IT THAT I WANTED OUR TEACHER TO LIVE.
IT'S PROBABLY BECAUSE WE'RE SISTERS THAT...
...WE BOTH FELT THE SAME WAY.
AND THAT'S WHY...
...I WANT TO PROTECT KORO SENSEI.
E Kaede Kayano
Blue
Save Faction
...
IS IT IN OUR DNA TO BE ATTRACTED TO ASSASSINS...?
Phew

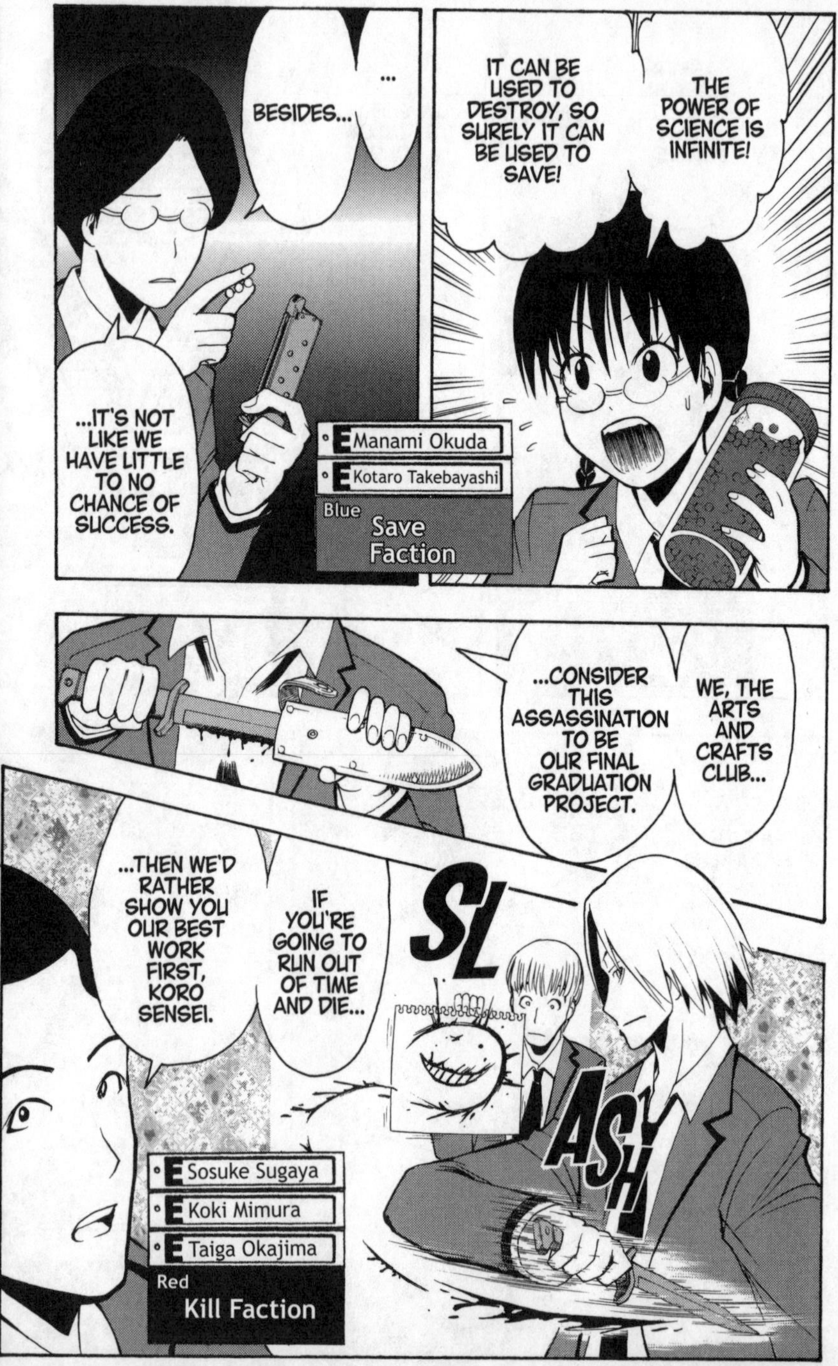
THE POWER OF SCIENCE IS INFINITE!
IT CAN BE USED TO DESTROY, SO SURELY IT CAN BE USED TO SAVE!
...
BESIDES...
...IT'S NOT LIKE WE HAVE LITTLE TO NO CHANCE OF SUCCESS.
E Manami Okuda
E Kotaro Takebayashi
Blue
Save Faction
WE, THE ARTS AND CRAFTS CLUB...
...CONSIDER THIS ASSASSINATION TO BE OUR FINAL GRADUATION PROJECT.
SLASH
IF YOU'RE GOING TO RUN OUT OF TIME AND DIE...
...THEN WE'D RATHER SHOW YOU OUR BEST WORK FIRST, KORO SENSEI.
E Sosuke Sugaya
E Koki Mimura
E Taiga Okajima
Red
Kill Faction

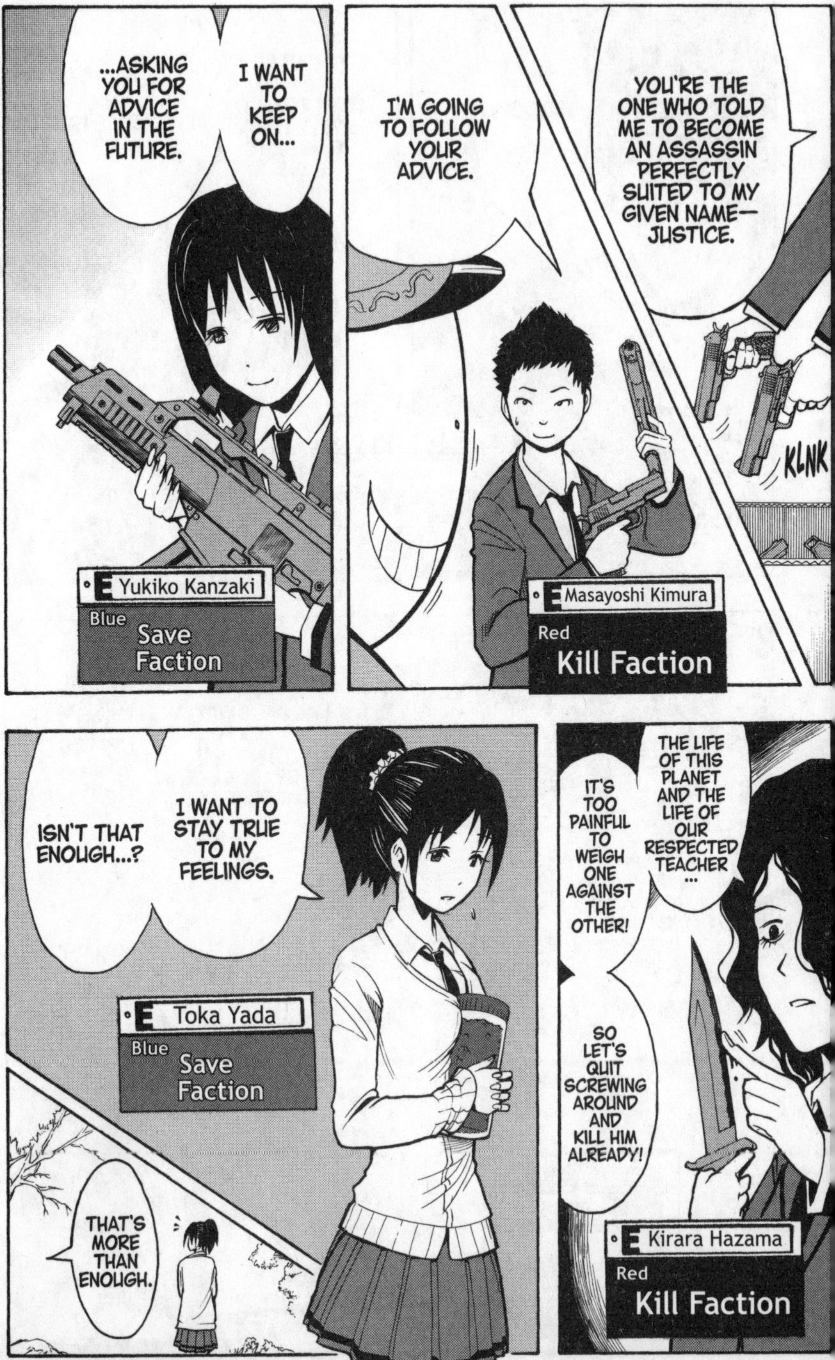
YOU'RE THE ONE WHO TOLD ME TO BECOME AN ASSASSIN PERFECTLY SUITED TO MY GIVEN NAME— JUSTICE.
KLNK
I'M GOING TO FOLLOW YOUR ADVICE.
Masayoshi Kimura
Red
Kill Faction
I WANT TO KEEP ON...
...ASKING YOU FOR ADVICE IN THE FUTURE.
Yukiko Kanzaki
Blue
Save Faction
THE LIFE OF THIS PLANET AND THE LIFE OF OUR RESPECTED TEACHER...
IT'S TOO PAINFUL TO WEIGH ONE AGAINST THE OTHER!
SO LET'S QUIT SCREWING AROUND AND KILL HIM ALREADY!
Kirara Hazama
Red
Kill Faction
I WANT TO STAY TRUE TO MY FEELINGS.
ISN'T THAT ENOUGH...?
Toka Yada
Blue
Save Faction
THAT'S MORE THAN ENOUGH.

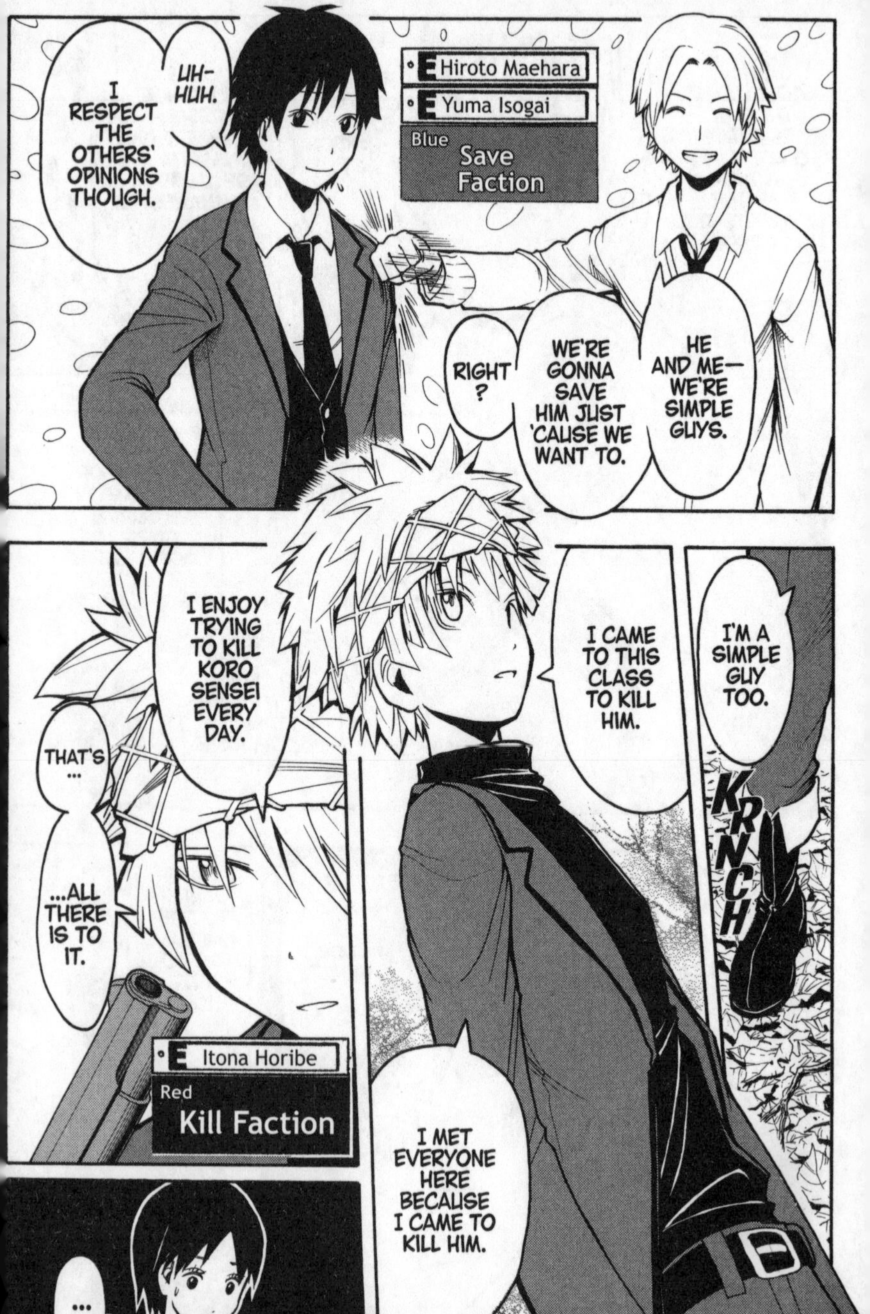

E Hiroto Maehara
E Yuma Isogai
Blue Save Faction
HE AND ME— WE'RE SIMPLE GUYS.
WE'RE GONNA SAVE HIM JUST 'CAUSE WE WANT TO.
RIGHT?
UH-HUH.
I RESPECT THE OTHERS' OPINIONS THOUGH.
I'M A SIMPLE GUY TOO.
KRNCH
I CAME TO THIS CLASS TO KILL HIM.
I MET EVERYONE HERE BECAUSE I CAME TO KILL HIM.
I ENJOY TRYING TO KILL KORO SENSEI EVERY DAY.
THAT'S...
...ALL THERE IS TO IT.
E Itona Horibe
Red Kill Faction
...

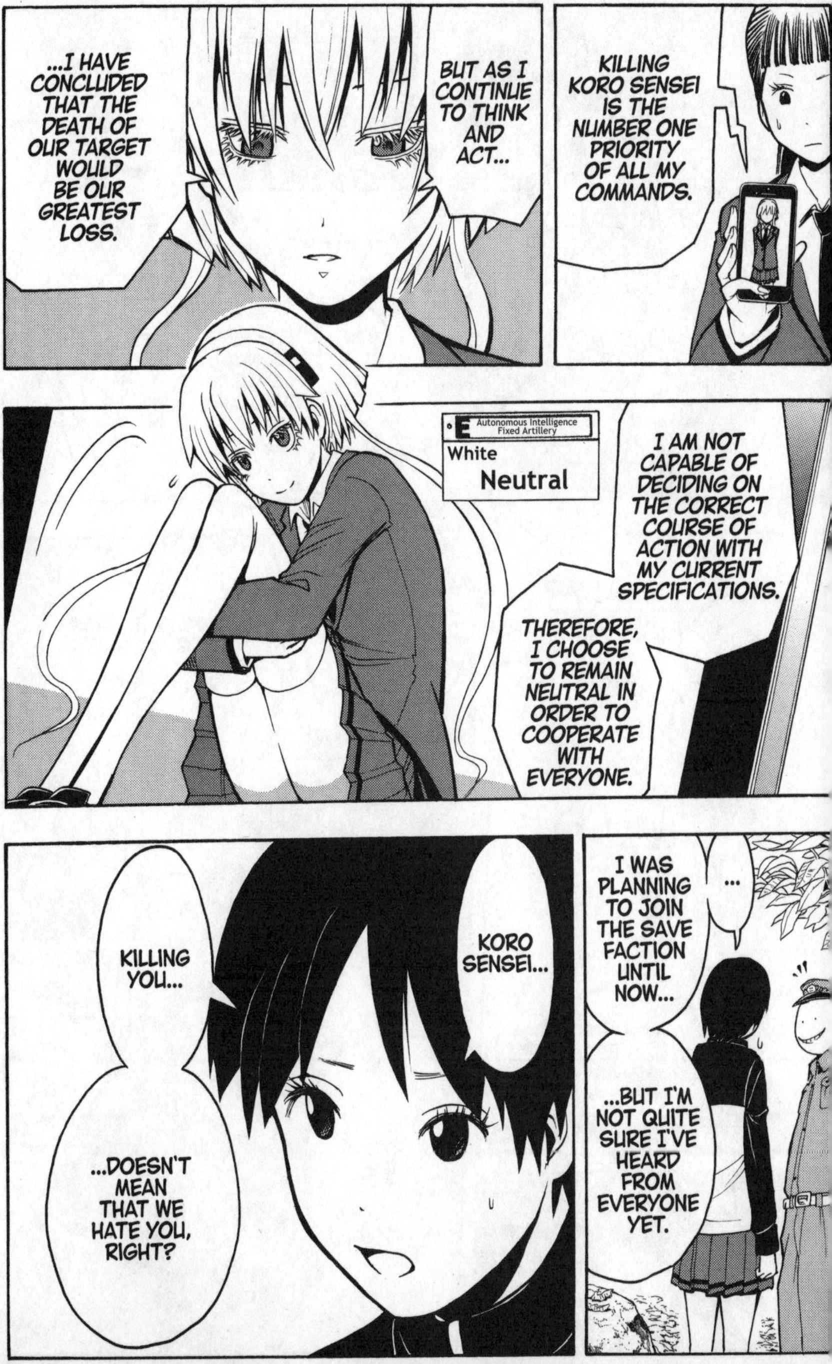
KILLING KORO SENSEI IS THE NUMBER ONE PRIORITY OF ALL MY COMMANDS.
BUT AS I CONTINUE TO THINK AND ACT...
...I HAVE CONCLUDED THAT THE DEATH OF OUR TARGET WOULD BE OUR GREATEST LOSS.
I AM NOT CAPABLE OF DECIDING ON THE CORRECT COURSE OF ACTION WITH MY CURRENT SPECIFICATIONS.
E Autonomous Intelligence Fixed Artillery
White
Neutral
THEREFORE, I CHOOSE TO REMAIN NEUTRAL IN ORDER TO COOPERATE WITH EVERYONE.
...
I WAS PLANNING TO JOIN THE SAVE FACTION UNTIL NOW...
...BUT I'M NOT QUITE SURE I'VE HEARD FROM EVERYONE YET.
KORO SENSEI...
KILLING YOU...
...DOESN'T MEAN THAT WE HATE YOU, RIGHT?

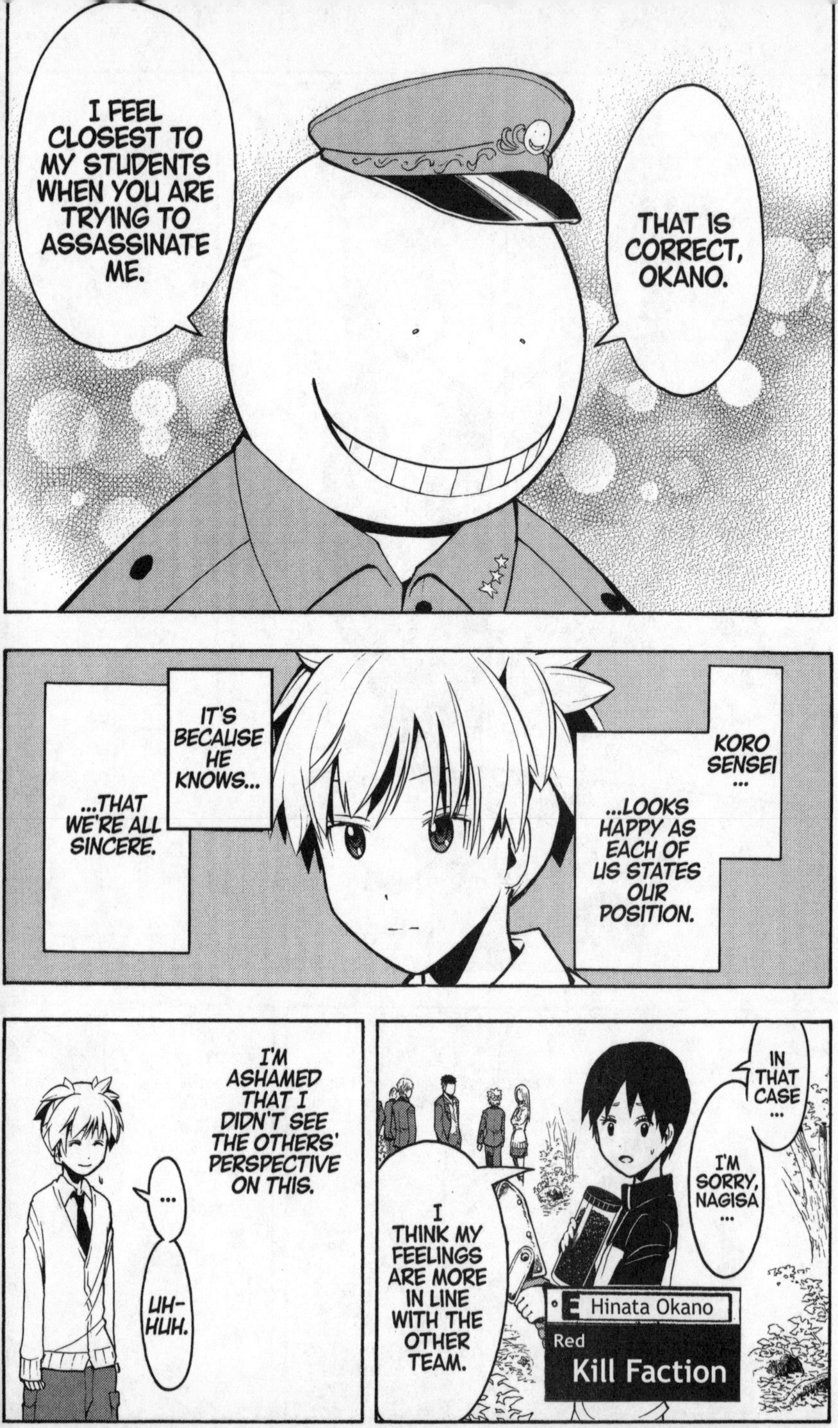
THAT IS CORRECT, OKANO.
I FEEL CLOSEST TO MY STUDENTS WHEN YOU ARE TRYING TO ASSASSINATE ME.
KORO SENSEI...
...LOOKS HAPPY AS EACH OF US STATES OUR POSITION.
IT'S BECAUSE HE KNOWS...
...THAT WE'RE ALL SINCERE.
IN THAT CASE...
I'M SORRY, NAGISA...
I THINK MY FEELINGS ARE MORE IN LINE WITH THE OTHER TEAM.
E Hinata Okano
Red
Kill Faction
I'M ASHAMED THAT I DIDN'T SEE THE OTHERS' PERSPECTIVE ON THIS.
...
UH-HUH.

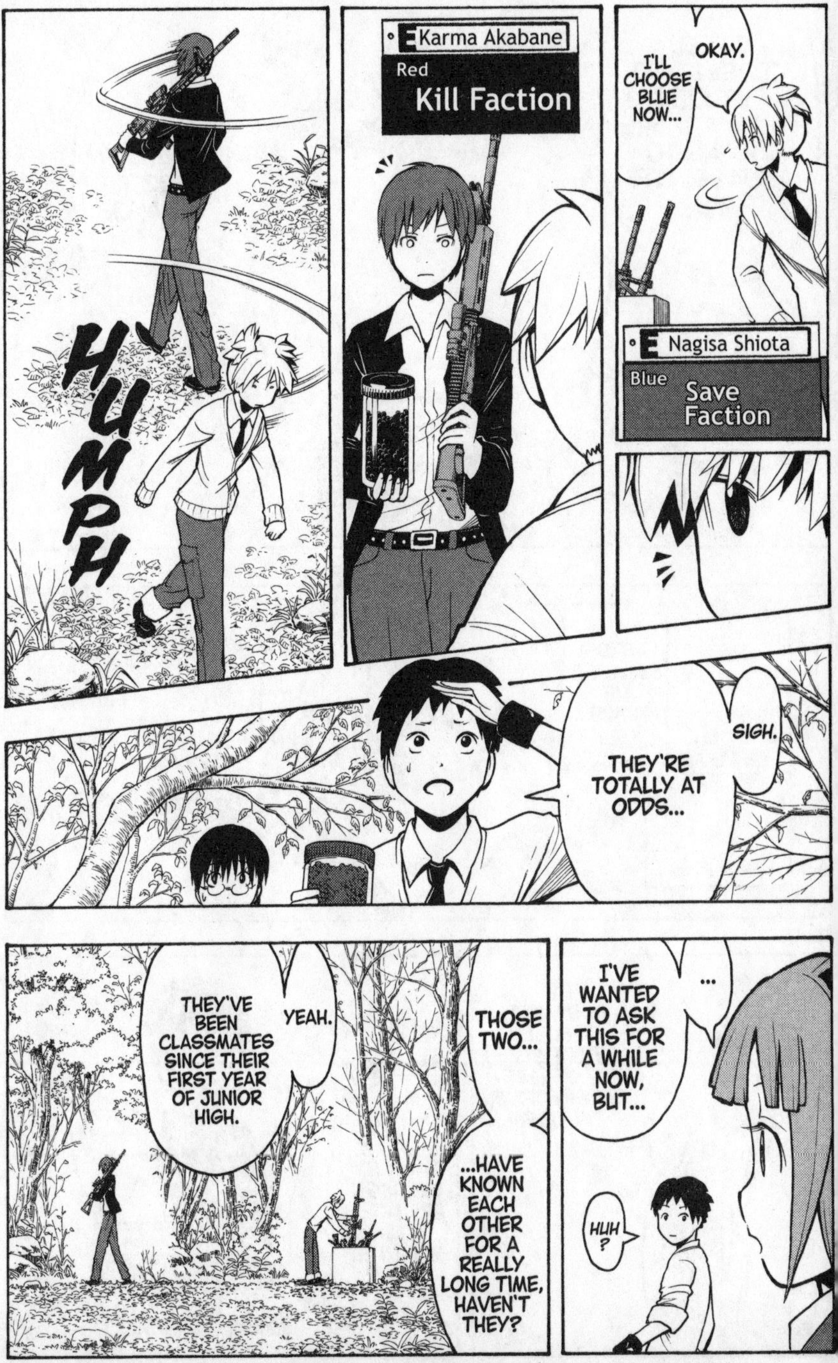
OKAY.
I'LL CHOOSE BLUE NOW...
E Nagisa Shiota
Blue
Save Faction
E Karma Akabane
Red
Kill Faction
HUMPH
SIGH.
THEY'RE TOTALLY AT ODDS...
...
I'VE WANTED TO ASK THIS FOR A WHILE NOW, BUT...
HUH?
THOSE TWO...
...HAVE KNOWN EACH OTHER FOR A REALLY LONG TIME, HAVEN'T THEY?
YEAH.
THEY'VE BEEN CLASSMATES SINCE THEIR FIRST YEAR OF JUNIOR HIGH.

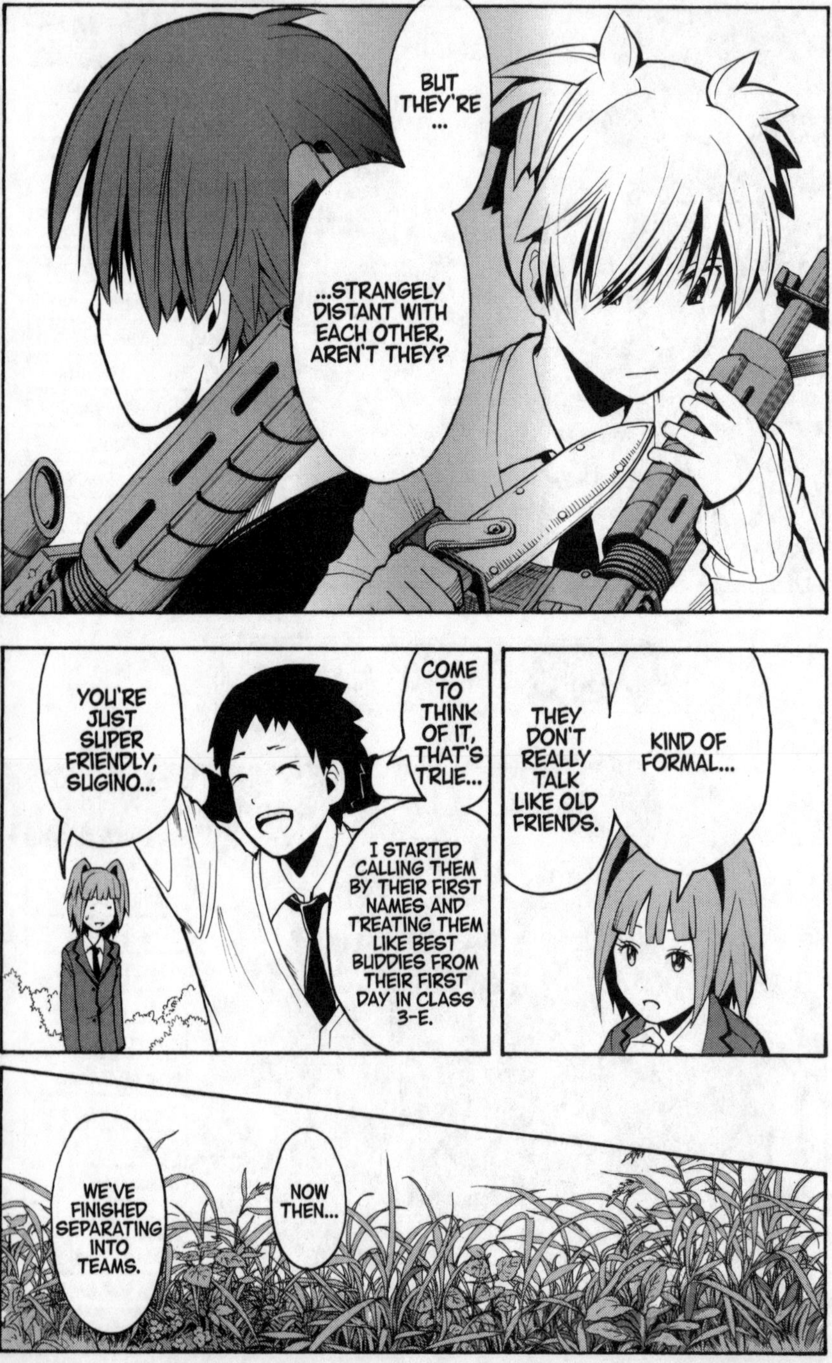
BUT THEY'RE ...
...STRANGELY DISTANT WITH EACH OTHER, AREN'T THEY?
KIND OF FORMAL...
THEY DON'T REALLY TALK LIKE OLD FRIENDS.
COME TO THINK OF IT, THAT'S TRUE...
I STARTED CALLING THEM BY THEIR FIRST NAMES AND TREATING THEM LIKE BEST BUDDIES FROM THEIR FIRST DAY IN CLASS 3-E.
YOU'RE JUST SUPER FRIENDLY, SUGINO...
NOW THEN...
WE'VE FINISHED SEPARATING INTO TEAMS.

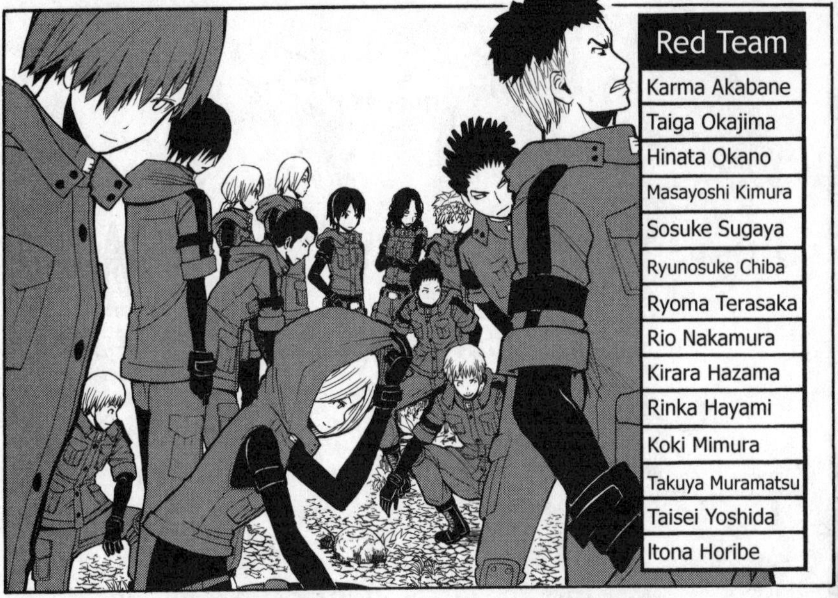
Red Team
Karma Akabane
Taiga Okajima
Hinata Okano
Masayoshi Kimura
Sosuke Sugaya
Ryunosuke Chiba
Ryoma Terasaka
Rio Nakamura
Kirara Hazama
Rinka Hayami
Koki Mimura
Takuya Muramatsu
Taisei Yoshida
Itona Horibe

CLASS 144 TIME FOR ASSASSINS

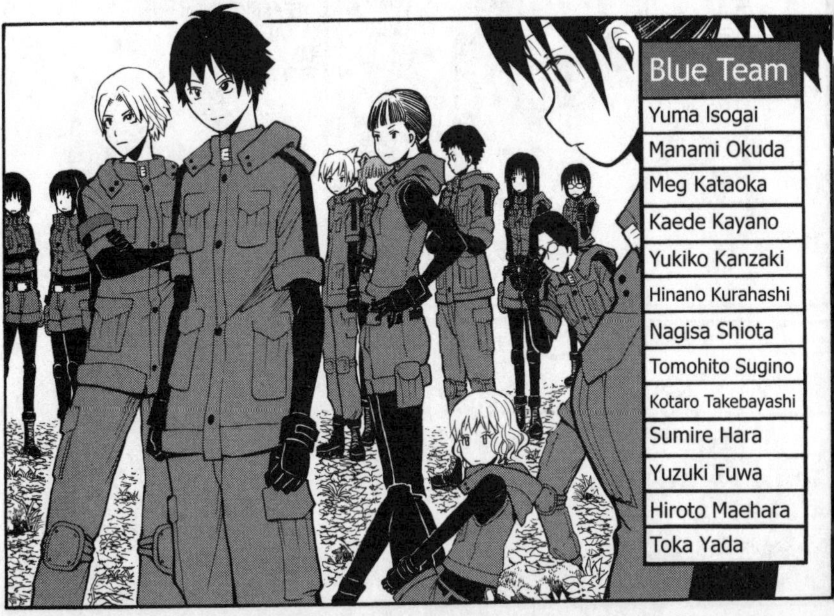
Blue Team
Yuma Isogai
Manami Okuda
Meg Kataoka
Kaede Kayano
Yukiko Kanzaki
Hinano Kurahashi
Nagisa Shiota
Tomohito Sugino
Kotaro Takebayashi
Sumire Hara
Yuzuki Fuwa
Hiroto Maehara
Toka Yada

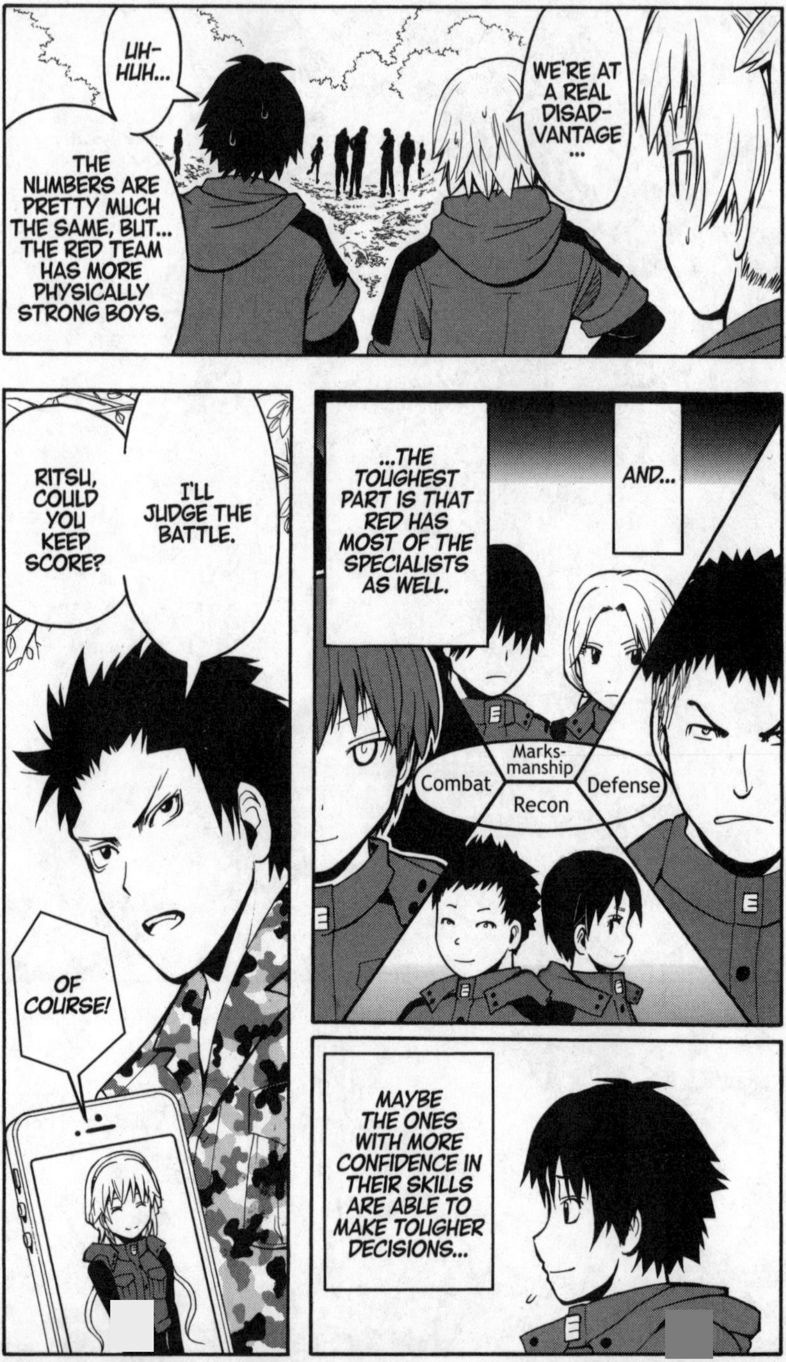
WE'RE AT A REAL DISADVANTAGE...
UH-HUH...
THE NUMBERS ARE PRETTY MUCH THE SAME, BUT... THE RED TEAM HAS MORE PHYSICALLY STRONG BOYS.
...THE TOUGHEST PART IS THAT RED HAS MOST OF THE SPECIALISTS AS WELL.
AND...
Marks-manship
Combat
Defense
Recon
MAYBE THE ONES WITH MORE CONFIDENCE IN THEIR SKILLS ARE ABLE TO MAKE TOUGHER DECISIONS...
I'LL JUDGE THE BATTLE.
RITSU, COULD YOU KEEP SCORE?
OF COURSE!

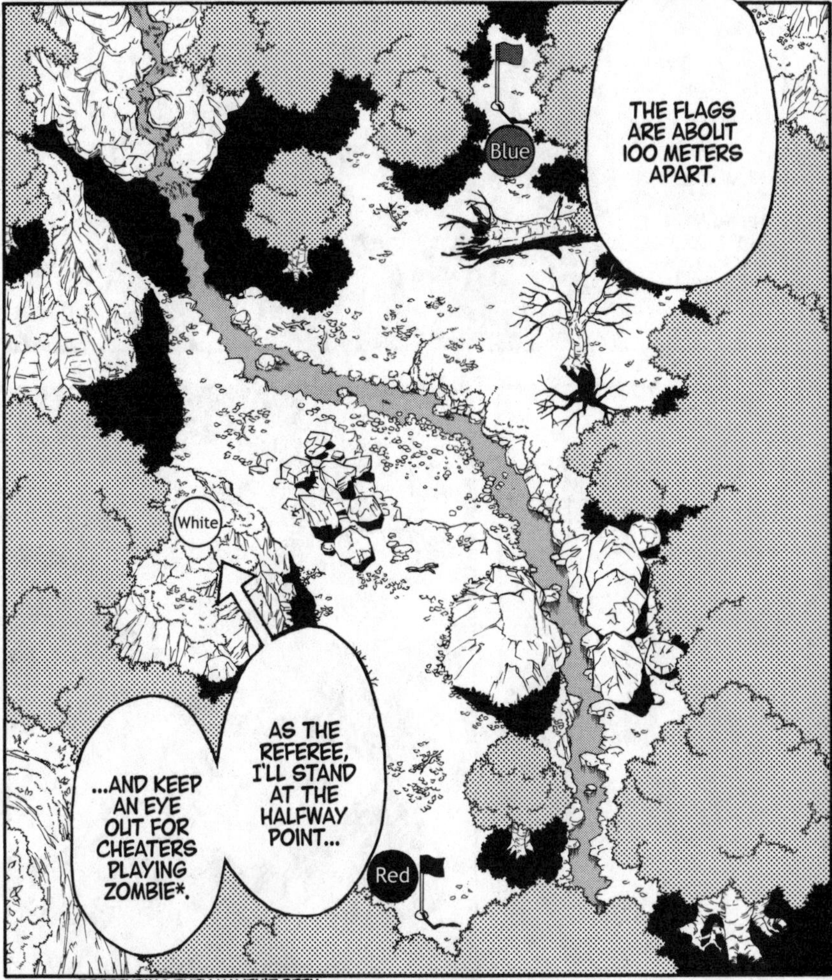
THE FLAGS ARE ABOUT 100 METERS APART.
Blue
White
AS THE REFEREE, I'LL STAND AT THE HALFWAY POINT...
...AND KEEP AN EYE OUT FOR CHEATERS PLAYING ZOMBIE*.
Red

*PRETENDING THEY HAVEN'T BEEN HIT AND CONTINUING TO FIGHT

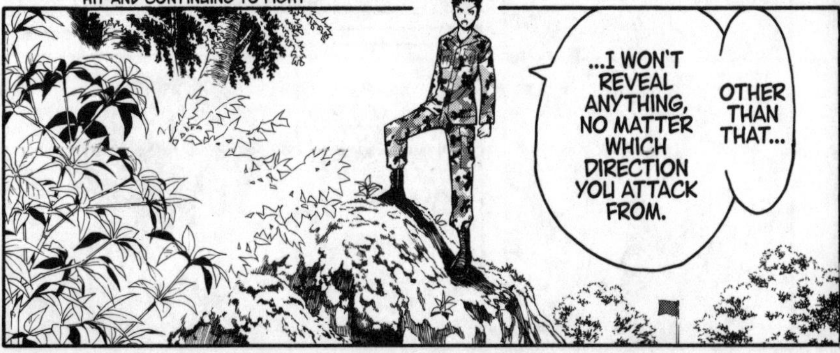
OTHER THAN THAT...
...I WON'T REVEAL ANYTHING, NO MATTER WHICH DIRECTION YOU ATTACK FROM.

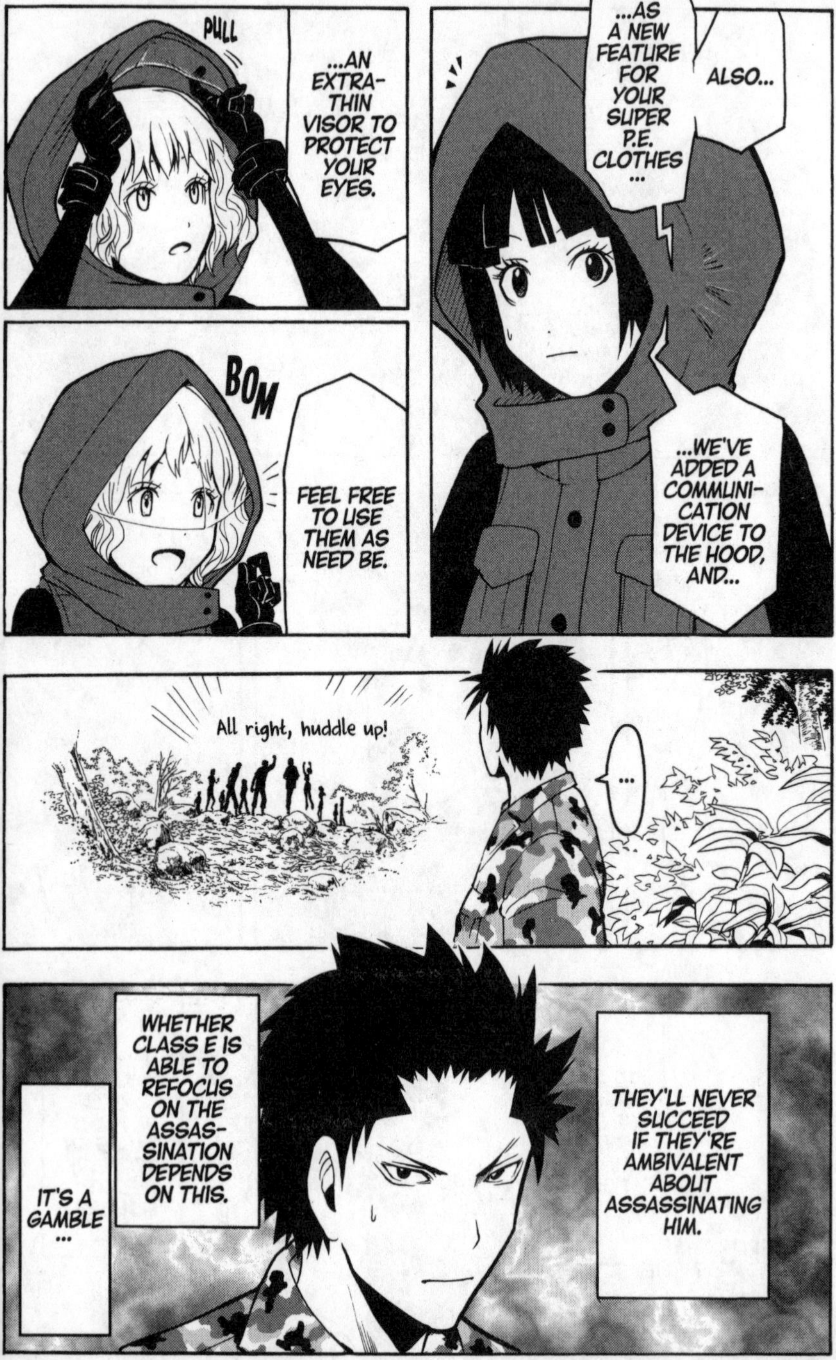
ALSO...
...AS A NEW FEATURE FOR YOUR SUPER P.E. CLOTHES ...
...WE'VE ADDED A COMMUNICATION DEVICE TO THE HOOD, AND...
...AN EXTRA-THIN VISOR TO PROTECT YOUR EYES.
PULL
FEEL FREE TO USE THEM AS NEED BE.
BOM
...
All right, huddle up!
THEY'LL NEVER SUCCEED IF THEY'RE AMBIVALENT ABOUT ASSASSINATING HIM.
WHETHER CLASS E IS ABLE TO REFOCUS ON THE ASSASSINATION DEPENDS ON THIS.
IT'S A GAMBLE ...

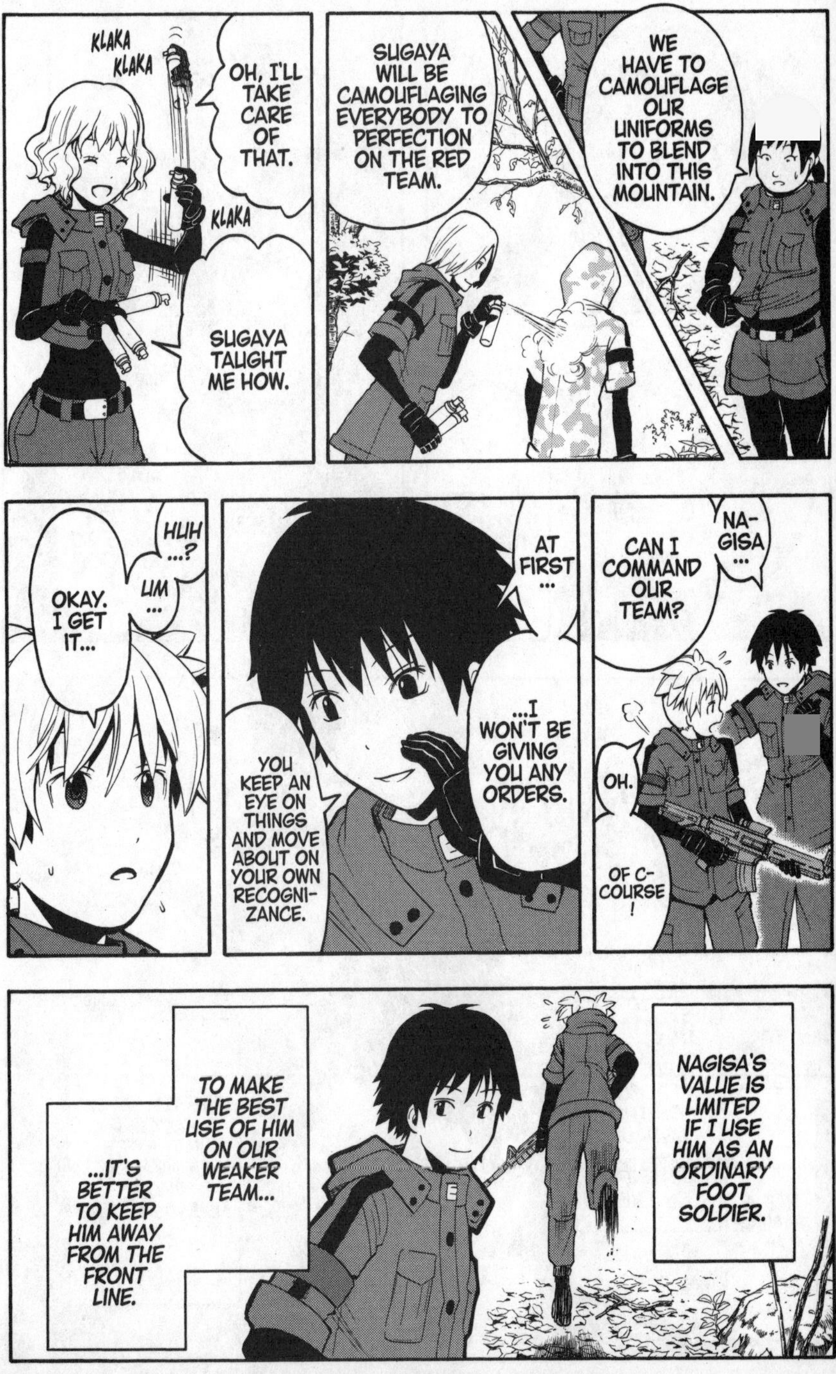
WE HAVE TO CAMOUFLAGE OUR UNIFORMS TO BLEND INTO THIS MOUNTAIN.
SUGAYA WILL BE CAMOUFLAGING EVERYBODY TO PERFECTION ON THE RED TEAM.
KLAKA KLAKA
OH, I'LL TAKE CARE OF THAT.
KLAKA
SUGAYA TAUGHT ME HOW.
NA-GISA...
CAN I COMMAND OUR TEAM?
OH.
OF C-COURSE!
AT FIRST...
...I WON'T BE GIVING YOU ANY ORDERS.
YOU KEEP AN EYE ON THINGS AND MOVE ABOUT ON YOUR OWN RECOGNI-ZANCE.
HUH...?
UM...
OKAY. I GET IT...
NAGISA'S VALUE IS LIMITED IF I USE HIM AS AN ORDINARY FOOT SOLDIER.
TO MAKE THE BEST USE OF HIM ON OUR WEAKER TEAM...
...IT'S BETTER TO KEEP HIM AWAY FROM THE FRONT LINE.

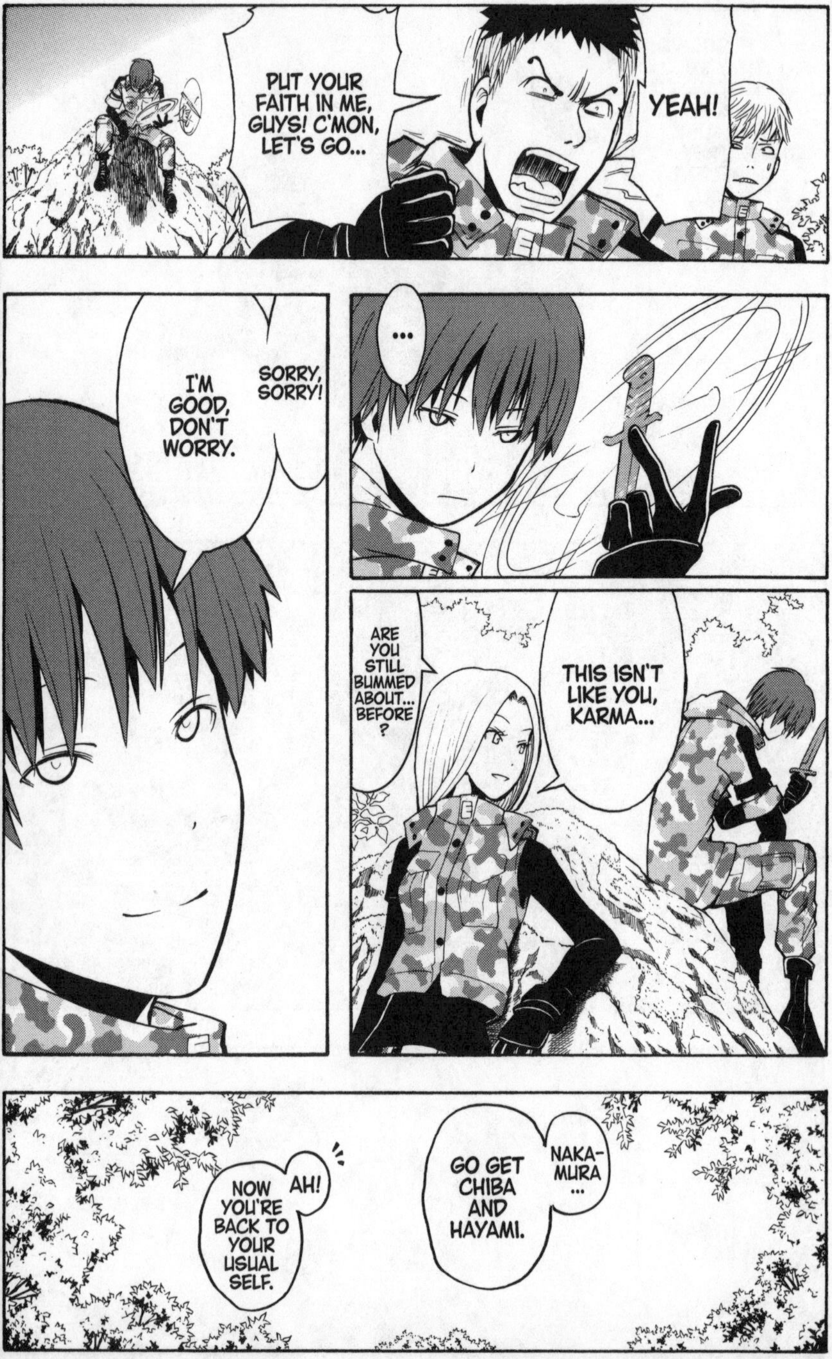
PUT YOUR FAITH IN ME, GUYS! C'MON, LET'S GO...
YEAH!
...
THIS ISN'T LIKE YOU, KARMA...
ARE YOU STILL BUMMED ABOUT... BEFORE?
SORRY, SORRY!
I'M GOOD, DON'T WORRY.
NAKA-MURA...
GO GET CHIBA AND HAYAMI.
AH!
NOW YOU'RE BACK TO YOUR USUAL SELF.

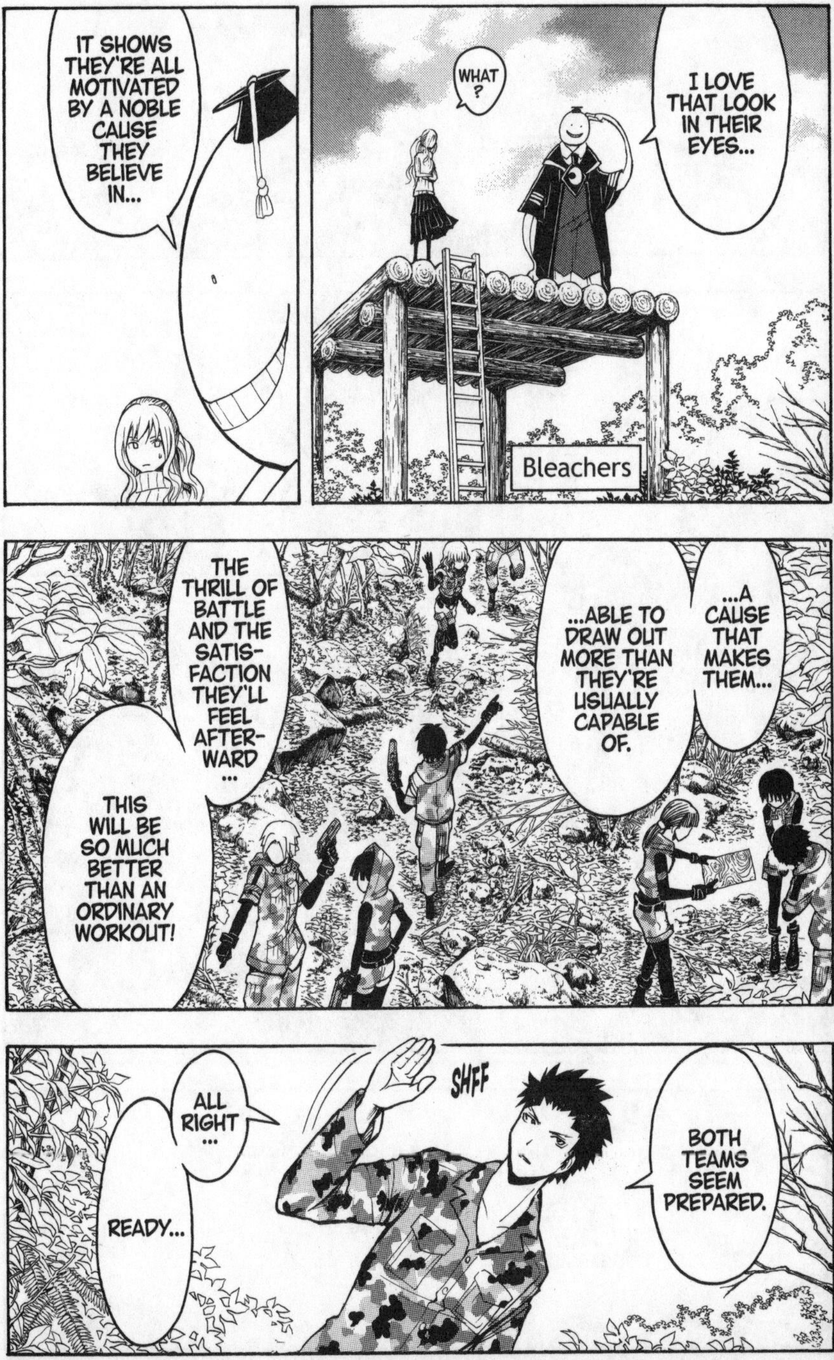
I LOVE THAT LOOK IN THEIR EYES...
WHAT?
Bleachers
IT SHOWS THEY'RE ALL MOTIVATED BY A NOBLE CAUSE THEY BELIEVE IN...
...A CAUSE THAT MAKES THEM...
...ABLE TO DRAW OUT MORE THAN THEY'RE USUALLY CAPABLE OF.
THE THRILL OF BATTLE AND THE SATISFACTION THEY'LL FEEL AFTERWARD...
THIS WILL BE SO MUCH BETTER THAN AN ORDINARY WORKOUT!
BOTH TEAMS SEEM PREPARED.
SHFF
ALL RIGHT...
READY...

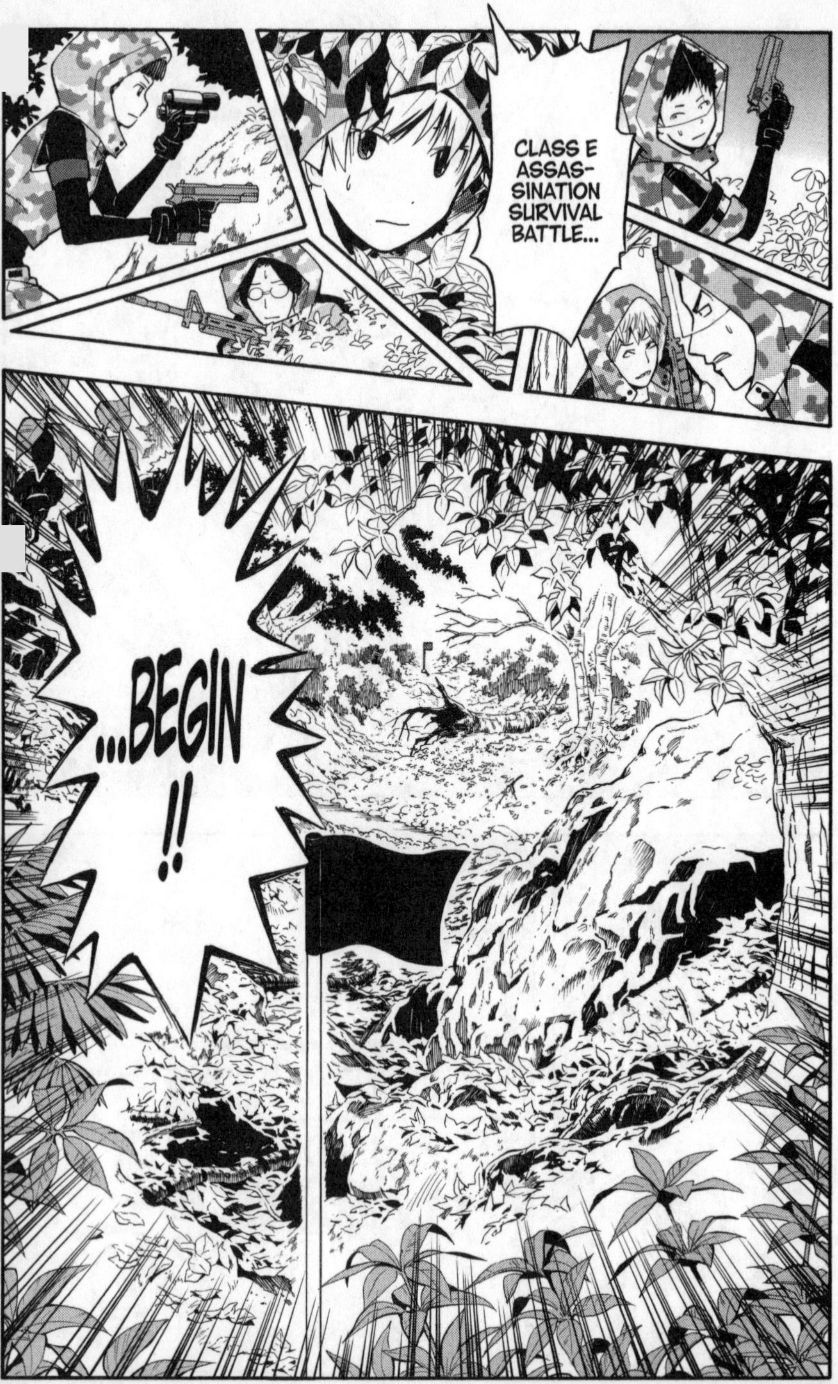
CLASS E ASSAS-SINATION SURVIVAL BATTLE...
...BEGIN !!

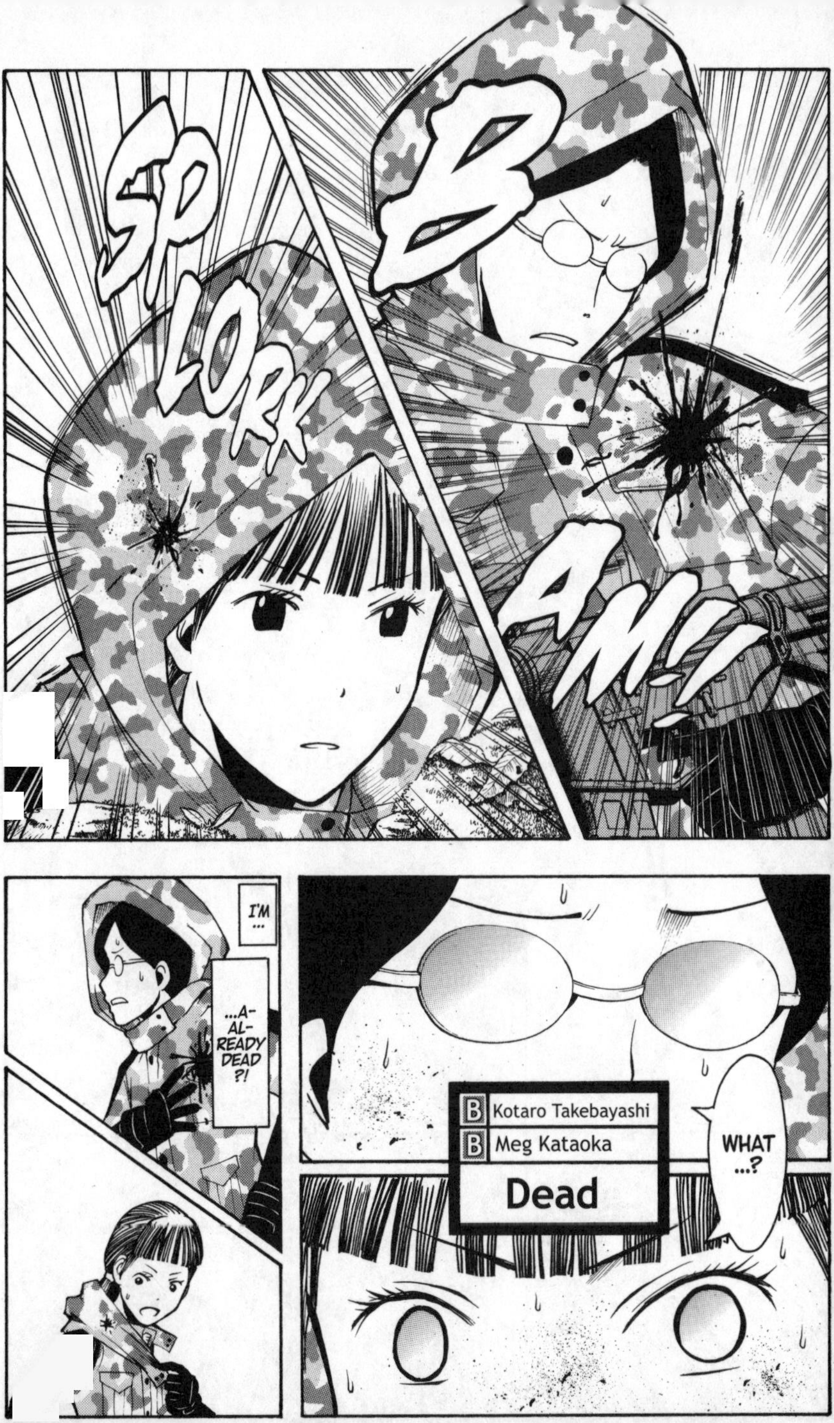
BAM!!
SPLORK
B Kotaro Takebayashi
B Meg Kataoka
Dead
WHAT ...?
I'M ...
...A-AL-READY DEAD ?!

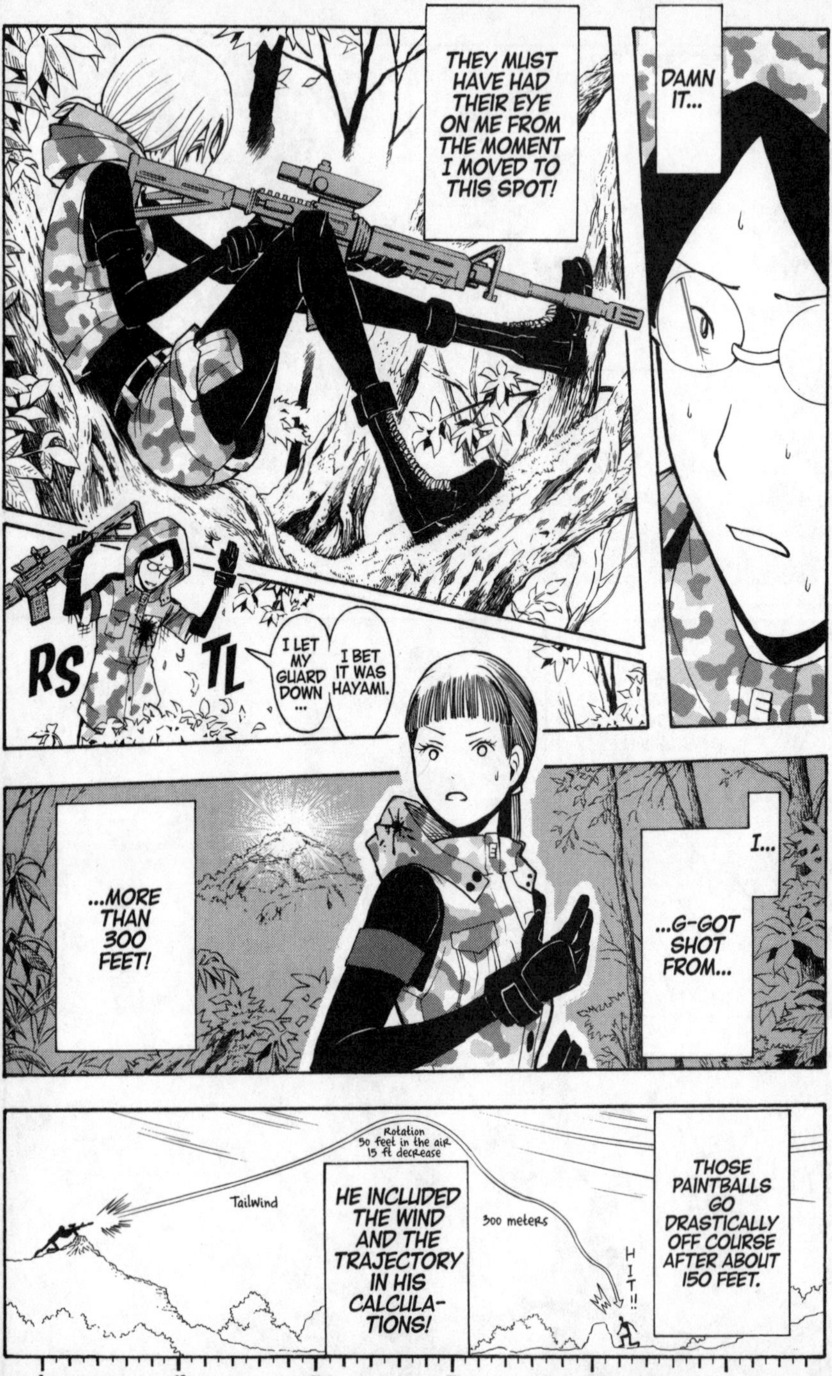

DAMN IT...
THEY MUST HAVE HAD THEIR EYE ON ME FROM THE MOMENT I MOVED TO THIS SPOT!
I BET IT WAS HAYAMI.
I LET MY GUARD DOWN...
RS
TL
I...
...G-GOT SHOT FROM...
...MORE THAN 300 FEET!
THOSE PAINTBALLS GO DRASTICALLY OFF COURSE AFTER ABOUT 150 FEET.
HE INCLUDED THE WIND AND THE TRAJECTORY IN HIS CALCULATIONS!
Rotation
50 feet in the air
15 ft decrease
Tailwind
300 meters
HIT!!
0m
25m
50m
75m
100m

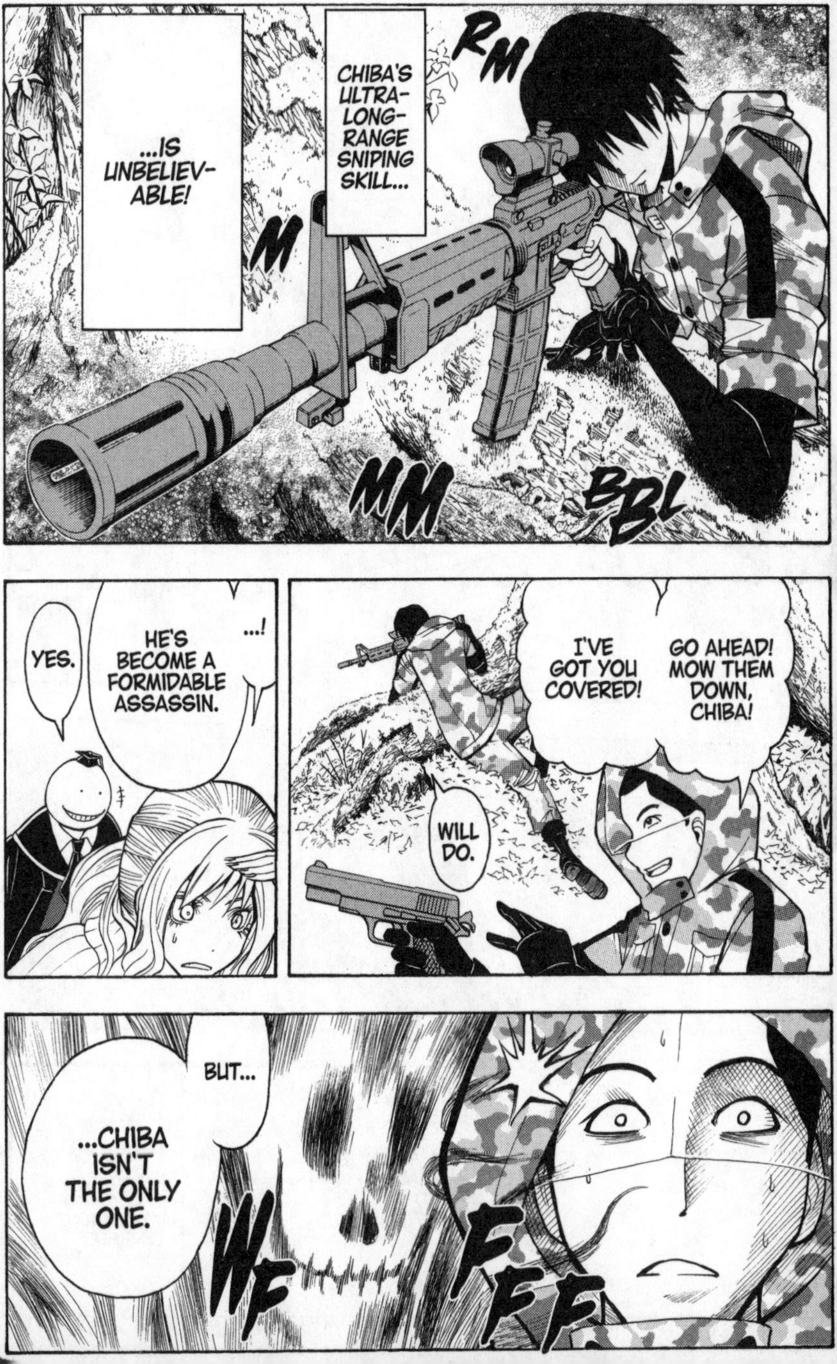
RM
CHIBA'S ULTRA-LONG-RANGE SNIPING SKILL...
...IS UNBELIEV-ABLE!
M
BBL
MM
GO AHEAD! MOW THEM DOWN, CHIBA!
I'VE GOT YOU COVERED!
WILL DO.
...!
HE'S BECOME A FORMIDABLE ASSASSIN.
YES.
BUT...
...CHIBA ISN'T THE ONLY ONE.
FF
WF

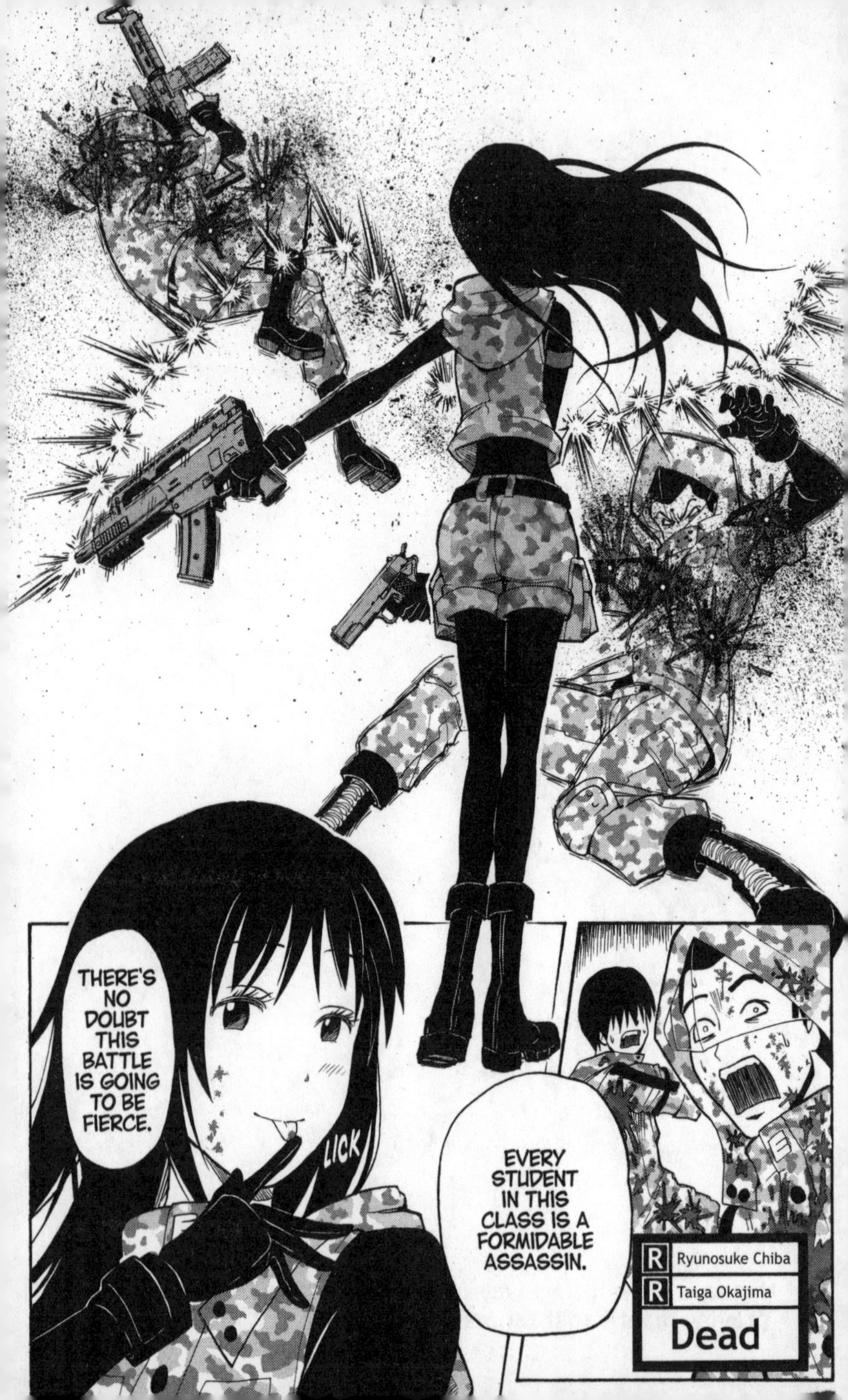
R Ryunosuke Chiba
R Taiga Okajima
Dead
EVERY STUDENT IN THIS CLASS IS A FORMIDABLE ASSASSIN.
THERE'S NO DOUBT THIS BATTLE IS GOING TO BE FIERCE.
LICK

Nagisa's Fighting Ability Checkup②

Fighting Spirit

Nagisa will even shy away from a praying mantis that taunts him.

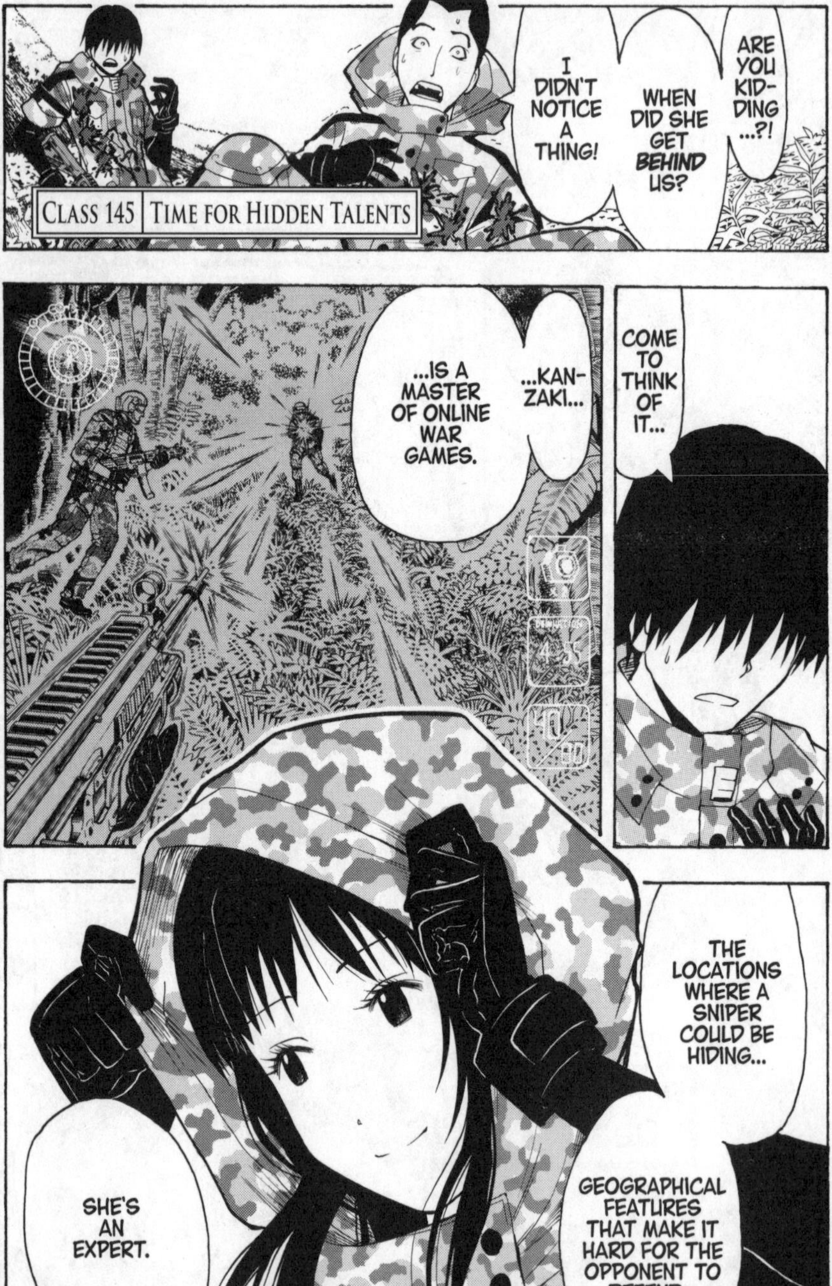
ARE YOU KIDDING...?!
WHEN DID SHE GET BEHIND US?
I DIDN'T NOTICE A THING!
CLASS 145 TIME FOR HIDDEN TALENTS
COME TO THINK OF IT...
...KANZAKI...
...IS A MASTER OF ONLINE WAR GAMES.
THE LOCATIONS WHERE A SNIPER COULD BE HIDING...
GEOGRAPHICAL FEATURES THAT MAKE IT HARD FOR THE OPPONENT TO DEFEND...
SHE'S AN EXPERT.

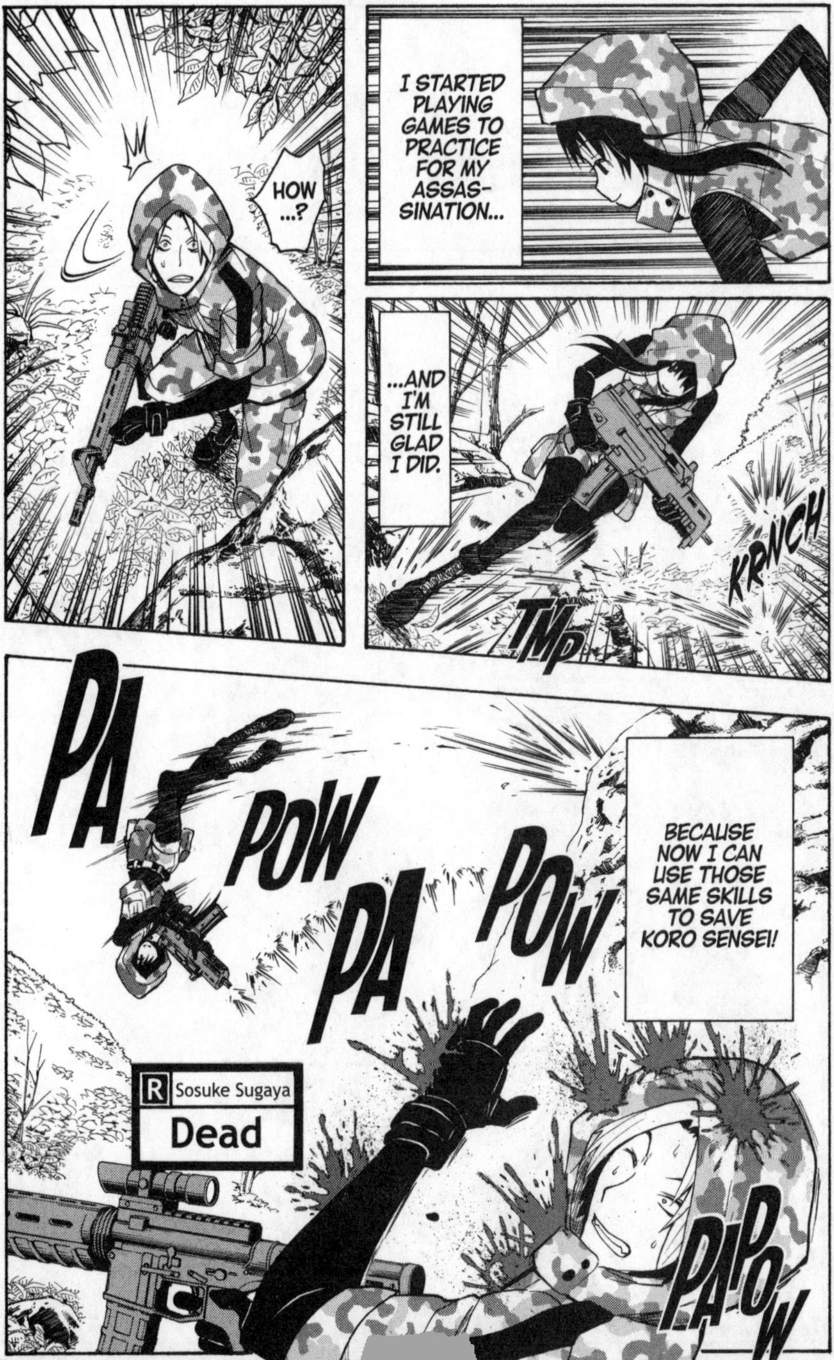
I STARTED PLAYING GAMES TO PRACTICE FOR MY ASSAS-SINATION...
...AND I'M STILL GLAD I DID.
KRNCH
TMP
HOW ...?
BECAUSE NOW I CAN USE THOSE SAME SKILLS TO SAVE KORO SENSEI!
PA POW
PA POW
R Sosuke Sugaya
Dead
PAPOW

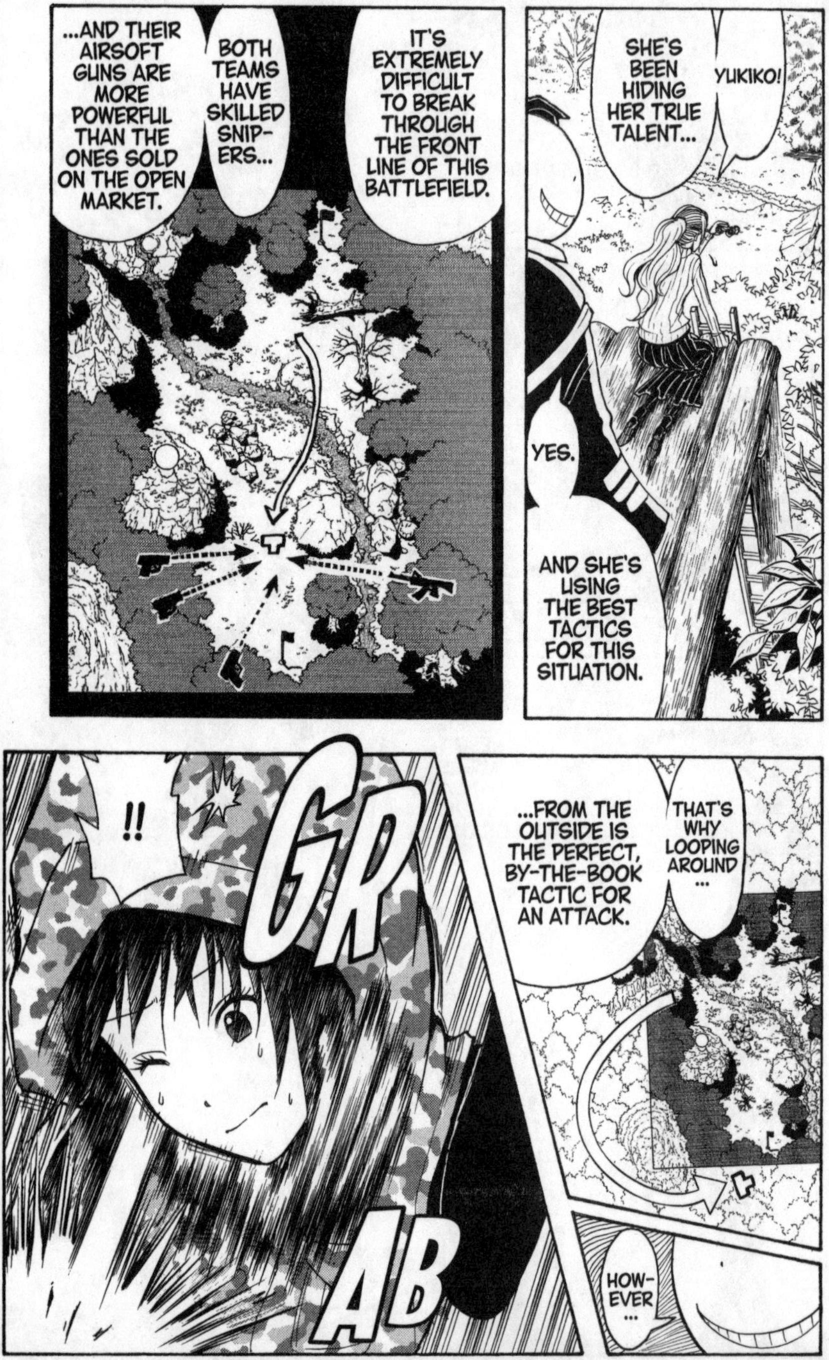
YUKIKO!
SHE'S BEEN HIDING HER TRUE TALENT...
YES.
AND SHE'S USING THE BEST TACTICS FOR THIS SITUATION.
IT'S EXTREMELY DIFFICULT TO BREAK THROUGH THE FRONT LINE OF THIS BATTLEFIELD.
BOTH TEAMS HAVE SKILLED SNIP-ERS...
...AND THEIR AIRSOFT GUNS ARE MORE POWERFUL THAN THE ONES SOLD ON THE OPEN MARKET.
THAT'S WHY LOOPING AROUND...
...FROM THE OUTSIDE IS THE PERFECT, BY-THE-BOOK TACTIC FOR AN ATTACK.
HOW-EVER...
!!
GRAB

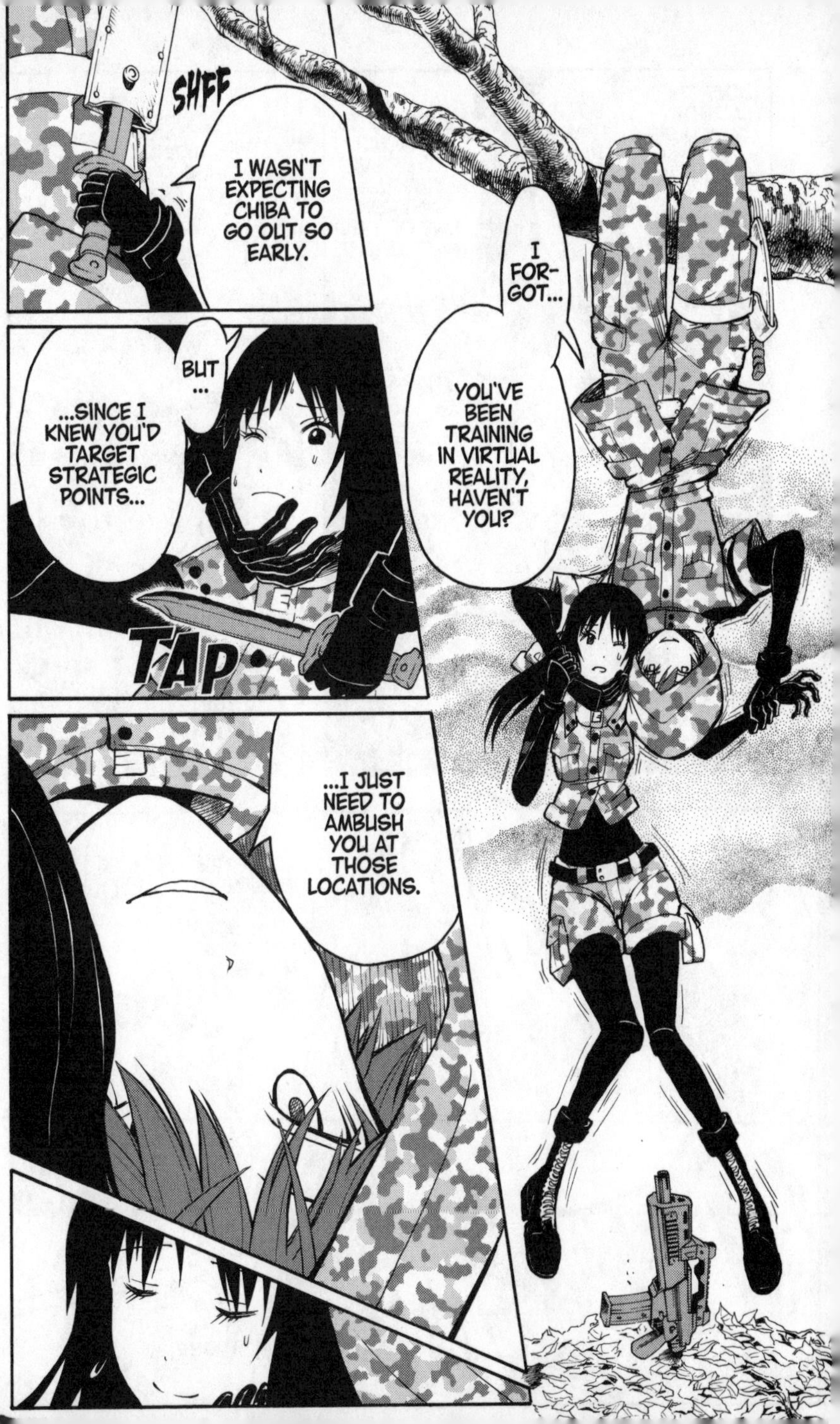
I FOR-GOT...
YOU'VE BEEN TRAINING IN VIRTUAL REALITY, HAVEN'T YOU?
SHFF
I WASN'T EXPECTING CHIBA TO GO OUT SO EARLY.
BUT ...
...SINCE I KNEW YOU'D TARGET STRATEGIC POINTS...
TAP
...I JUST NEED TO AMBUSH YOU AT THOSE LOCATIONS.

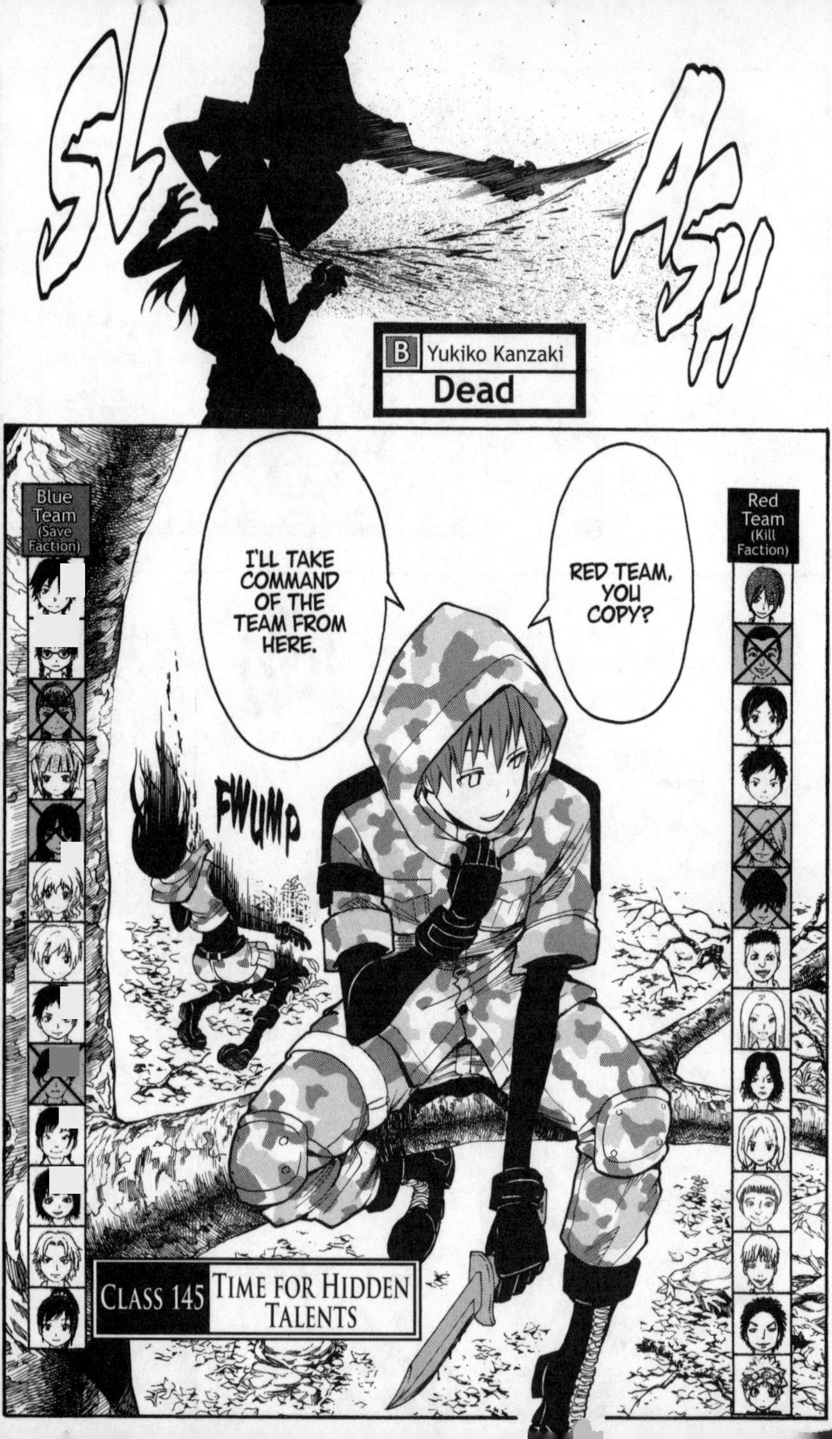
SLASH
B Yukiko Kanzaki
Dead
Red Team (Kill Faction)
RED TEAM, YOU COPY?
I'LL TAKE COMMAND OF THE TEAM FROM HERE.
Blue Team (Save Faction)
FWUMP
CLASS 145 TIME FOR HIDDEN TALENTS

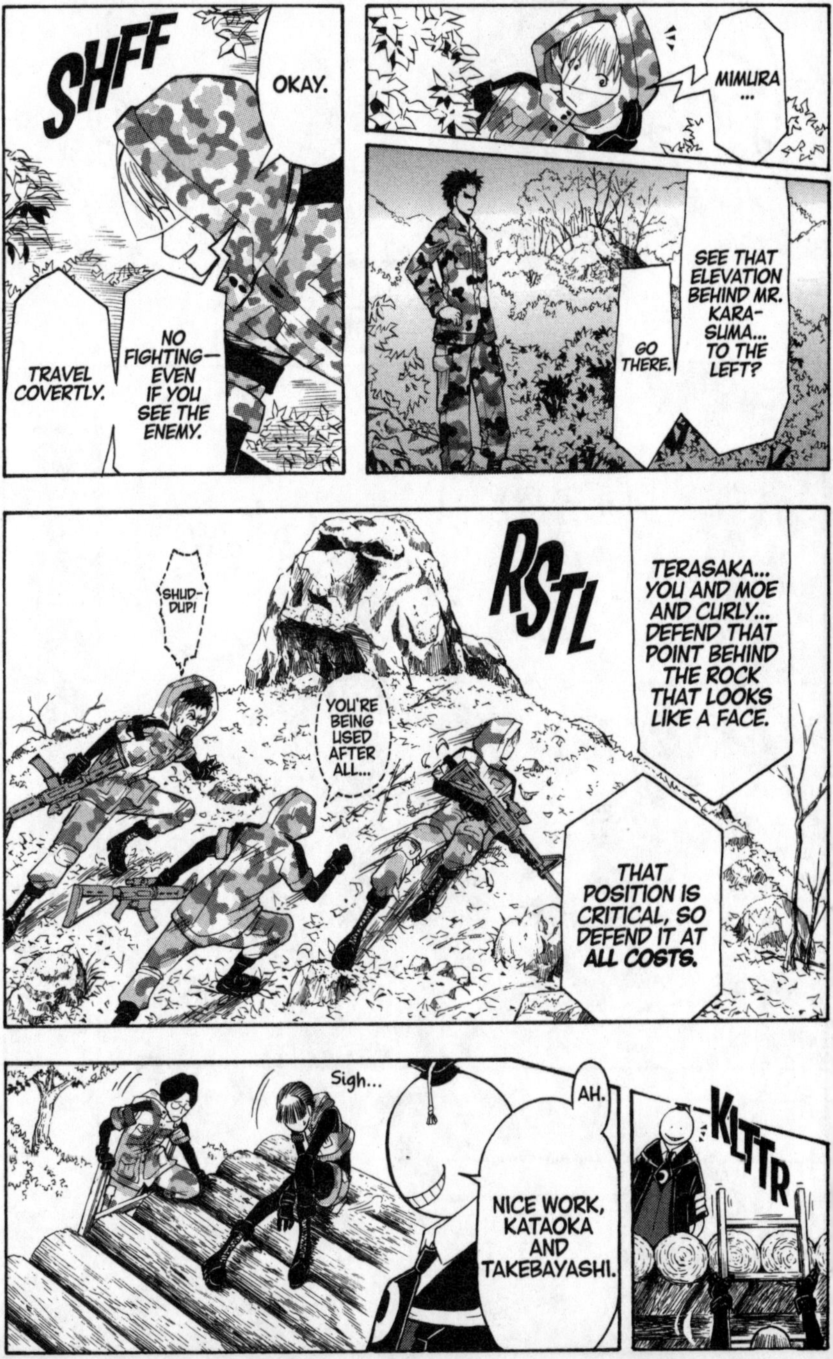
MIMURA ...
SEE THAT ELEVATION BEHIND MR. KARASUMA... TO THE LEFT?
GO THERE.
OKAY.
SHFF
NO FIGHTING— EVEN IF YOU SEE THE ENEMY.
TRAVEL COVERTLY.
TERASAKA... YOU AND MOE AND CURLY... DEFEND THAT POINT BEHIND THE ROCK THAT LOOKS LIKE A FACE.
RSTL
THAT POSITION IS CRITICAL, SO DEFEND IT AT ALL COSTS.
YOU'RE BEING USED AFTER ALL...
SHUD-DUP!
KLTTR
AH.
NICE WORK, KATAOKA AND TAKEBAYASHI.
Sigh...

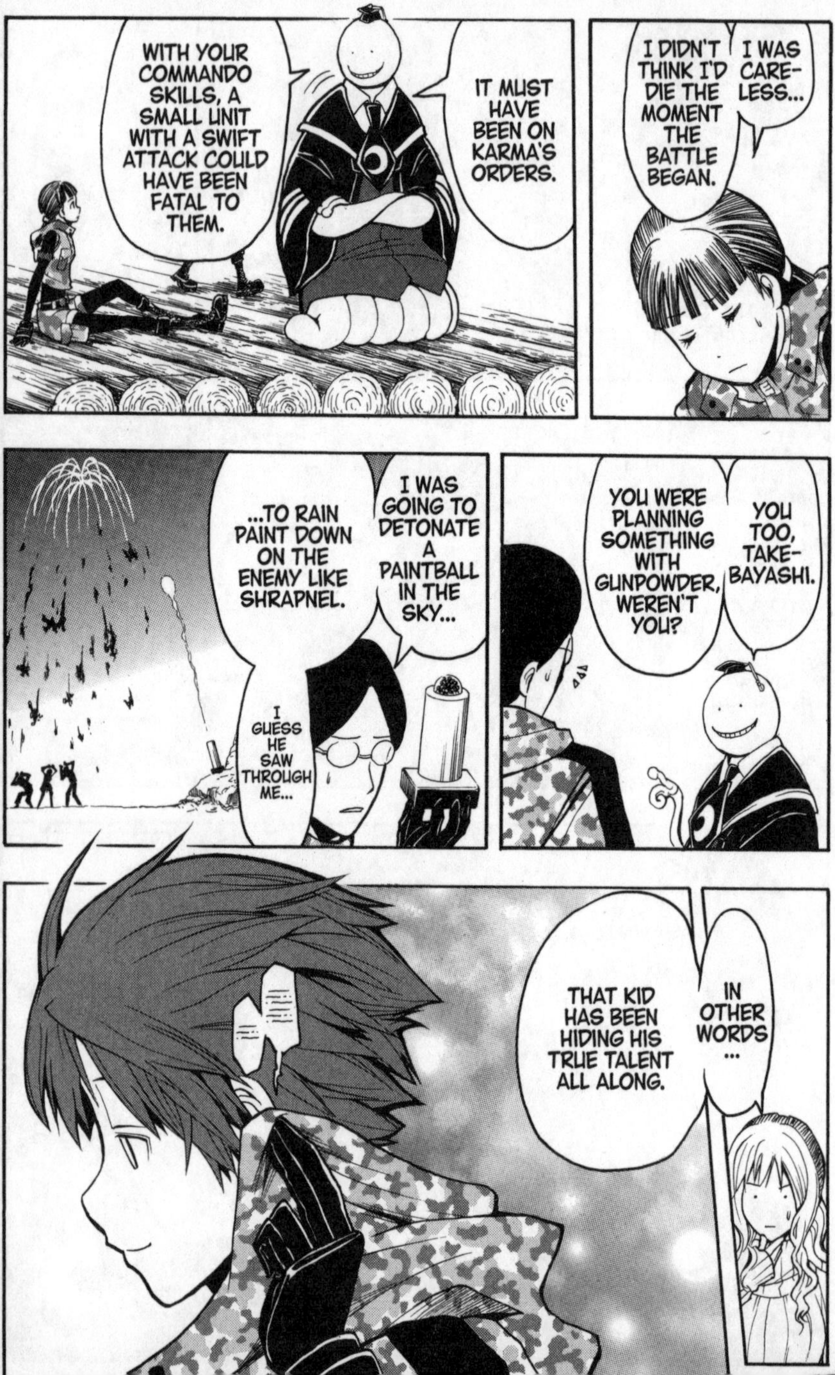
I WAS CARELESS...
I DIDN'T THINK I'D DIE THE MOMENT THE BATTLE BEGAN.
IT MUST HAVE BEEN ON KARMA'S ORDERS.
WITH YOUR COMMANDO SKILLS, A SMALL UNIT WITH A SWIFT ATTACK COULD HAVE BEEN FATAL TO THEM.
YOU TOO, TAKEBAYASHI.
YOU WERE PLANNING SOMETHING WITH GUNPOWDER, WEREN'T YOU?
I WAS GOING TO DETONATE A PAINTBALL IN THE SKY...
...TO RAIN PAINT DOWN ON THE ENEMY LIKE SHRAPNEL.
I GUESS HE SAW THROUGH ME...
IN OTHER WORDS...
THAT KID HAS BEEN HIDING HIS TRUE TALENT ALL ALONG.

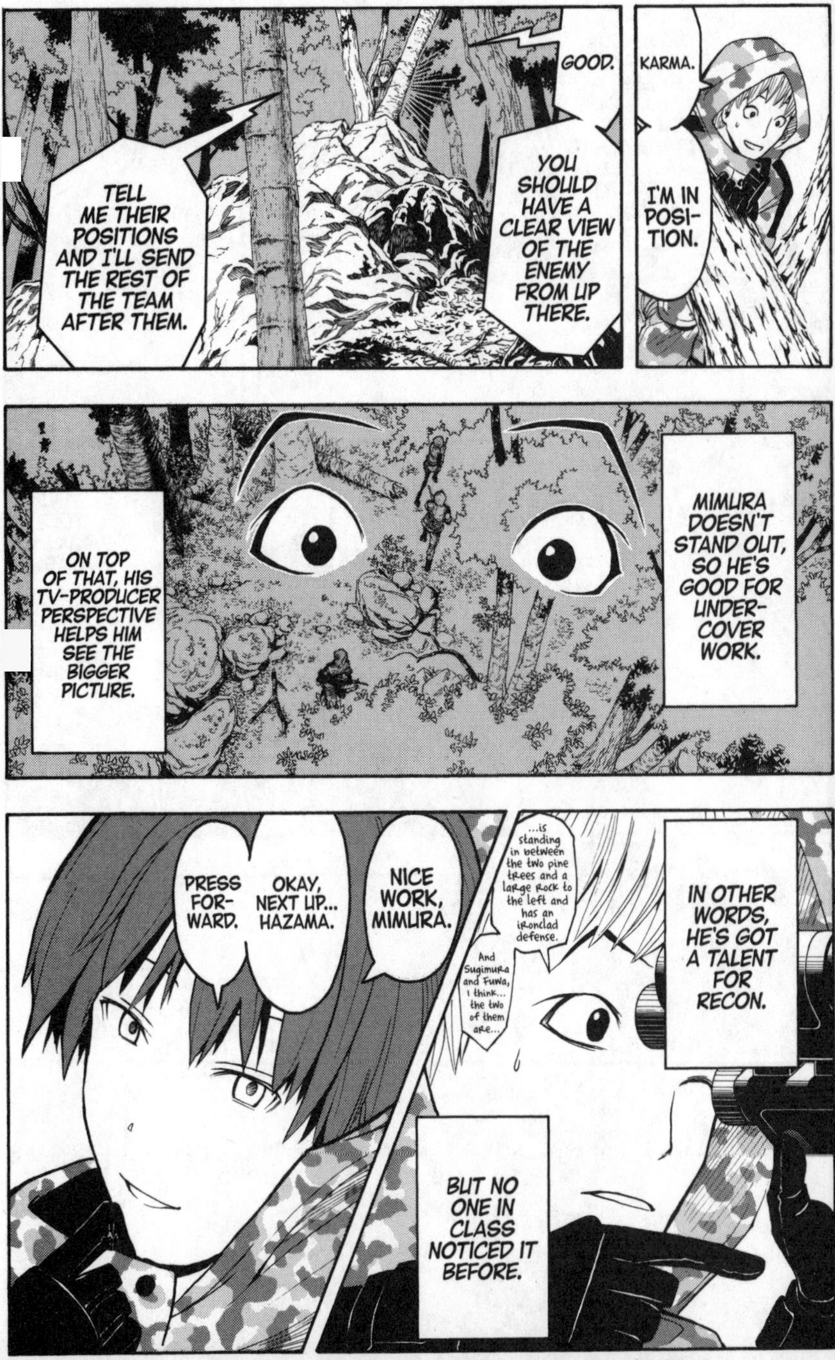
KARMA.
I'M IN POSI-TION.
GOOD.
YOU SHOULD HAVE A CLEAR VIEW OF THE ENEMY FROM UP THERE.
TELL ME THEIR POSITIONS AND I'LL SEND THE REST OF THE TEAM AFTER THEM.
MIMURA DOESN'T STAND OUT, SO HE'S GOOD FOR UNDER-COVER WORK.
ON TOP OF THAT, HIS TV-PRODUCER PERSPECTIVE HELPS HIM SEE THE BIGGER PICTURE.
IN OTHER WORDS, HE'S GOT A TALENT FOR RECON.
...is standing in between the two pine trees and a large rock to the left and has an ironclad defense.
And Sugimura and Fuwa, I think... the two of them are...
BUT NO ONE IN CLASS NOTICED IT BEFORE.
NICE WORK, MIMURA.
OKAY, NEXT UP... HAZAMA.
PRESS FOR-WARD.

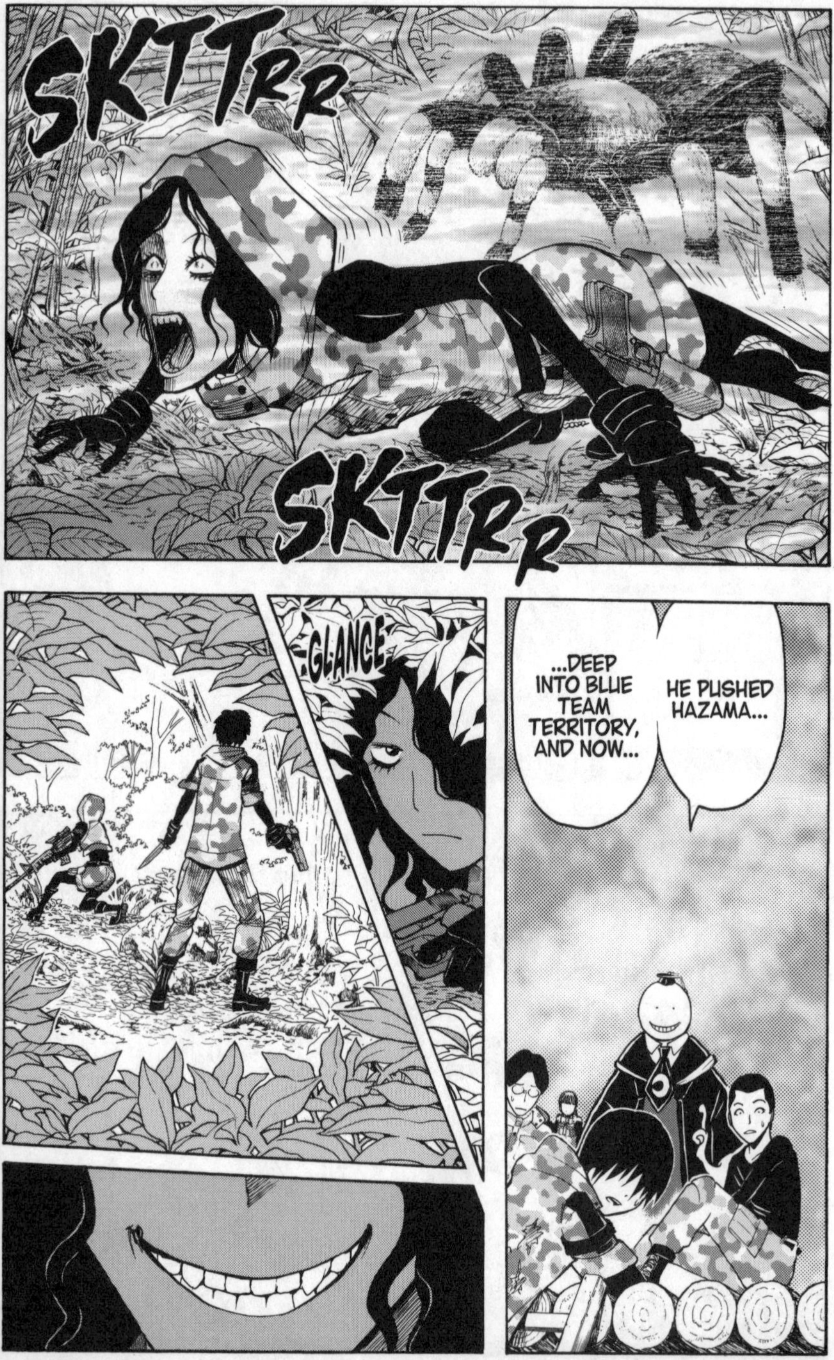
SKTTRR
SKTTRR
HE PUSHED HAZAMA...
...DEEP INTO BLUE TEAM TERRITORY, AND NOW...
GLANCE

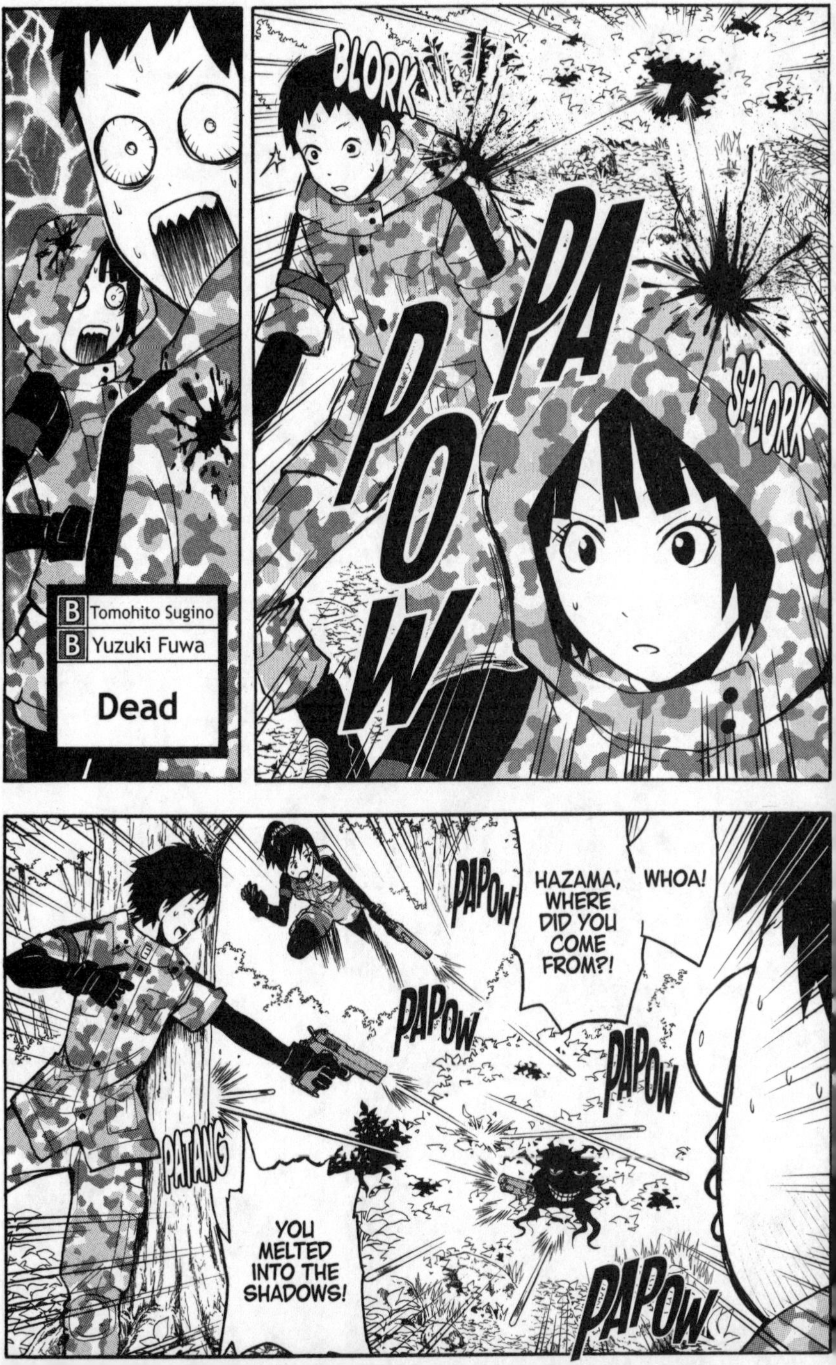
BLORK
PAPOW
SPLORK
B Tomohito Sugino
B Yuzuki Fuwa
Dead
WHOA!
HAZAMA, WHERE DID YOU COME FROM?!
PAPOW
PAPOW
PAPOW
PAPOW
PATANG
YOU MELTED INTO THE SHADOWS!

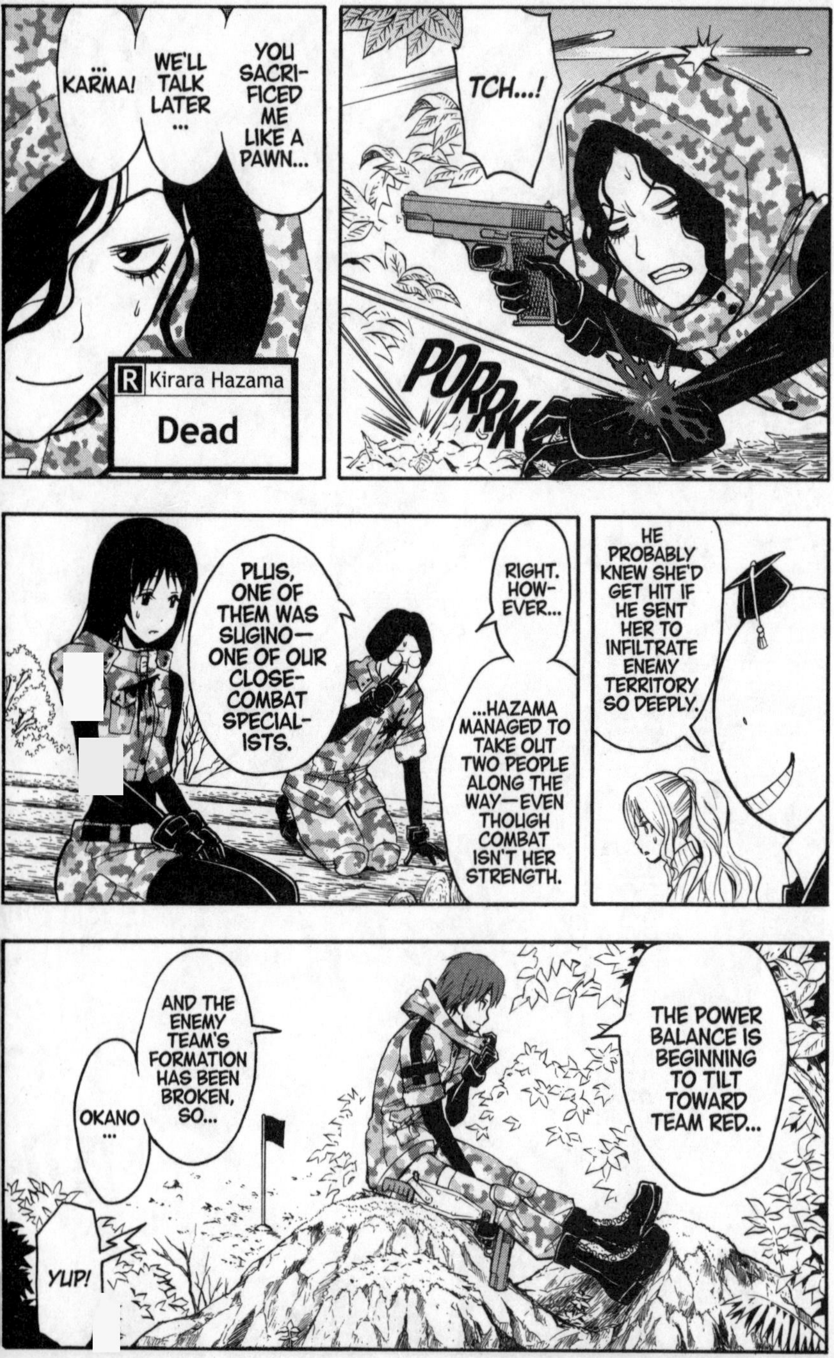
TCH...!
PORRK
YOU SACRIFICED ME LIKE A PAWN...
WE'LL TALK LATER...
...KARMA!
R Kirara Hazama
Dead
HE PROBABLY KNEW SHE'D GET HIT IF HE SENT HER TO INFILTRATE ENEMY TERRITORY SO DEEPLY.
RIGHT. HOWEVER...
...HAZAMA MANAGED TO TAKE OUT TWO PEOPLE ALONG THE WAY—EVEN THOUGH COMBAT ISN'T HER STRENGTH.
PLUS, ONE OF THEM WAS SUGINO—ONE OF OUR CLOSE-COMBAT SPECIALISTS.
THE POWER BALANCE IS BEGINNING TO TILT TOWARD TEAM RED...
AND THE ENEMY TEAM'S FORMATION HAS BEEN BROKEN, SO...
OKANO...
YUP!

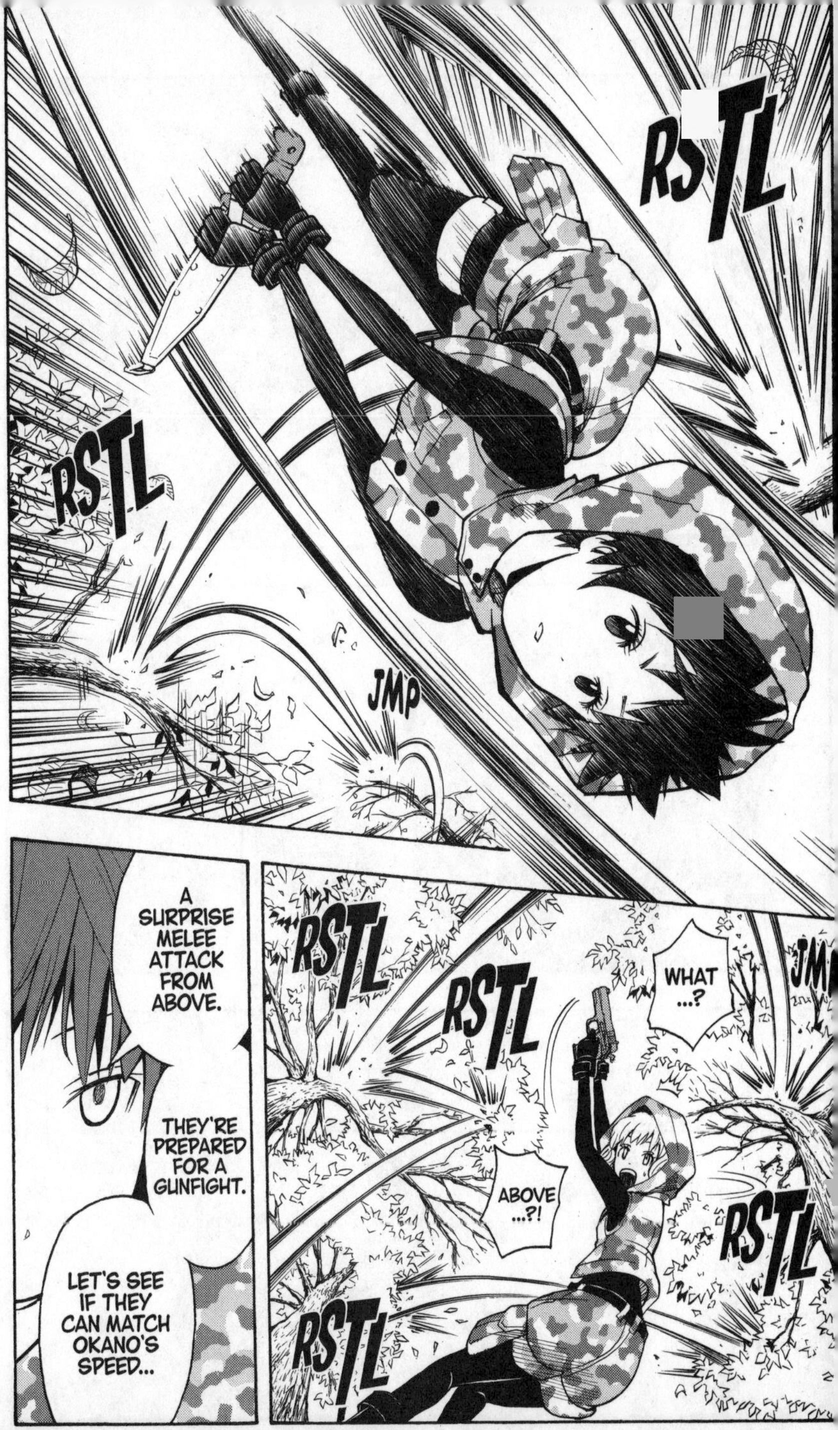

RSTL
RSTL
JMP
WHAT ...?
RSTL
RSTL
ABOVE ...?!
RSTL
RSTL
A SURPRISE MELEE ATTACK FROM ABOVE.
THEY'RE PREPARED FOR A GUNFIGHT.
LET'S SEE IF THEY CAN MATCH OKANO'S SPEED...

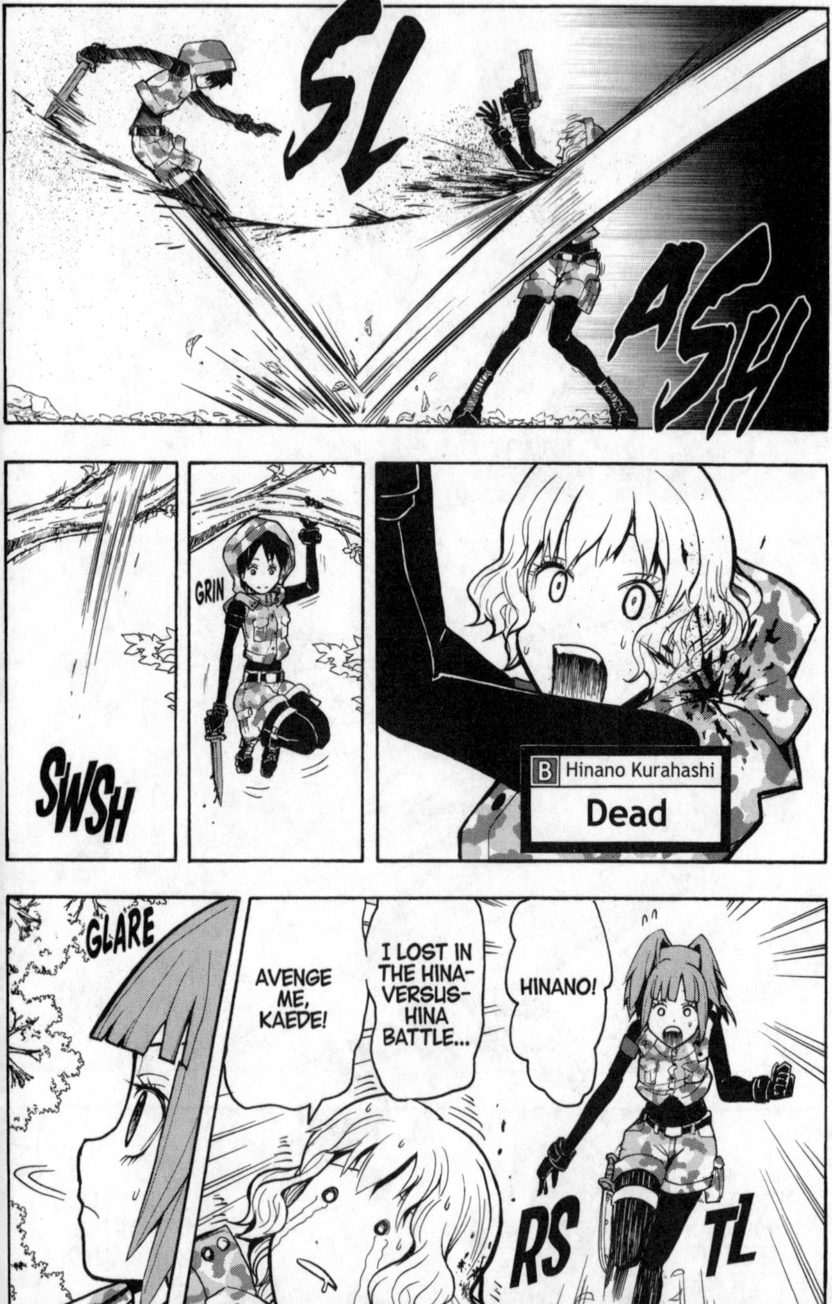
SL
ASH
Hinano Kurahashi
B
Dead
GRIN
SWSH
HINANO!
I LOST IN THE HINA-VERSUS-HINA BATTLE...
AVENGE ME, KAEDE!
GLARE
RS
TL

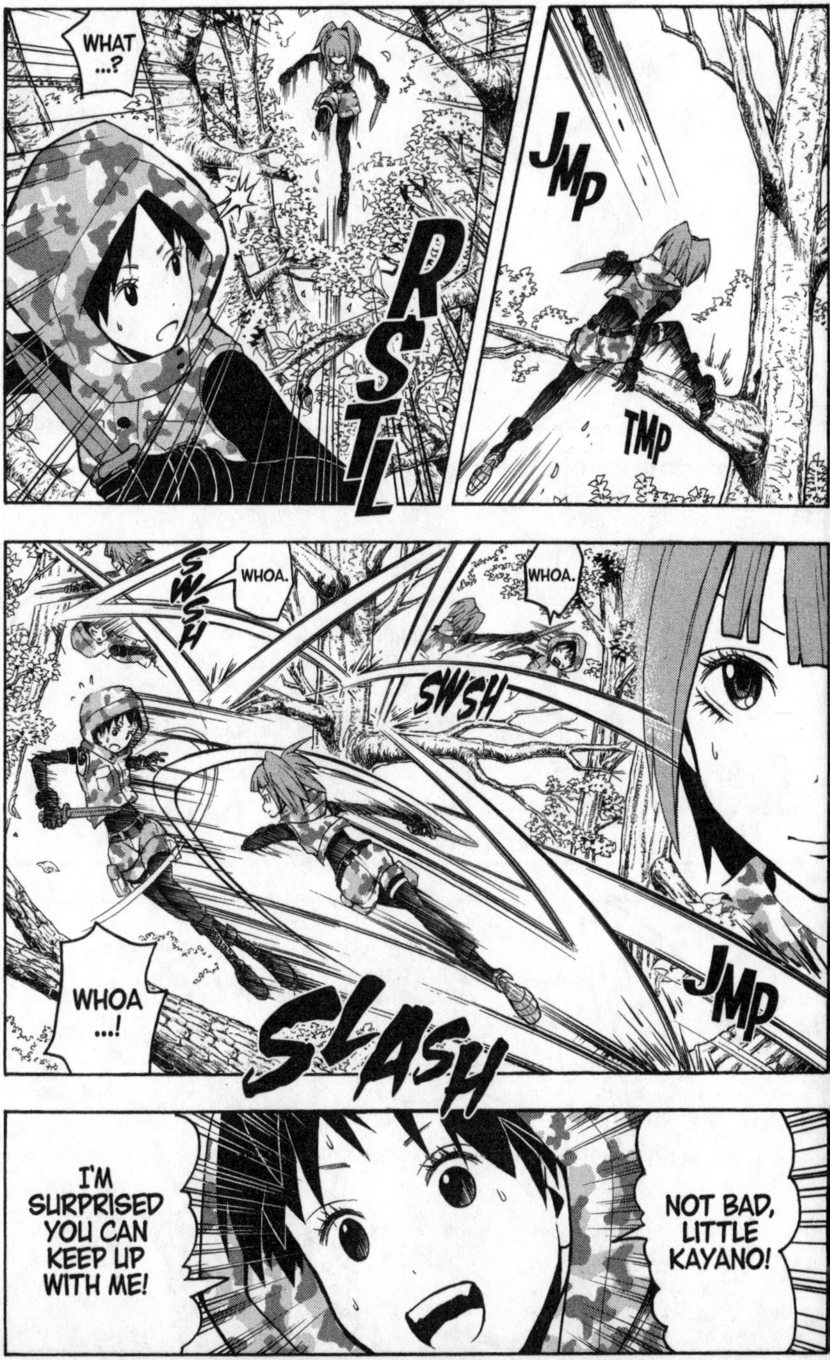
JMP
TMP
WHAT ...?
RSTL
WHOA.
JMP
SWSH
WHOA.
SWSH
WHOA ...!
SLASH
NOT BAD, LITTLE KAYANO!
I'M SURPRISED YOU CAN KEEP UP WITH ME!

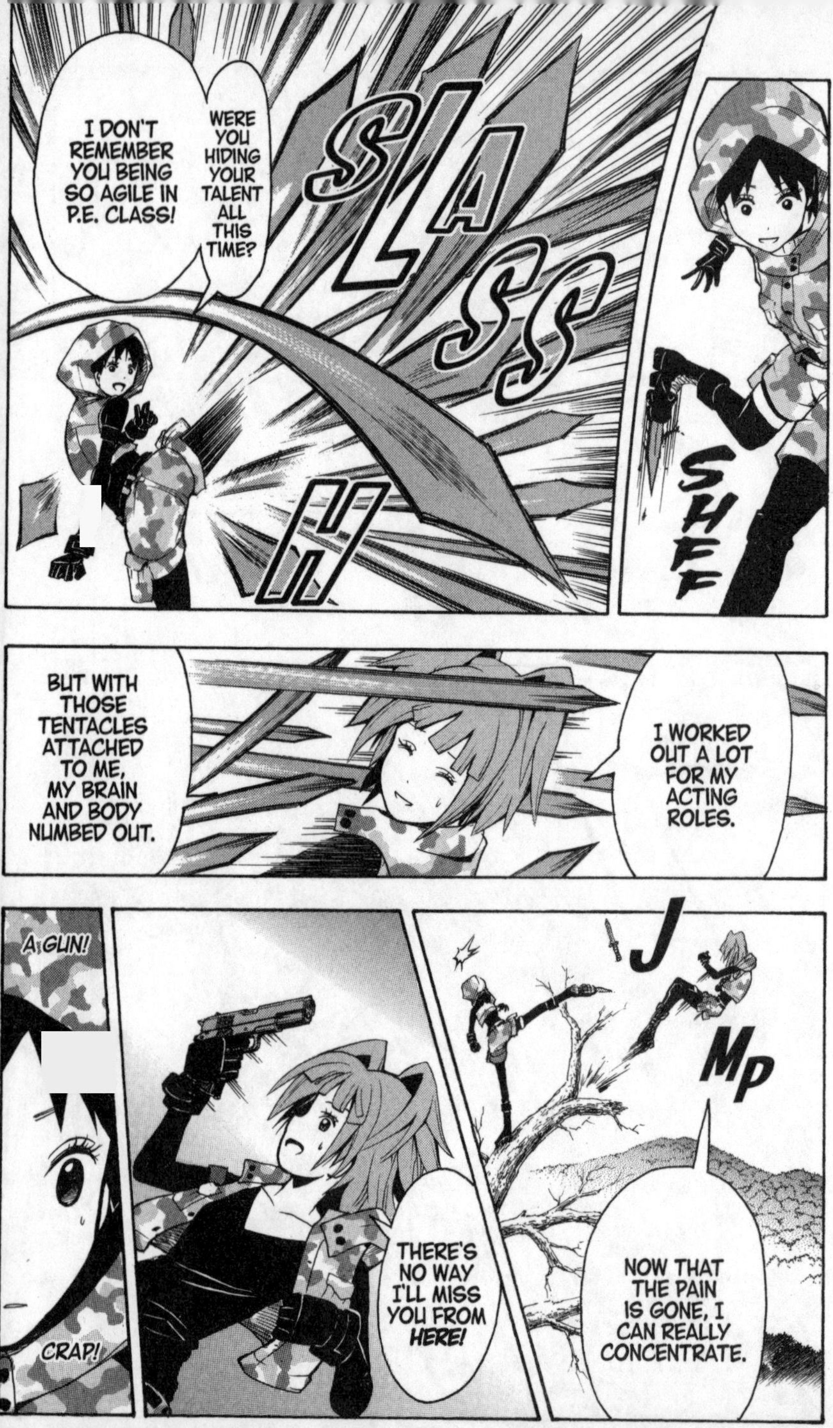
SHFF
WERE YOU HIDING YOUR TALENT ALL THIS TIME?
I DON'T REMEMBER YOU BEING SO AGILE IN P.E. CLASS!
SLASSH
I WORKED OUT A LOT FOR MY ACTING ROLES.
BUT WITH THOSE TENTACLES ATTACHED TO ME, MY BRAIN AND BODY NUMBED OUT.
JUMP
NOW THAT THE PAIN IS GONE, I CAN REALLY CONCENTRATE.
THERE'S NO WAY I'LL MISS YOU FROM HERE!
A GUN!
CRAP!

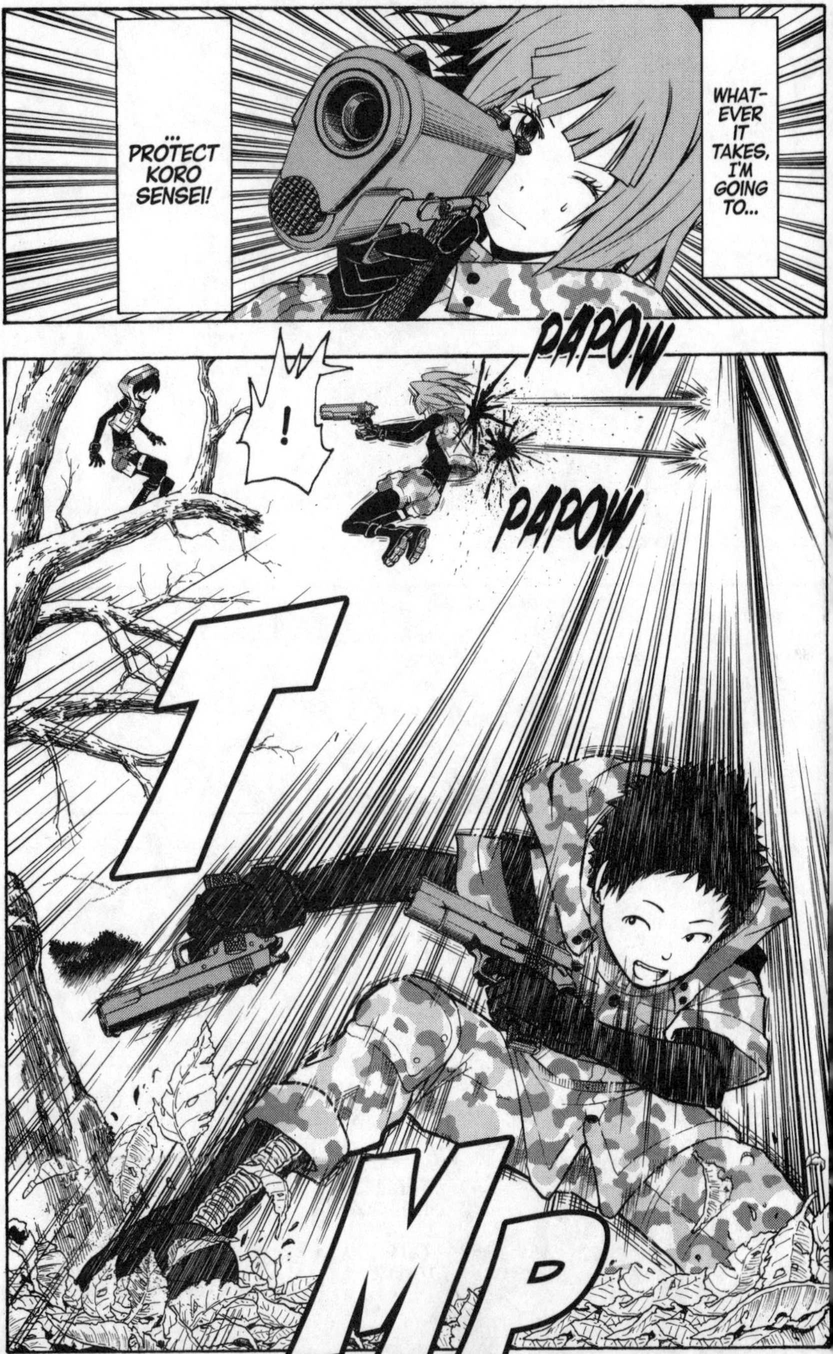
WHAT-EVER IT TAKES, I'M GOING TO...
...PROTECT KORO SENSEI!
PAPOW
PAPOW
!
TMP

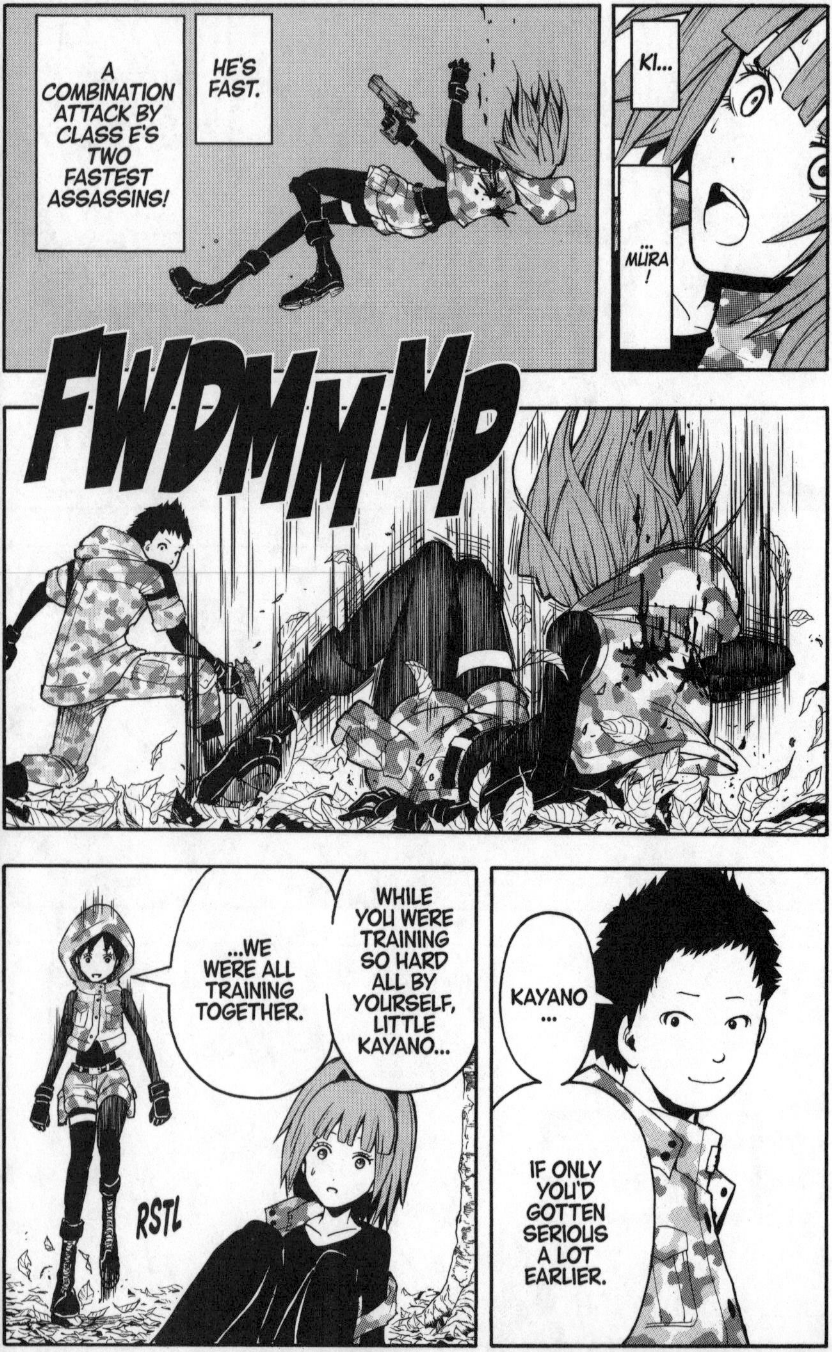
KI...
...MŪRA!
HE'S FAST.
A COMBINATION ATTACK BY CLASS E'S TWO FASTEST ASSASSINS!
FWDMMMP
KAYANO...
IF ONLY YOU'D GOTTEN SERIOUS A LOT EARLIER.
WHILE YOU WERE TRAINING SO HARD ALL BY YOURSELF, LITTLE KAYANO...
...WE WERE ALL TRAINING TOGETHER.
RSTL

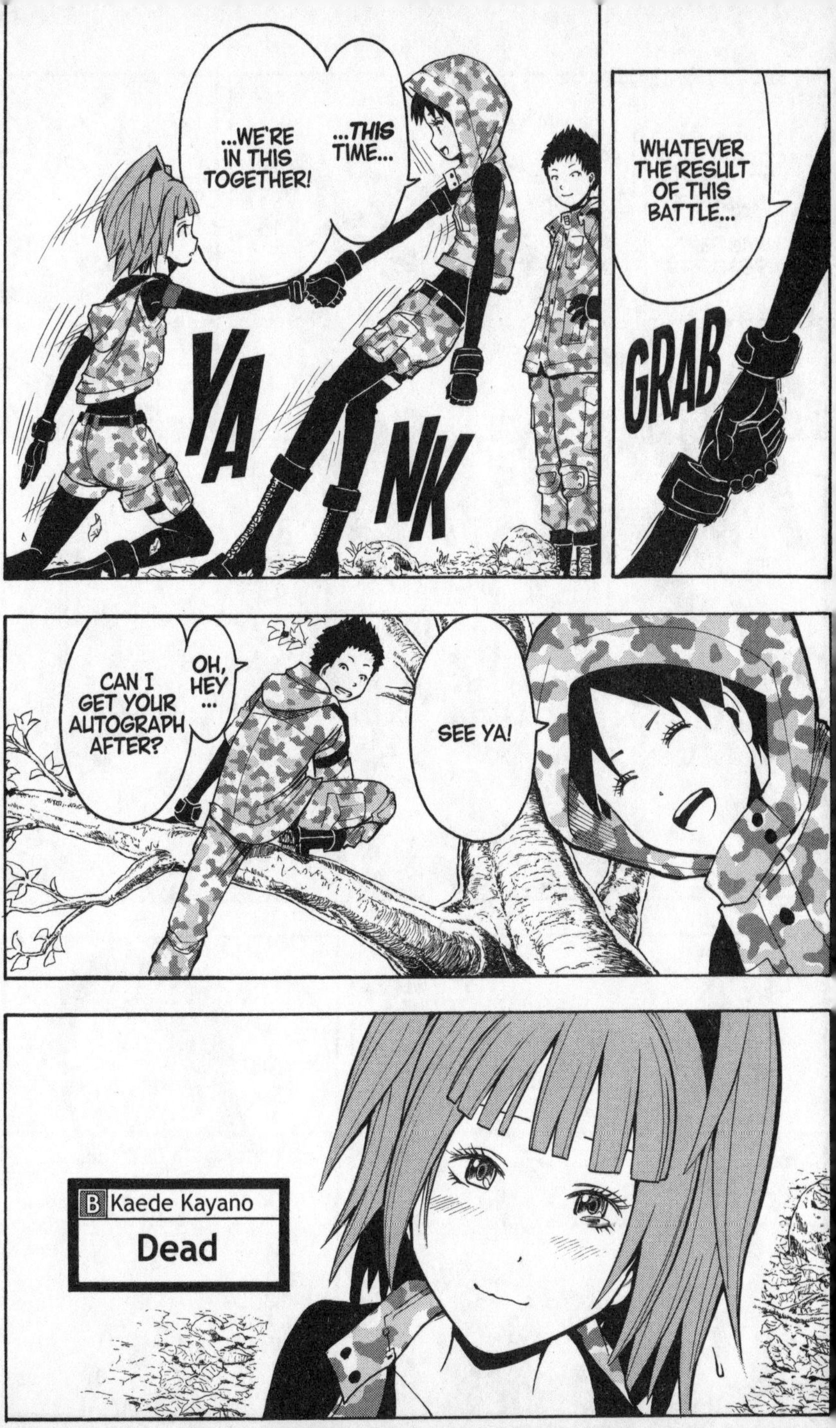
WHATEVER THE RESULT OF THIS BATTLE...
GRAB
...THIS TIME...
...WE'RE IN THIS TOGETHER!
YANK
SEE YA!
OH, HEY...
CAN I GET YOUR AUTOGRAPH AFTER?
B Kaede Kayano
Dead

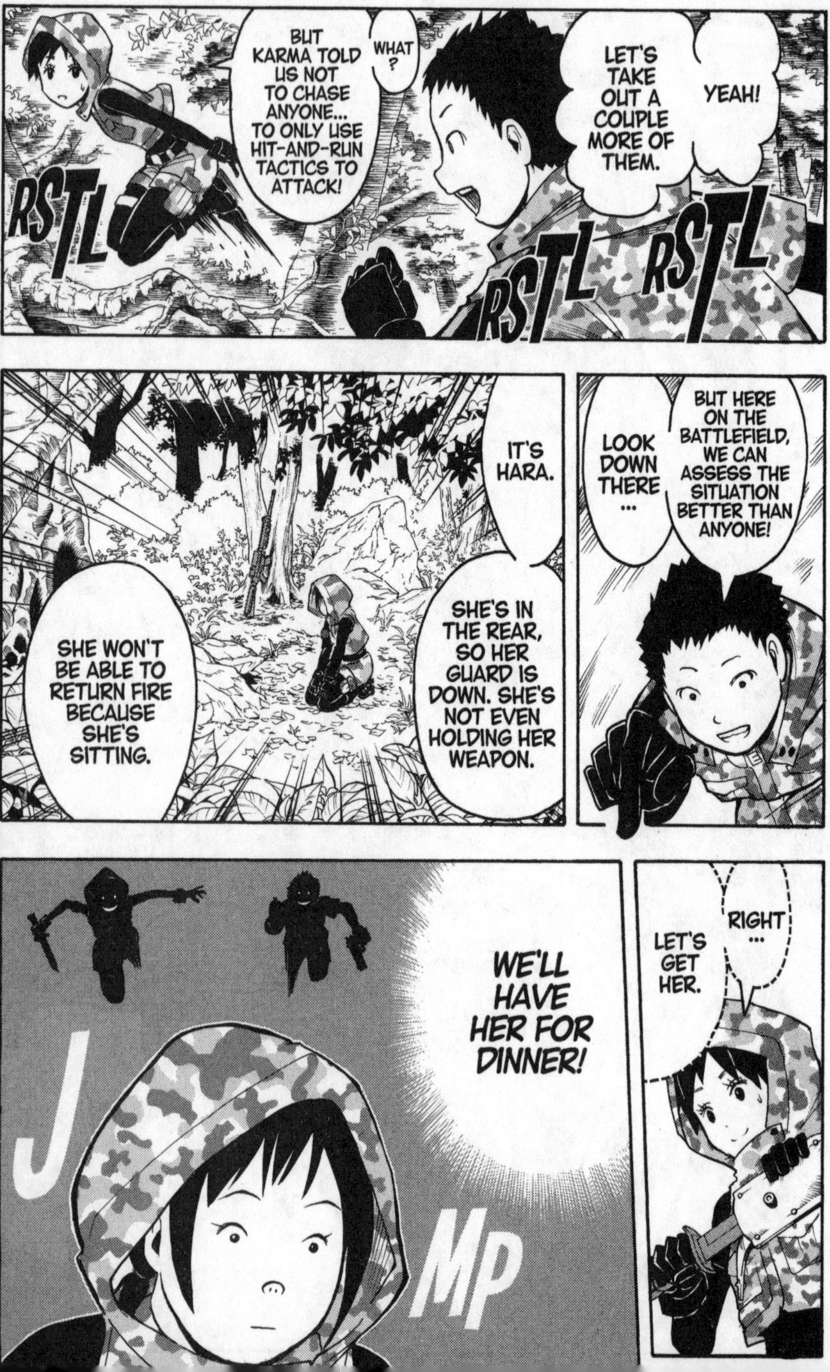
YEAH!
LET'S TAKE OUT A COUPLE MORE OF THEM.
WHAT?
BUT KARMA TOLD US NOT TO CHASE ANYONE... TO ONLY USE HIT-AND-RUN TACTICS TO ATTACK!
RSTL
RSTL
RSTL
BUT HERE ON THE BATTLEFIELD, WE CAN ASSESS THE SITUATION BETTER THAN ANYONE!
LOOK DOWN THERE...
IT'S HARA.
SHE'S IN THE REAR, SO HER GUARD IS DOWN. SHE'S NOT EVEN HOLDING HER WEAPON.
SHE WON'T BE ABLE TO RETURN FIRE BECAUSE SHE'S SITTING.
RIGHT...
LET'S GET HER.
WE'LL HAVE HER FOR DINNER!
JUMP

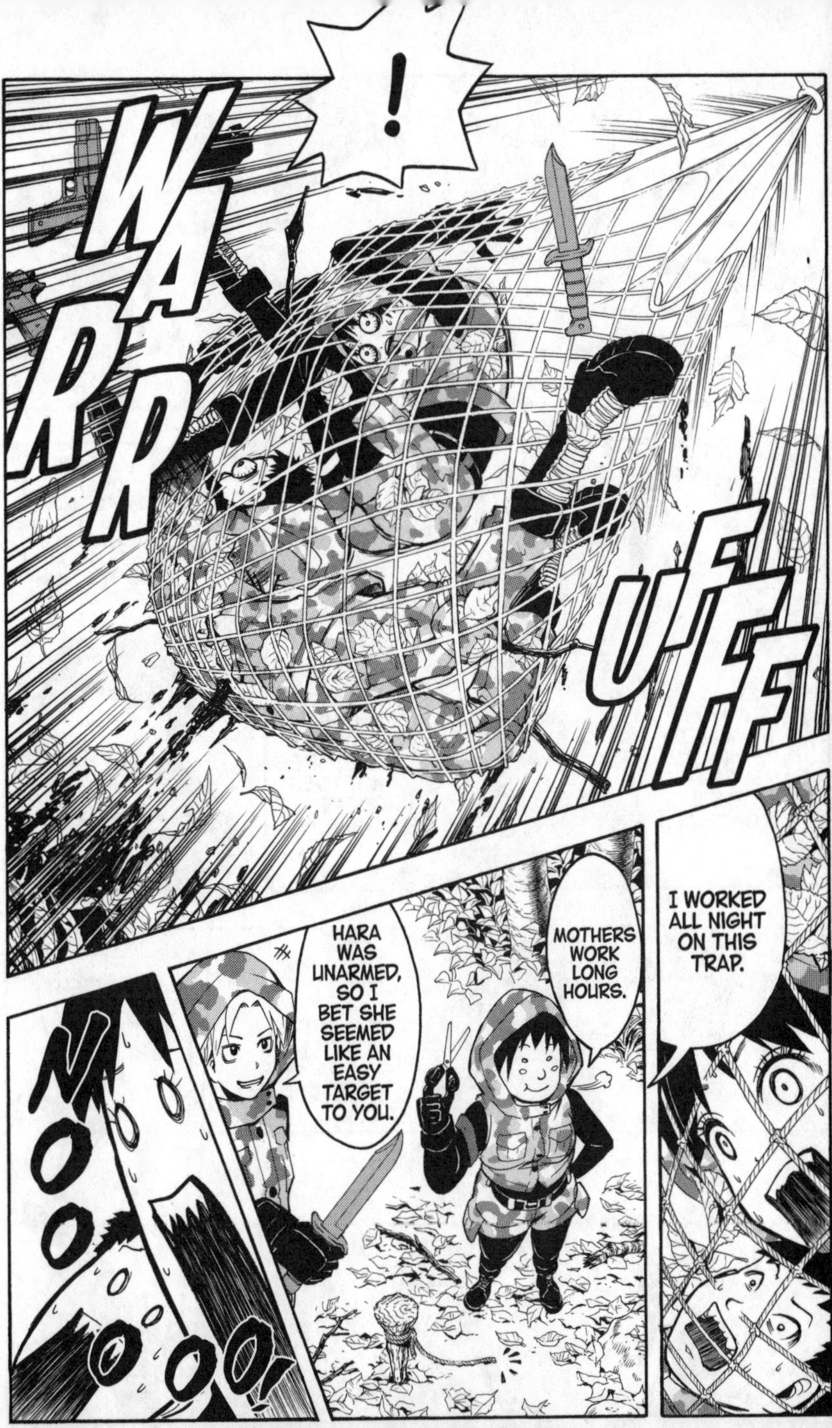
!
WARR
UFFF
I WORKED ALL NIGHT ON THIS TRAP.
MOTHERS WORK LONG HOURS.
HARA WAS UNARMED, SO I BET SHE SEEMED LIKE AN EASY TARGET TO YOU.
NOOOOOOOO!

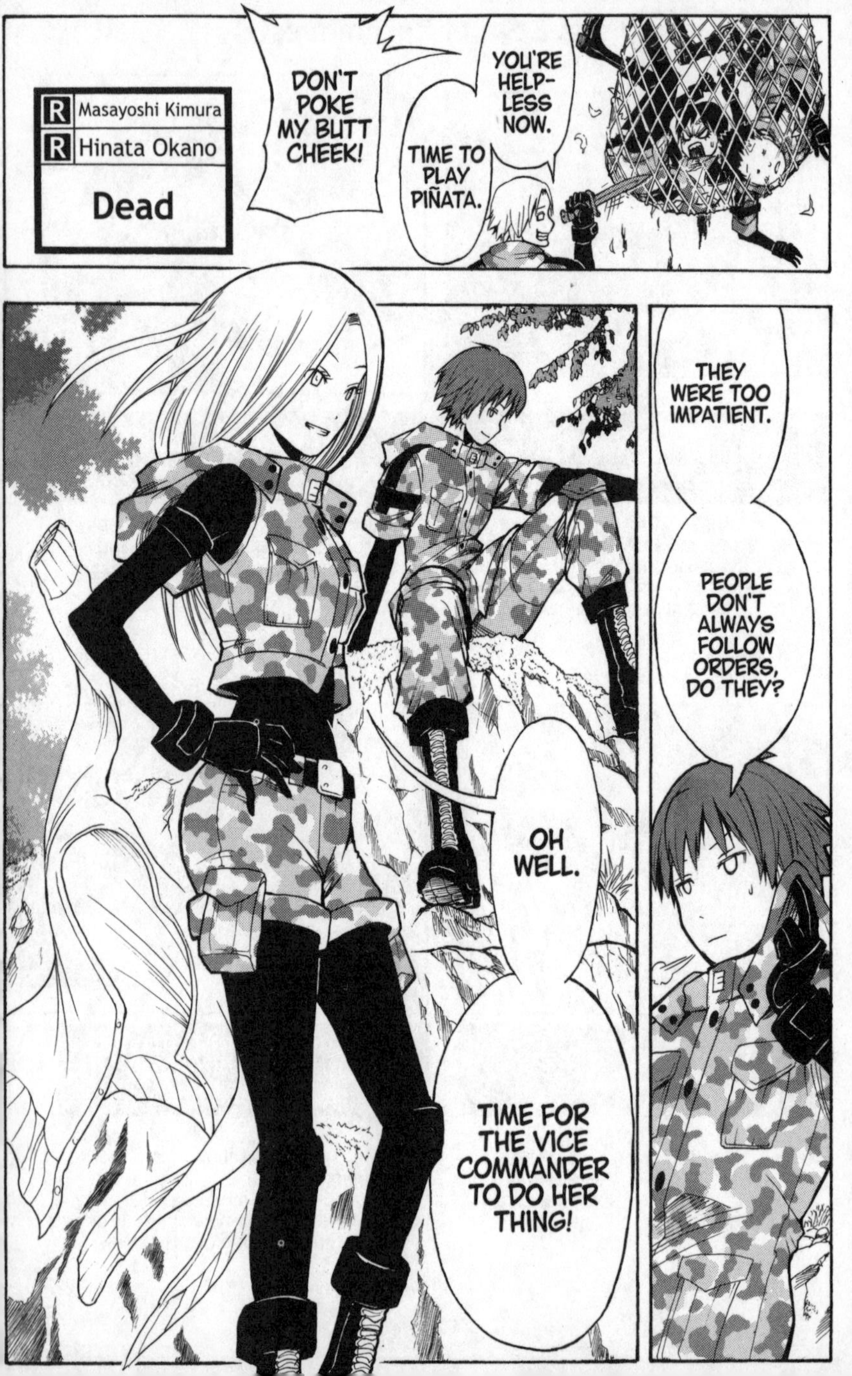
YOU'RE HELP-LESS NOW.
TIME TO PLAY PIÑATA.
DON'T POKE MY BUTT CHEEK!
R Masayoshi Kimura
R Hinata Okano
Dead
THEY WERE TOO IMPATIENT.
PEOPLE DON'T ALWAYS FOLLOW ORDERS, DO THEY?
OH WELL.
TIME FOR THE VICE COMMANDER TO DO HER THING!

Class E Super Techniques①

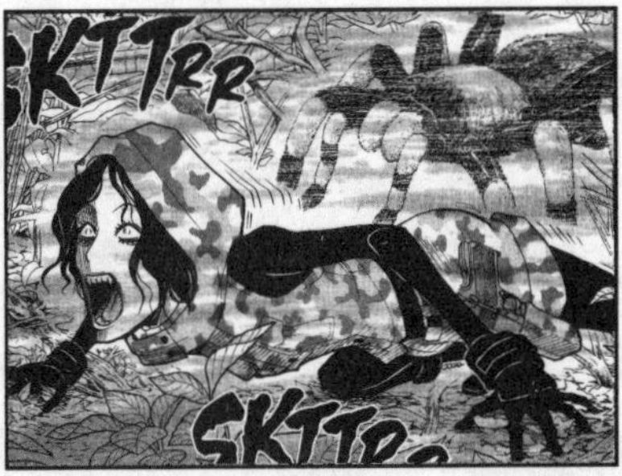
SKTTRR

Kirara Hazama's Poison Spider Subterfuge

She uses her slim arms and legs to slither and slide though narrow gaps. Because she is mimicking her pet tarantula, you could call this an animal-style martial art.

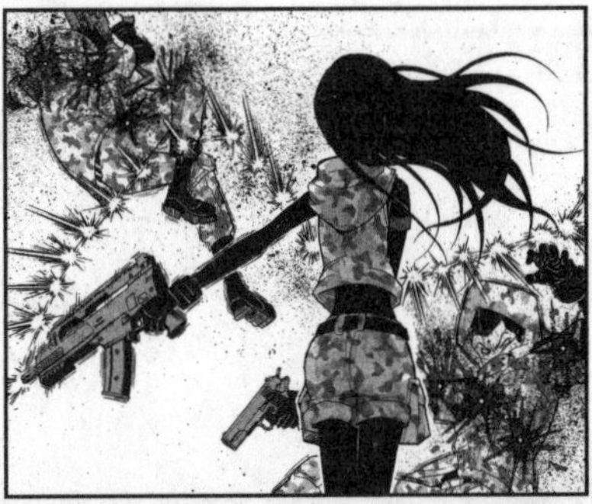

Yukiko Kanzaki's Ladylike Liquidation

Her gentle smile and impeccable posture make even trees and animals neglect to raise their guard. And then she massacres them.

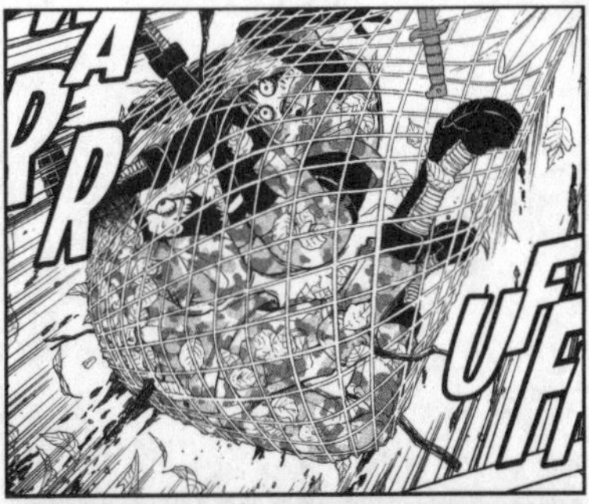

Sumire Hara's Dish of the Day

"If they were wild boar, this would be even better." Hearing these words as they were captured, these two felt a chill run down their spines and saw death standing before them.

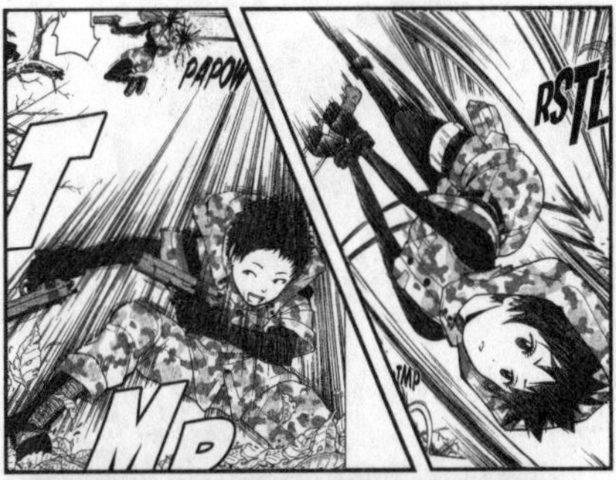
PAPOW
RSTL
TMP

Masayoshi Kimura & Hinata Okano's Four-Dimensional Killer Takedown

A combination attack by two acrobats with formidable athletic skills. Both of them are most effective on the front line, so how much damage they deal will depend on how skillfully the commander deploys them.

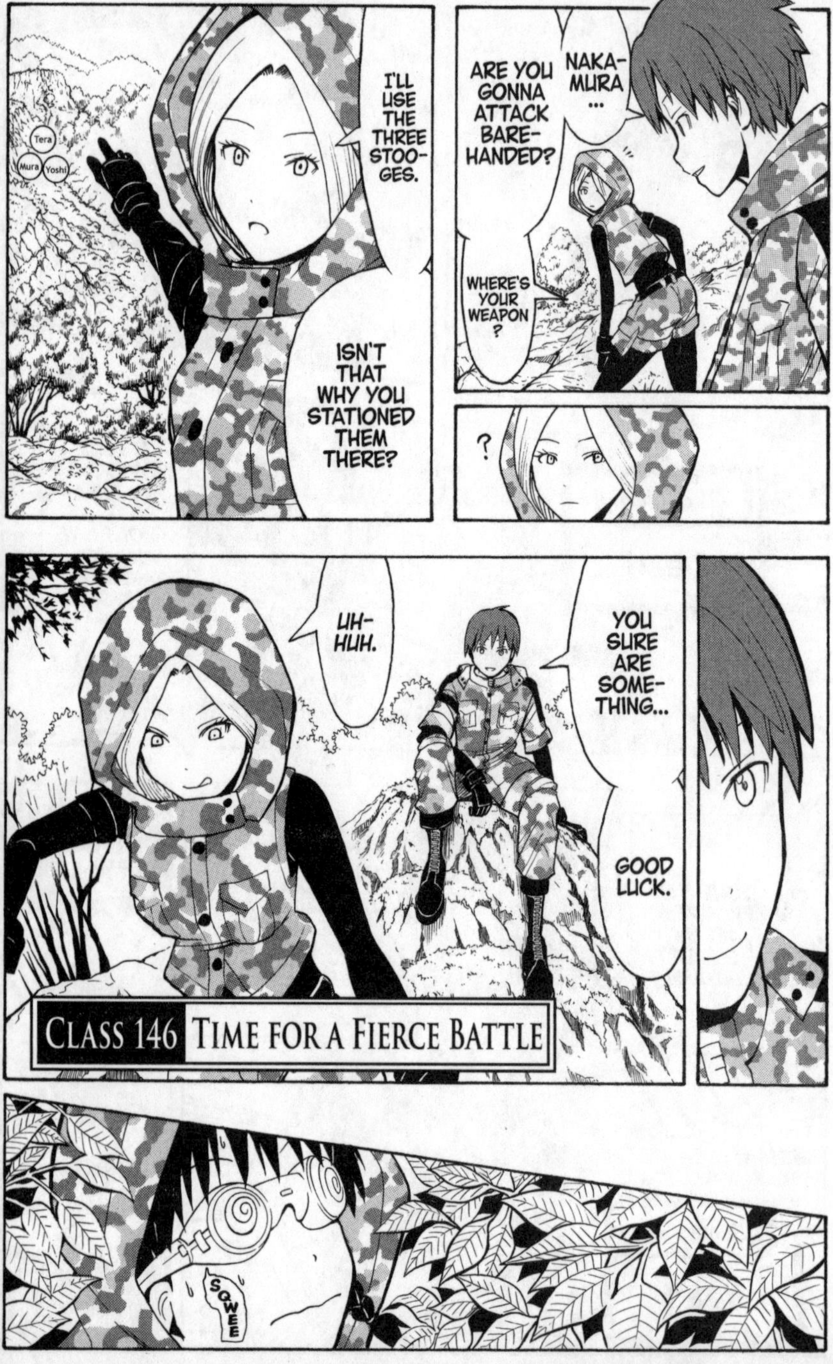
NAKA-MURA...
ARE YOU GONNA ATTACK BARE-HANDED?
WHERE'S YOUR WEAPON?
?
Tera
Mura
Yoshi
I'LL USE THE THREE STOOGES.
ISN'T THAT WHY YOU STATIONED THEM THERE?
YOU SURE ARE SOME-THING...
GOOD LUCK.
UH-HUH.
CLASS 146 TIME FOR A FIERCE BATTLE
SQWEE

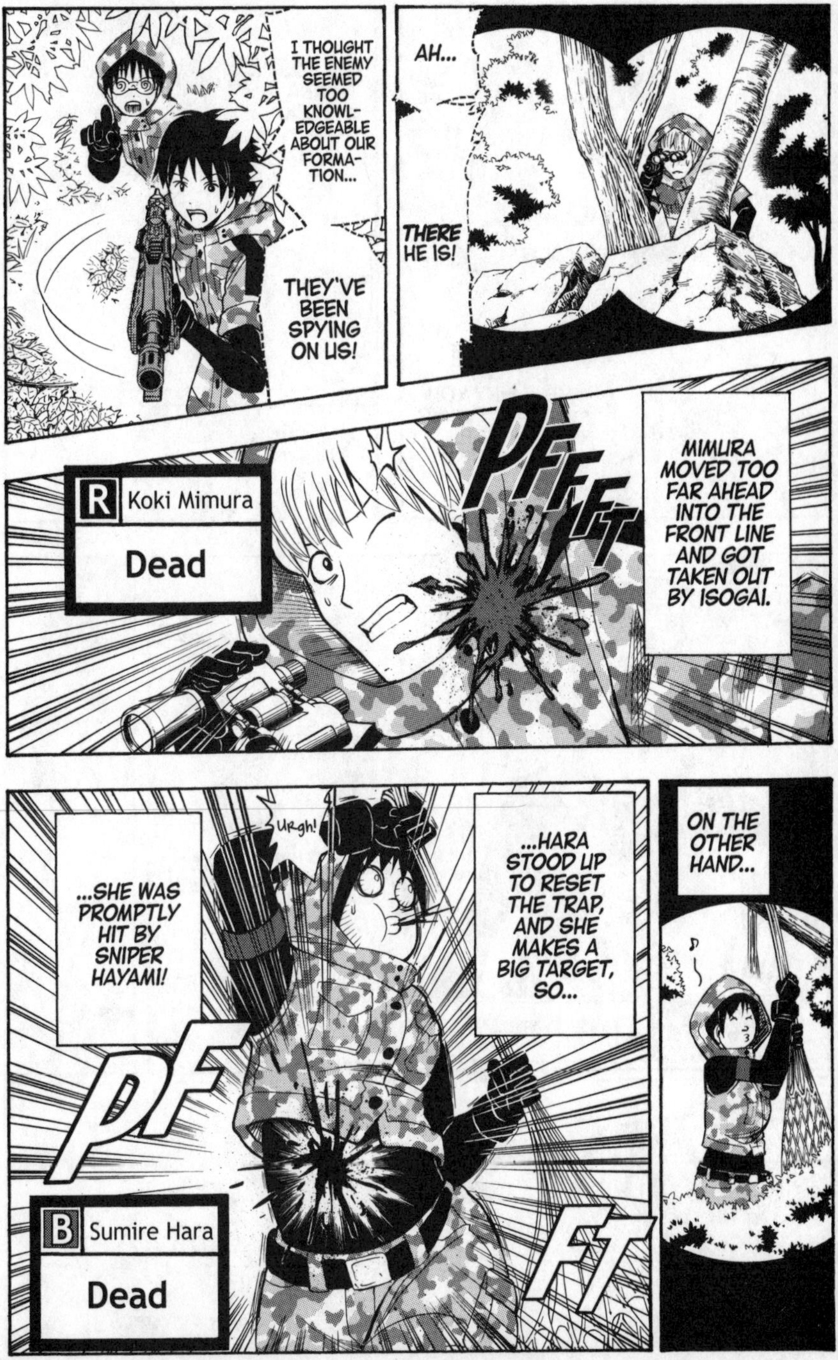
AH...
THERE HE IS!
I THOUGHT THE ENEMY SEEMED TOO KNOWL-EDGEABLE ABOUT OUR FORMA-TION...
THEY'VE BEEN SPYING ON US!
MIMURA MOVED TOO FAR AHEAD INTO THE FRONT LINE AND GOT TAKEN OUT BY ISOGAI.
PFFFFT
R Koki Mimura
Dead
ON THE OTHER HAND...
...HARA STOOD UP TO RESET THE TRAP, AND SHE MAKES A BIG TARGET, SO...
Urgh!
...SHE WAS PROMPTLY HIT BY SNIPER HAYAMI!
PF
FT
B Sumire Hara
Dead

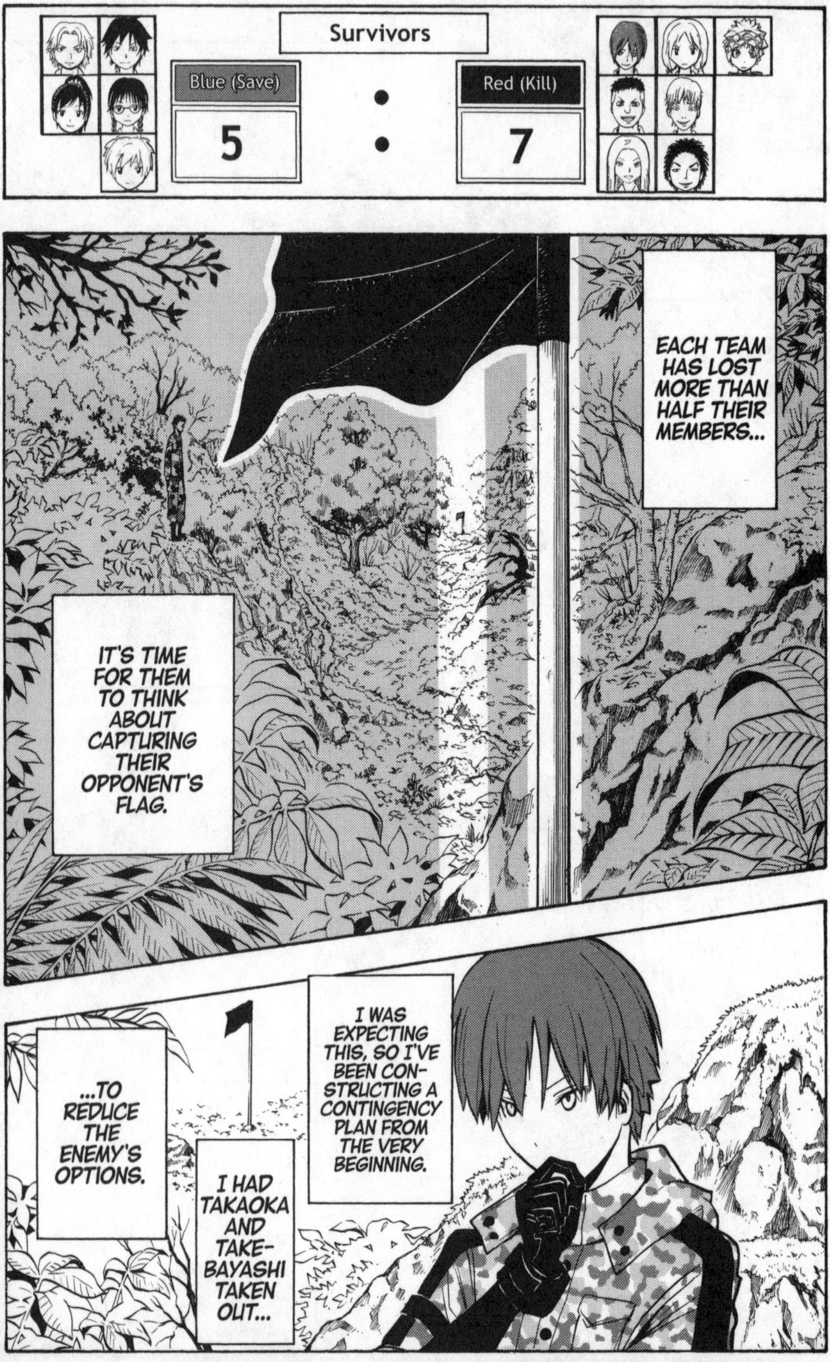
Survivors
Red (Kill)
7
Blue (Save)
5
EACH TEAM HAS LOST MORE THAN HALF THEIR MEMBERS...
IT'S TIME FOR THEM TO THINK ABOUT CAPTURING THEIR OPPONENT'S FLAG.
I WAS EXPECTING THIS, SO I'VE BEEN CON-STRUCTING A CONTINGENCY PLAN FROM THE VERY BEGINNING.
I HAD TAKAOKA AND TAKE-BAYASHI TAKEN OUT...
...TO REDUCE THE ENEMY'S OPTIONS.

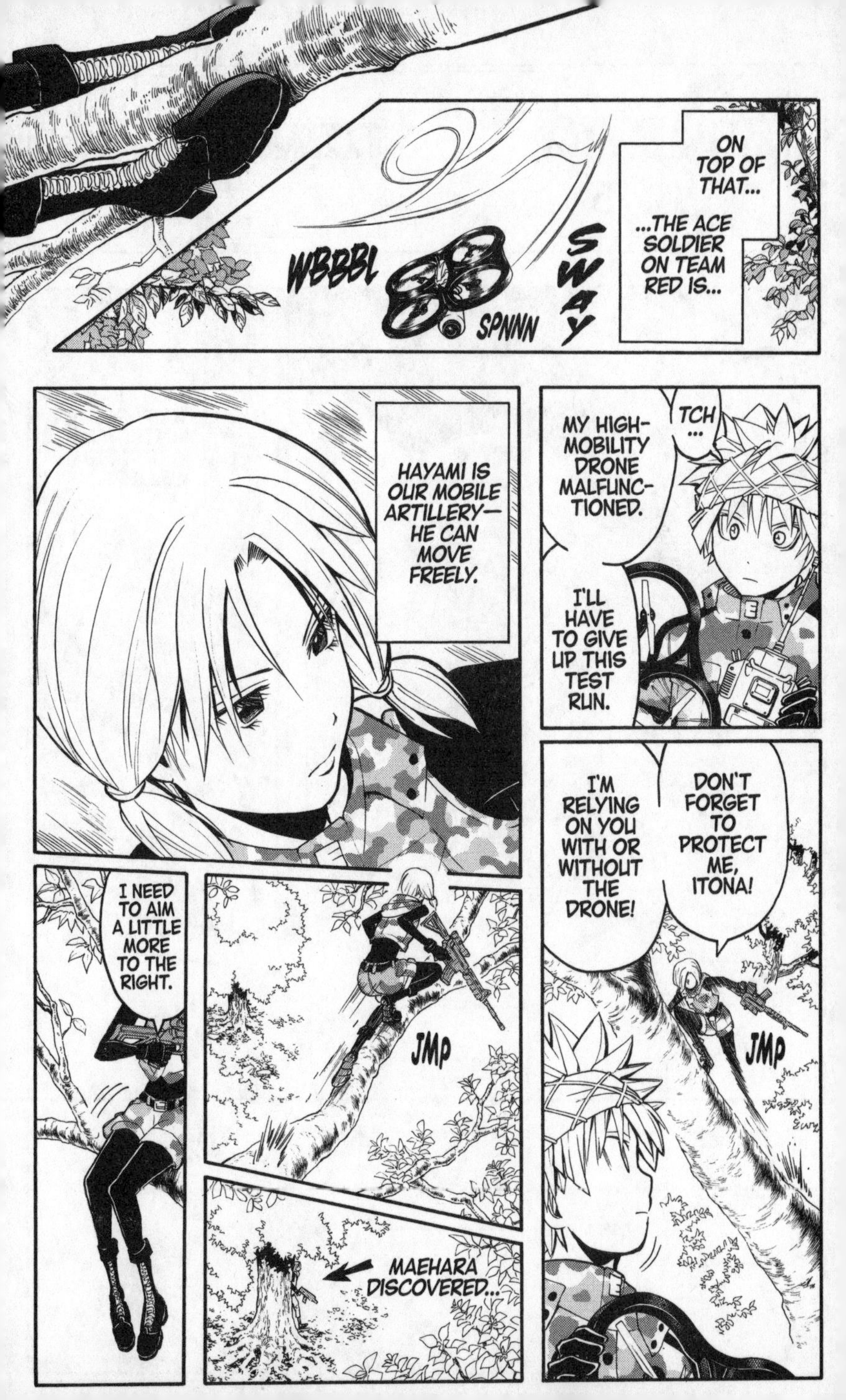

ON TOP OF THAT...
...THE ACE SOLDIER ON TEAM RED IS...
SWAY
SPNNN
WBBBL
TCH...
MY HIGH-MOBILITY DRONE MALFUNCTIONED.
I'LL HAVE TO GIVE UP THIS TEST RUN.
HAYAMI IS OUR MOBILE ARTILLERY—HE CAN MOVE FREELY.
DON'T FORGET TO PROTECT ME, ITONA!
I'M RELYING ON YOU WITH OR WITHOUT THE DRONE!
JMP
JMP
MAEHARA DISCOVERED...
I NEED TO AIM A LITTLE MORE TO THE RIGHT.

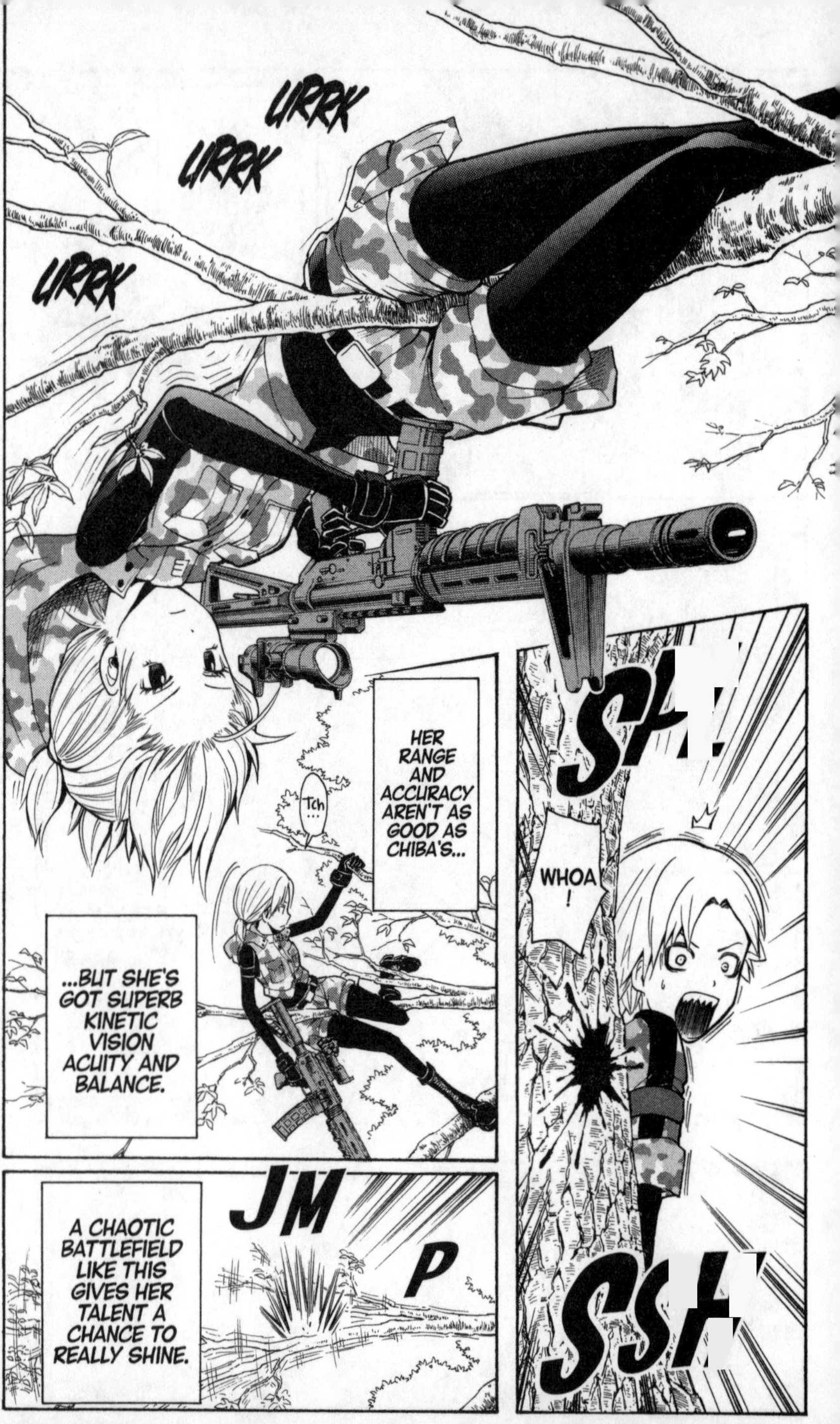
URRK
URRK
URRK
HER RANGE AND ACCURACY AREN'T AS GOOD AS CHIBA'S...
Tch...
...BUT SHE'S GOT SUPERB KINETIC VISION ACUITY AND BALANCE.
SH
WHOA!
SSH
A CHAOTIC BATTLEFIELD LIKE THIS GIVES HER TALENT A CHANCE TO REALLY SHINE.
JM
P

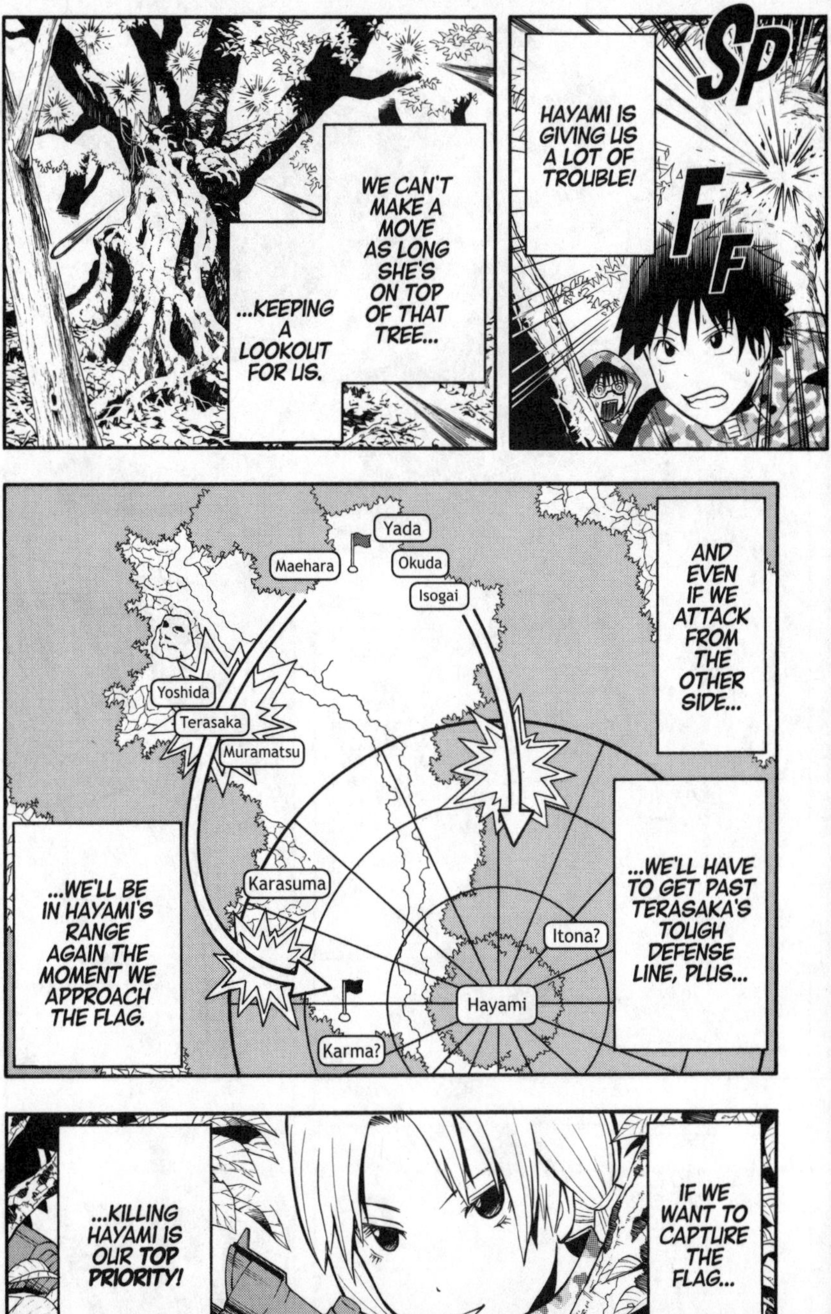
SP
FF
HAYAMI IS GIVING US A LOT OF TROUBLE!
WE CAN'T MAKE A MOVE AS LONG SHE'S ON TOP OF THAT TREE...
...KEEPING A LOOKOUT FOR US.
AND EVEN IF WE ATTACK FROM THE OTHER SIDE...
Yada
Maehara
Okuda
Isogai
Yoshida
Terasaka
Muramatsu
Karasuma
Itona?
Hayami
Karma?
...WE'LL HAVE TO GET PAST TERASAKA'S TOUGH DEFENSE LINE, PLUS...
...WE'LL BE IN HAYAMI'S RANGE AGAIN THE MOMENT WE APPROACH THE FLAG.
IF WE WANT TO CAPTURE THE FLAG...
...KILLING HAYAMI IS OUR TOP PRIORITY!

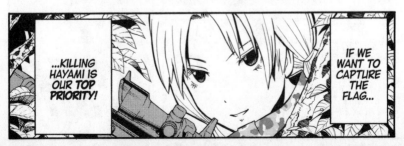

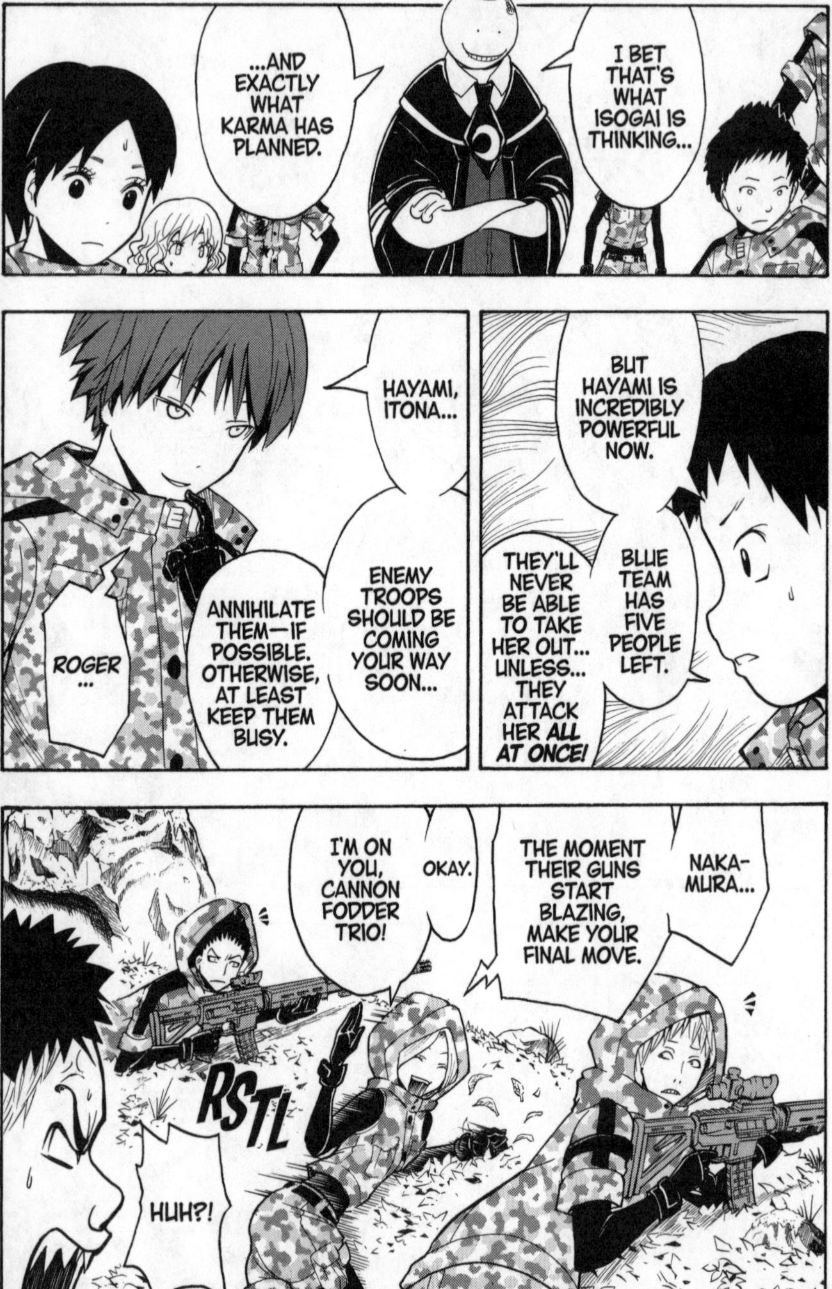
I BET THAT'S WHAT ISOGAI IS THINKING...
...AND EXACTLY WHAT KARMA HAS PLANNED.
BUT HAYAMI IS INCREDIBLY POWERFUL NOW.
BLUE TEAM HAS FIVE PEOPLE LEFT.
THEY'LL NEVER BE ABLE TO TAKE HER OUT... UNLESS... THEY ATTACK HER ALL AT ONCE!
HAYAMI, ITONA...
ENEMY TROOPS SHOULD BE COMING YOUR WAY SOON...
ANNIHILATE THEM—IF POSSIBLE. OTHERWISE, AT LEAST KEEP THEM BUSY.
ROGER...
NAKA-MURA...
THE MOMENT THEIR GUNS START BLAZING, MAKE YOUR FINAL MOVE.
OKAY.
I'M ON YOU, CANNON FODDER TRIO!
RSTL
HUH?!

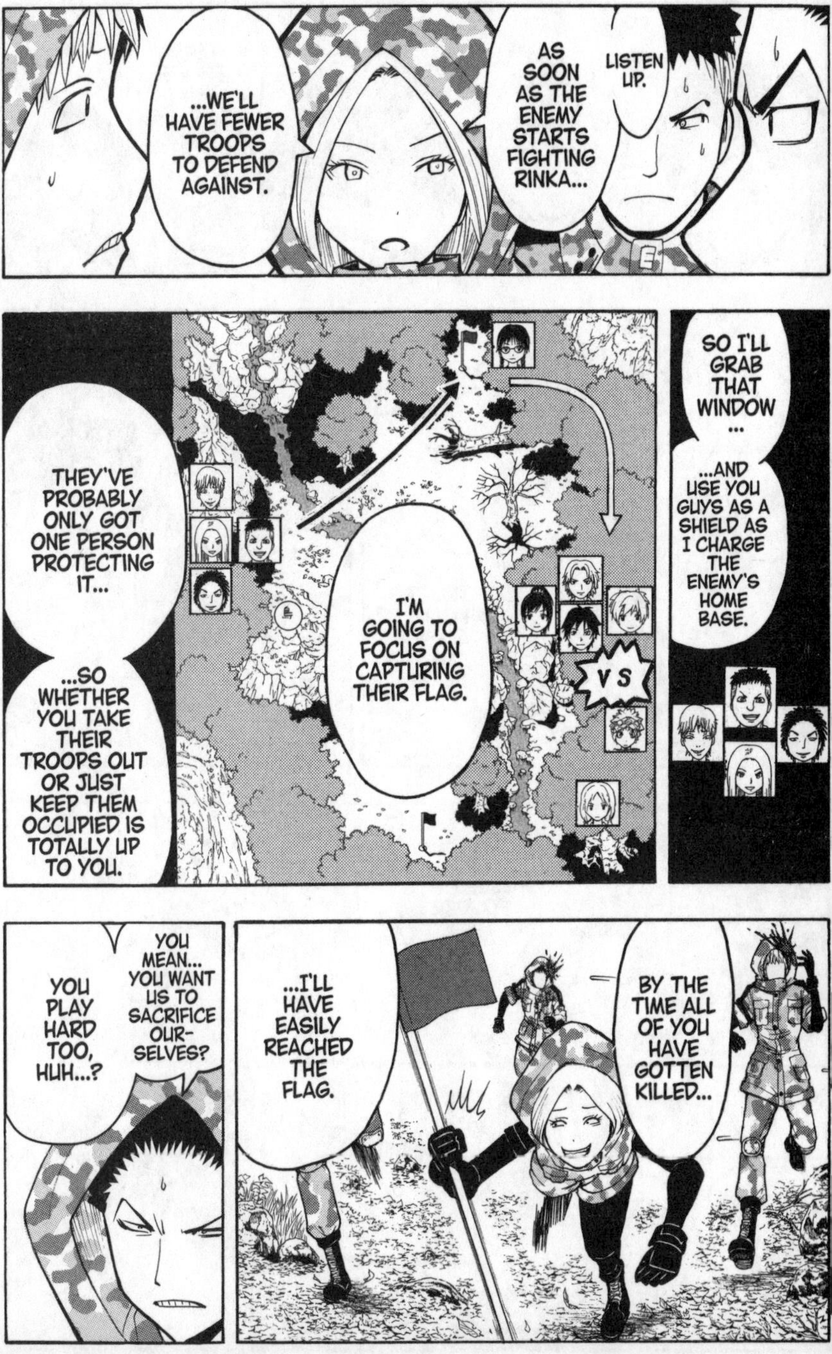
LISTEN UP.
AS SOON AS THE ENEMY STARTS FIGHTING RINKA...
...WE'LL HAVE FEWER TROOPS TO DEFEND AGAINST.
SO I'LL GRAB THAT WINDOW...
...AND USE YOU GUYS AS A SHIELD AS I CHARGE THE ENEMY'S HOME BASE.
VS
I'M GOING TO FOCUS ON CAPTURING THEIR FLAG.
THEY'VE PROBABLY ONLY GOT ONE PERSON PROTECTING IT...
...SO WHETHER YOU TAKE THEIR TROOPS OUT OR JUST KEEP THEM OCCUPIED IS TOTALLY UP TO YOU.
BY THE TIME ALL OF YOU HAVE GOTTEN KILLED...
...I'LL HAVE EASILY REACHED THE FLAG.
YOU MEAN... YOU WANT US TO SACRIFICE OUR-SELVES?
YOU PLAY HARD TOO, HUH...?

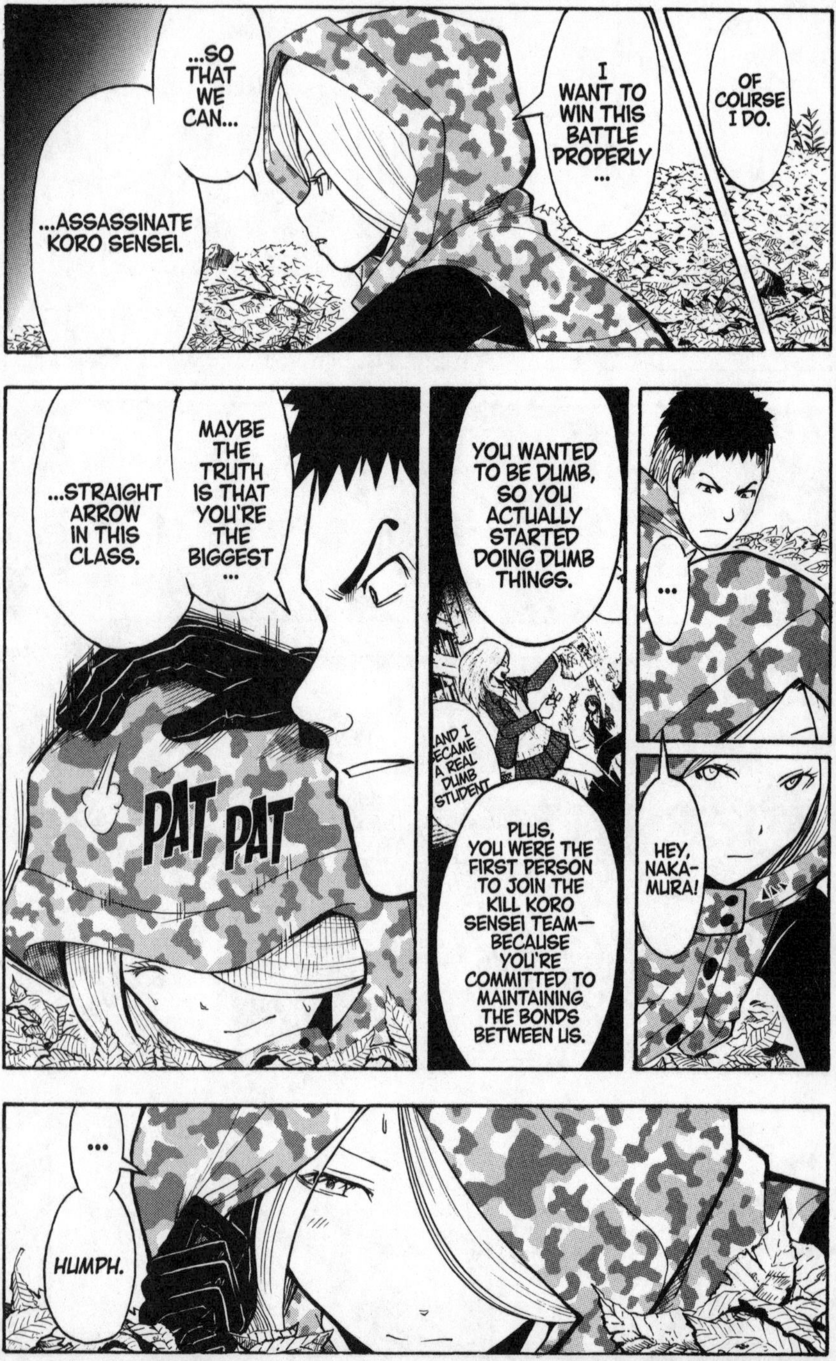
OF COURSE I DO.
I WANT TO WIN THIS BATTLE PROPERLY...
...SO THAT WE CAN...
...ASSASSINATE KORO SENSEI.
...
HEY, NAKAMURA!
YOU WANTED TO BE DUMB, SO YOU ACTUALLY STARTED DOING DUMB THINGS.
AND I ECAME A REAL DUMB STUDENT
PLUS, YOU WERE THE FIRST PERSON TO JOIN THE KILL KORO SENSEI TEAM—BECAUSE YOU'RE COMMITTED TO MAINTAINING THE BONDS BETWEEN US.
MAYBE THE TRUTH IS THAT YOU'RE THE BIGGEST...
...STRAIGHT ARROW IN THIS CLASS.
PAT PAT
...
HUMPH.

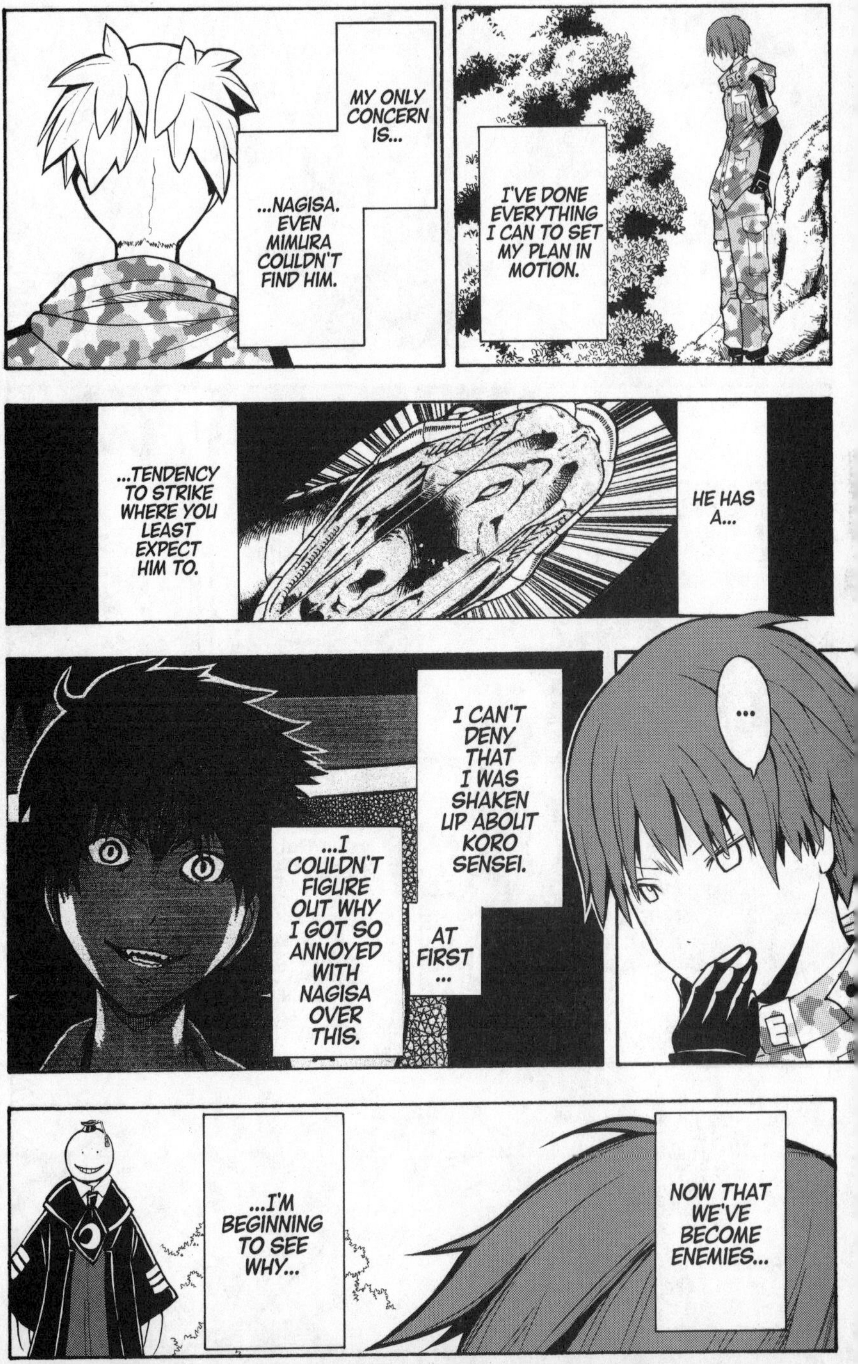
I'VE DONE EVERYTHING I CAN TO SET MY PLAN IN MOTION.
MY ONLY CONCERN IS...
...NAGISA. EVEN MIMURA COULDN'T FIND HIM.
HE HAS A...
...TENDENCY TO STRIKE WHERE YOU LEAST EXPECT HIM TO.
...
I CAN'T DENY THAT I WAS SHAKEN UP ABOUT KORO SENSEI.
AT FIRST...
...I COULDN'T FIGURE OUT WHY I GOT SO ANNOYED WITH NAGISA OVER THIS.
NOW THAT WE'VE BECOME ENEMIES...
...I'M BEGINNING TO SEE WHY...

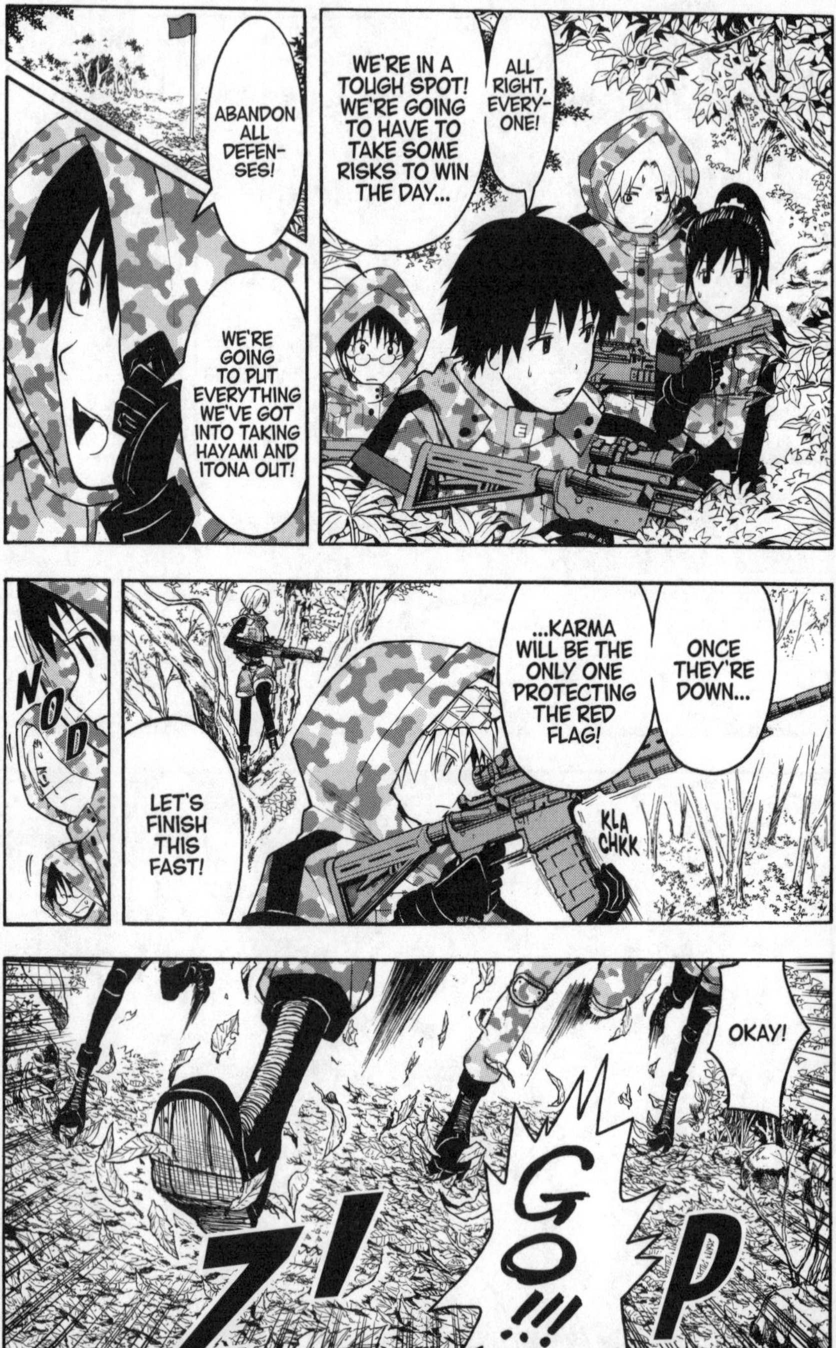
ALL RIGHT, EVERYONE!
WE'RE IN A TOUGH SPOT! WE'RE GOING TO HAVE TO TAKE SOME RISKS TO WIN THE DAY...
ABANDON ALL DEFENSES!
WE'RE GOING TO PUT EVERYTHING WE'VE GOT INTO TAKING HAYAMI AND ITONA OUT!
ONCE THEY'RE DOWN...
...KARMA WILL BE THE ONLY ONE PROTECTING THE RED FLAG!
KLA CHKK
LET'S FINISH THIS FAST!
NOD
OKAY!
GO!!!
ZIP

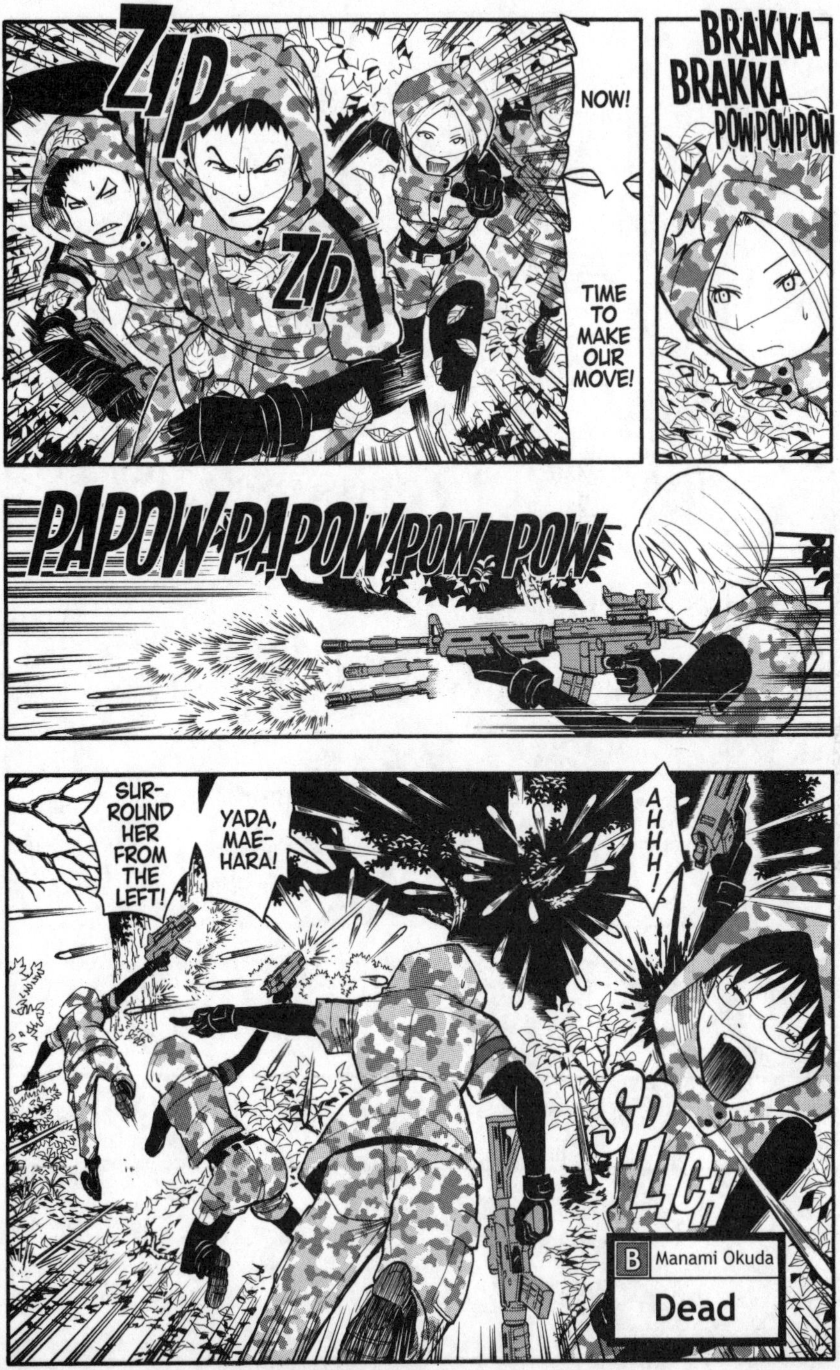
BRAKKA
BRAKKA
POWPOWPOW
NOW!
TIME TO MAKE OUR MOVE!
ZIP
ZIP
PAPOW PAPOW POW POW
AHHH!
YADA, MAE-HARA!
SUR-ROUND HER FROM THE LEFT!
SPLICH
B Manami Okuda
Dead

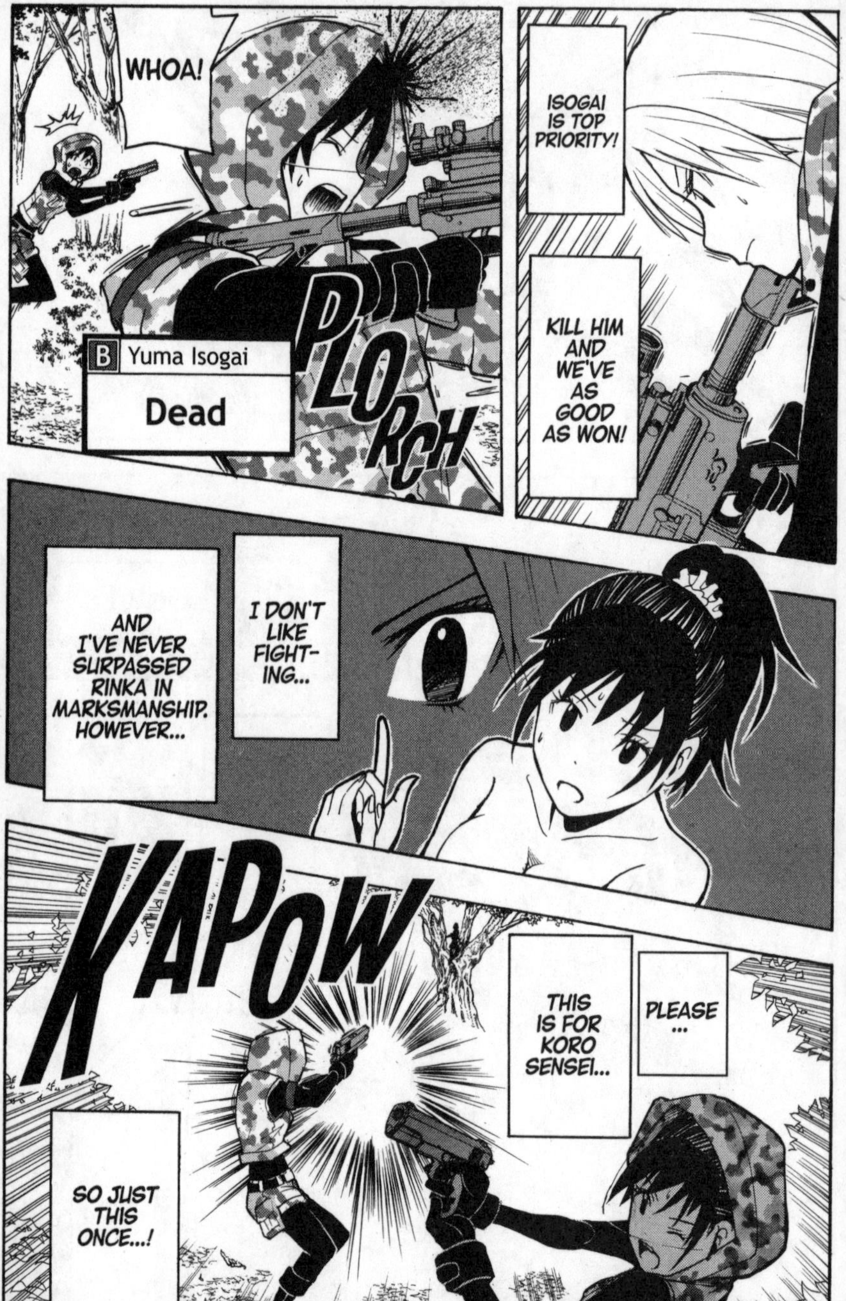
ISOGAI IS TOP PRIORITY!
KILL HIM AND WE'VE AS GOOD AS WON!
WHOA!
PLORCH
B Yuma Isogai
Dead
I DON'T LIKE FIGHTING...
AND I'VE NEVER SURPASSED RINKA IN MARKSMANSHIP. HOWEVER...
PLEASE...
THIS IS FOR KORO SENSEI...
KAPOW
SO JUST THIS ONCE...!

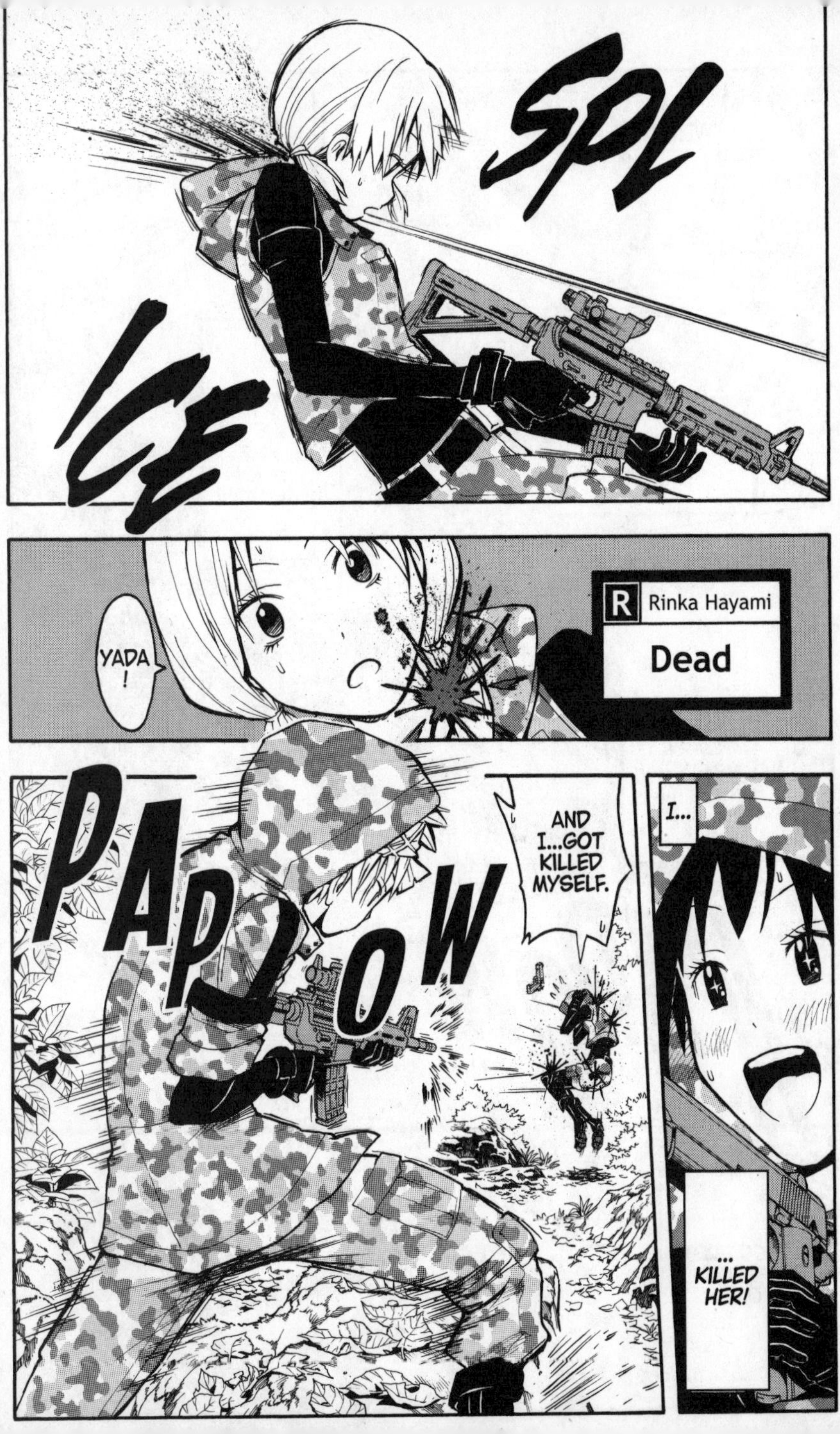
SPL
ICE
R Rinka Hayami
Dead
YADA!
I...
...KILLED HER!
AND I...GOT KILLED MYSELF.
PAPOW

I KNEW IT. I'M BETTER WITH KNIVES.

HFF

HFF

I CAN'T HIT YOU GUYS WITH A GUN.

B	Toka Yada
R	Itona Horibe

Dead

ZLIP

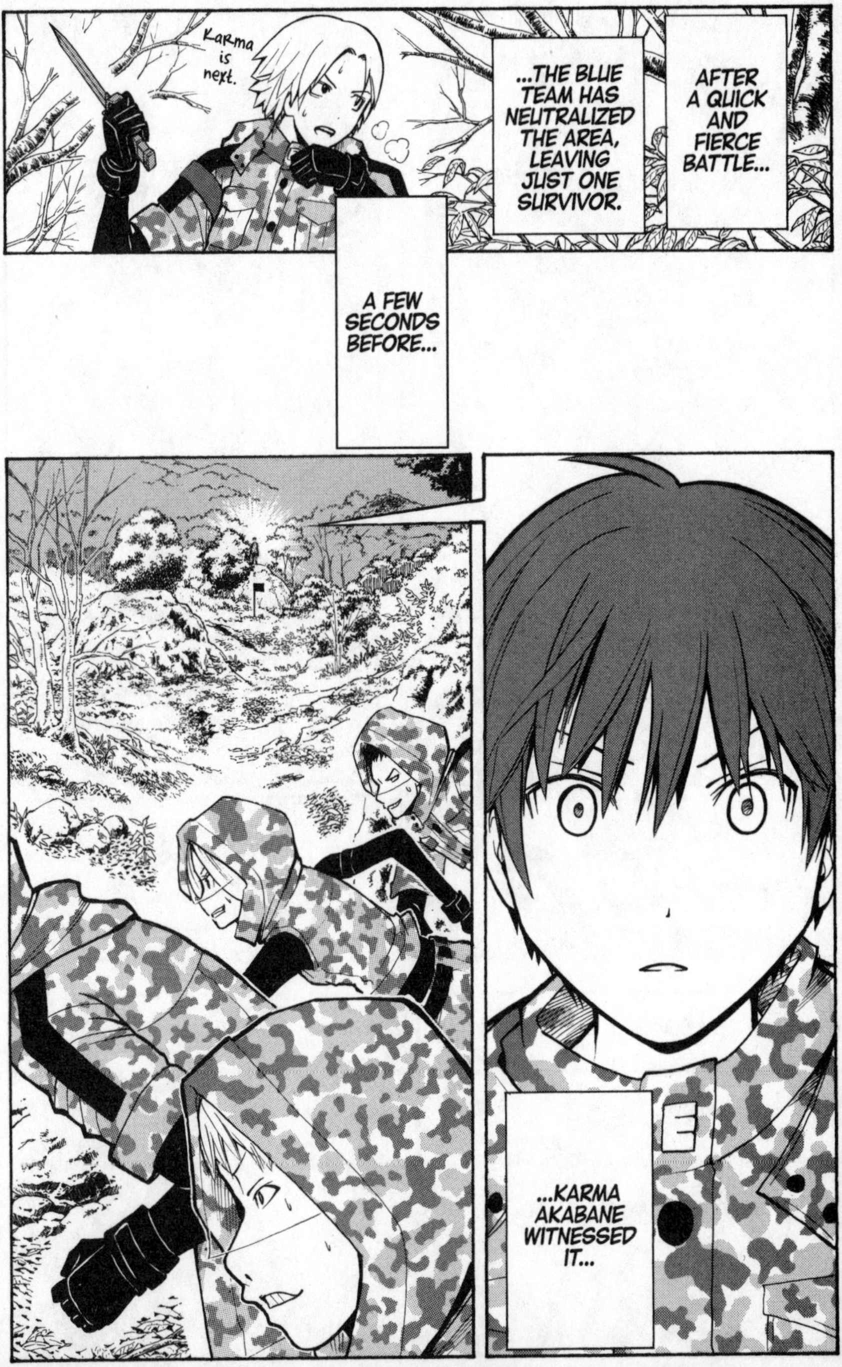
AFTER A QUICK AND FIERCE BATTLE...
...THE BLUE TEAM HAS NEUTRALIZED THE AREA, LEAVING JUST ONE SURVIVOR.
Karma is next.
A FEW SECONDS BEFORE...
...KARMA AKABANE WITNESSED IT...

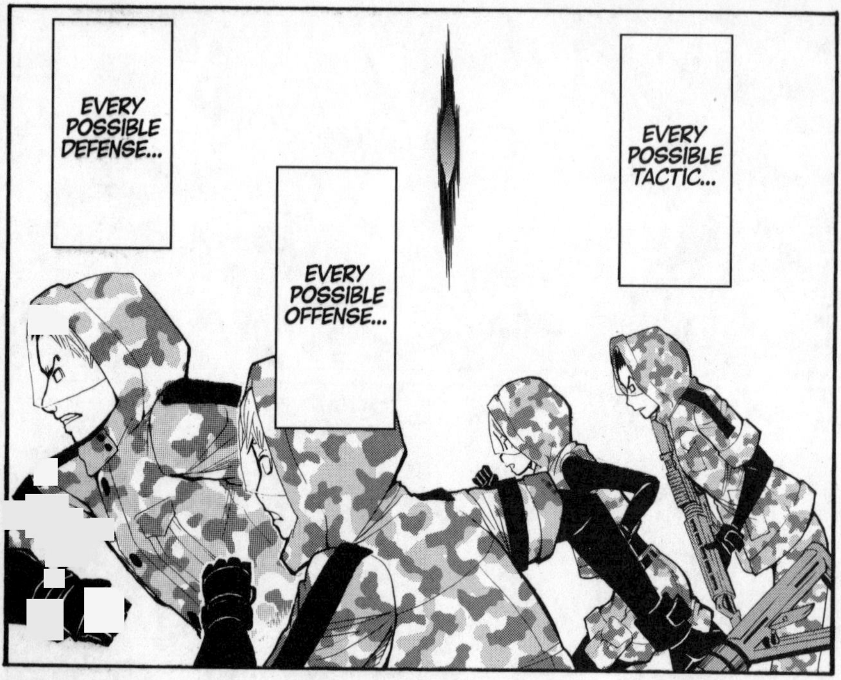
EVERY POSSIBLE TACTIC...
EVERY POSSIBLE OFFENSE...
EVERY POSSIBLE DEFENSE...
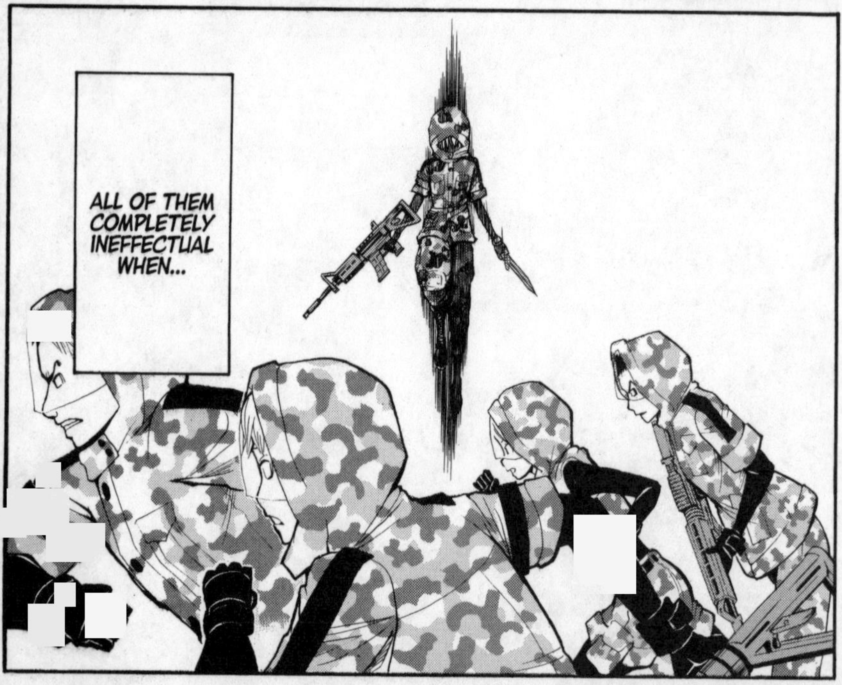
ALL OF THEM COMPLETELY INEFFECTUAL WHEN...

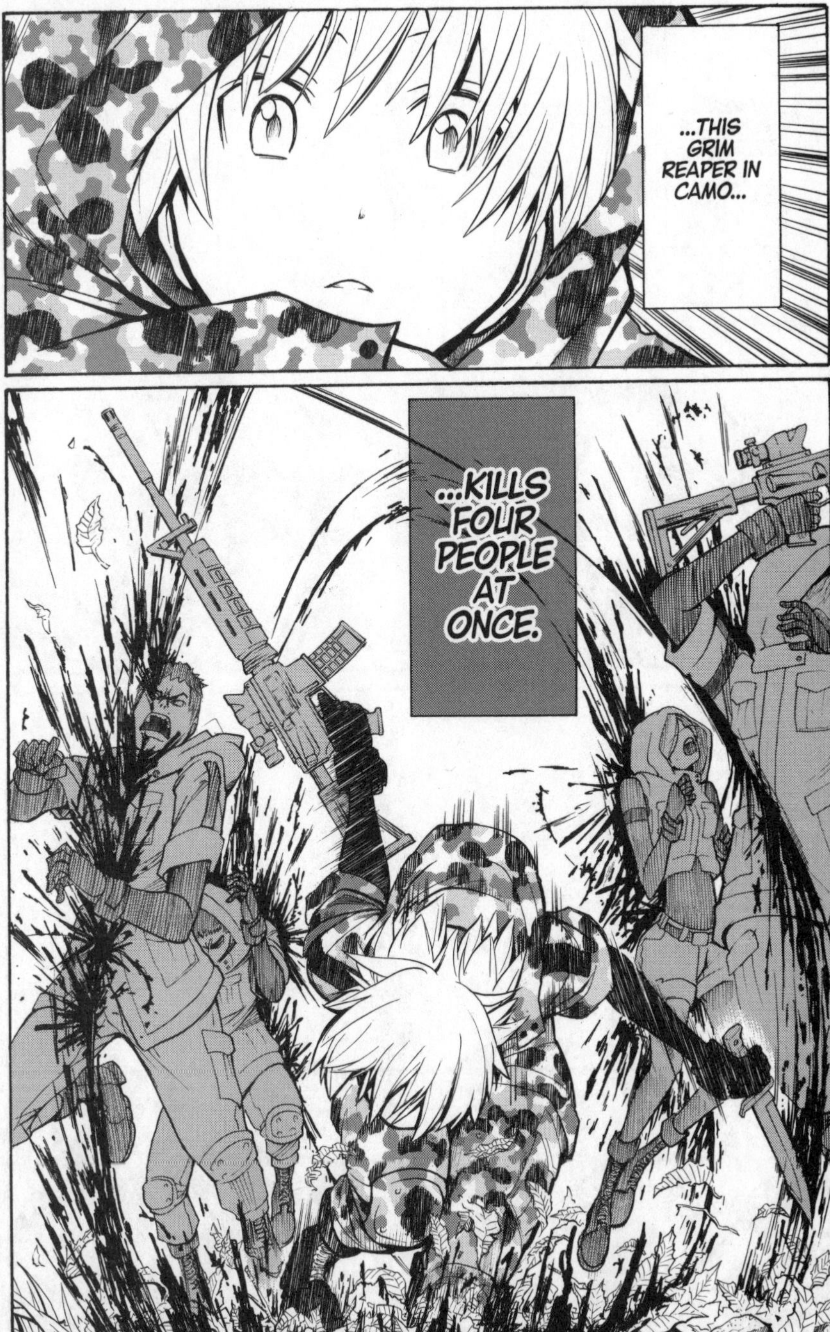
...THIS GRIM REAPER IN CAMO...
...KILLS FOUR PEOPLE AT ONCE.

R	Rio Nakamura
R	Ryoma Terasaka
R	Taisei Yoshida
R	Takuya Muramatsu
	Dead

FW UMP

NO ONE WAS THERE UNTIL A MOMENT AGO...

H-HE APPEARED OUT OF NOWHERE!

...GOT ATTACKED FROM BEHIND... IN CLOSE COMBAT?!

W-WE...

SO THAT'S HOW...

...

SHFF

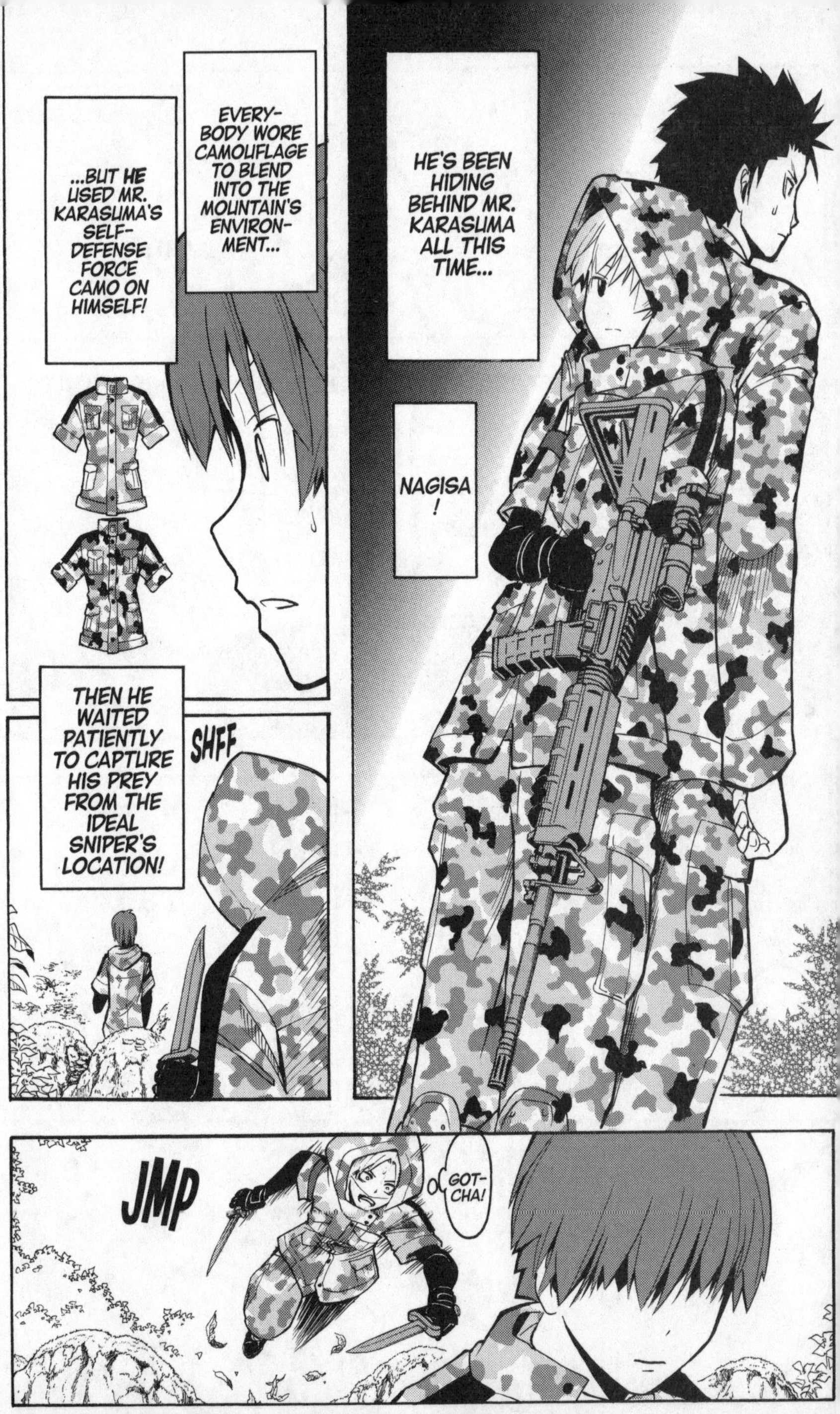
HE'S BEEN HIDING BEHIND MR. KARASUMA ALL THIS TIME...
NAGISA!
EVERYBODY WORE CAMOUFLAGE TO BLEND INTO THE MOUNTAIN'S ENVIRONMENT...
...BUT HE USED MR. KARASUMA'S SELF-DEFENSE FORCE CAMO ON HIMSELF!
THEN HE WAITED PATIENTLY TO CAPTURE HIS PREY FROM THE IDEAL SNIPER'S LOCATION!
SHFF
GOTCHA!
JMP

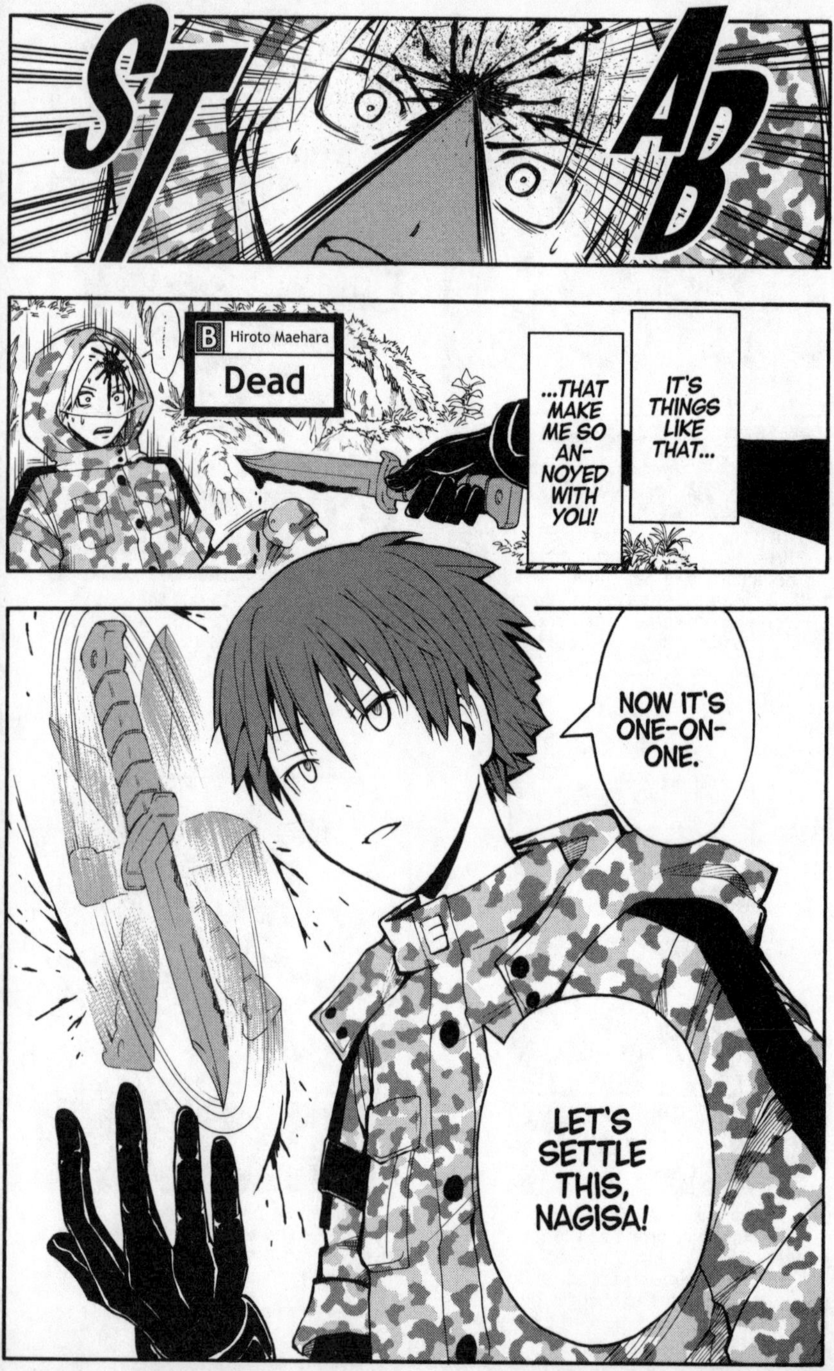
STAB
IT'S THINGS LIKE THAT...
...THAT MAKE ME SO AN-NOYED WITH YOU!
B Hiroto Maehara
Dead
...
NOW IT'S ONE-ON-ONE.
LET'S SETTLE THIS, NAGISA!

Class E Super Techniques②

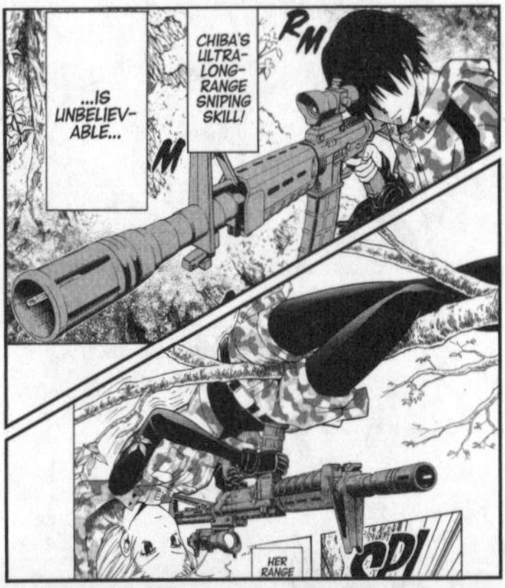
RM
CHIBA'S ULTRA-LONG-RANGE SNIPING SKILL!
...IS UNBELIEV-ABLE...
M
HER RANGE

Ryunosuke Chiba/Rinka Hayami's Ultra-Long-Range & High Mobility Sniping

It goes without saying that these are master snipers with mad skills. Chiba is in the habit of taking off his gloves for an ultra-long-range shot.

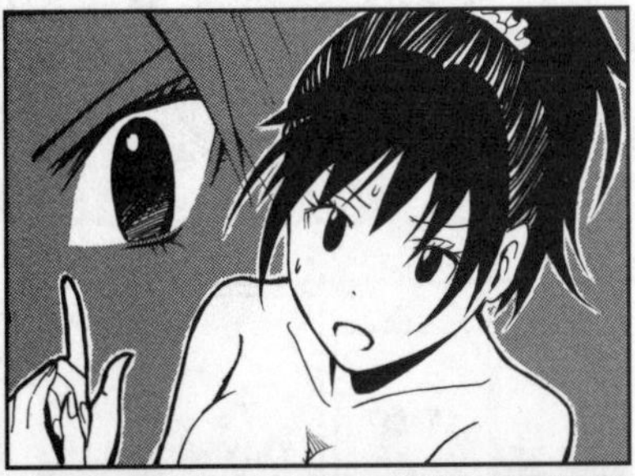

Toka Yada's Curvature Correction

When the bouncing of her bosom and the shaking of her hands are in sync, the accuracy of her shots skyrockets. If she were to practice this technique for another three years, she might master it to perfection.

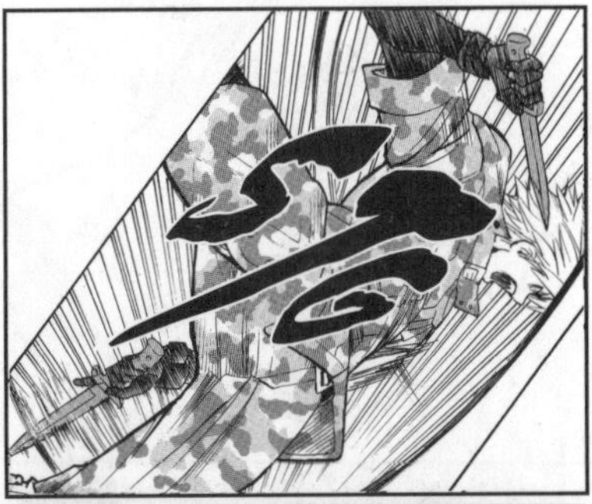

Hiroto Maehara's Bi-Blade

This is the pinnacle of his knife technique. The technique's name might give the impression that he's into both guys and girls, but that's not what it means.

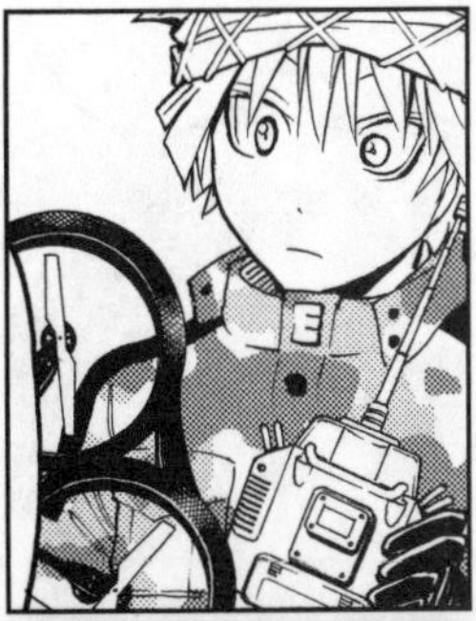

Itona Horibe's Itona Experiment

Itona is developing this high-mobility drone as the final form of his Itona Series. This time, it failed. Will he be able to successfully complete it by March...?

CLASS 147 TIME FOR THE STAGE

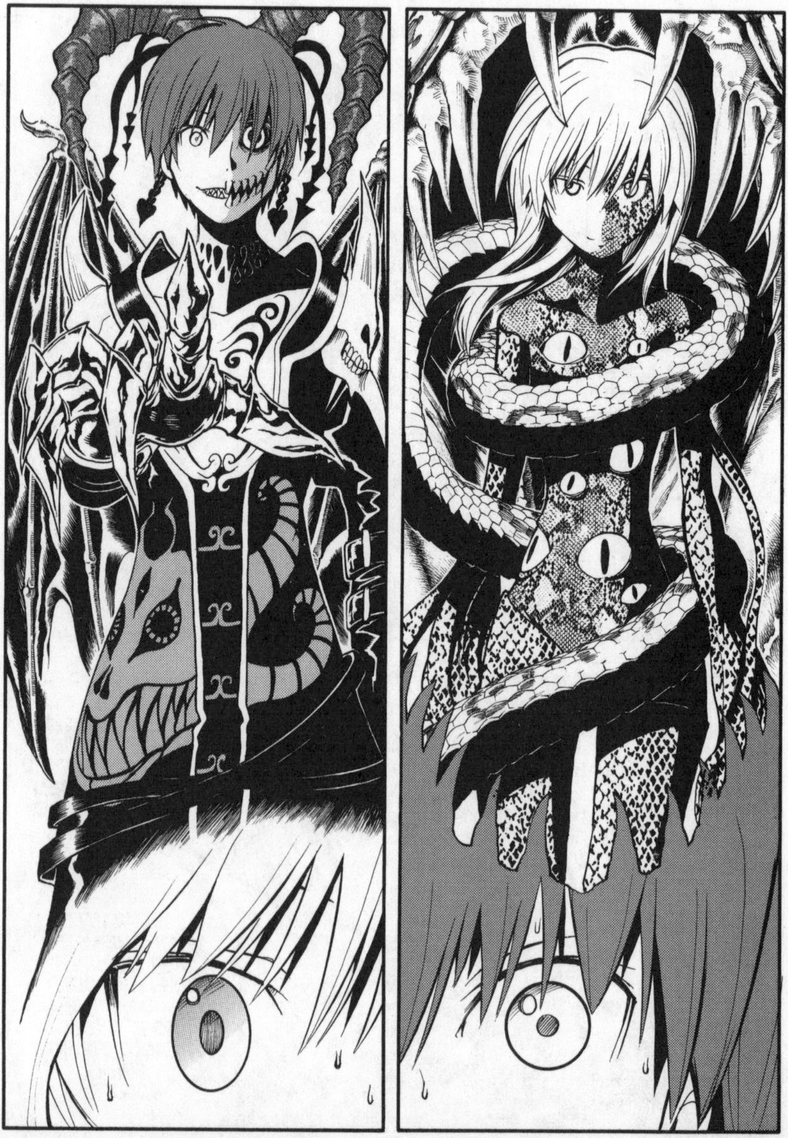

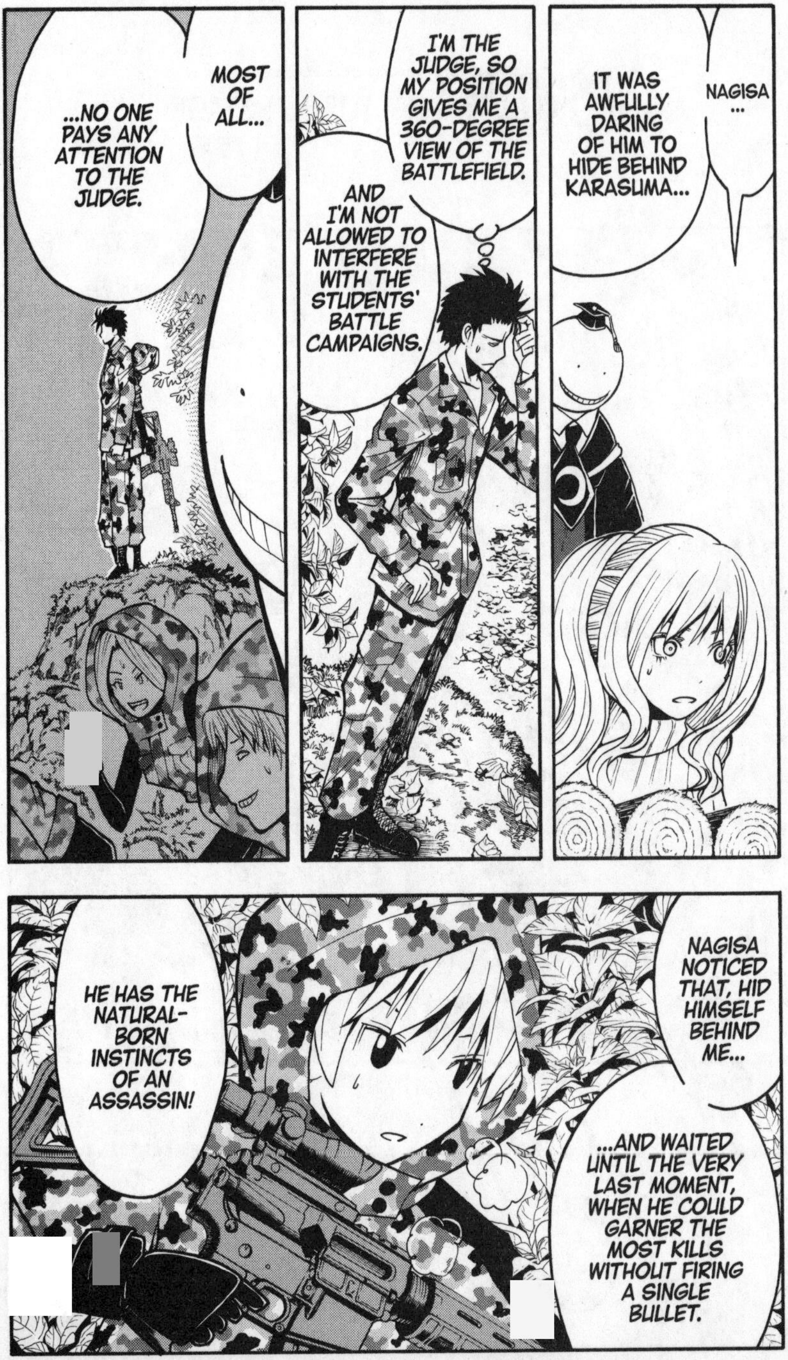
NAGISA...
IT WAS AWFULLY DARING OF HIM TO HIDE BEHIND KARASUMA...
I'M THE JUDGE, SO MY POSITION GIVES ME A 360-DEGREE VIEW OF THE BATTLEFIELD.
AND I'M NOT ALLOWED TO INTERFERE WITH THE STUDENTS' BATTLE CAMPAIGNS.
MOST OF ALL...
...NO ONE PAYS ANY ATTENTION TO THE JUDGE.
NAGISA NOTICED THAT, HID HIMSELF BEHIND ME...
...AND WAITED UNTIL THE VERY LAST MOMENT, WHEN HE COULD GARNER THE MOST KILLS WITHOUT FIRING A SINGLE BULLET.
HE HAS THE NATURAL-BORN INSTINCTS OF AN ASSASSIN!

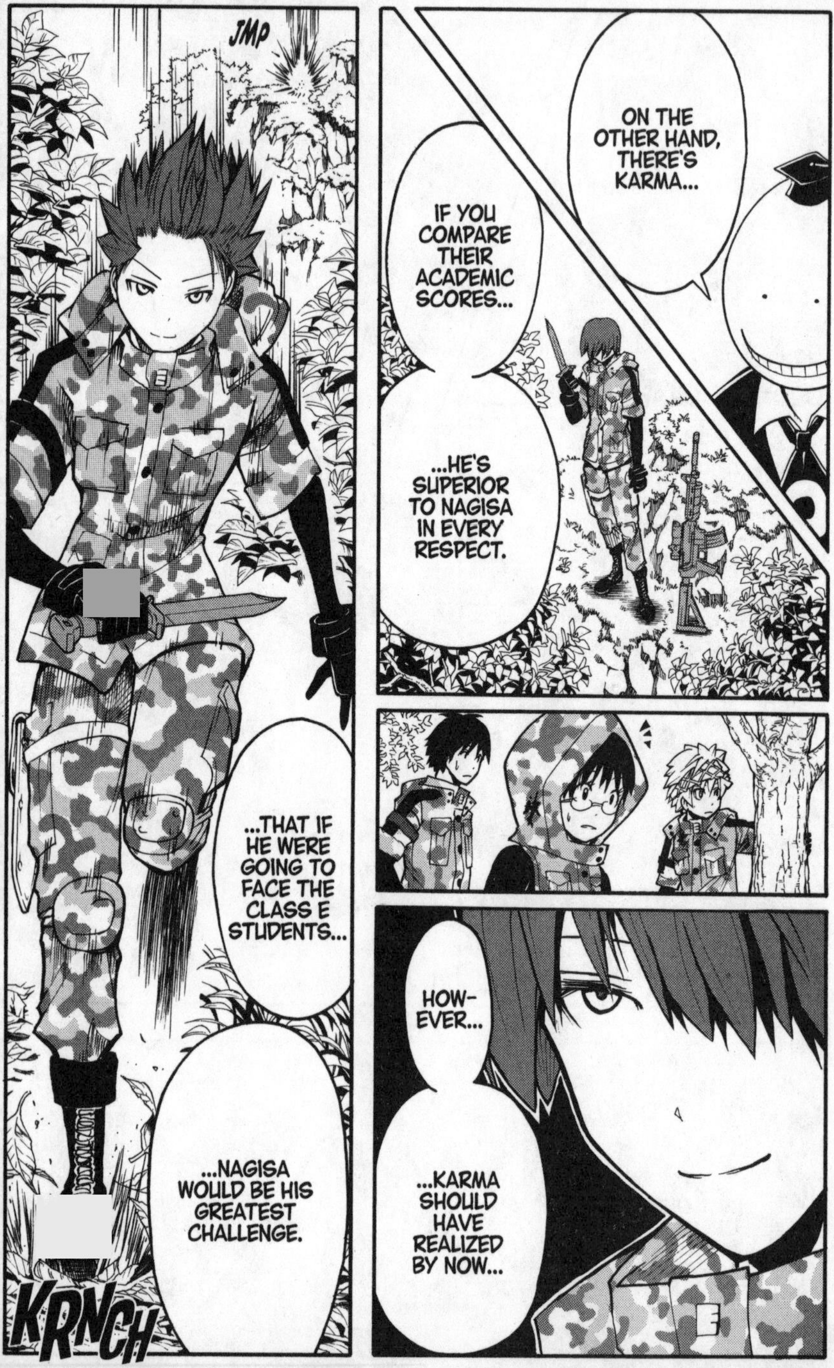
ON THE OTHER HAND, THERE'S KARMA...
IF YOU COMPARE THEIR ACADEMIC SCORES...
...HE'S SUPERIOR TO NAGISA IN EVERY RESPECT.
HOW-EVER...
...KARMA SHOULD HAVE REALIZED BY NOW...
JMP
...THAT IF HE WERE GOING TO FACE THE CLASS E STUDENTS...
...NAGISA WOULD BE HIS GREATEST CHALLENGE.
KRNCH

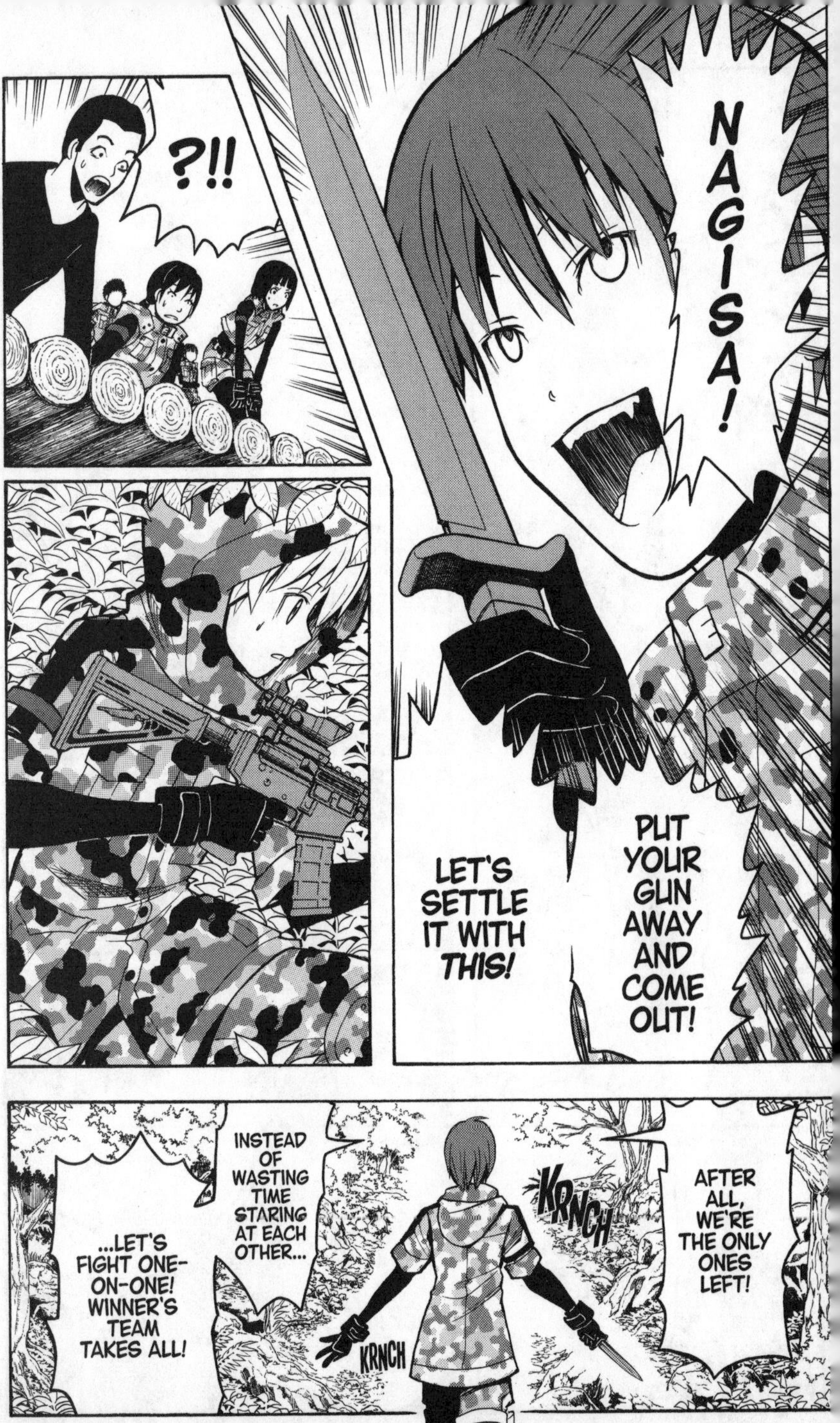
NAGISA!
PUT YOUR GUN AWAY AND COME OUT!
LET'S SETTLE IT WITH *THIS!*
?!!
AFTER ALL, WE'RE THE ONLY ONES LEFT!
KRNCH
INSTEAD OF WASTING TIME STARING AT EACH OTHER...
...LET'S FIGHT ONE-ON-ONE! WINNER'S TEAM TAKES ALL!
KRNCH

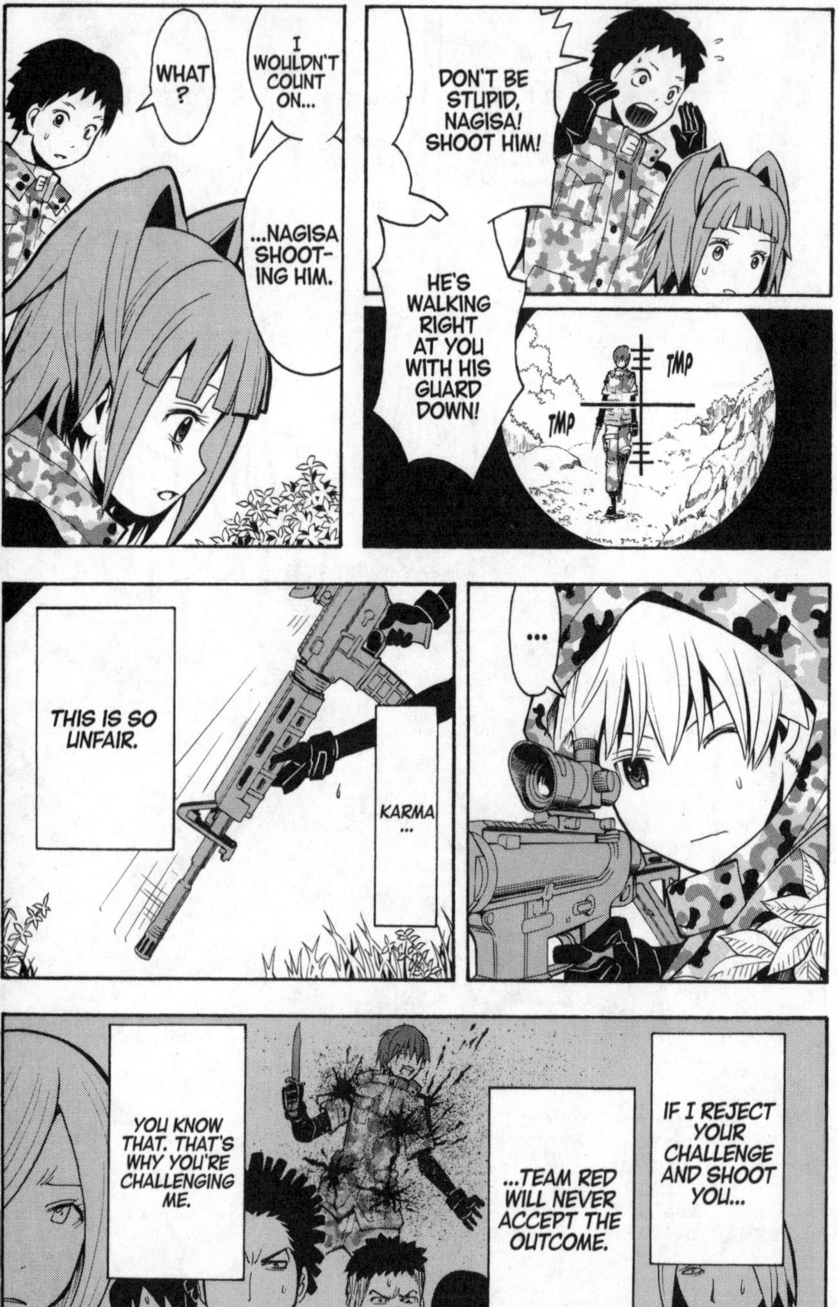
DON'T BE STUPID, NAGISA! SHOOT HIM!
HE'S WALKING RIGHT AT YOU WITH HIS GUARD DOWN!
TMP
TMP
I WOULDN'T COUNT ON...
WHAT ?
...NAGISA SHOOTING HIM.
...
KARMA ...
THIS IS SO UNFAIR.
IF I REJECT YOUR CHALLENGE AND SHOOT YOU...
...TEAM RED WILL NEVER ACCEPT THE OUTCOME.
YOU KNOW THAT. THAT'S WHY YOU'RE CHALLENGING ME.

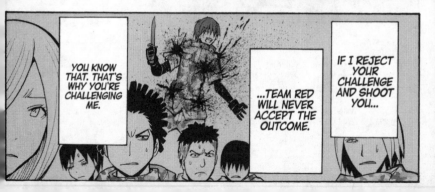

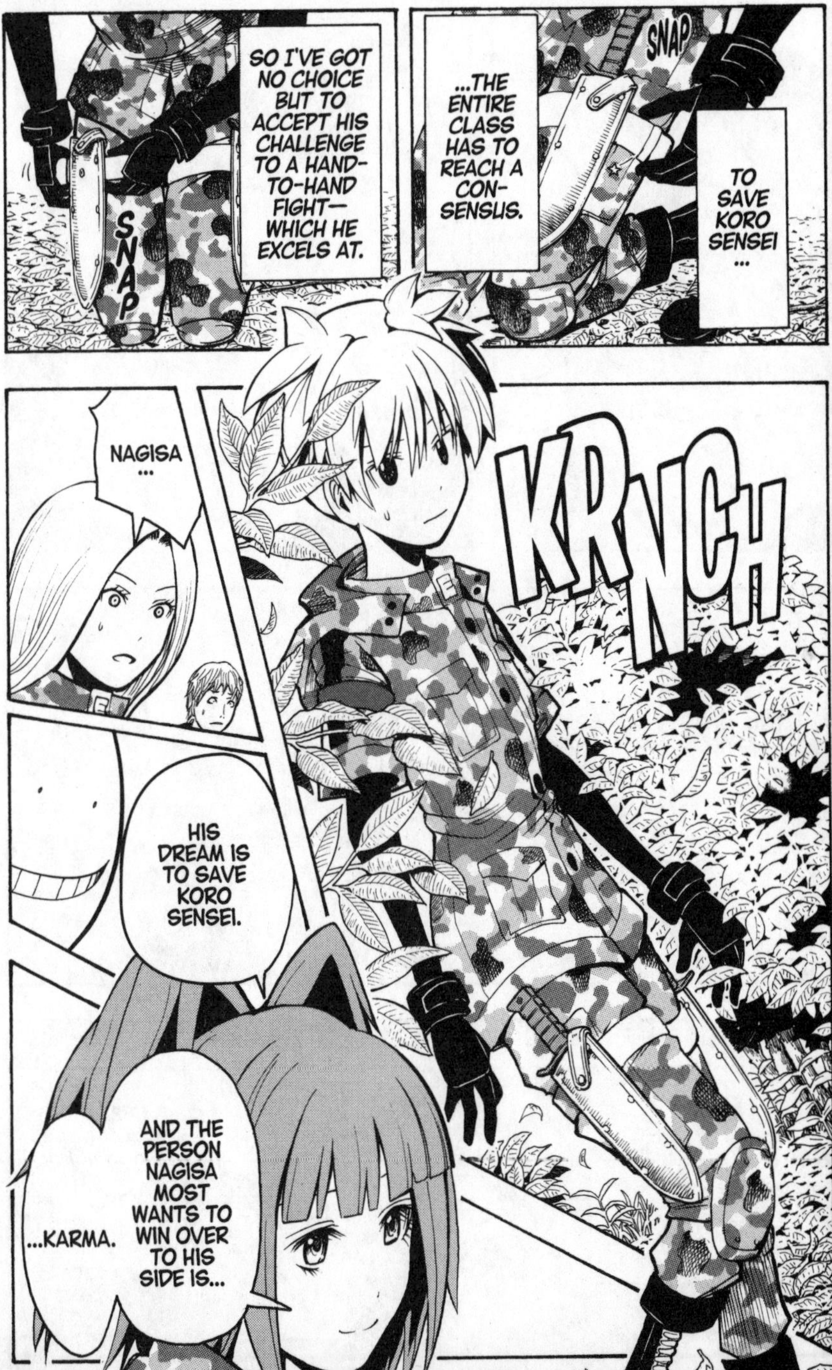
SNAP
TO SAVE KORO SENSEI...
...THE ENTIRE CLASS HAS TO REACH A CON-SENSUS.
SO I'VE GOT NO CHOICE BUT TO ACCEPT HIS CHALLENGE TO A HAND-TO-HAND FIGHT—WHICH HE EXCELS AT.
SNAP
KRNCH
NAGISA...
HIS DREAM IS TO SAVE KORO SENSEI.
AND THE PERSON NAGISA MOST WANTS TO WIN OVER TO HIS SIDE IS...
...KARMA.

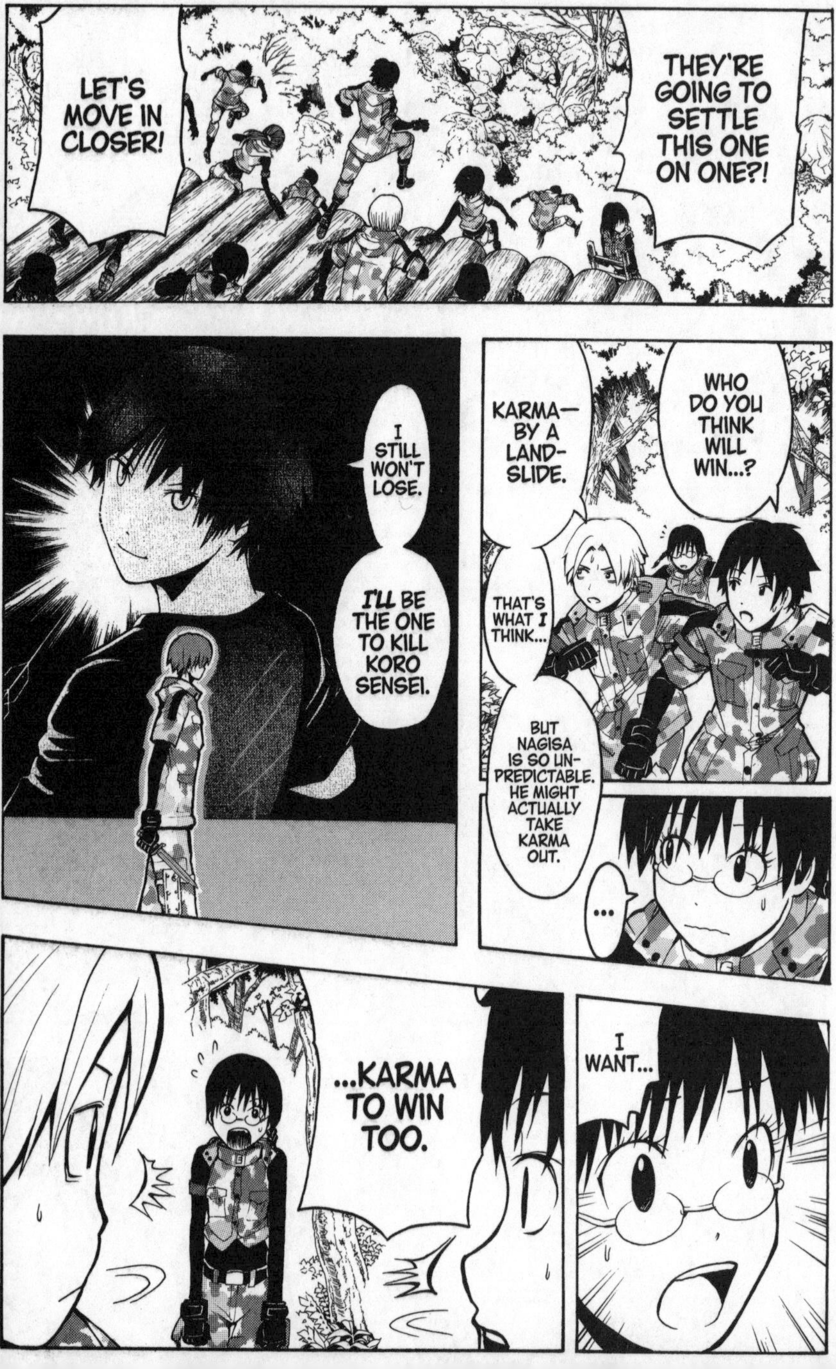
THEY'RE GOING TO SETTLE THIS ONE ON ONE?!
LET'S MOVE IN CLOSER!
WHO DO YOU THINK WILL WIN...?
KARMA— BY A LAND-SLIDE.
THAT'S WHAT I THINK...
BUT NAGISA IS SO UN-PREDICTABLE. HE MIGHT ACTUALLY TAKE KARMA OUT.
...
I STILL WON'T LOSE.
I'LL BE THE ONE TO KILL KORO SENSEI.
I WANT...
...KARMA TO WIN TOO.

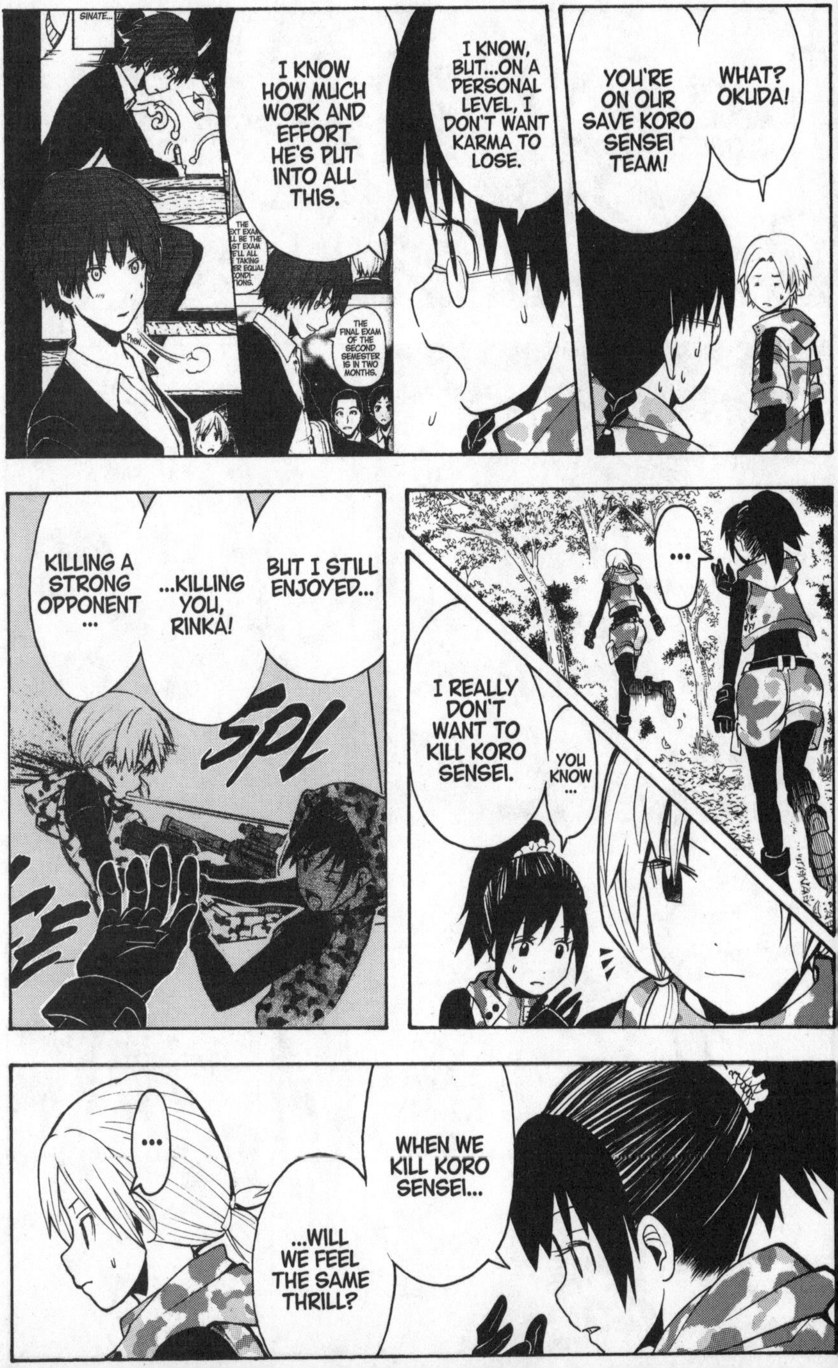
WHAT? OKUDA!
YOU'RE ON OUR SAVE KORO SENSEI TEAM!
I KNOW, BUT...ON A PERSONAL LEVEL, I DON'T WANT KARMA TO LOSE.
I KNOW HOW MUCH WORK AND EFFORT HE'S PUT INTO ALL THIS.
THE FINAL EXAM OF THE SECOND SEMESTER IS IN TWO MONTHS.
PHEW...
...
YOU KNOW ...
I REALLY DON'T WANT TO KILL KORO SENSEI.
BUT I STILL ENJOYED...
...KILLING YOU, RINKA!
KILLING A STRONG OPPONENT ...
SPL
WHEN WE KILL KORO SENSEI...
...WILL WE FEEL THE SAME THRILL?
...

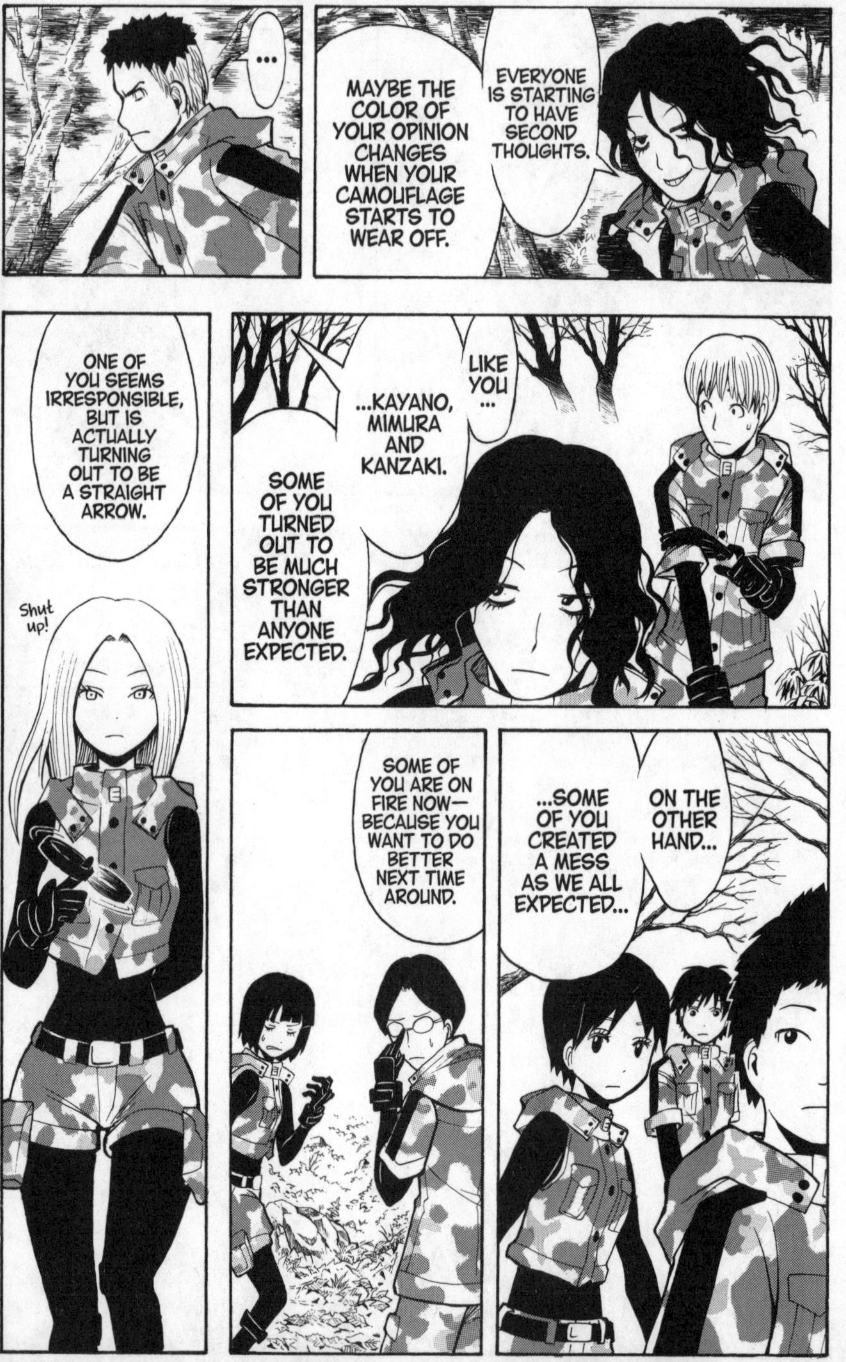
EVERYONE IS STARTING TO HAVE SECOND THOUGHTS.
MAYBE THE COLOR OF YOUR OPINION CHANGES WHEN YOUR CAMOUFLAGE STARTS TO WEAR OFF.
...
LIKE YOU...
...KAYANO, MIMURA AND KANZAKI.
SOME OF YOU TURNED OUT TO BE MUCH STRONGER THAN ANYONE EXPECTED.
ON THE OTHER HAND...
...SOME OF YOU CREATED A MESS AS WE ALL EXPECTED...
SOME OF YOU ARE ON FIRE NOW—BECAUSE YOU WANT TO DO BETTER NEXT TIME AROUND.
ONE OF YOU SEEMS IRRESPONSIBLE, BUT IS ACTUALLY TURNING OUT TO BE A STRAIGHT ARROW.
Shut up!

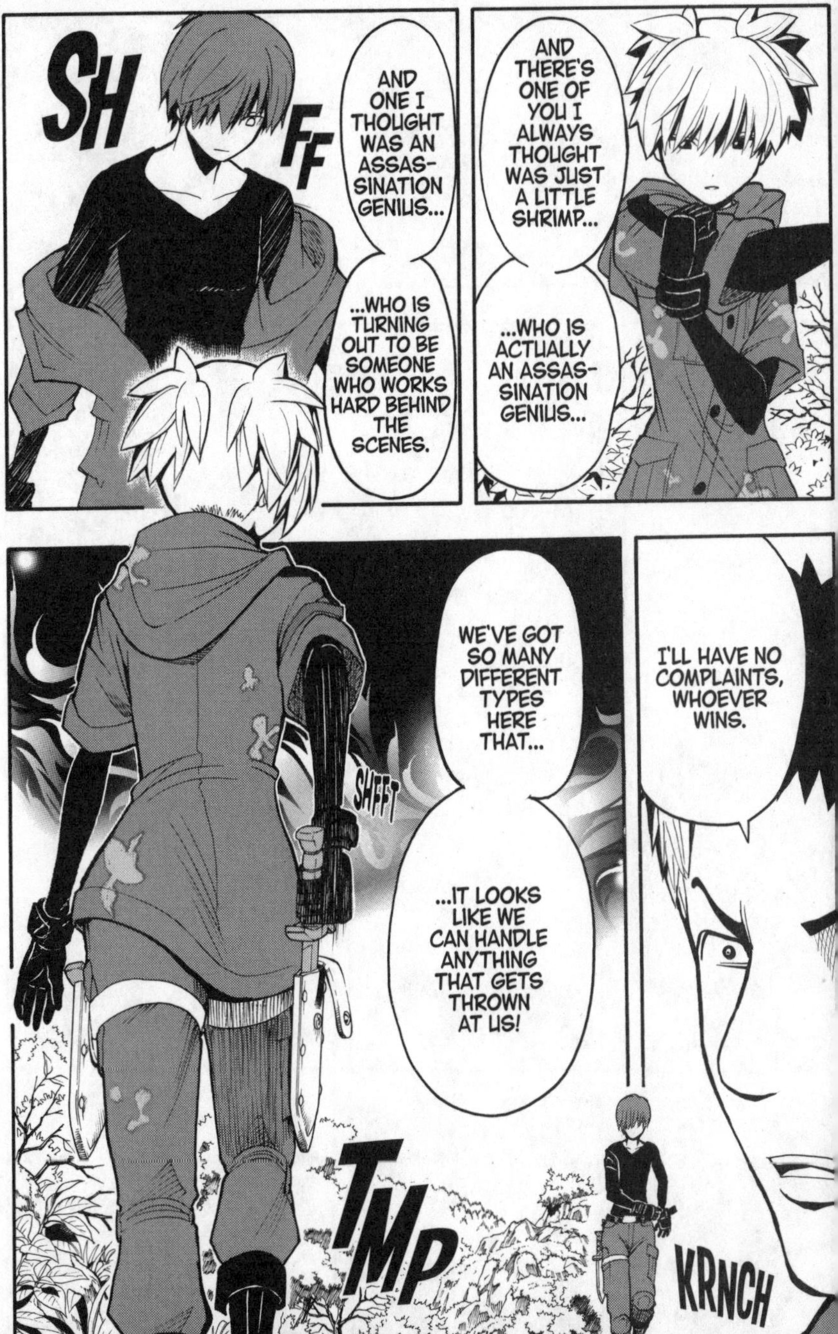
AND THERE'S ONE OF YOU I ALWAYS THOUGHT WAS JUST A LITTLE SHRIMP...
...WHO IS ACTUALLY AN ASSASSINATION GENIUS...
SHFF
AND ONE I THOUGHT WAS AN ASSASSINATION GENIUS...
...WHO IS TURNING OUT TO BE SOMEONE WHO WORKS HARD BEHIND THE SCENES.
I'LL HAVE NO COMPLAINTS, WHOEVER WINS.
KRNCH
WE'VE GOT SO MANY DIFFERENT TYPES HERE THAT...
...IT LOOKS LIKE WE CAN HANDLE ANYTHING THAT GETS THROWN AT US!
SHFFT
TMP

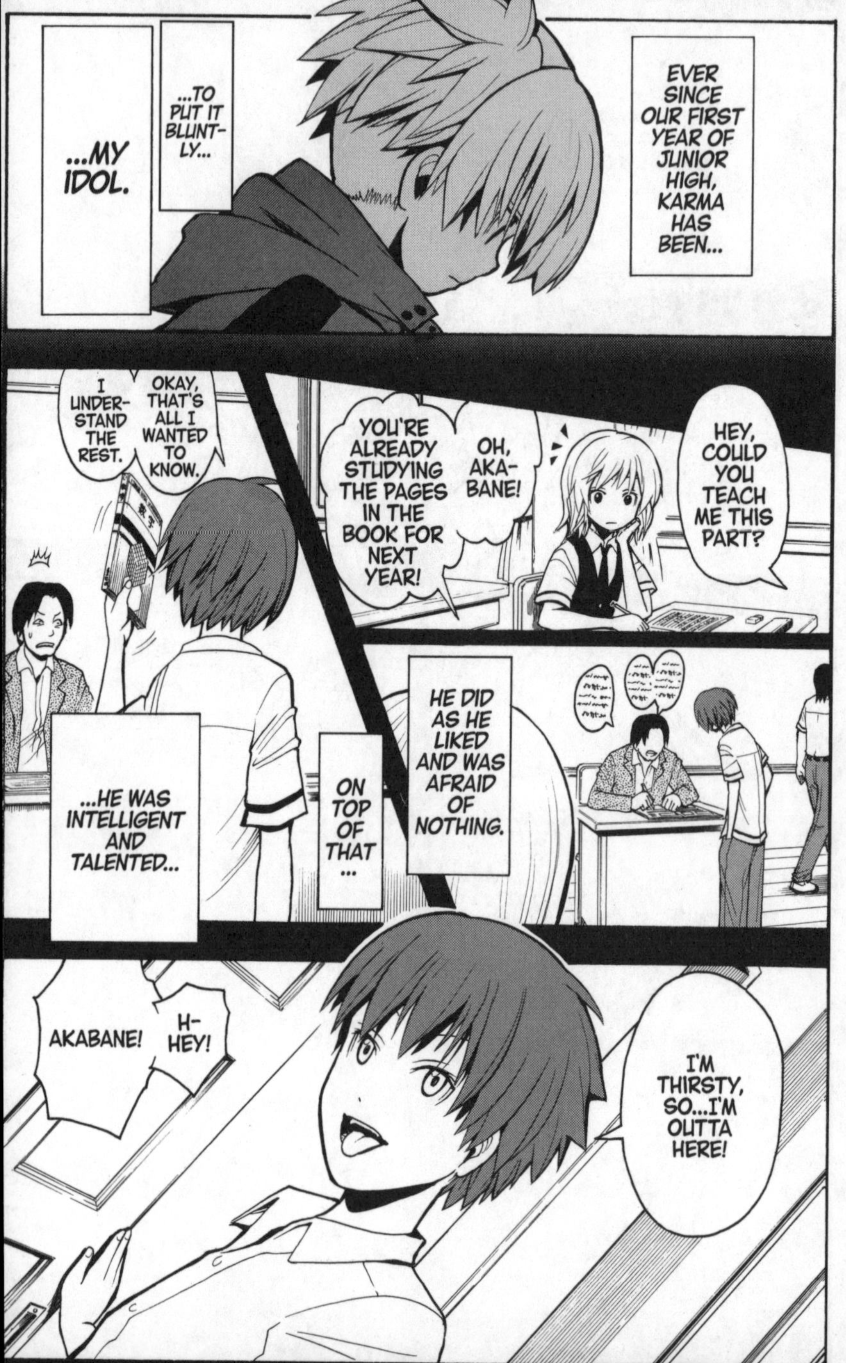
EVER SINCE OUR FIRST YEAR OF JUNIOR HIGH, KARMA HAS BEEN...
...TO PUT IT BLUNTLY...
...MY IDOL.
HEY, COULD YOU TEACH ME THIS PART?
OH, AKABANE!
YOU'RE ALREADY STUDYING THE PAGES IN THE BOOK FOR NEXT YEAR!
HE DID AS HE LIKED AND WAS AFRAID OF NOTHING.
OKAY, THAT'S ALL I WANTED TO KNOW.
I UNDERSTAND THE REST.
ON TOP OF THAT...
...HE WAS INTELLIGENT AND TALENTED...
I'M THIRSTY, SO...I'M OUTTA HERE!
H-HEY!
AKABANE!

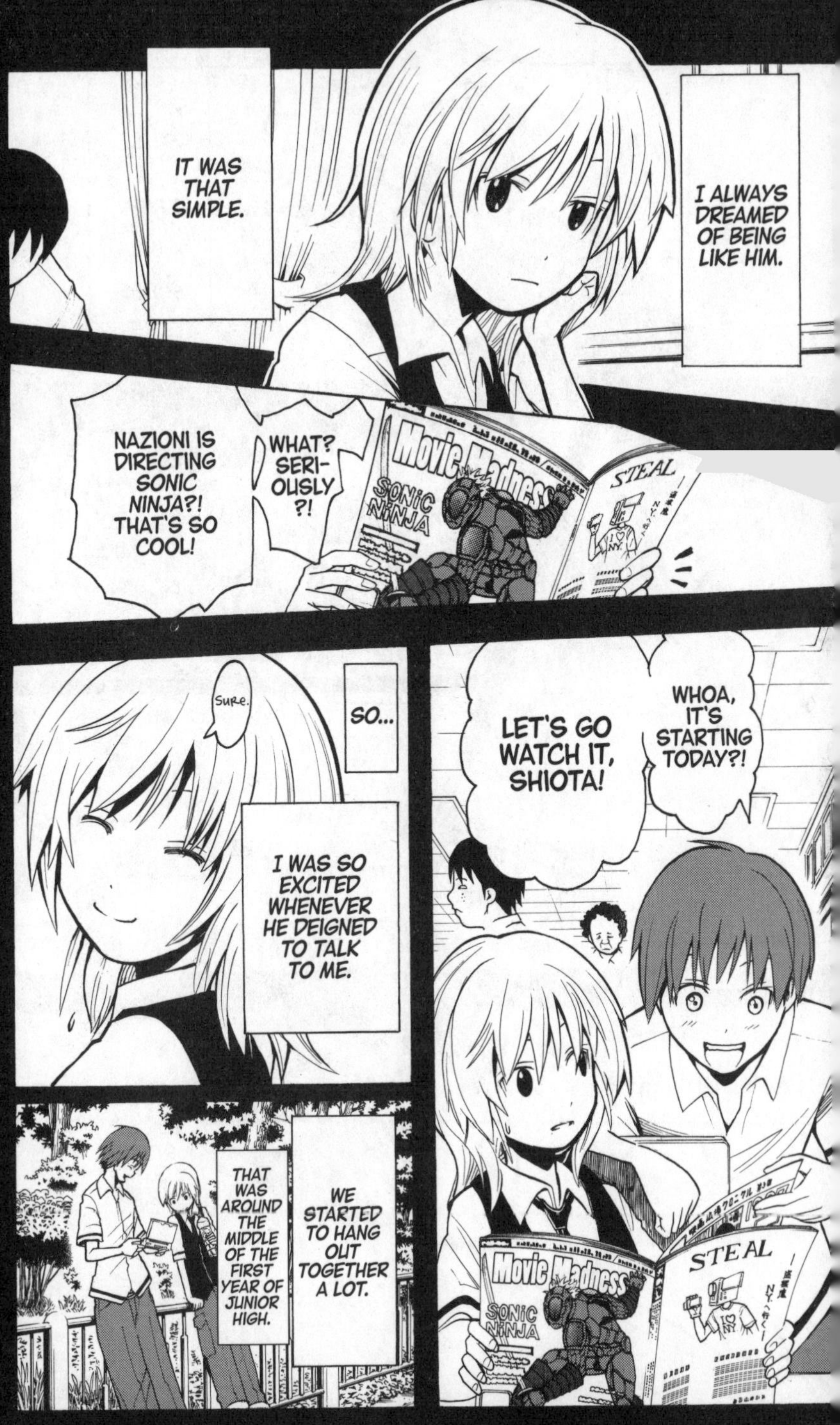
I ALWAYS DREAMED OF BEING LIKE HIM.
IT WAS THAT SIMPLE.
WHAT? SERIOUSLY?!
NAZIONI IS DIRECTING SONIC NINJA?! THAT'S SO COOL!
Movie Madness
SONIC NINJA
STEAL
WHOA, IT'S STARTING TODAY?!
LET'S GO WATCH IT, SHIOTA!
Movie Madness
SONIC NINJA
STEAL
SO...
Sure.
I WAS SO EXCITED WHENEVER HE DEIGNED TO TALK TO ME.
WE STARTED TO HANG OUT TOGETHER A LOT.
THAT WAS AROUND THE MIDDLE OF THE FIRST YEAR OF JUNIOR HIGH.

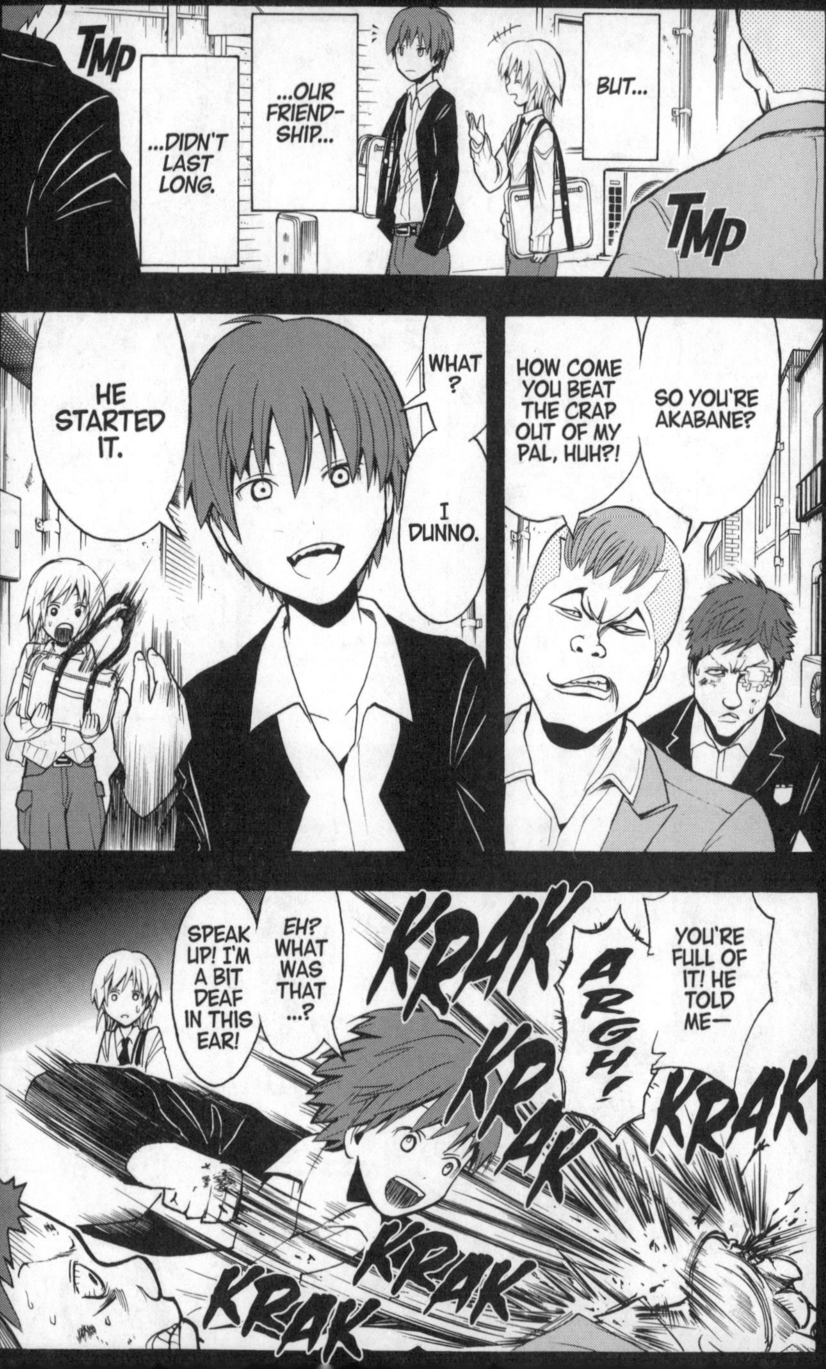
BUT...
...OUR FRIEND-SHIP...
...DIDN'T LAST LONG.
TMP
TMP
SO YOU'RE AKABANE?
HOW COME YOU BEAT THE CRAP OUT OF MY PAL, HUH?!
WHAT?
I DUNNO.
HE STARTED IT.
YOU'RE FULL OF IT! HE TOLD ME—
KRAK
ARGH!
KRAK
EH? WHAT WAS THAT ...?
SPEAK UP! I'M A BIT DEAF IN THIS EAR!
KRAK
KRAK
KRAK
KRAK
KRAK

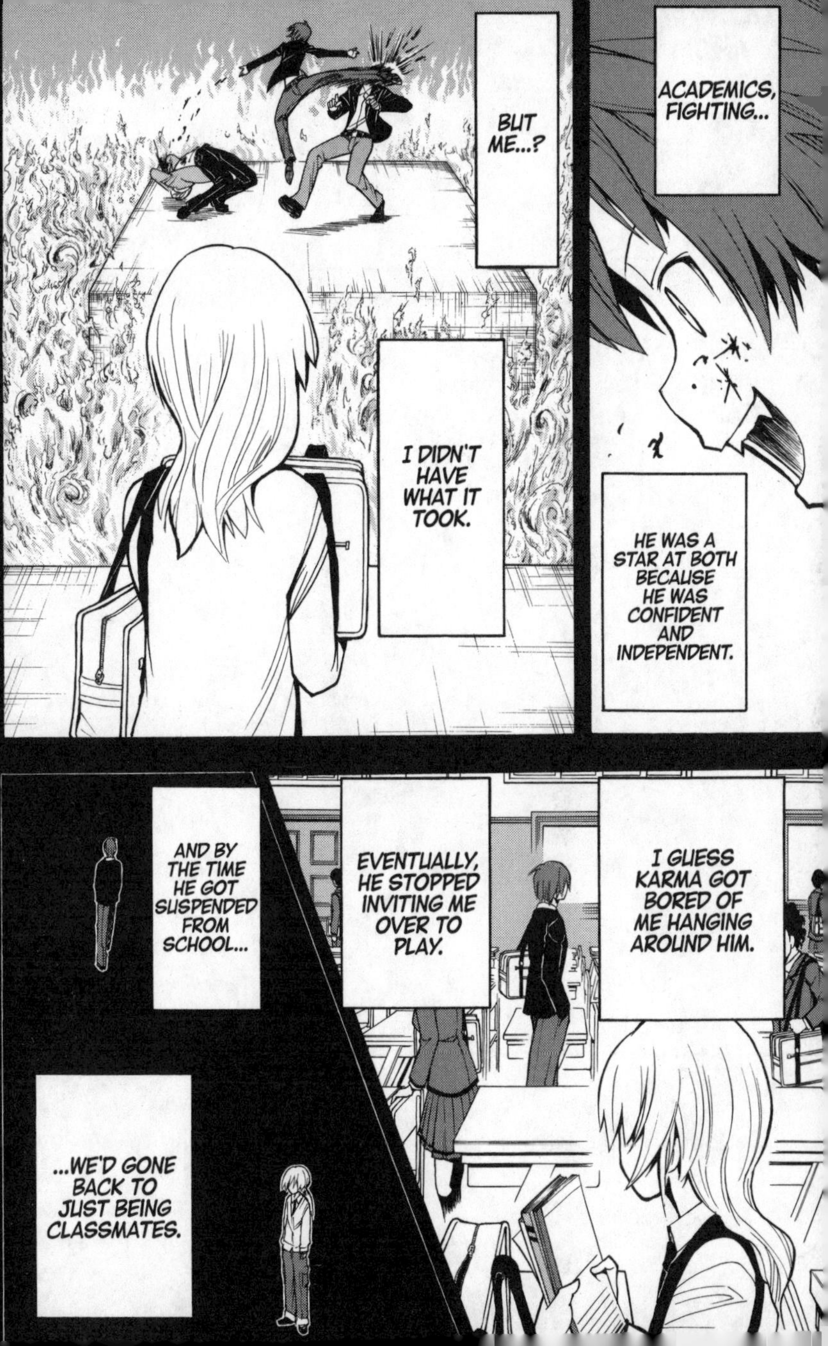
ACADEMICS, FIGHTING...
HE WAS A STAR AT BOTH BECAUSE HE WAS CONFIDENT AND INDEPENDENT.
BUT ME...?
I DIDN'T HAVE WHAT IT TOOK.
I GUESS KARMA GOT BORED OF ME HANGING AROUND HIM.
EVENTUALLY, HE STOPPED INVITING ME OVER TO PLAY.
AND BY THE TIME HE GOT SUSPENDED FROM SCHOOL...
...WE'D GONE BACK TO JUST BEING CLASSMATES.

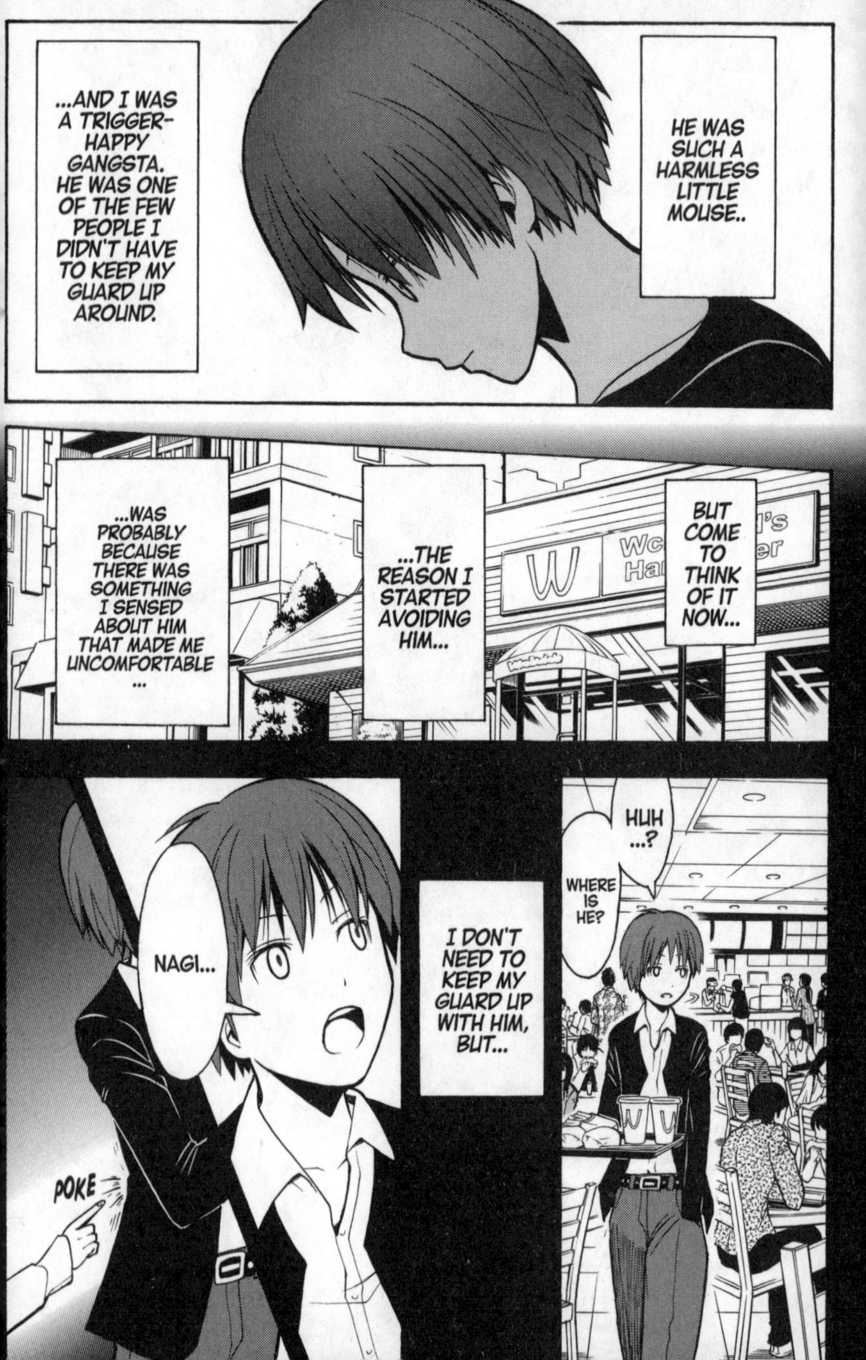
HE WAS SUCH A HARMLESS LITTLE MOUSE..
...AND I WAS A TRIGGER-HAPPY GANGSTA. HE WAS ONE OF THE FEW PEOPLE I DIDN'T HAVE TO KEEP MY GUARD UP AROUND.
BUT COME TO THINK OF IT NOW...
...THE REASON I STARTED AVOIDING HIM...
...WAS PROBABLY BECAUSE THERE WAS SOMETHING I SENSED ABOUT HIM THAT MADE ME UNCOMFORTABLE ...
HUH ...?
WHERE IS HE?
I DON'T NEED TO KEEP MY GUARD UP WITH HIM, BUT...
NAGI...
POKE

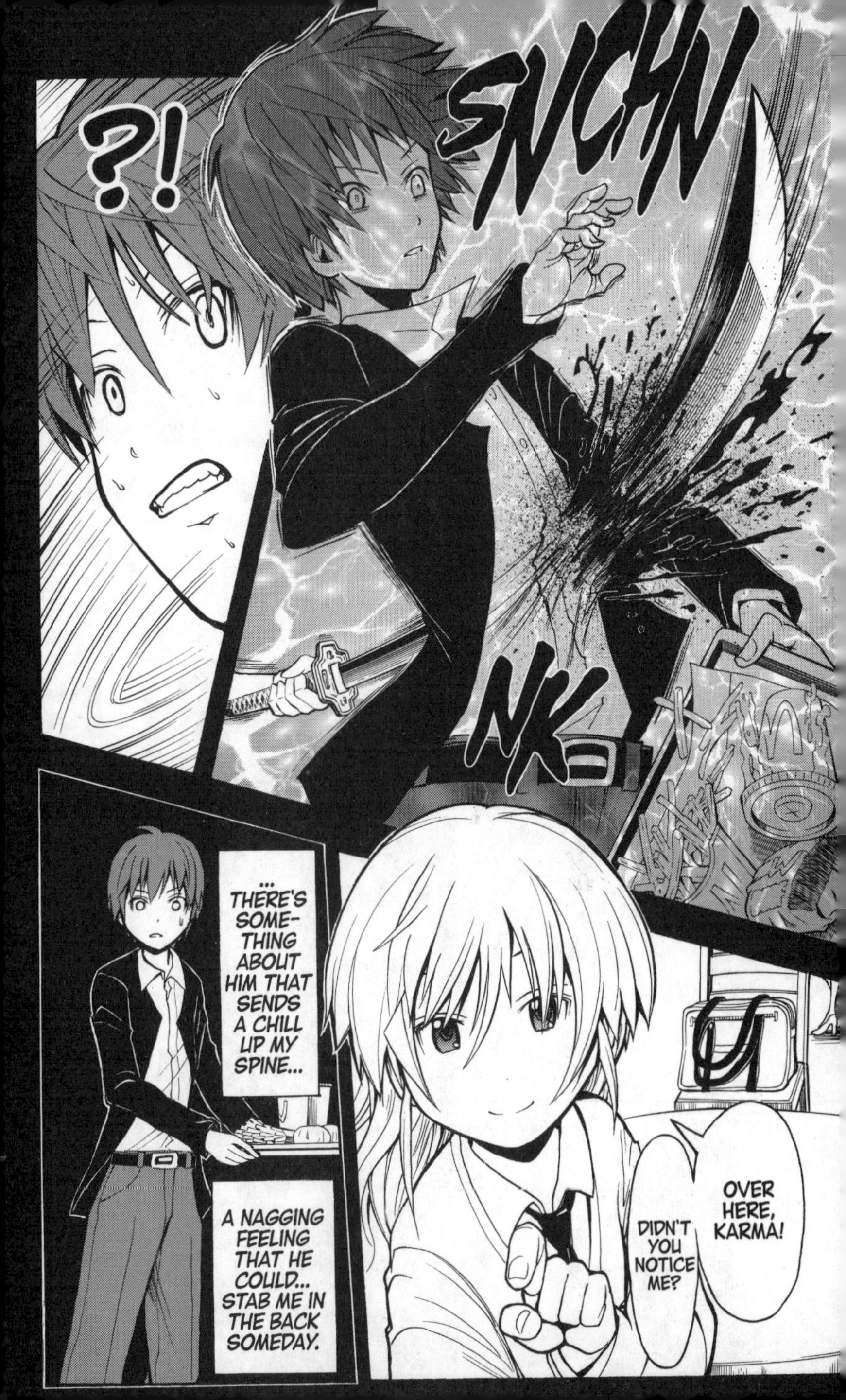
SNCHN
NK
?!
OVER HERE, KARMA!
DIDN'T YOU NOTICE ME?
... THERE'S SOME-THING ABOUT HIM THAT SENDS A CHILL UP MY SPINE...
A NAGGING FEELING THAT HE COULD... STAB ME IN THE BACK SOMEDAY.

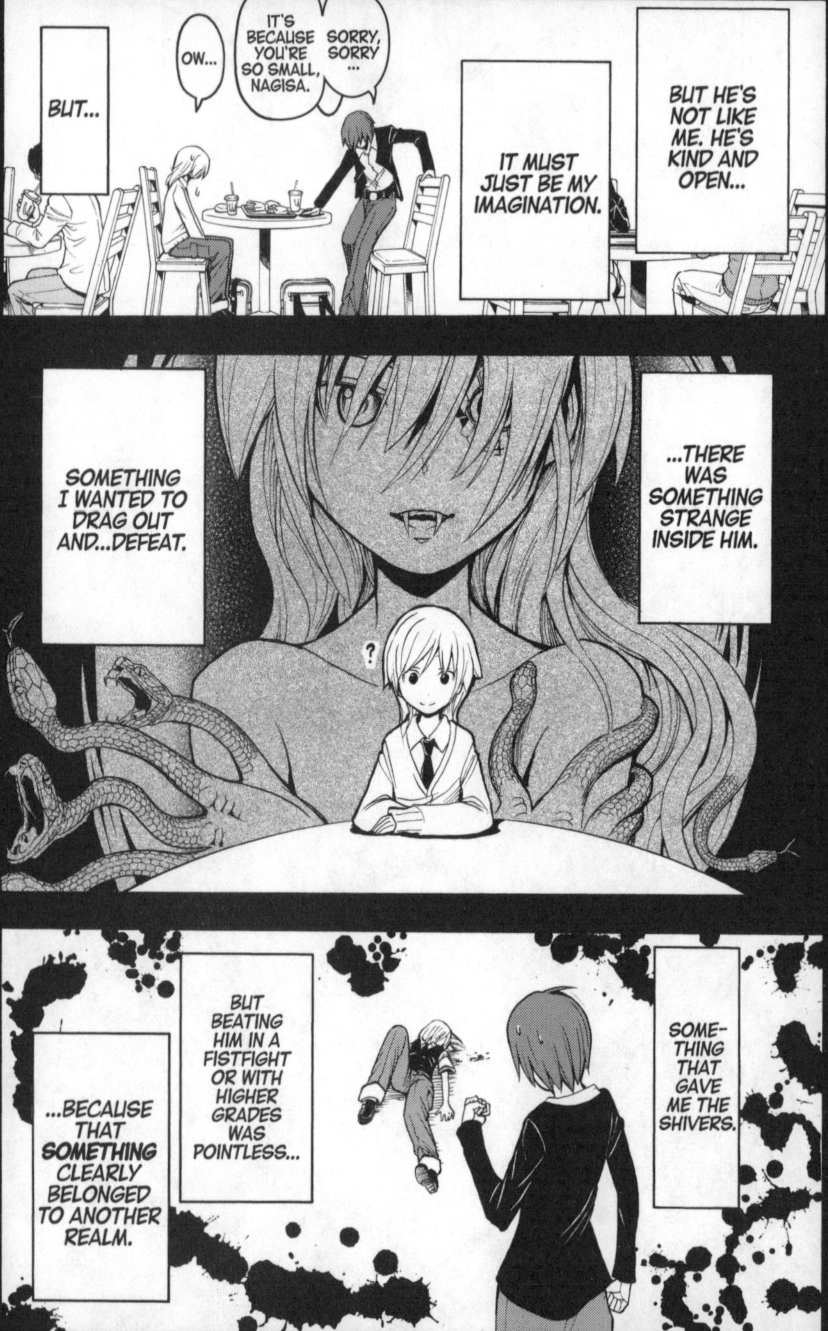
BUT HE'S NOT LIKE ME. HE'S KIND AND OPEN...
IT MUST JUST BE MY IMAGINATION.
SORRY, SORRY ...
IT'S BECAUSE YOU'RE SO SMALL, NAGISA.
OW...
BUT...
...THERE WAS SOMETHING STRANGE INSIDE HIM.
?
SOMETHING I WANTED TO DRAG OUT AND...DEFEAT.
SOME-THING THAT GAVE ME THE SHIVERS.
BUT BEATING HIM IN A FISTFIGHT OR WITH HIGHER GRADES WAS POINTLESS...
...BECAUSE THAT SOMETHING CLEARLY BELONGED TO ANOTHER REALM.

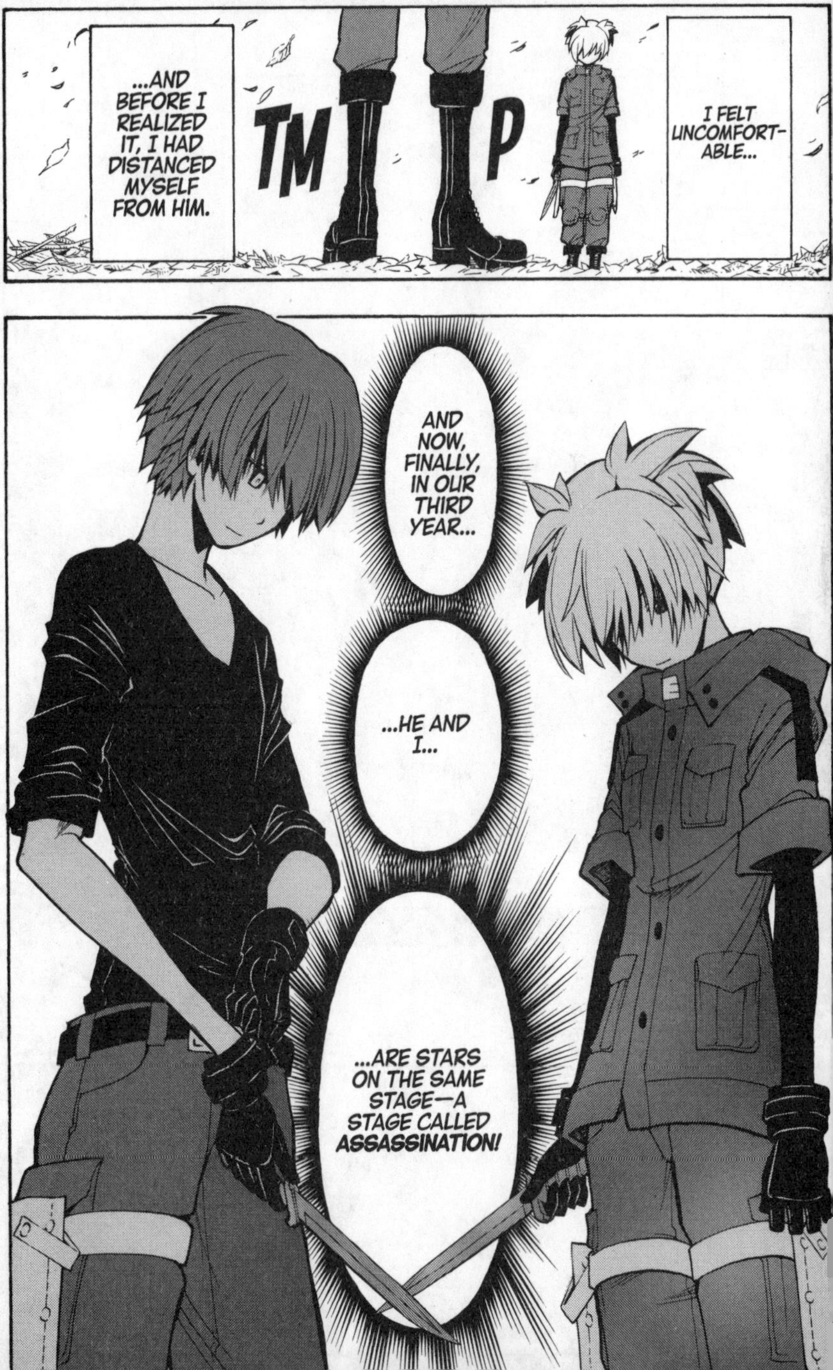
I FELT UNCOMFORT-ABLE...
TMP
...AND BEFORE I REALIZED IT, I HAD DISTANCED MYSELF FROM HIM.
AND NOW, FINALLY, IN OUR THIRD YEAR...
...HE AND I...
...ARE STARS ON THE SAME STAGE—A STAGE CALLED ASSASSINATION!

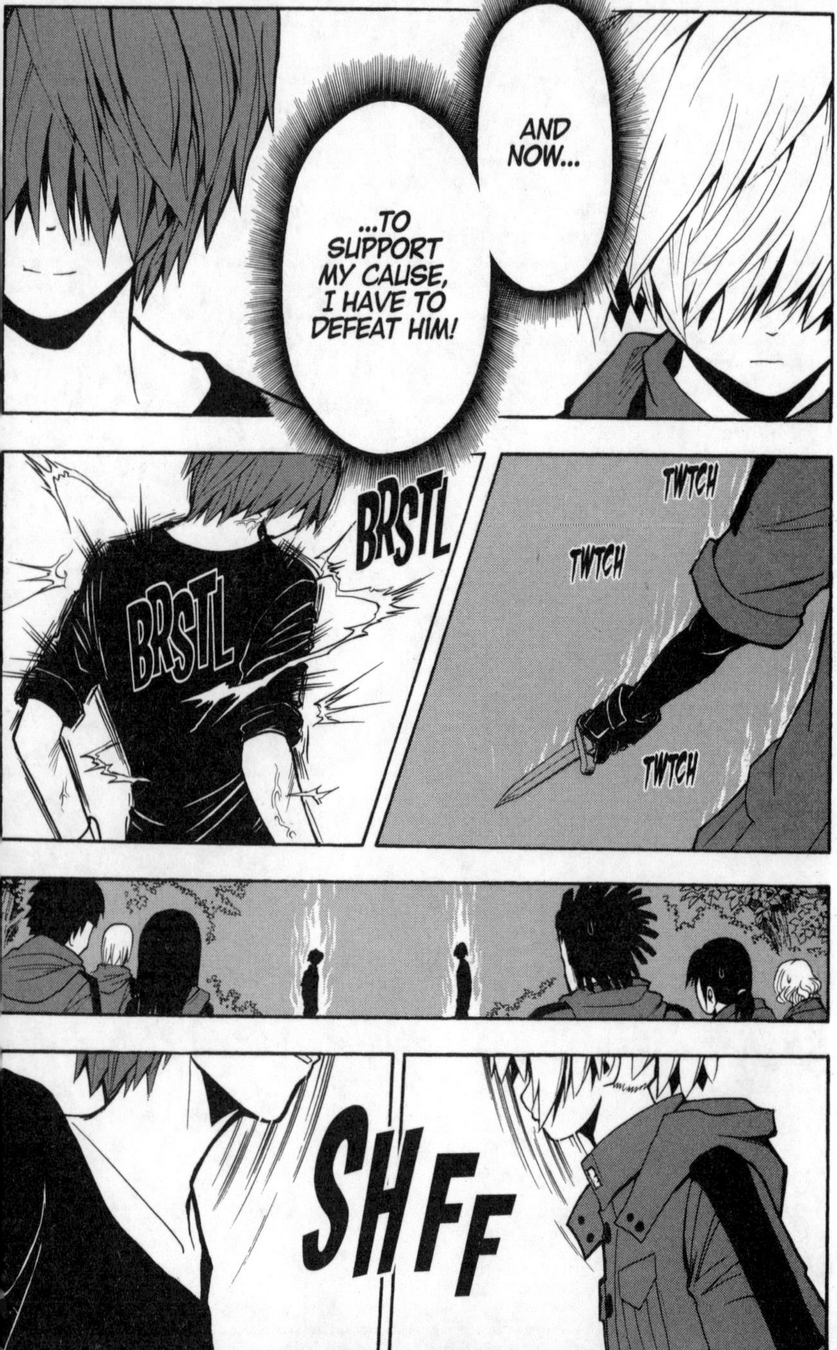
AND NOW...
...TO SUPPORT MY CAUSE, I HAVE TO DEFEAT HIM!
TWTCH
TWTCH
TWTCH
BRSTL
BRSTL
SHFF

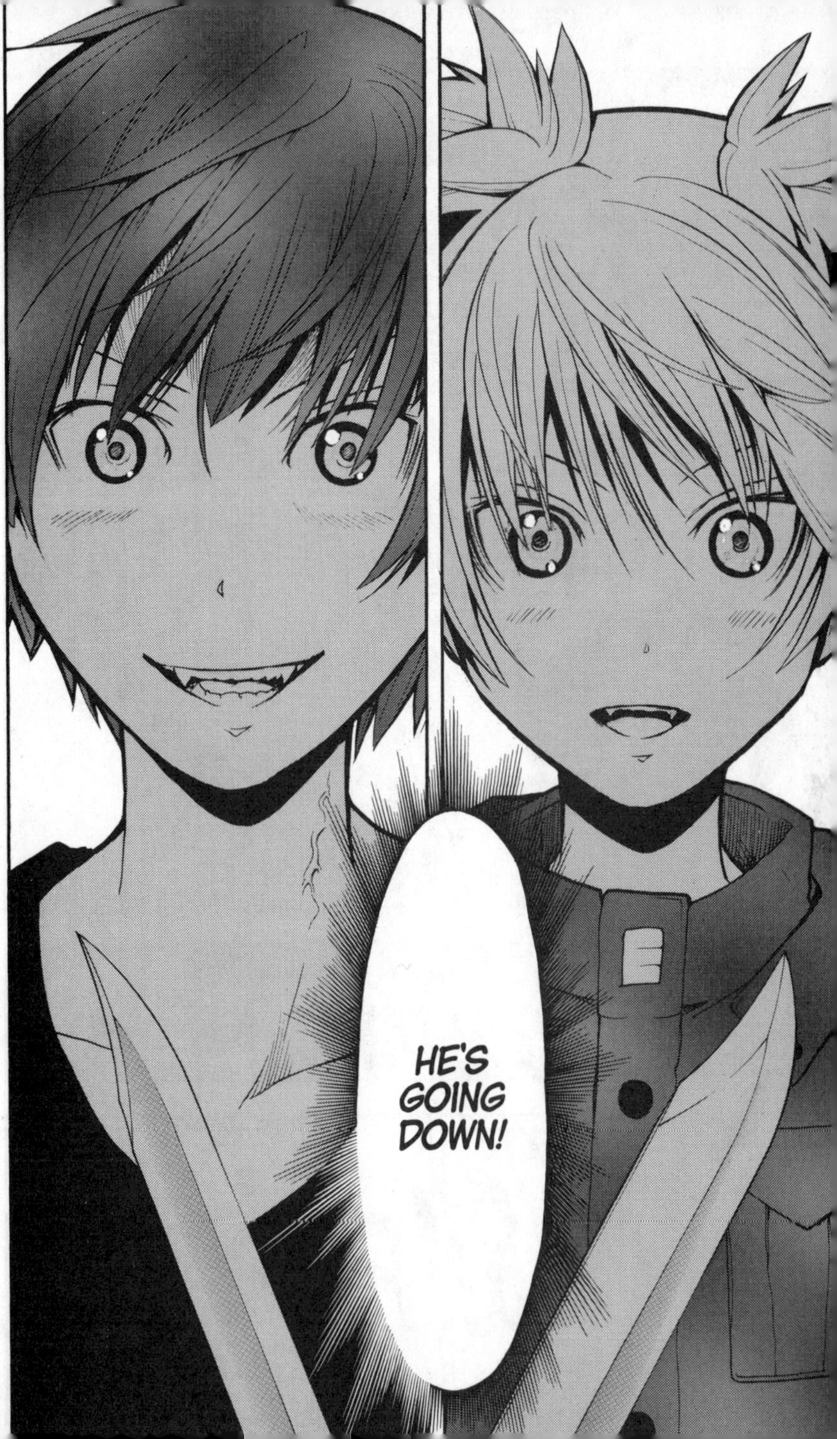
HE'S GOING DOWN!

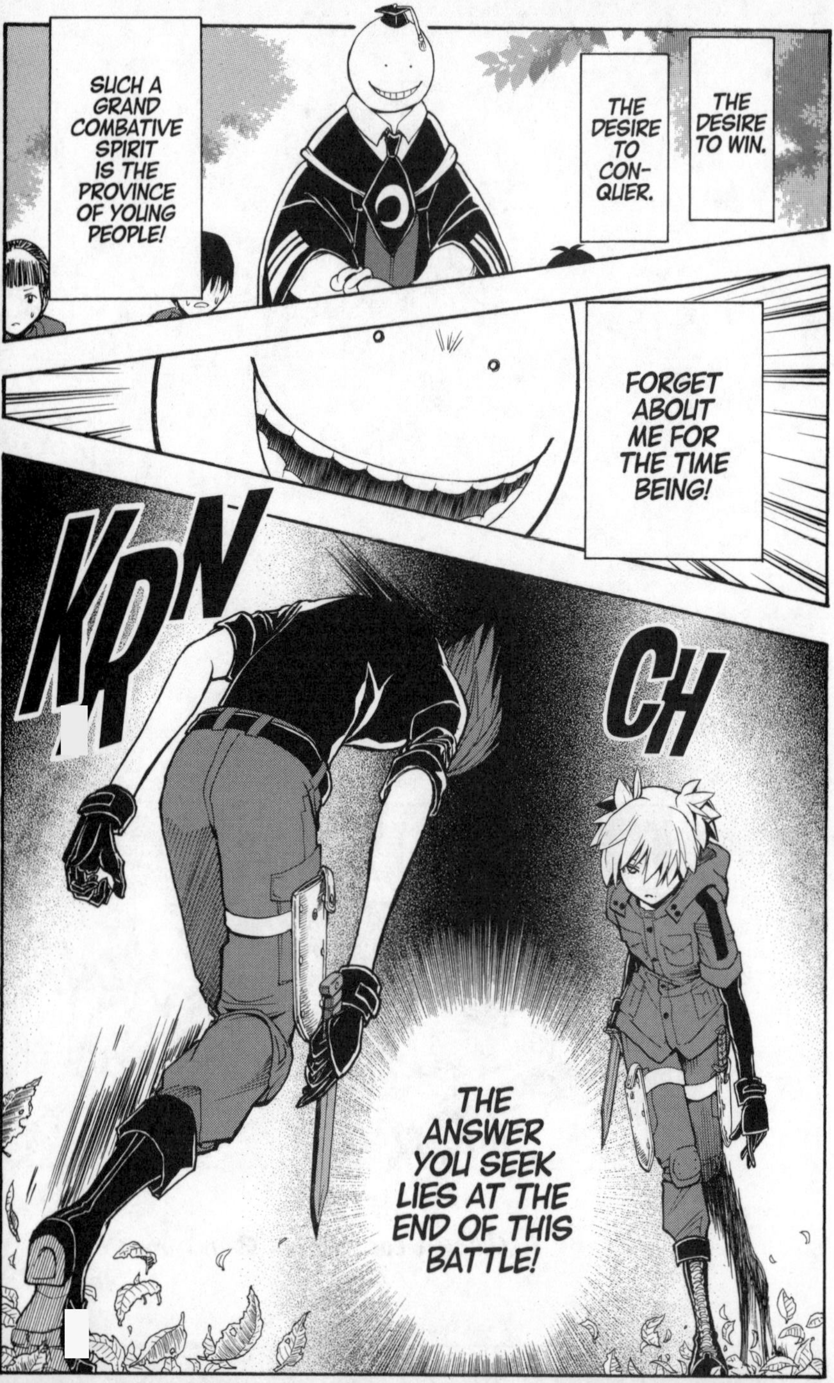
THE DESIRE TO WIN.
THE DESIRE TO CON-QUER.
SUCH A GRAND COMBATIVE SPIRIT IS THE PROVINCE OF YOUNG PEOPLE!
FORGET ABOUT ME FOR THE TIME BEING!
KRN
CH
THE ANSWER YOU SEEK LIES AT THE END OF THIS BATTLE!

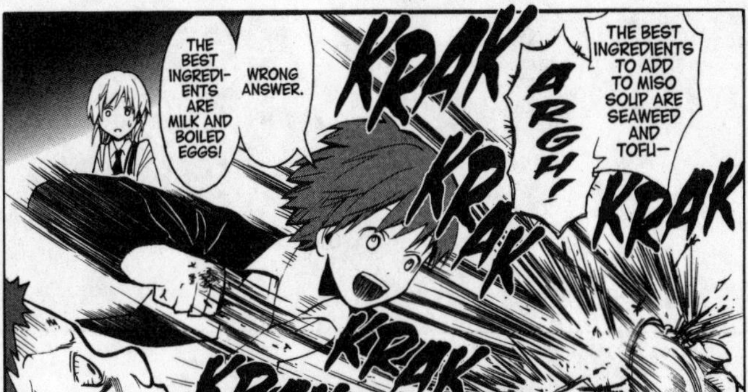
THE BEST INGREDIENTS TO ADD TO MISO SOUP ARE SEAWEED AND TOFU—
KRAK
ARGH!
KRAK
WRONG ANSWER.
THE BEST INGREDI-ENTS ARE MILK AND BOILED EGGS!
KRAK
KRAK
KRAK
KRAK

A stage I can never stand on.

Class 148 Time for the Process

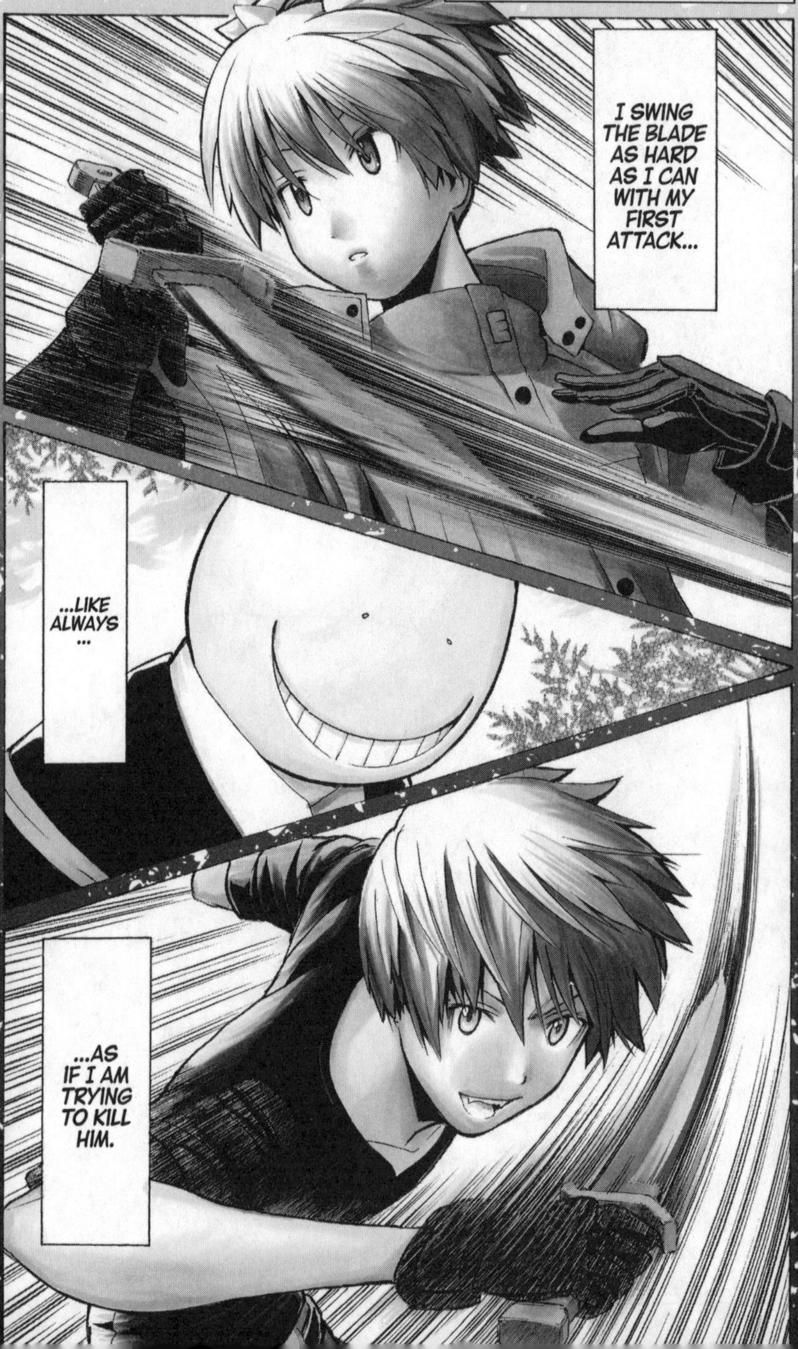
I SWING THE BLADE AS HARD AS I CAN WITH MY FIRST ATTACK...
...LIKE ALWAYS ...
...AS IF I AM TRYING TO KILL HIM.

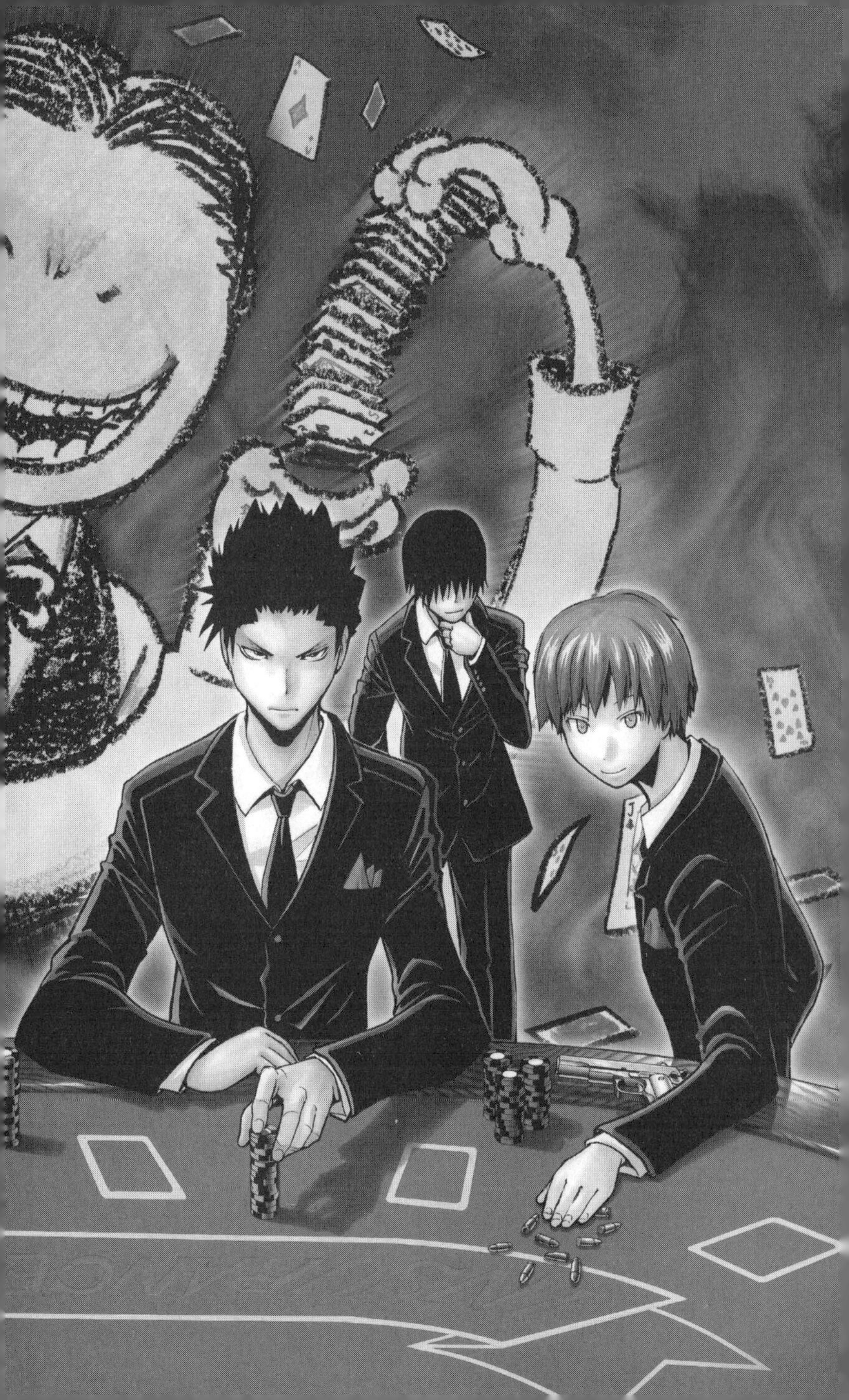

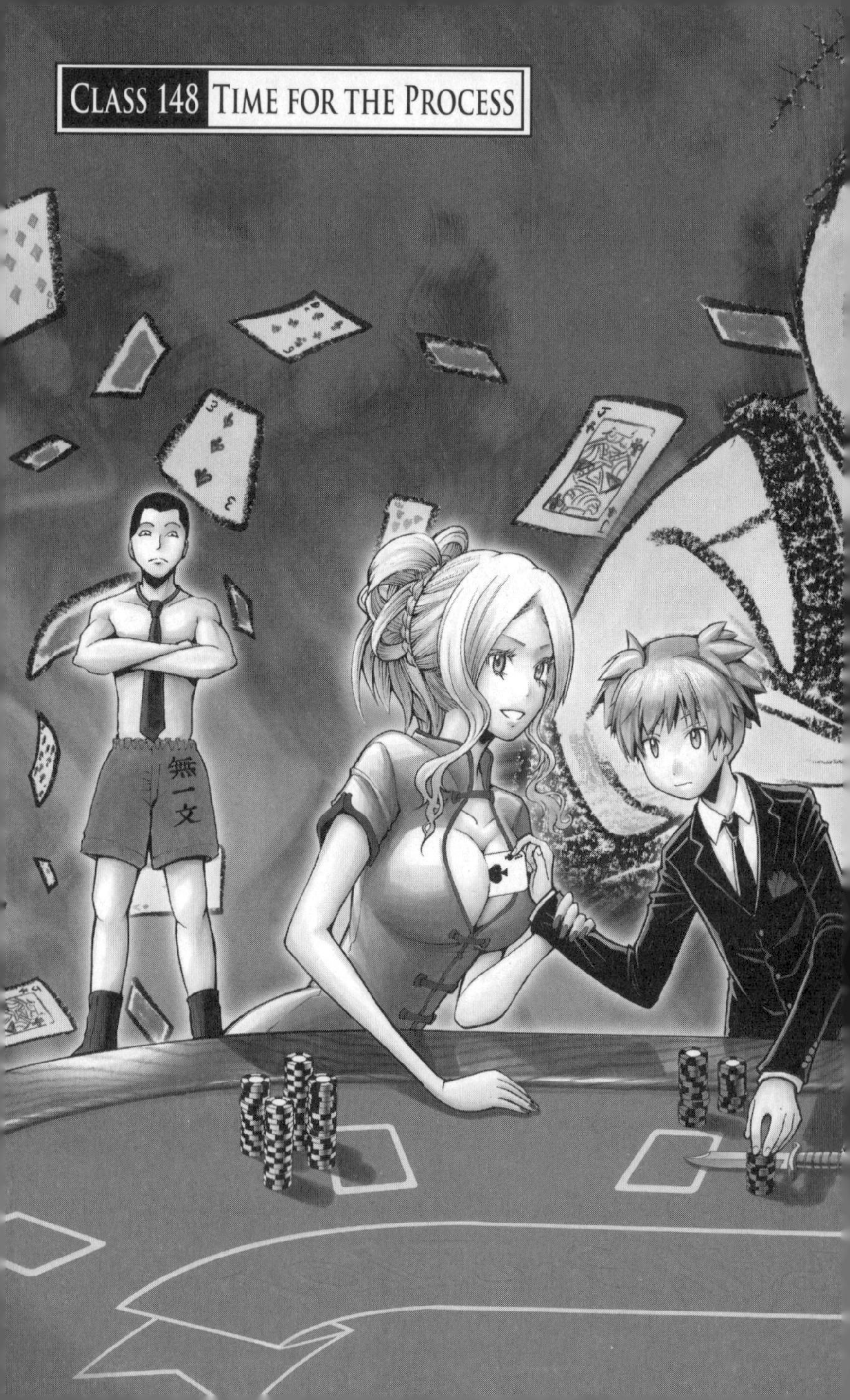
CLASS 148 TIME FOR THE PROCESS
無一文

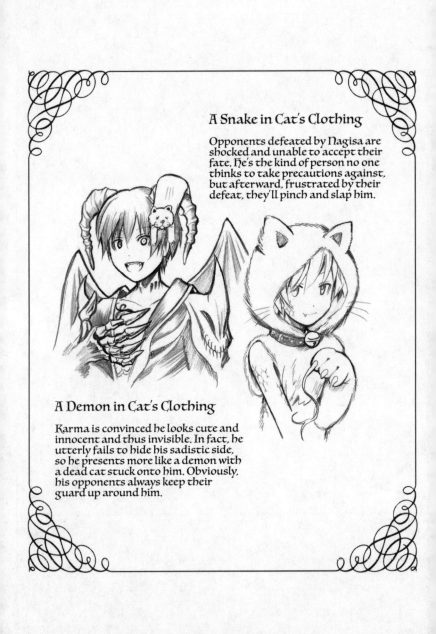

A Snake in Cat's Clothing

Opponents defeated by Nagisa are shocked and unable to accept their fate. He's the kind of person no one thinks to take precautions against, but afterward, frustrated by their defeat, they'll pinch and slap him.

A Demon in Cat's Clothing

Karma is convinced he looks cute and innocent and thus invisible. In fact, he utterly fails to hide his sadistic side, so he presents more like a demon with a dead cat stuck onto him. Obviously, his opponents always keep their guard up around him.

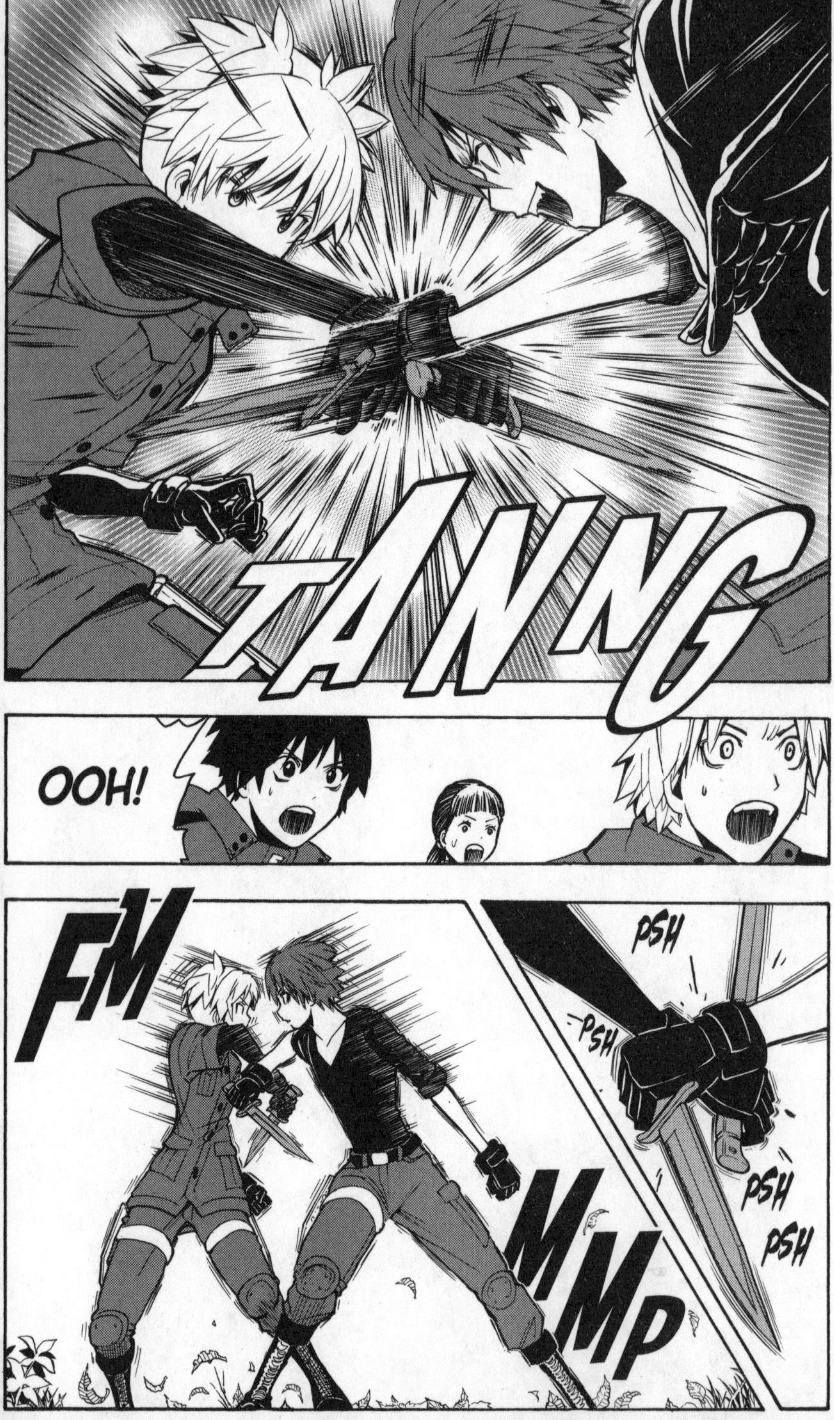
TANNG
OOH!
PSH
PSH
PSH
PSH
FM
MMP

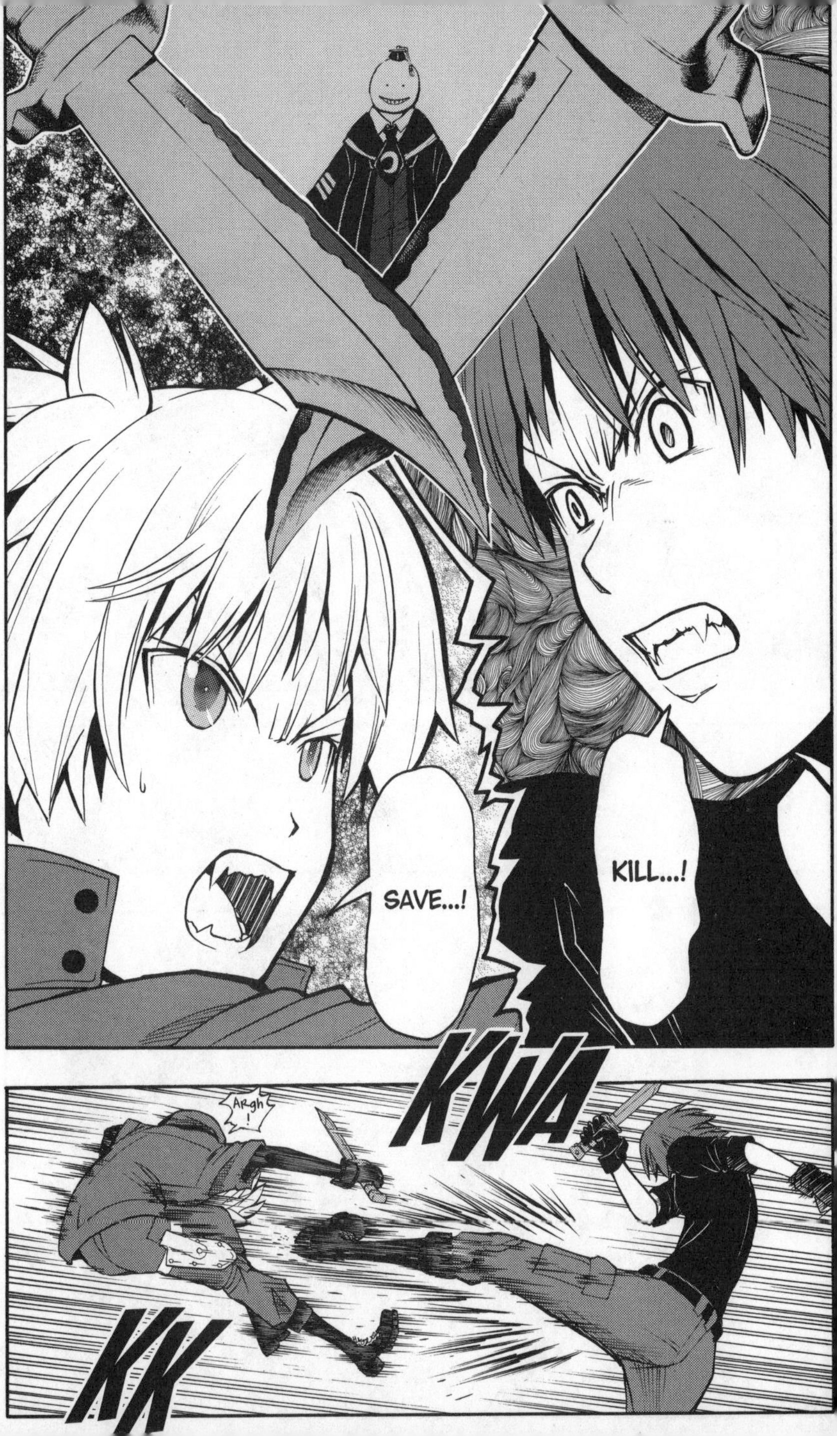
KILL...!
SAVE...!
KWA
Argh!
KK

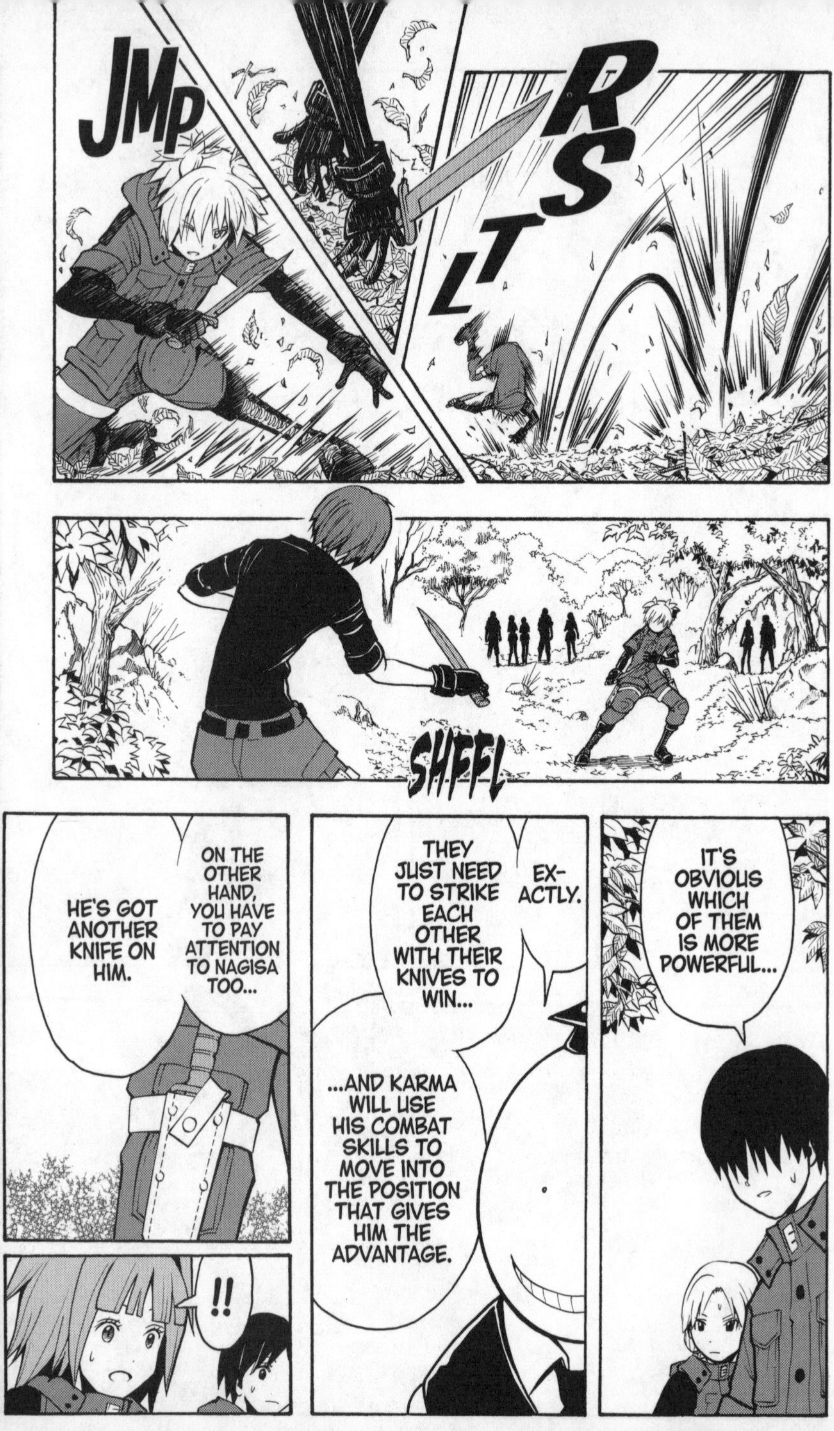
RSTL
JMP
SHFFL
IT'S OBVIOUS WHICH OF THEM IS MORE POWERFUL...
EX-ACTLY.
THEY JUST NEED TO STRIKE EACH OTHER WITH THEIR KNIVES TO WIN...
...AND KARMA WILL USE HIS COMBAT SKILLS TO MOVE INTO THE POSITION THAT GIVES HIM THE ADVANTAGE.
ON THE OTHER HAND, YOU HAVE TO PAY ATTENTION TO NAGISA TOO...
HE'S GOT ANOTHER KNIFE ON HIM.
!!

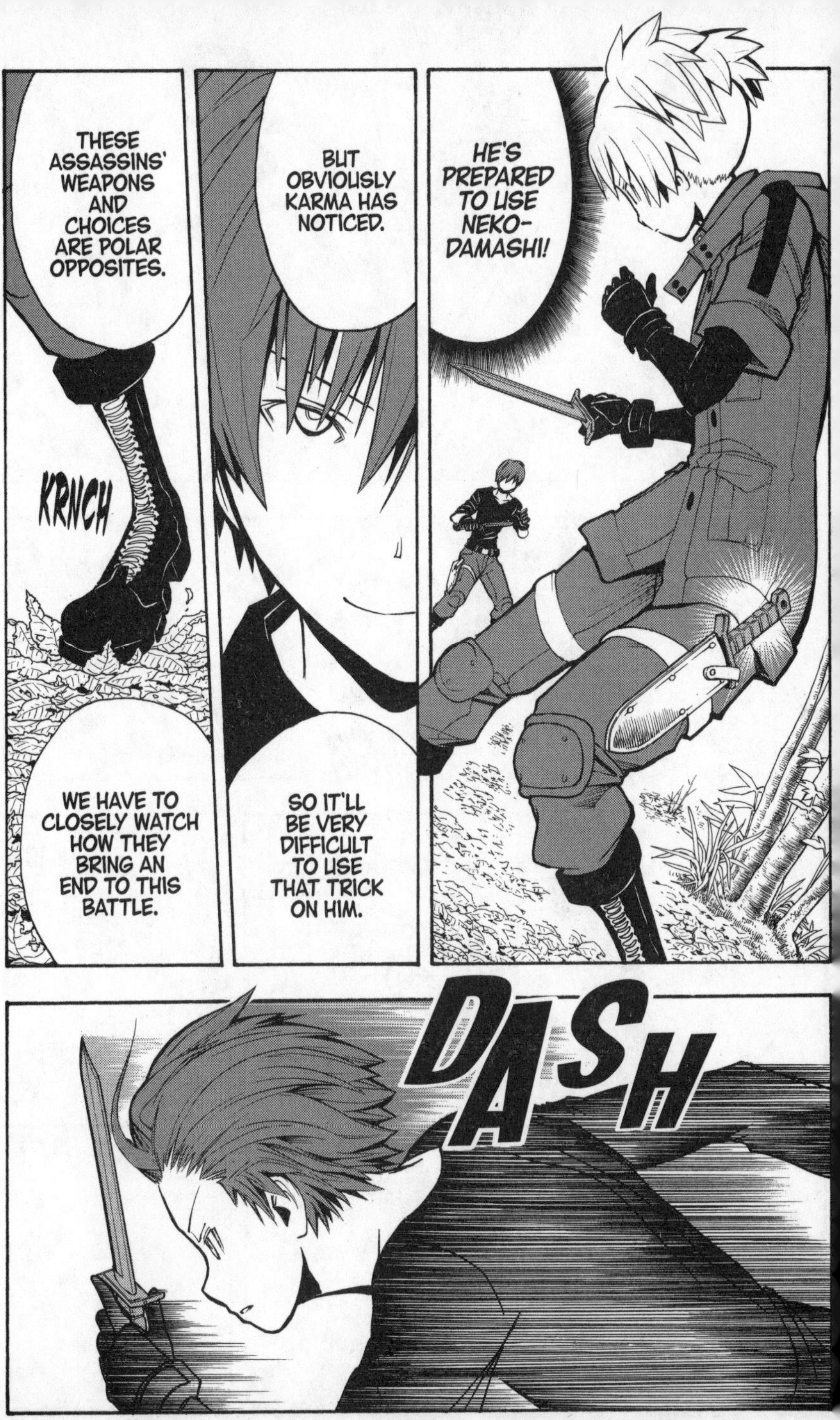
HE'S PREPARED TO USE NEKO-DAMASHI!
BUT OBVIOUSLY KARMA HAS NOTICED.
SO IT'LL BE VERY DIFFICULT TO USE THAT TRICK ON HIM.
THESE ASSASSINS' WEAPONS AND CHOICES ARE POLAR OPPOSITES.
KRNCH
WE HAVE TO CLOSELY WATCH HOW THEY BRING AN END TO THIS BATTLE.
DASH

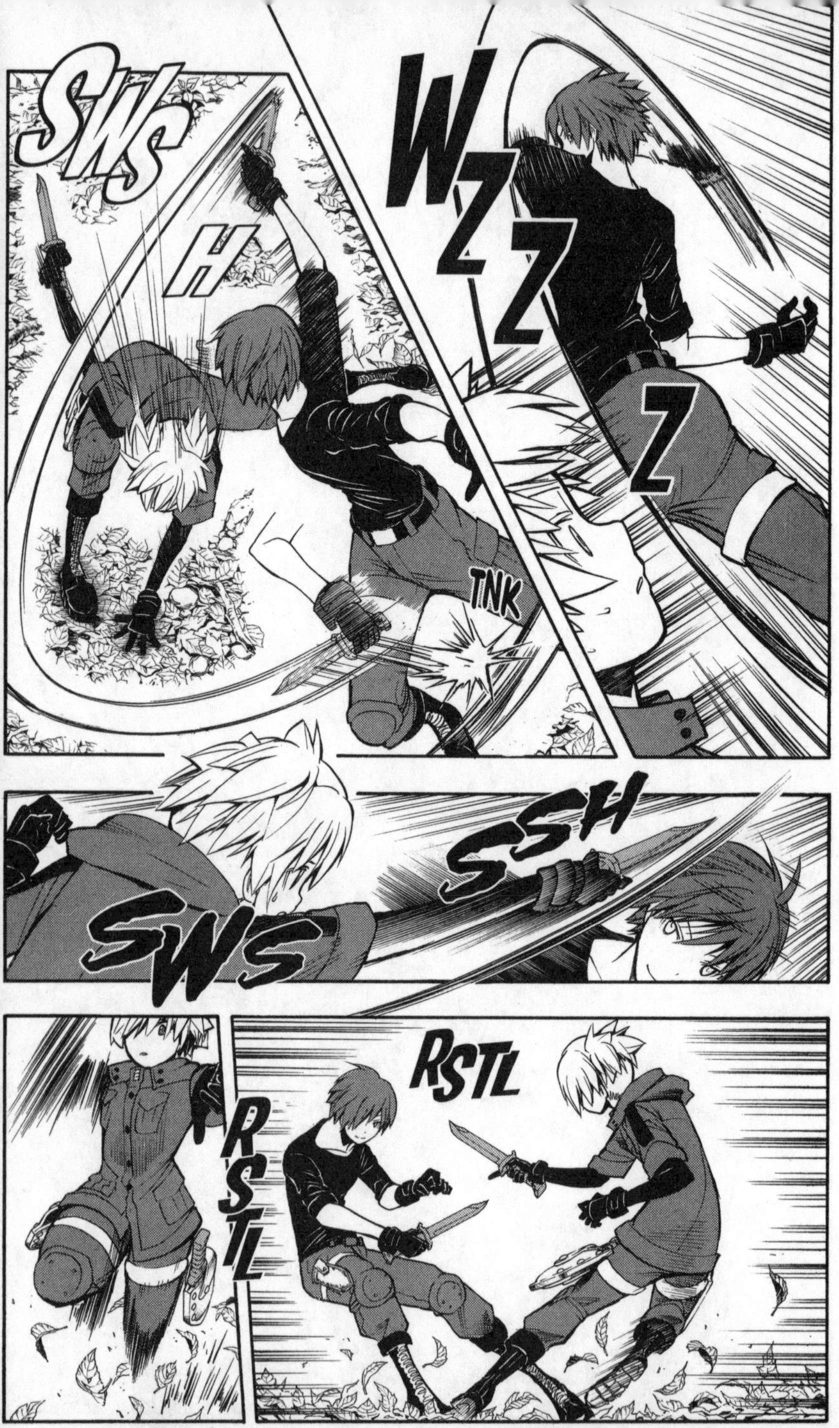
WZZZ
SWSH
TNK
SSH
SWS
RSTL
RSTL

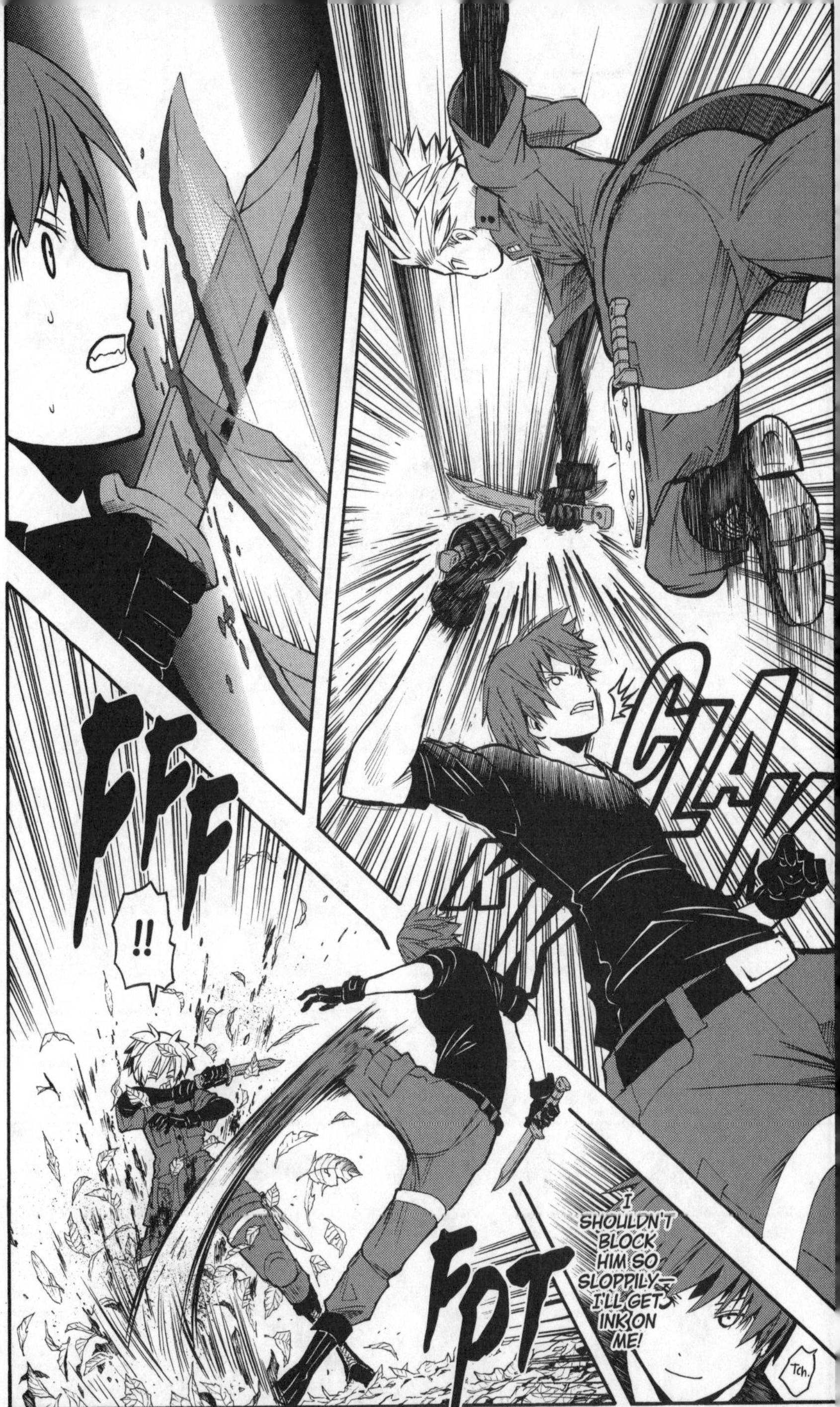
CLA
I SHOULDN'T BLOCK HIM SO SLOPPILY— I'LL GET INK ON ME!
Tch.
FPT
FFF
!!

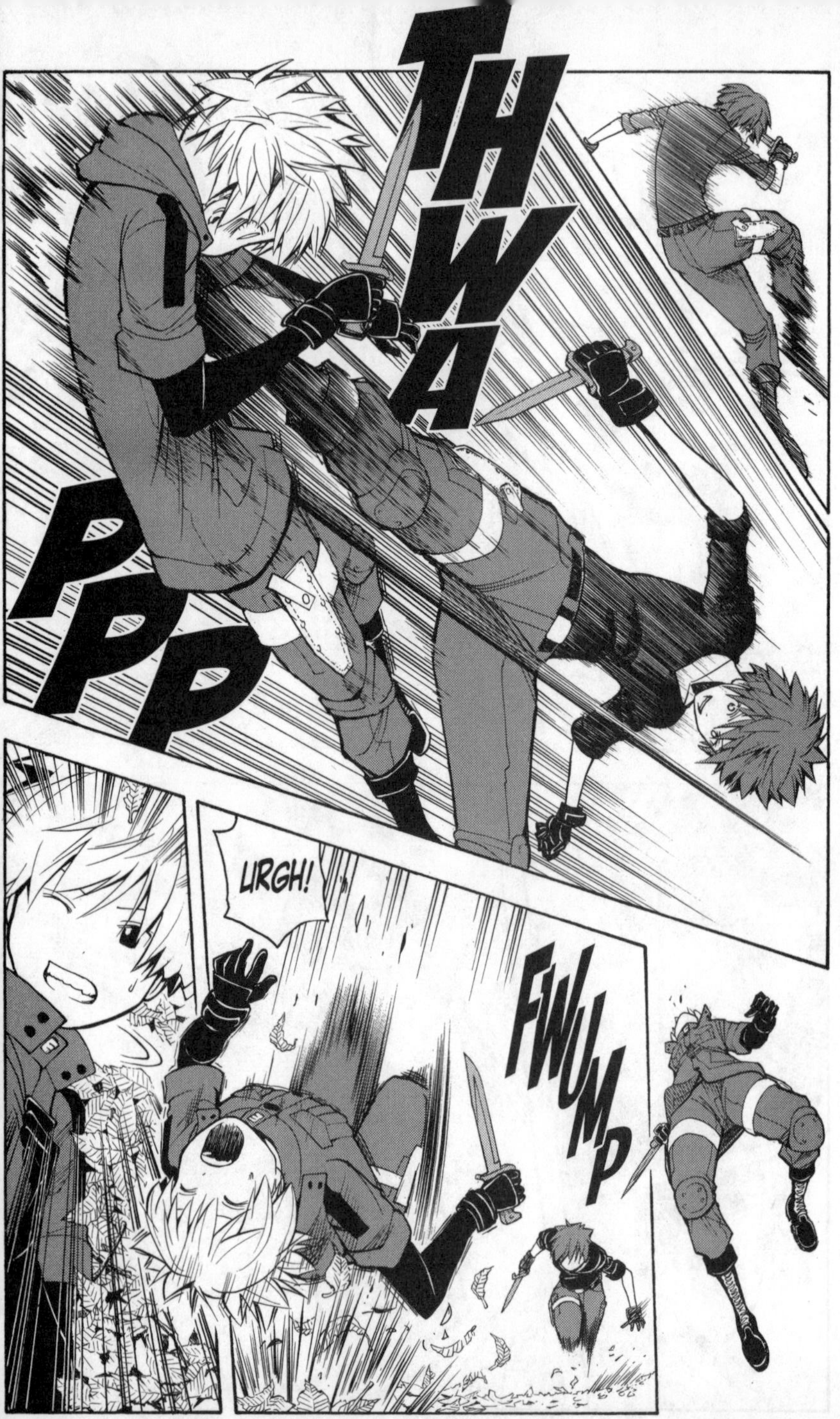
THWAPPP
URGH!
FWUMP

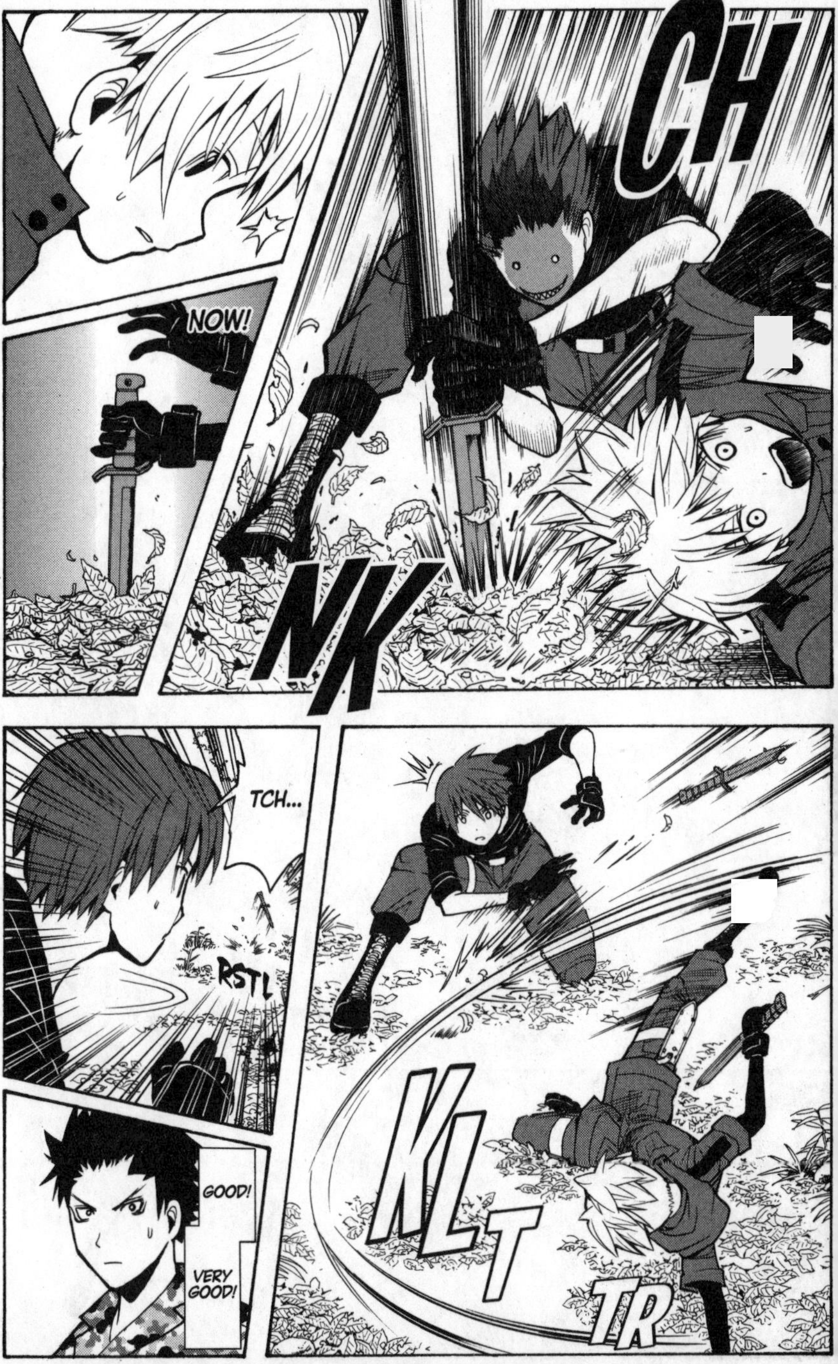
CH
NK
NOW!
KL
T
TR
TCH...
RSTL
GOOD!
VERY GOOD!

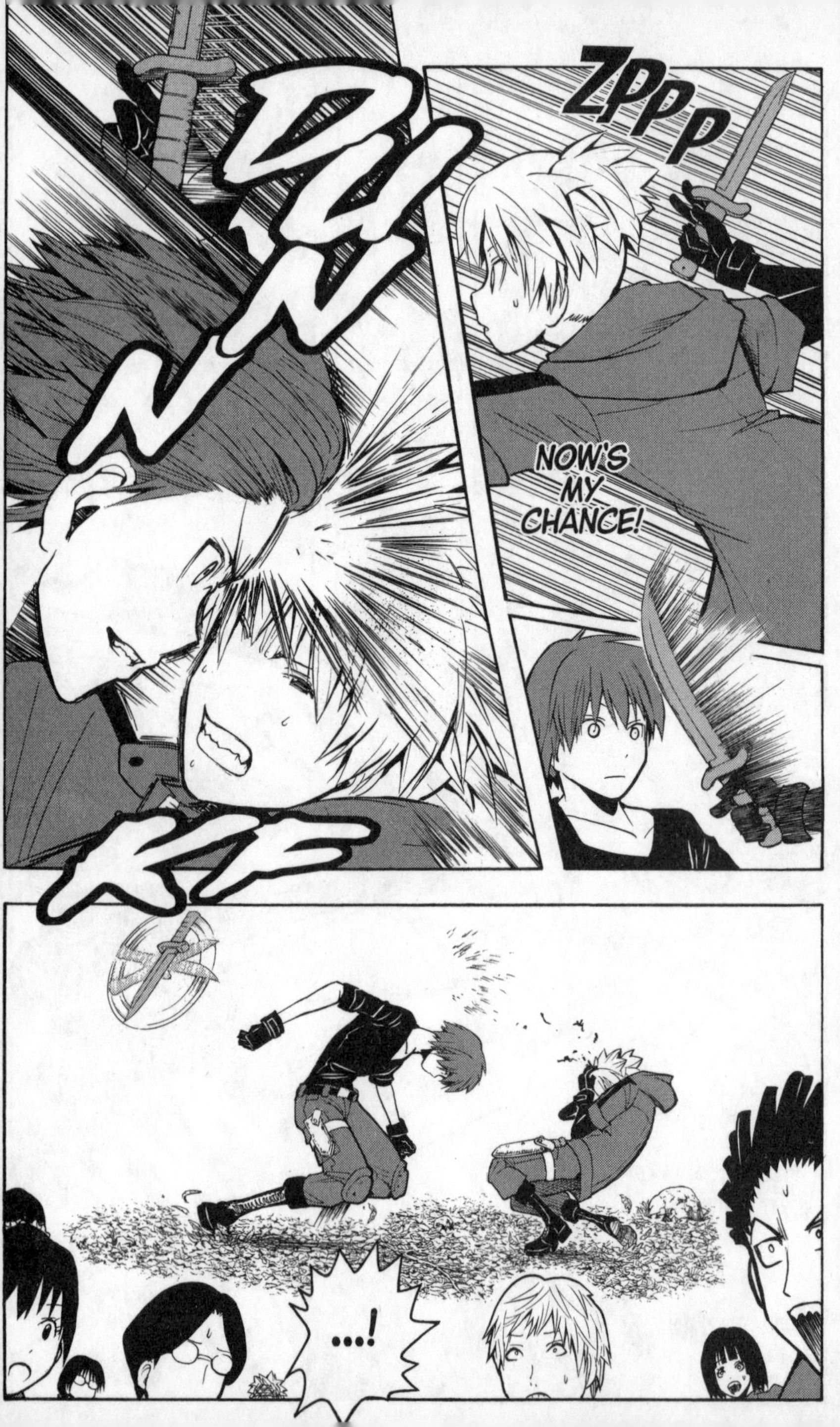
ZPPP
NOW'S MY CHANCE!
...!

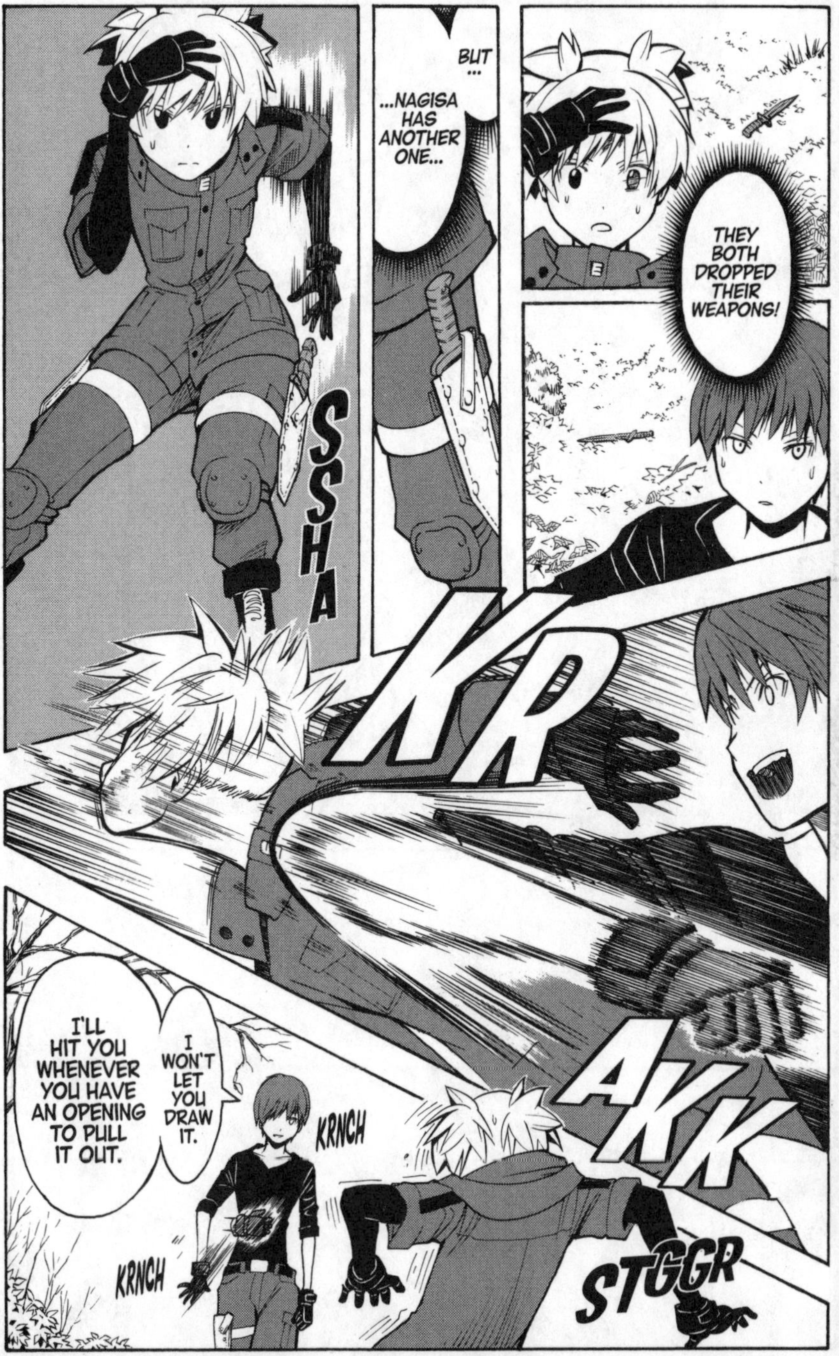
THEY BOTH DROPPED THEIR WEAPONS!
BUT ...
...NAGISA HAS ANOTHER ONE...
SSHA
KR
AKK
STGGR
KRNCH
I WON'T LET YOU DRAW IT.
I'LL HIT YOU WHENEVER YOU HAVE AN OPENING TO PULL IT OUT.
KRNCH

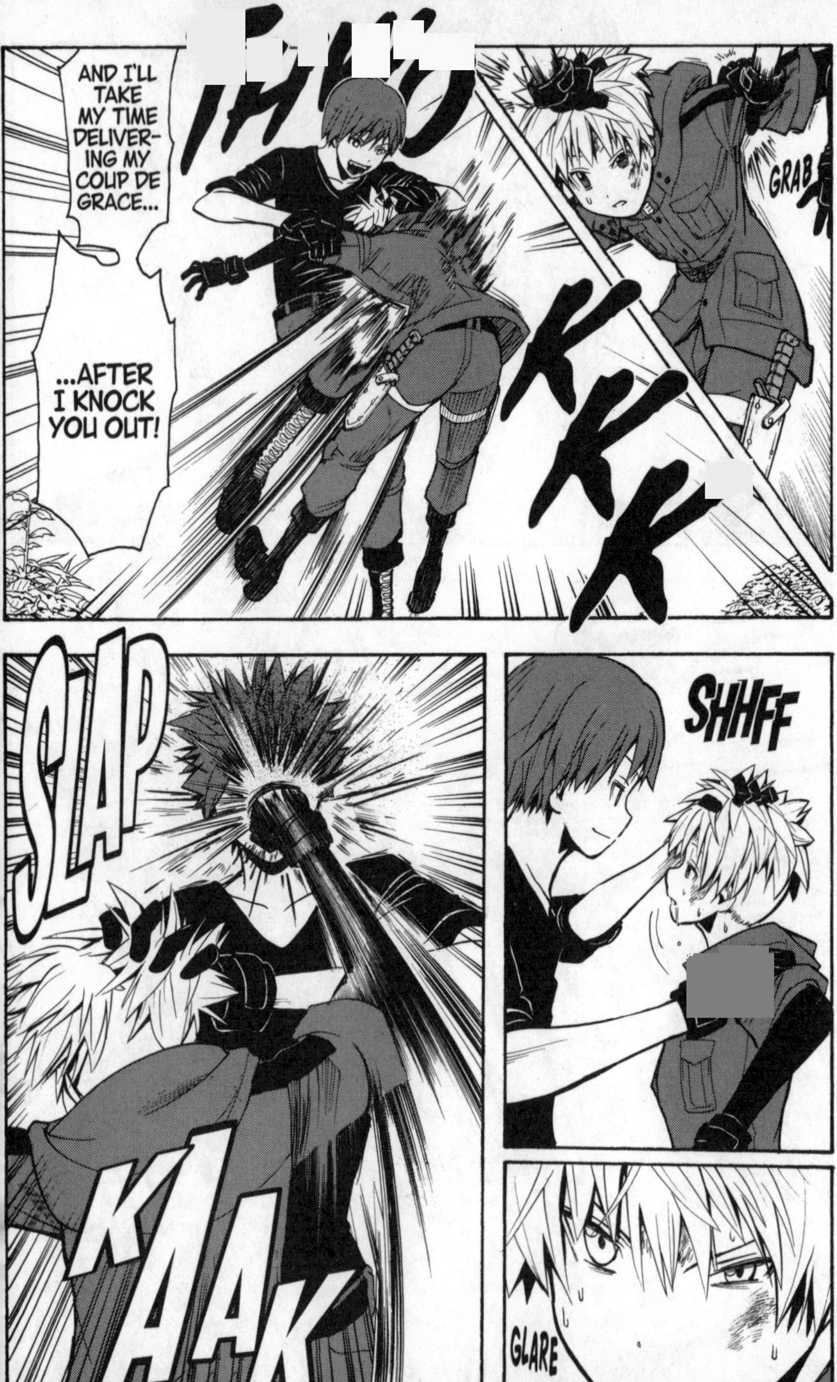
GRAB
AND I'LL TAKE MY TIME DELIVERING MY COUP DE GRACE...
...AFTER I KNOCK YOU OUT!
SHHFF
GLARE
SLAP
KAAK

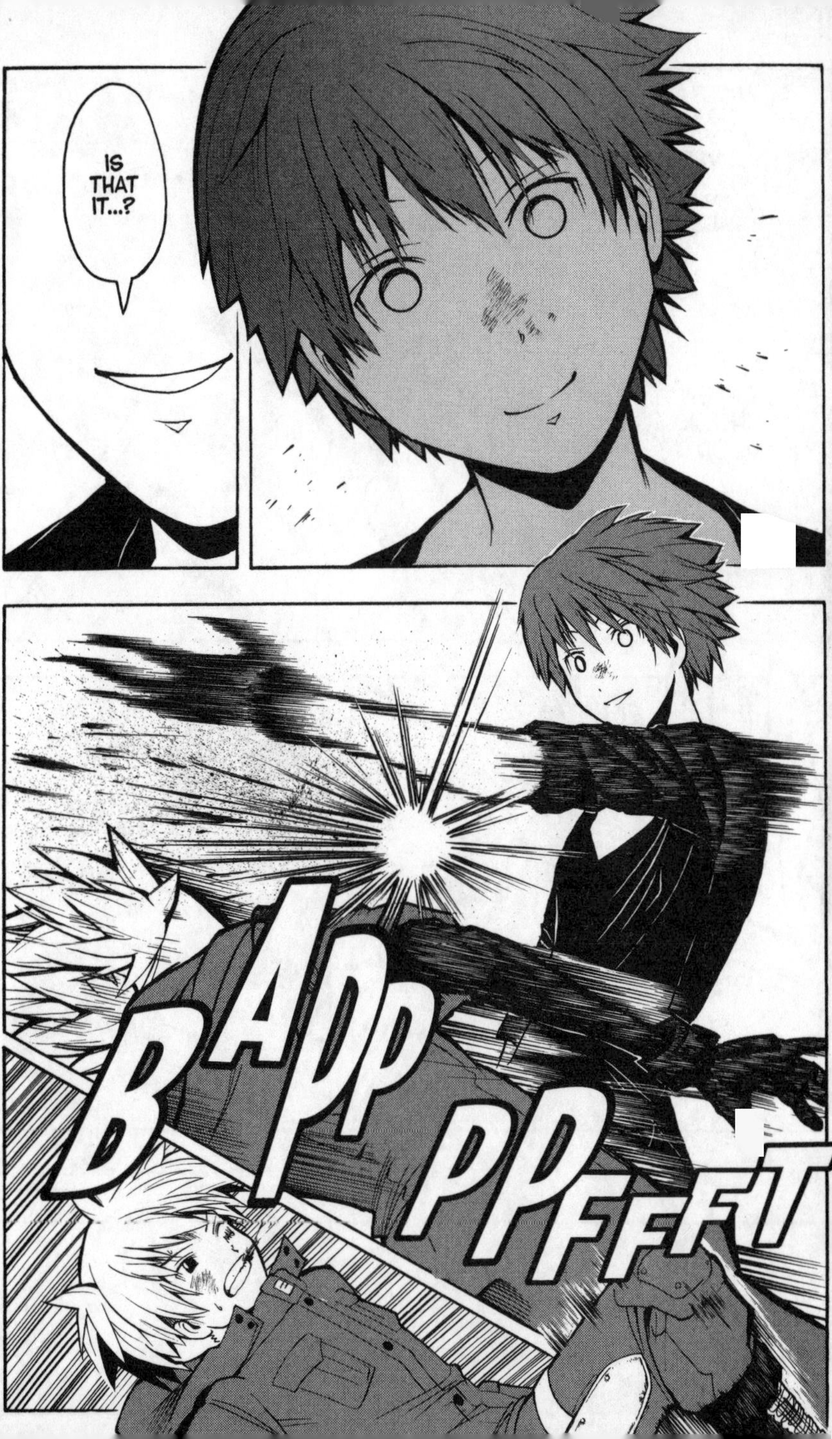
IS THAT IT...?
BAPP PPFFFT

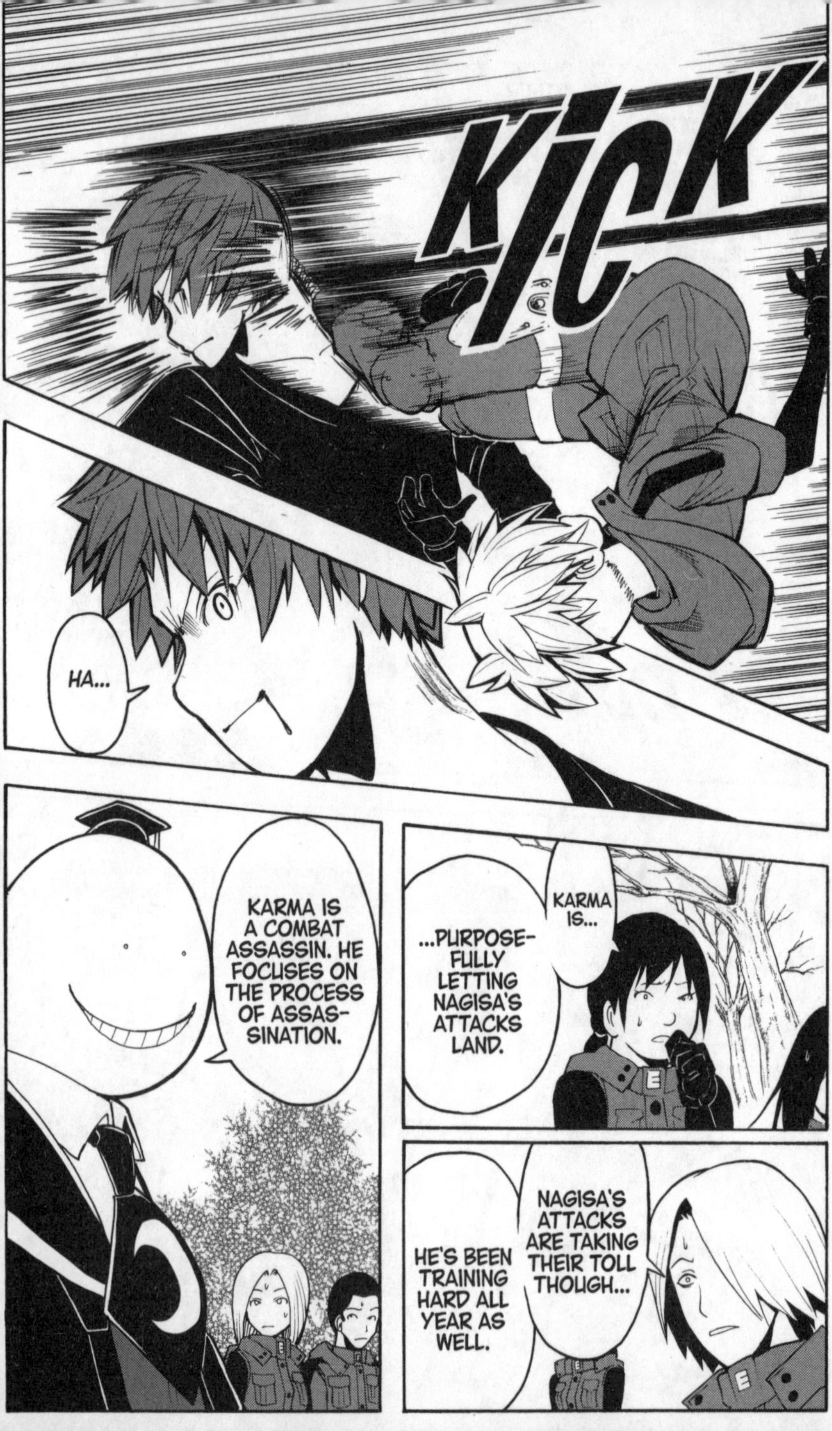
KICK
HA...
KARMA IS...
...PURPOSE-FULLY LETTING NAGISA'S ATTACKS LAND.
NAGISA'S ATTACKS ARE TAKING THEIR TOLL THOUGH...
HE'S BEEN TRAINING HARD ALL YEAR AS WELL.
KARMA IS A COMBAT ASSASSIN. HE FOCUSES ON THE PROCESS OF ASSAS-SINATION.

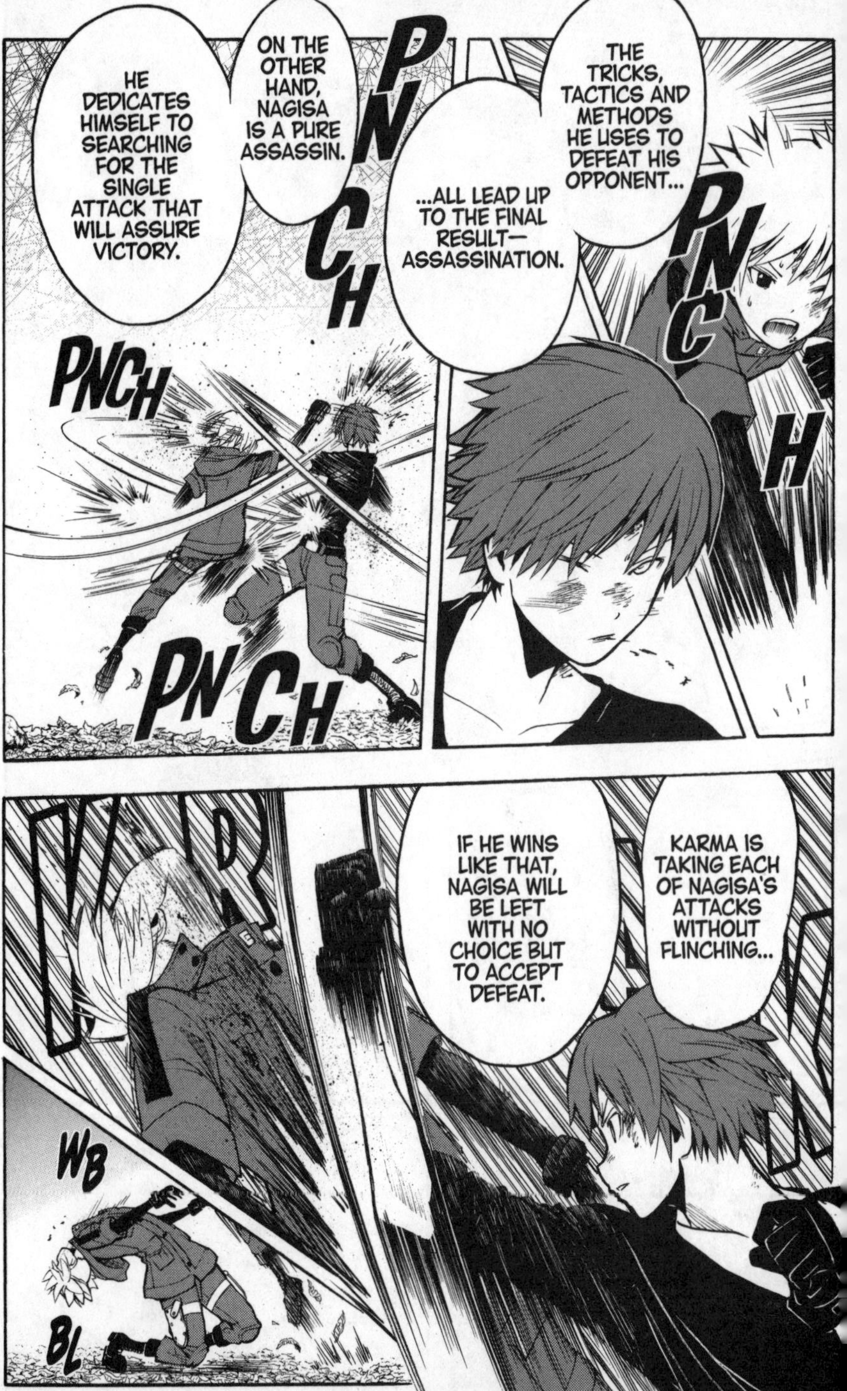
PNCH
THE TRICKS, TACTICS AND METHODS HE USES TO DEFEAT HIS OPPONENT...
...ALL LEAD UP TO THE FINAL RESULT—ASSASSINATION.
H
PNCH
ON THE OTHER HAND, NAGISA IS A PURE ASSASSIN.
HE DEDICATES HIMSELF TO SEARCHING FOR THE SINGLE ATTACK THAT WILL ASSURE VICTORY.
PNCH
PNCH
KARMA IS TAKING EACH OF NAGISA'S ATTACKS WITHOUT FLINCHING...
IF HE WINS LIKE THAT, NAGISA WILL BE LEFT WITH NO CHOICE BUT TO ACCEPT DEFEAT.
D
WB
BL

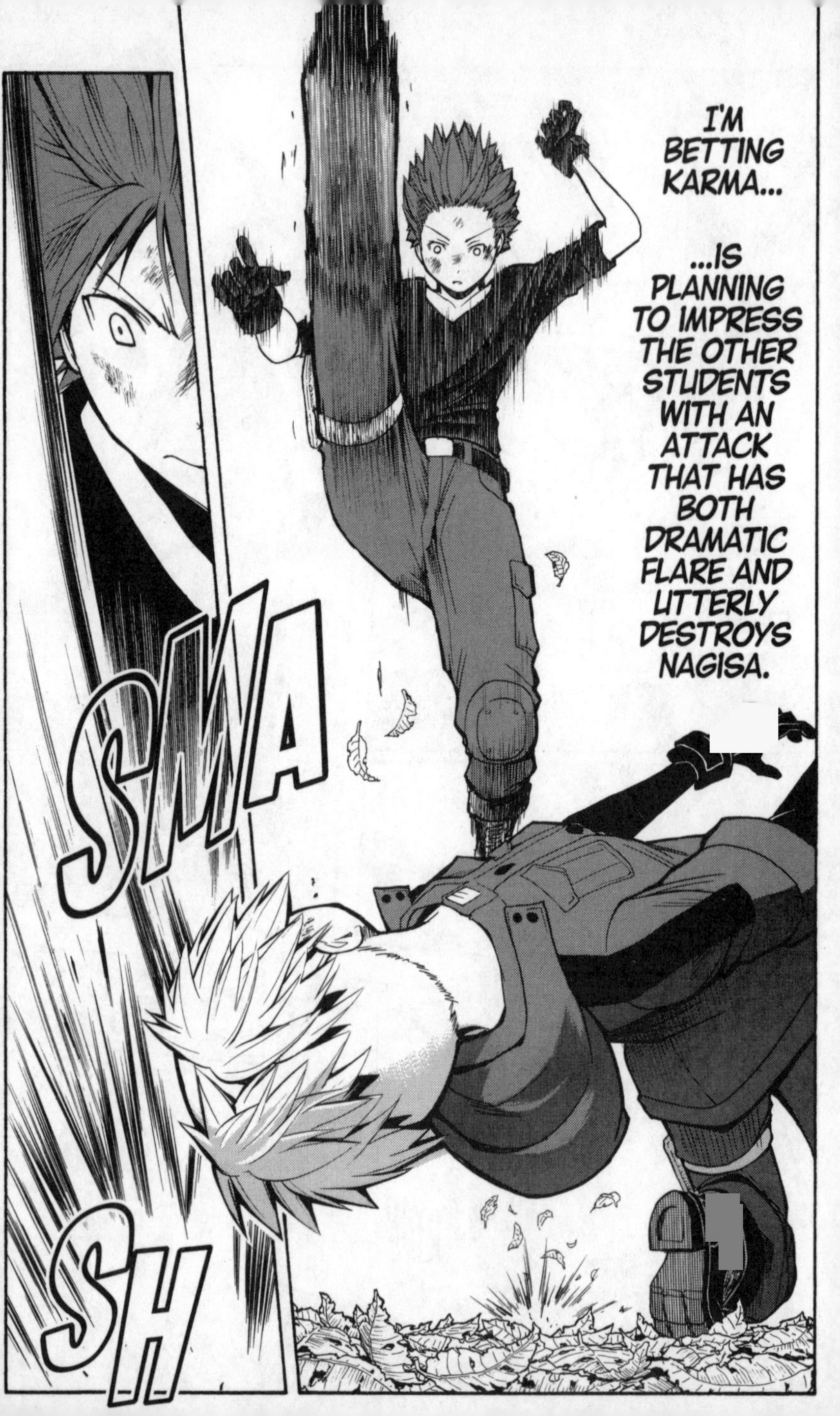
I'M BETTING KARMA...
...IS PLANNING TO IMPRESS THE OTHER STUDENTS WITH AN ATTACK THAT HAS BOTH DRAMATIC FLARE AND UTTERLY DESTROYS NAGISA.
SMA
SH

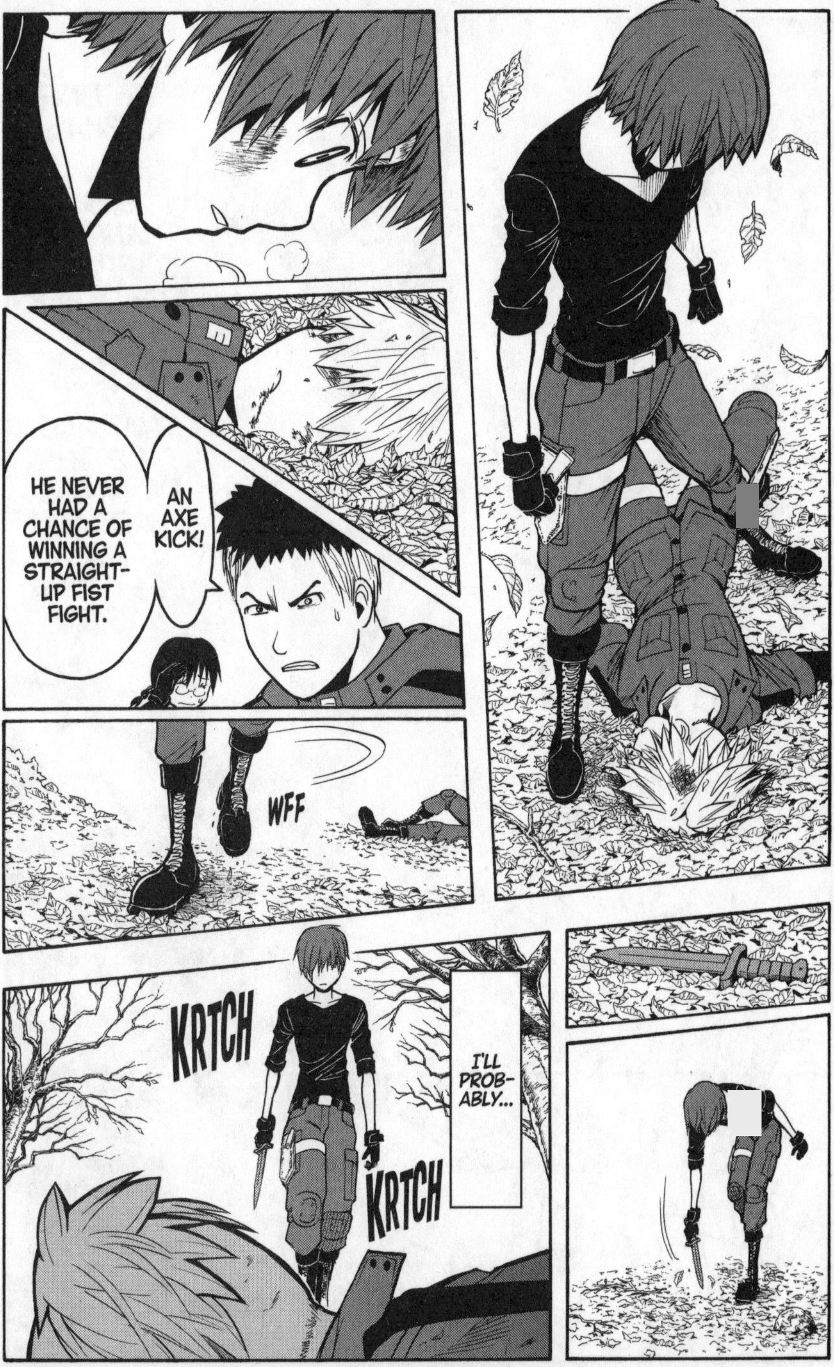

AN AXE KICK!
HE NEVER HAD A CHANCE OF WINNING A STRAIGHT-UP FIST FIGHT.
WFF
I'LL PROBABLY...
KRTCH
KRTCH

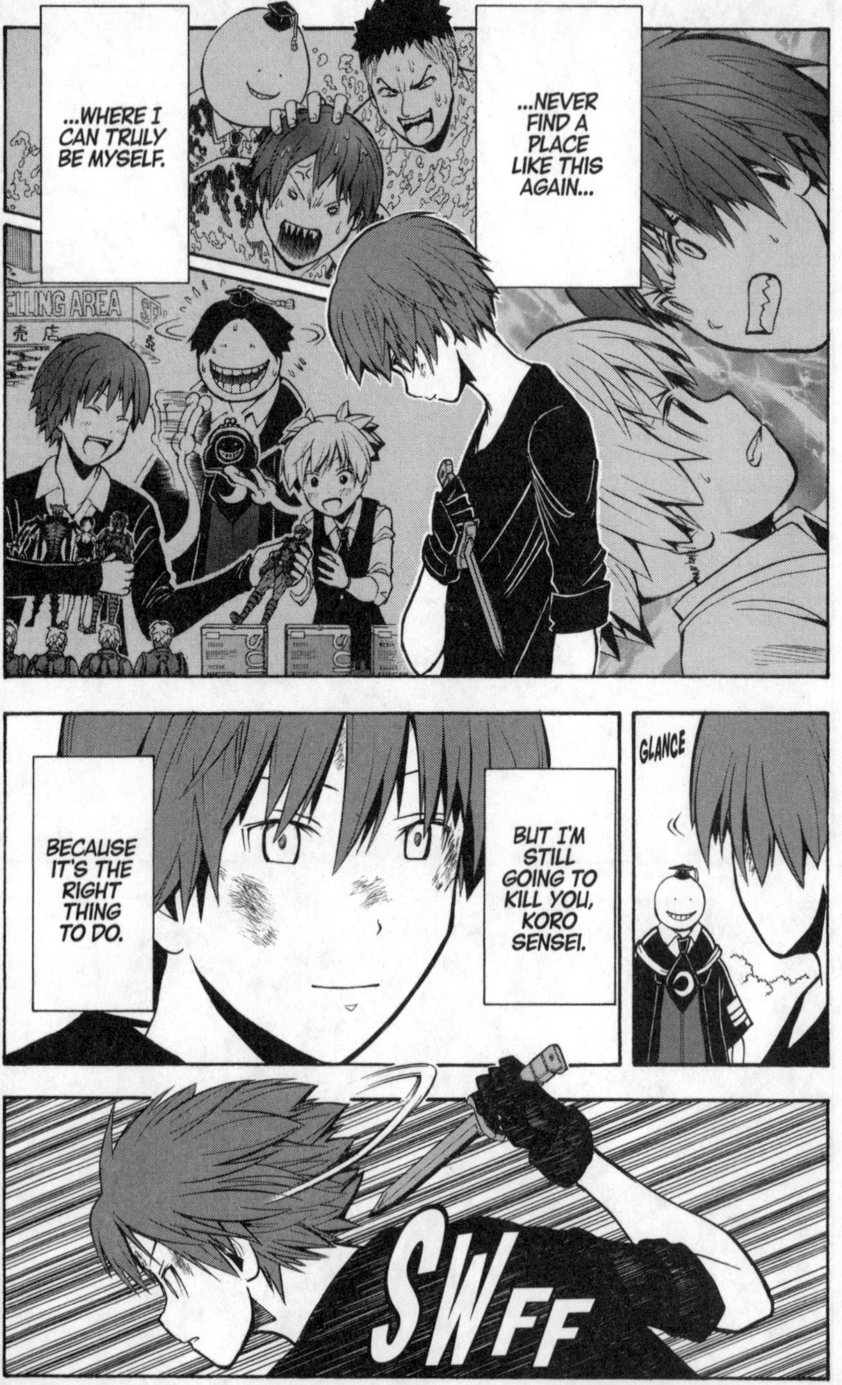
...NEVER FIND A PLACE LIKE THIS AGAIN...
...WHERE I CAN TRULY BE MYSELF.
ELLING AREA
売店
GLANCE
BUT I'M STILL GOING TO KILL YOU, KORO SENSEI.
BECAUSE IT'S THE RIGHT THING TO DO.
SWFF

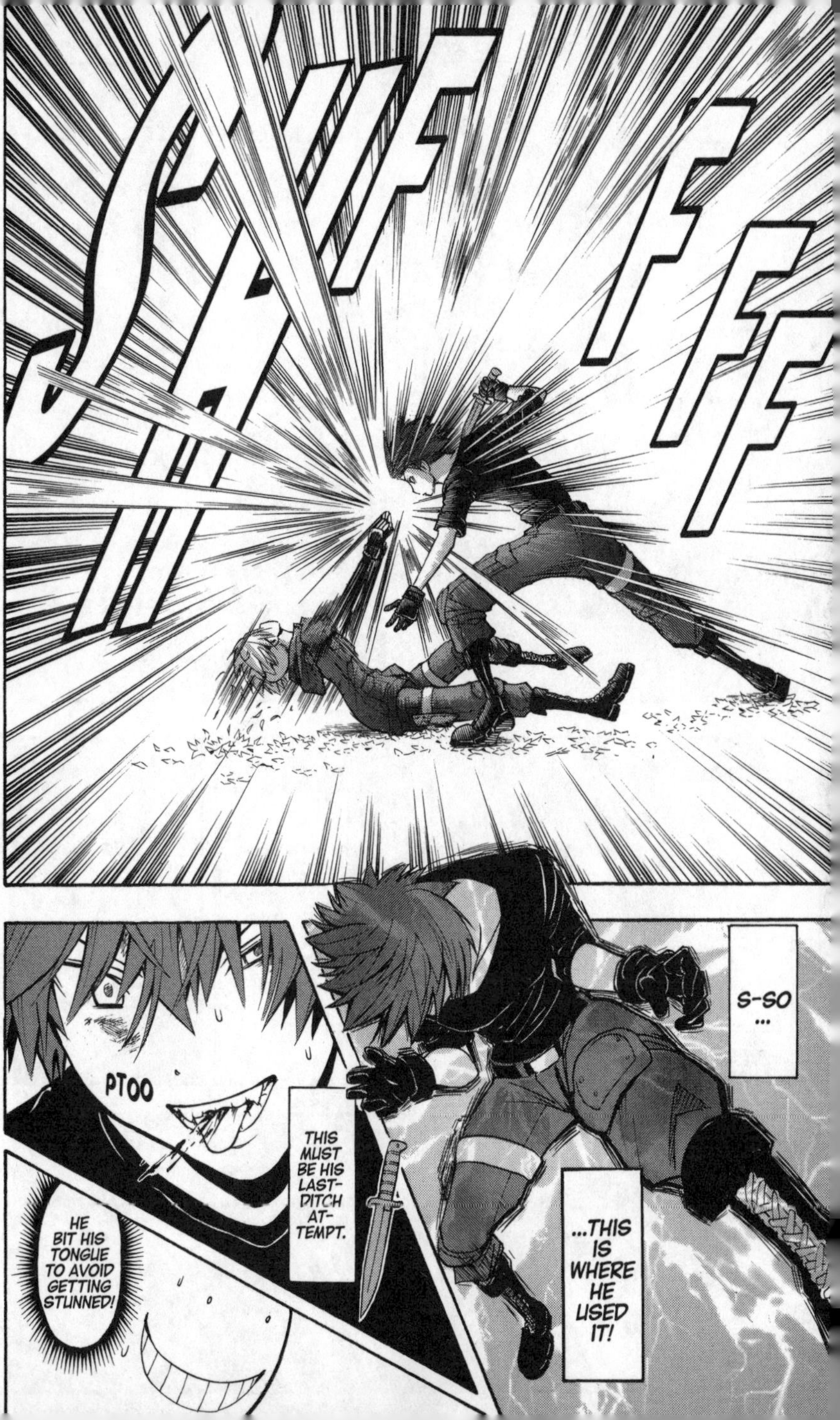

SHUFFFFF
S-SO ...
...THIS IS WHERE HE USED IT!
THIS MUST BE HIS LAST-DITCH AT-TEMPT.
PTOO
HE BIT HIS TONGUE TO AVOID GETTING STUNNED!

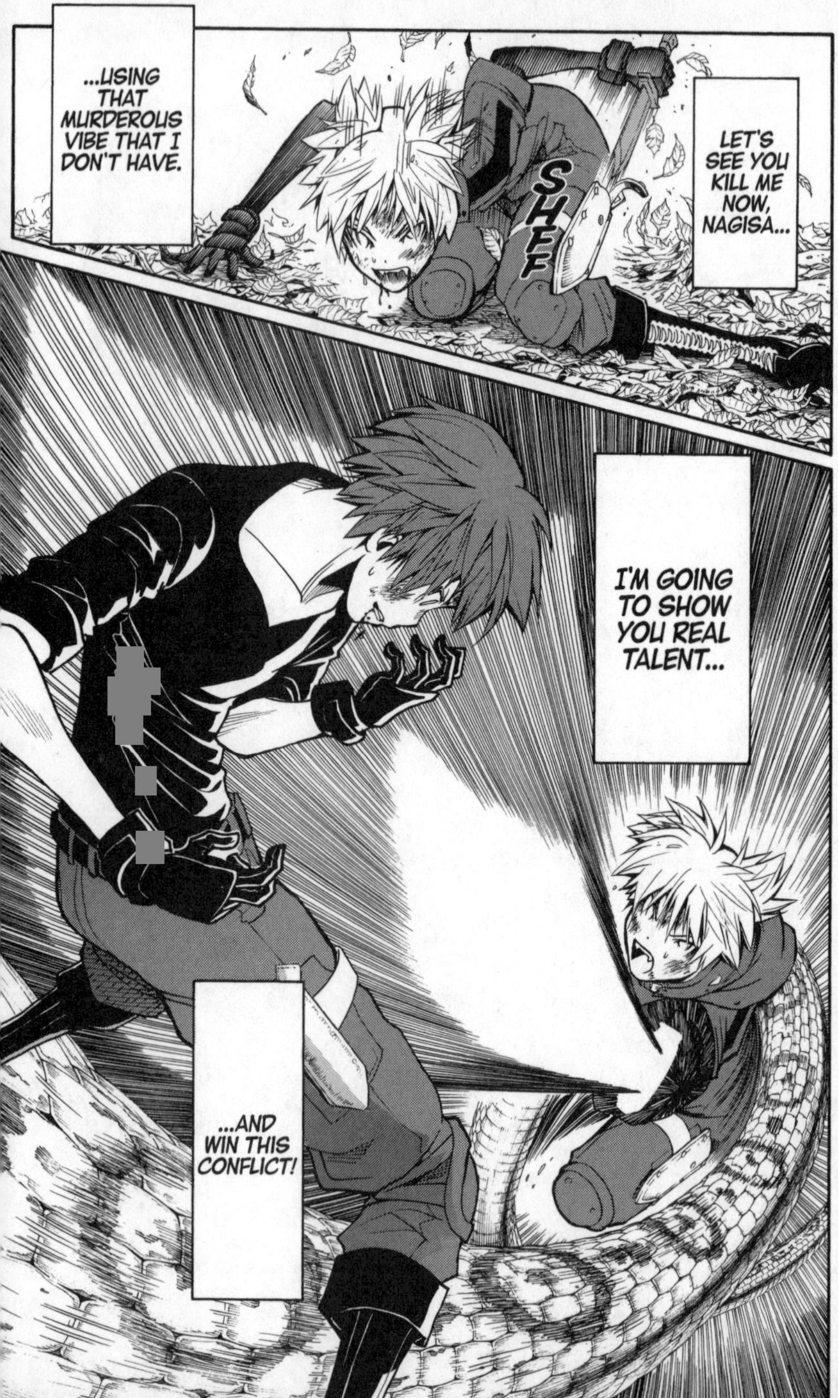
LET'S SEE YOU KILL ME NOW, NAGISA...
SHFF
...USING THAT MURDEROUS VIBE THAT I DON'T HAVE.
I'M GOING TO SHOW YOU REAL TALENT...
...AND WIN THIS CONFLICT!

Th–this is...

...turning
into a shonen
manga.

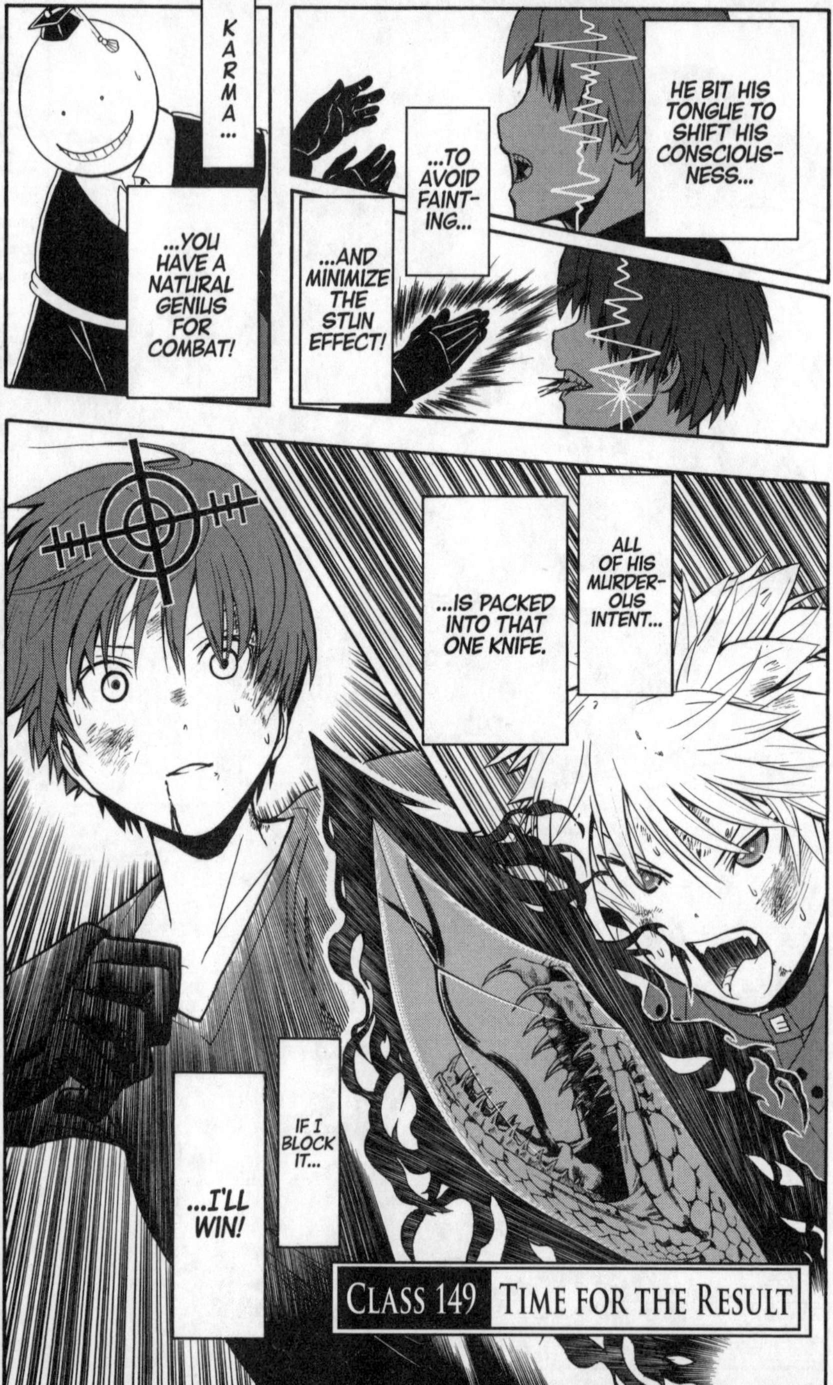
HE BIT HIS TONGUE TO SHIFT HIS CONSCIOUSNESS...
...TO AVOID FAINTING...
...AND MINIMIZE THE STUN EFFECT!
KARMA...
...YOU HAVE A NATURAL GENIUS FOR COMBAT!
ALL OF HIS MURDEROUS INTENT...
...IS PACKED INTO THAT ONE KNIFE.
IF I BLOCK IT...
...I'LL WIN!
CLASS 149 TIME FOR THE RESULT

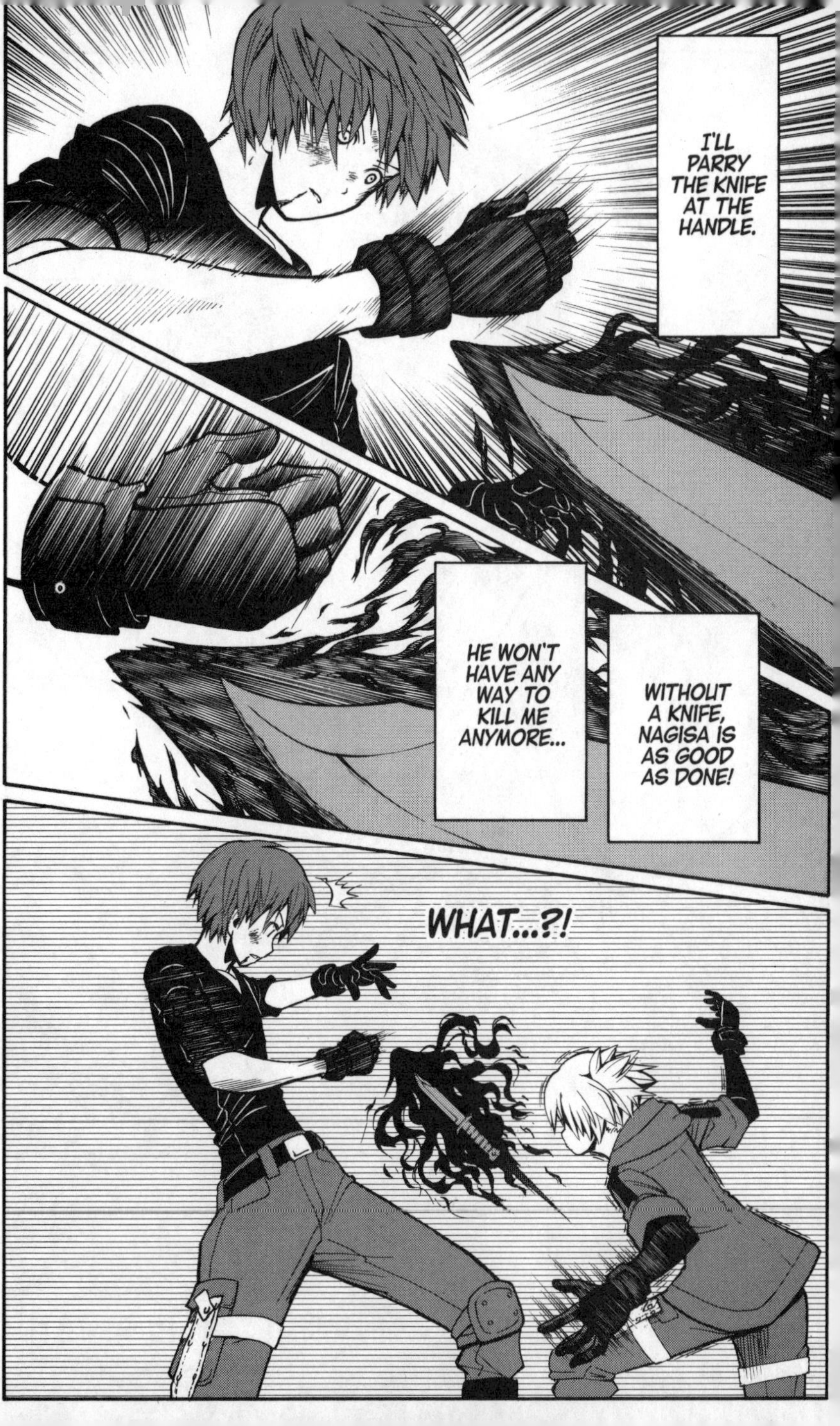
I'LL PARRY THE KNIFE AT THE HANDLE.
WITHOUT A KNIFE, NAGISA IS AS GOOD AS DONE!
HE WON'T HAVE ANY WAY TO KILL ME ANYMORE...
WHAT...?!

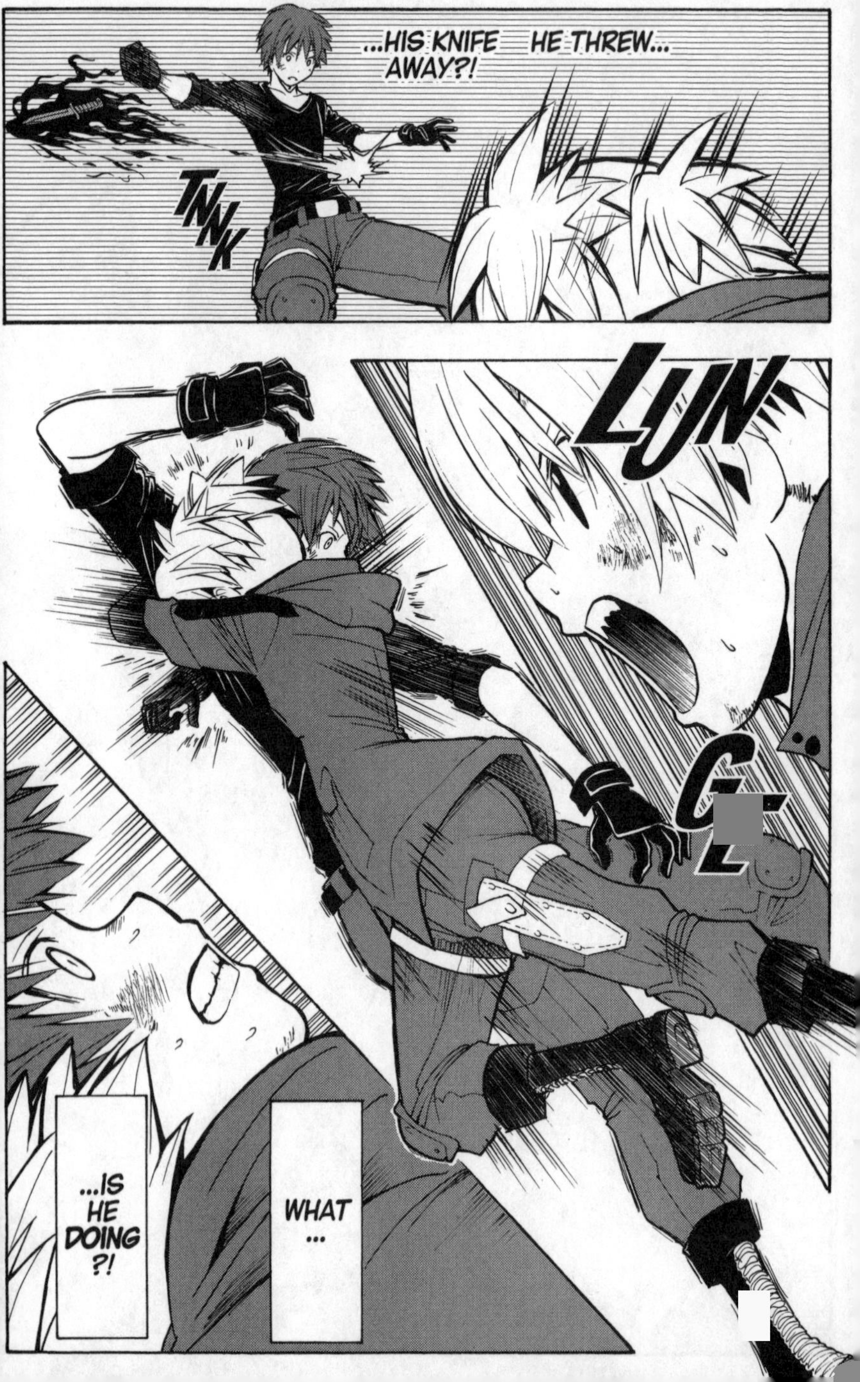
HE THREW...
...HIS KNIFE AWAY?!
TNNK
LUN-
G-
WHAT...
...IS HE DOING?!

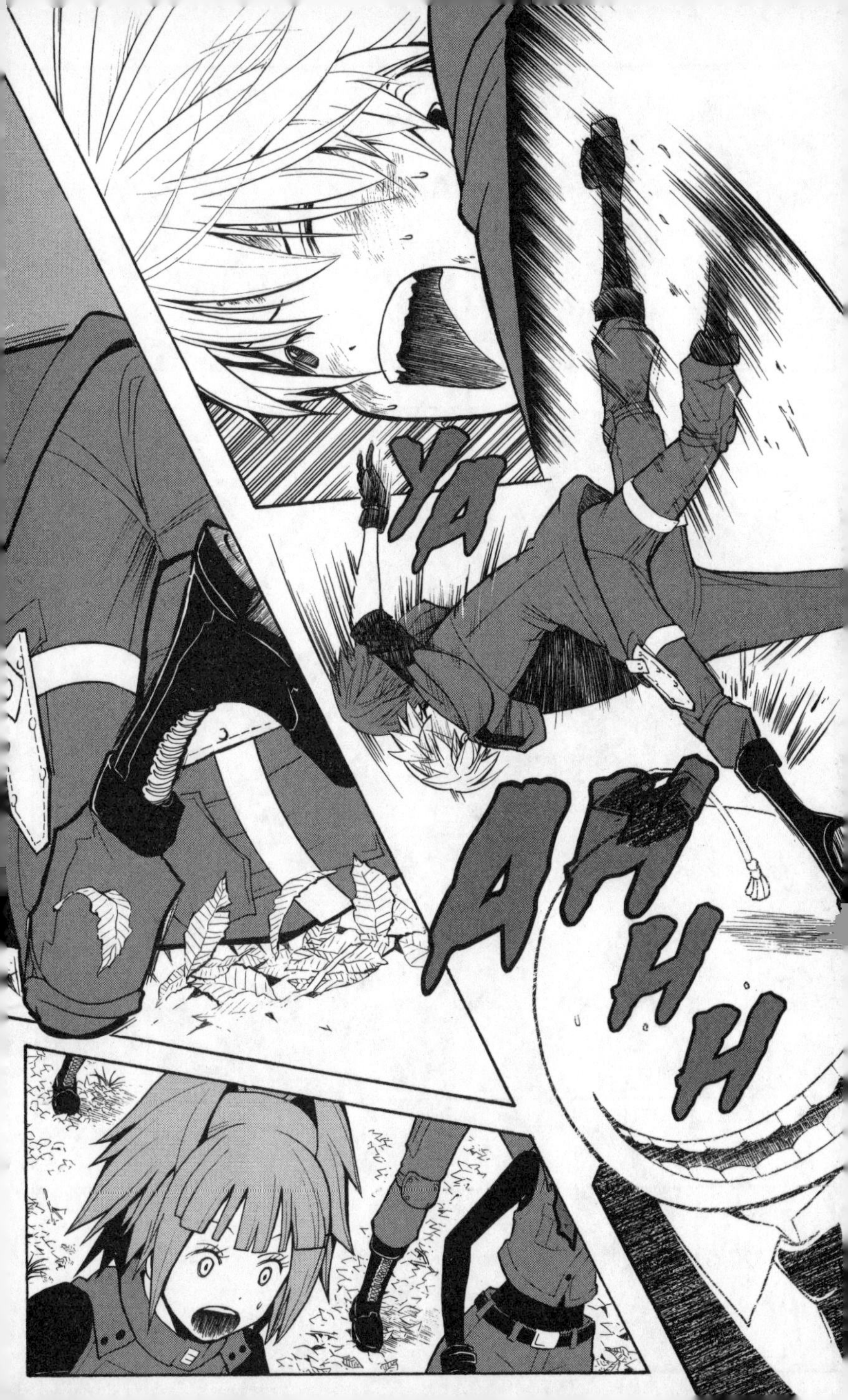
YAAHHH

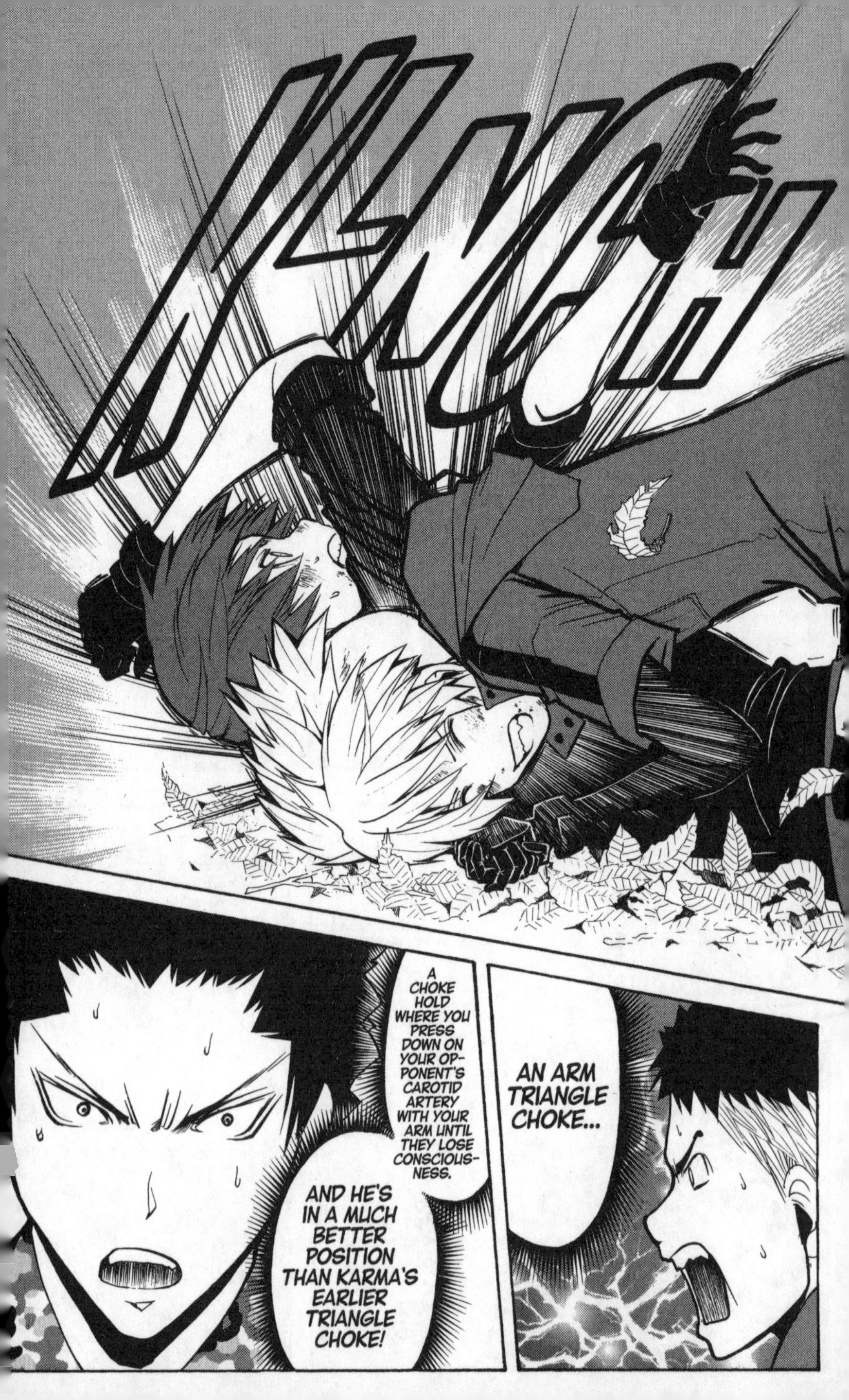
AN ARM TRIANGLE CHOKE...
A CHOKE HOLD WHERE YOU PRESS DOWN ON YOUR OP-PONENT'S CAROTID ARTERY WITH YOUR ARM UNTIL THEY LOSE CONSCIOUS-NESS.
AND HE'S IN A MUCH BETTER POSITION THAN KARMA'S EARLIER TRIANGLE CHOKE!

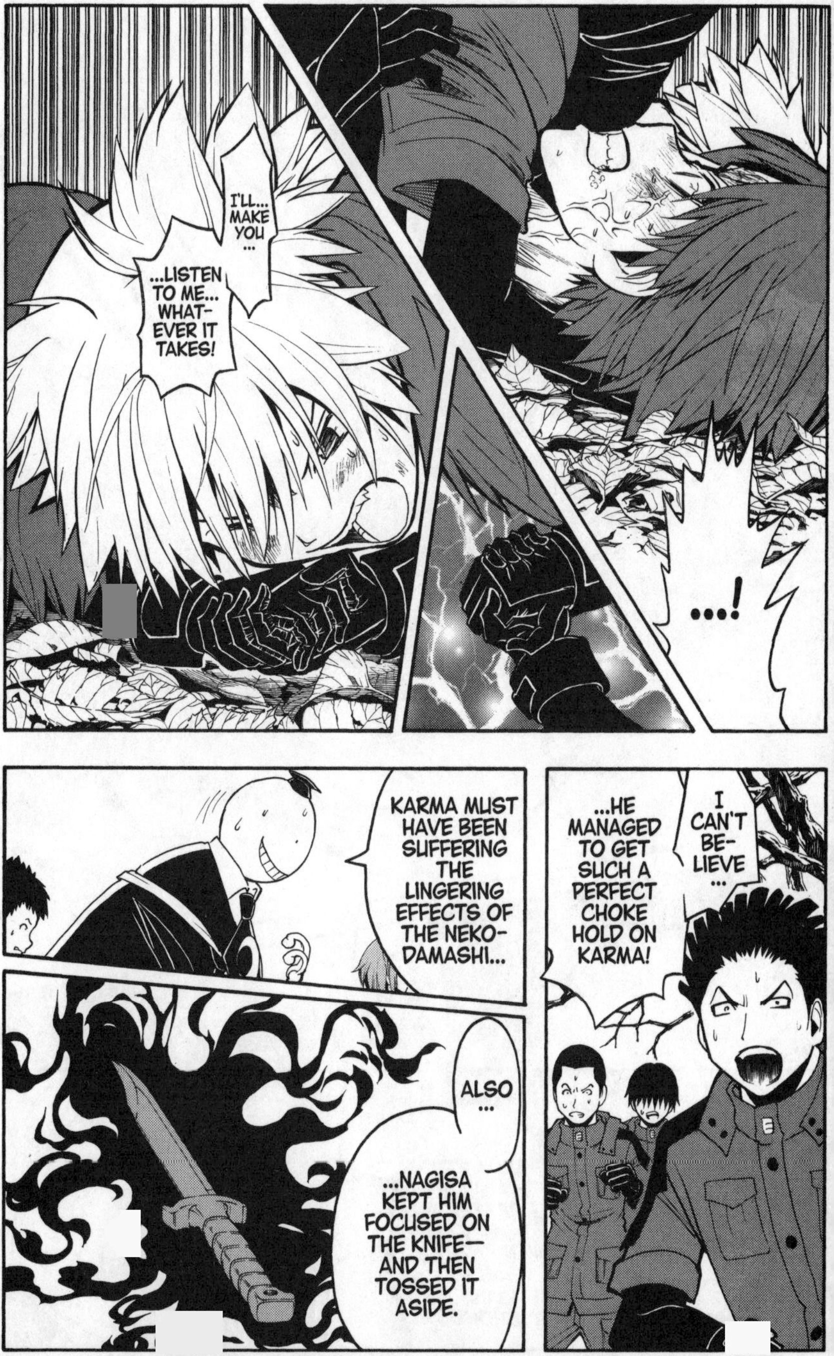
...!
I'LL... MAKE YOU...
...LISTEN TO ME... WHATEVER IT TAKES!
I CAN'T BELIEVE...
...HE MANAGED TO GET SUCH A PERFECT CHOKE HOLD ON KARMA!
KARMA MUST HAVE BEEN SUFFERING THE LINGERING EFFECTS OF THE NEKO-DAMASHI...
ALSO...
...NAGISA KEPT HIM FOCUSED ON THE KNIFE—AND THEN TOSSED IT ASIDE.

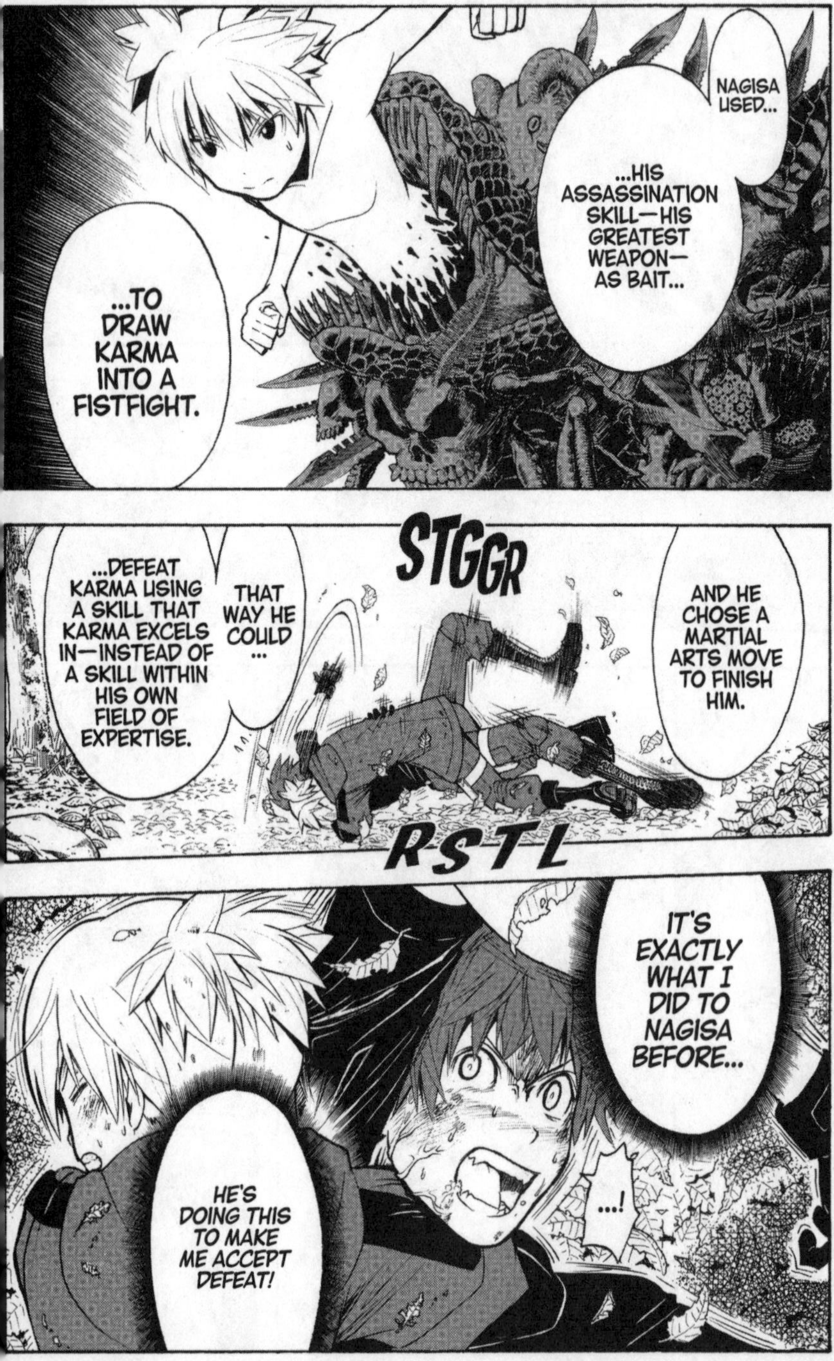
NAGISA USED...
...HIS ASSASSINATION SKILL—HIS GREATEST WEAPON—AS BAIT...
...TO DRAW KARMA INTO A FISTFIGHT.
AND HE CHOSE A MARTIAL ARTS MOVE TO FINISH HIM.
STGGR
THAT WAY HE COULD ...
...DEFEAT KARMA USING A SKILL THAT KARMA EXCELS IN—INSTEAD OF A SKILL WITHIN HIS OWN FIELD OF EXPERTISE.
RSTL
IT'S EXACTLY WHAT I DID TO NAGISA BEFORE...
...!
HE'S DOING THIS TO MAKE ME ACCEPT DEFEAT!

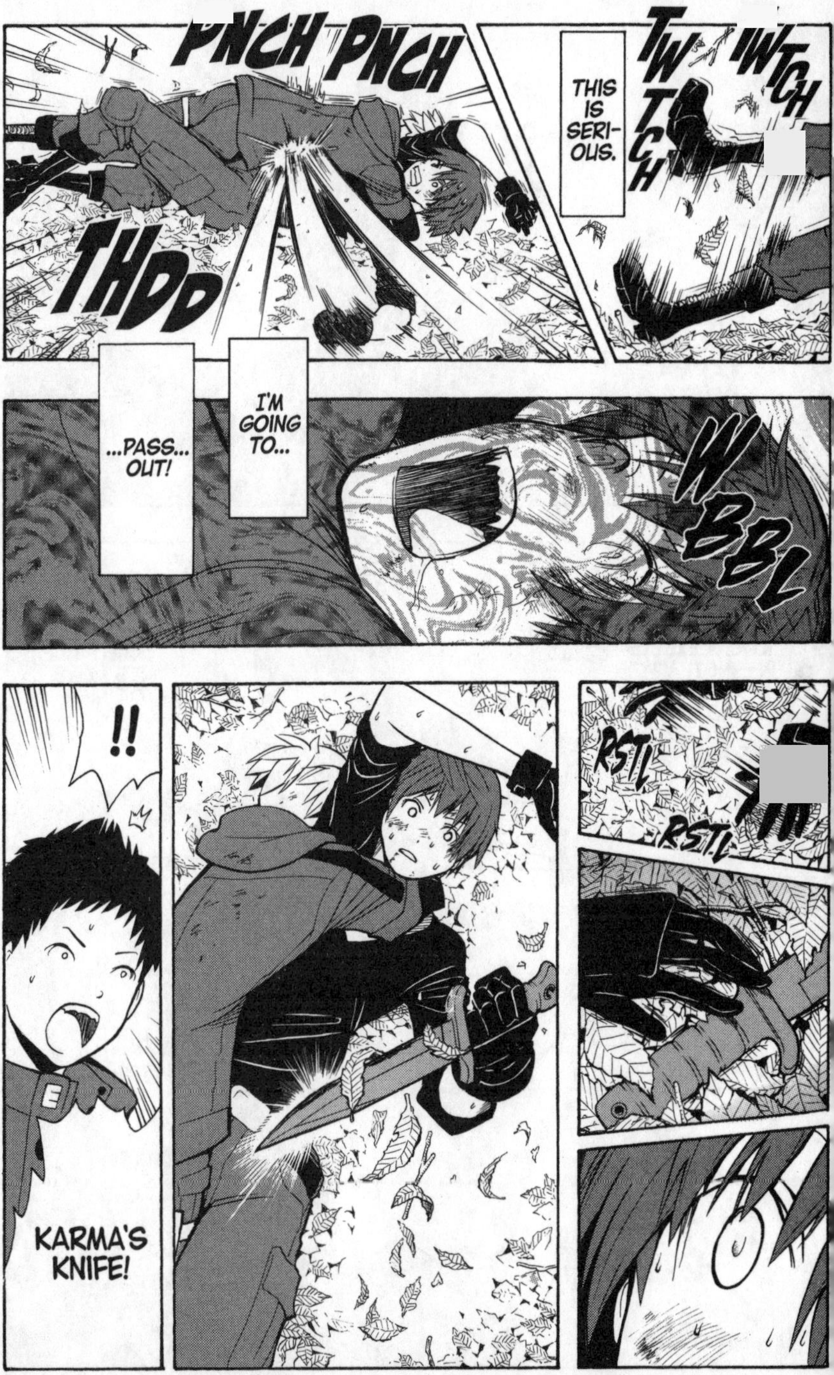
TWITCH TWITCH
THIS IS SERI-OUS.
PNCH PNCH
THDD
WBBL
I'M GOING TO...
...PASS... OUT!
RSTL
RSTL
!!
KARMA'S KNIFE!

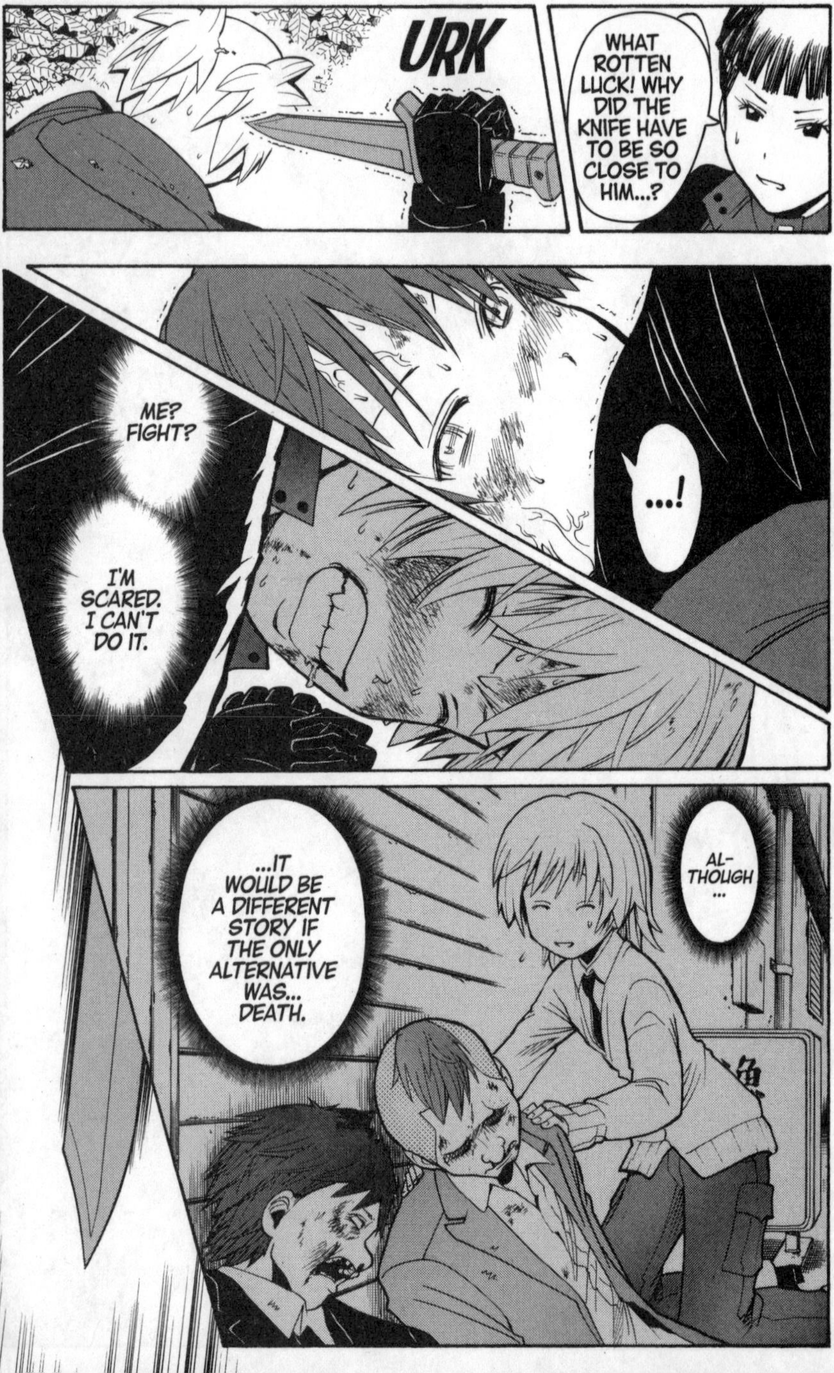
WHAT ROTTEN LUCK! WHY DID THE KNIFE HAVE TO BE SO CLOSE TO HIM...?
URK
...!
ME? FIGHT?
I'M SCARED. I CAN'T DO IT.
AL-THOUGH ...
...IT WOULD BE A DIFFERENT STORY IF THE ONLY ALTERNATIVE WAS... DEATH.

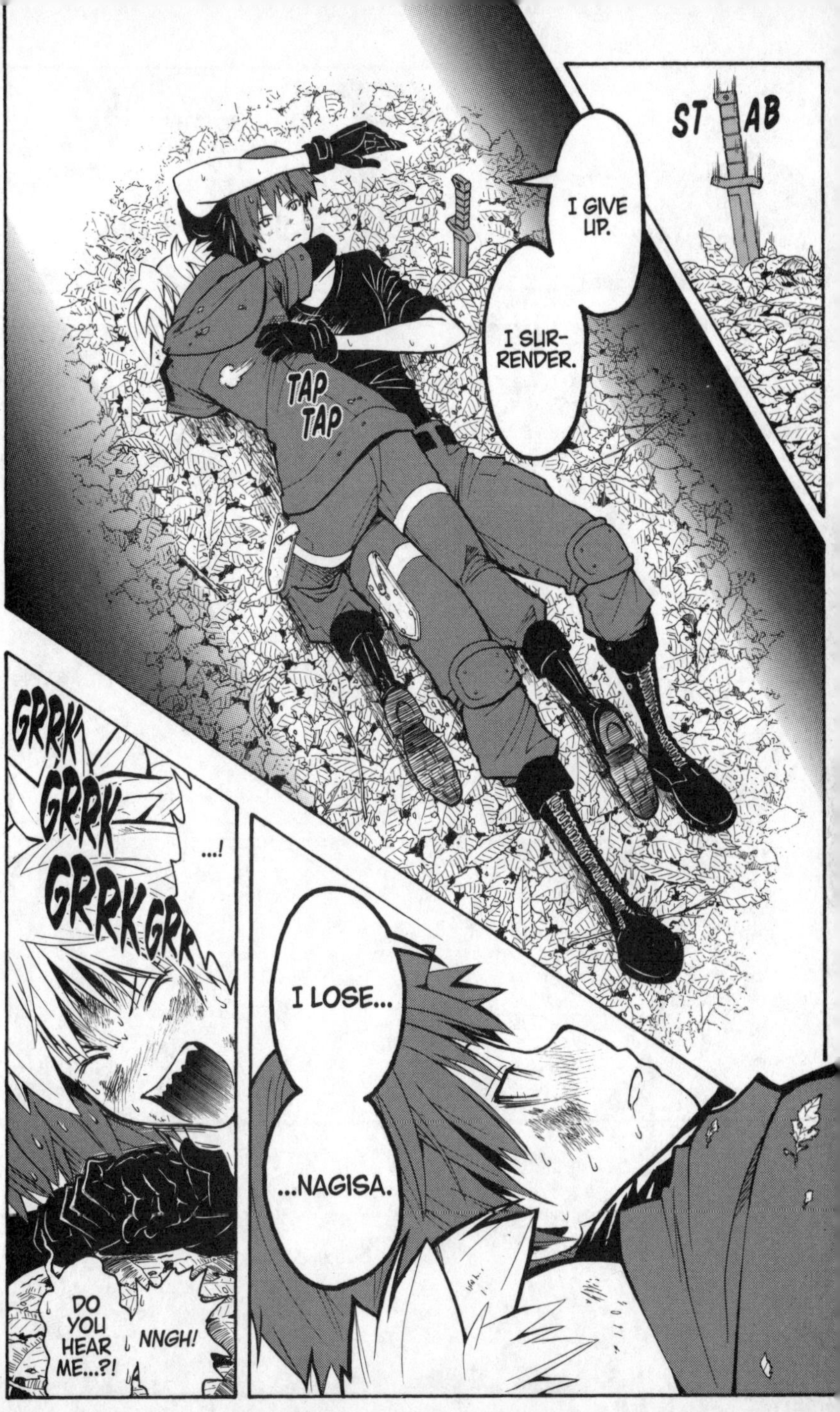
STAB
I GIVE UP.
I SURRENDER.
TAP TAP
I LOSE...
...NAGISA.
GRRK GRRK GRRK GRR
...!
NNGH!
DO YOU HEAR ME...?!

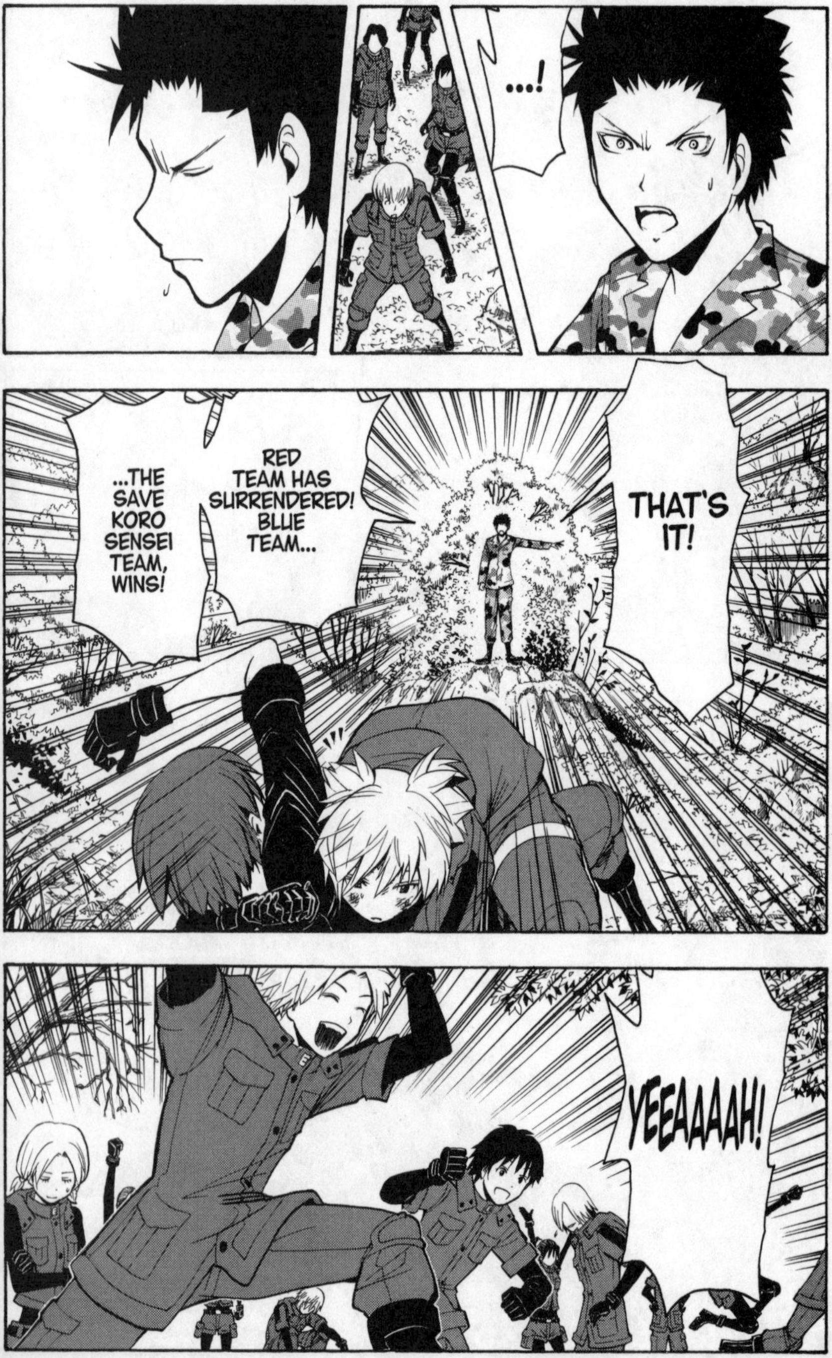
...!
THAT'S IT!
RED TEAM HAS SURRENDERED! BLUE TEAM...
...THE SAVE KORO SENSEI TEAM, WINS!
YEEAAAAH!

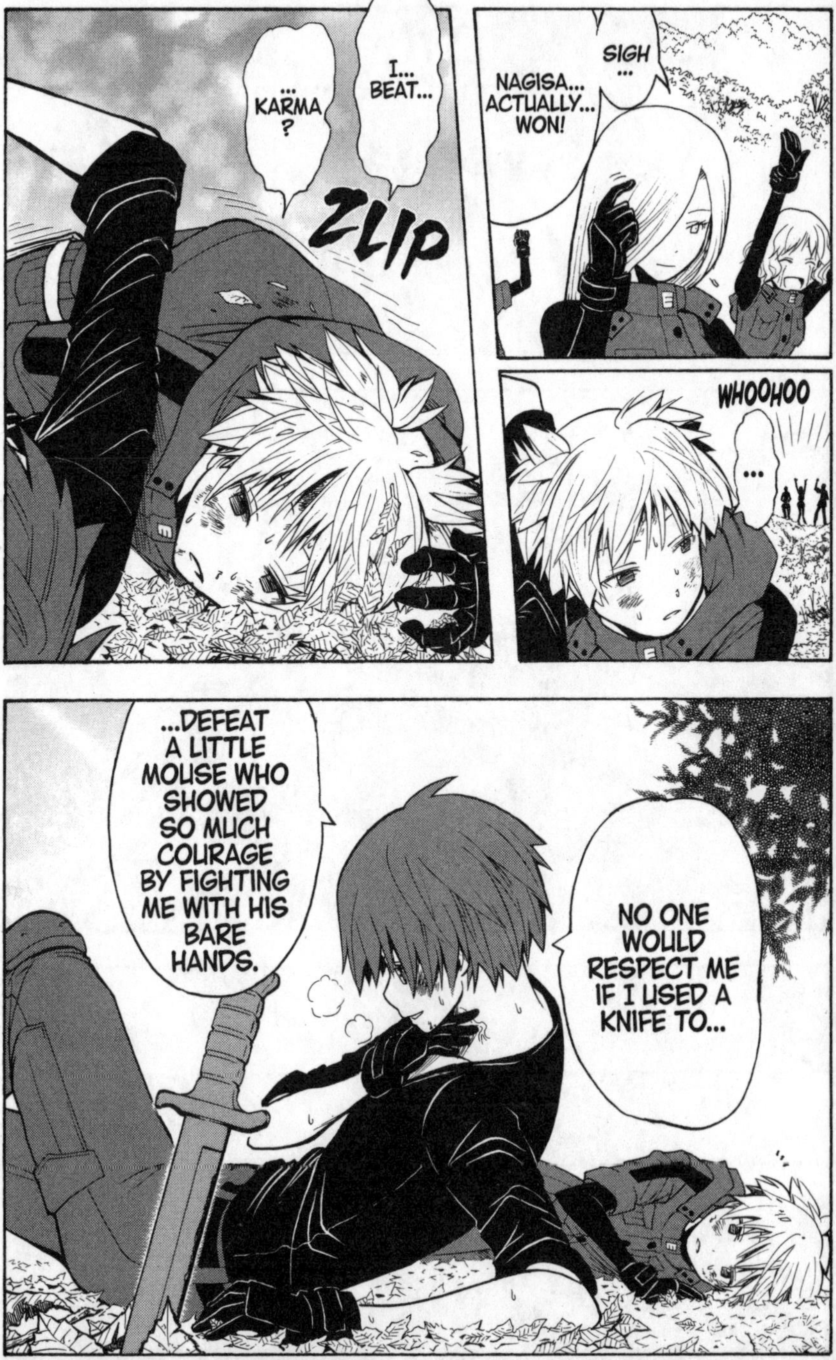
SIGH ...
NAGISA... ACTUALLY... WON!
WHOOHOO
...
I... BEAT...
... KARMA ?
ZLIP
NO ONE WOULD RESPECT ME IF I USED A KNIFE TO...
...DEFEAT A LITTLE MOUSE WHO SHOWED SO MUCH COURAGE BY FIGHTING ME WITH HIS BARE HANDS.

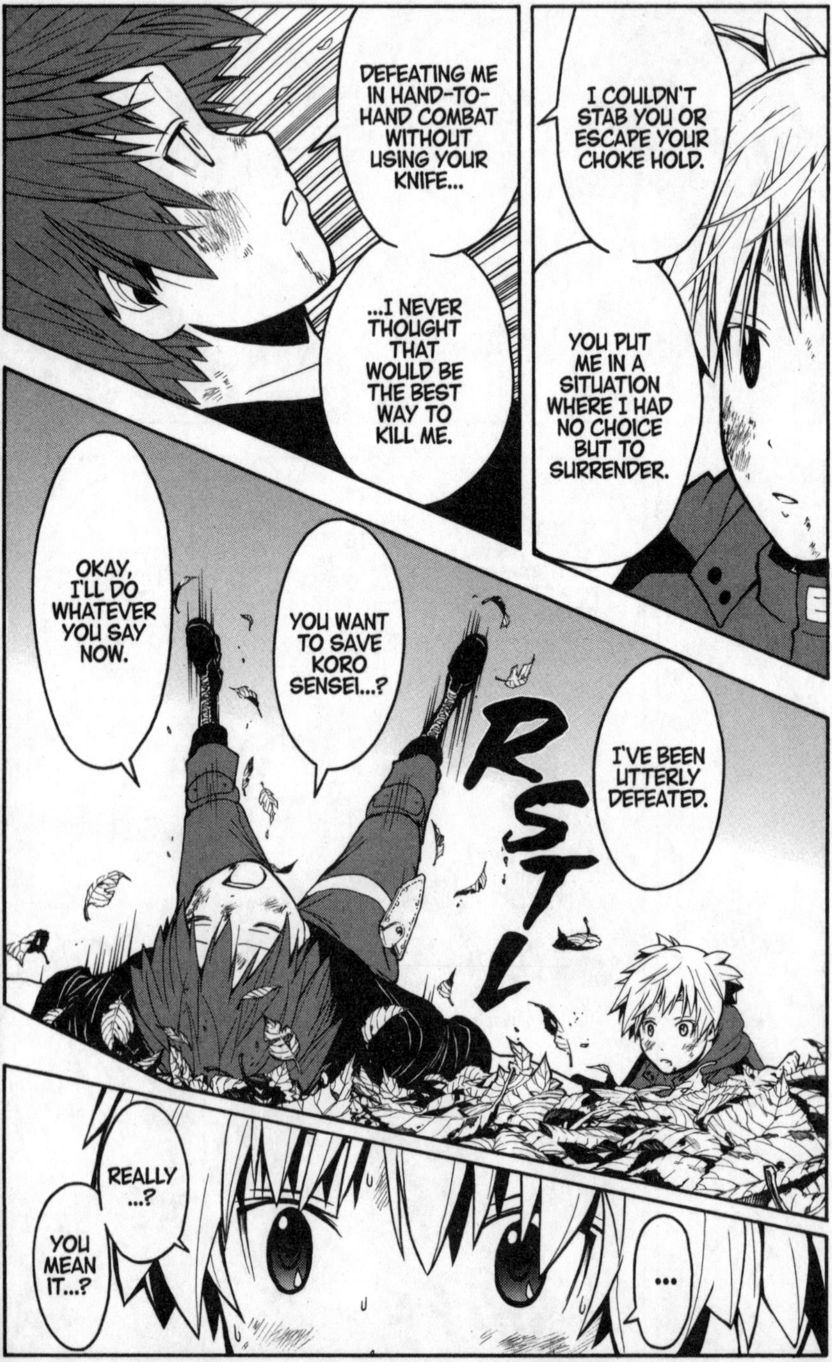
I COULDN'T STAB YOU OR ESCAPE YOUR CHOKE HOLD.
YOU PUT ME IN A SITUATION WHERE I HAD NO CHOICE BUT TO SURRENDER.
DEFEATING ME IN HAND-TO-HAND COMBAT WITHOUT USING YOUR KNIFE...
...I NEVER THOUGHT THAT WOULD BE THE BEST WAY TO KILL ME.
I'VE BEEN UTTERLY DEFEATED.
RSTL
YOU WANT TO SAVE KORO SENSEI...?
OKAY, I'LL DO WHATEVER YOU SAY NOW.
...
REALLY ...?
YOU MEAN IT...?

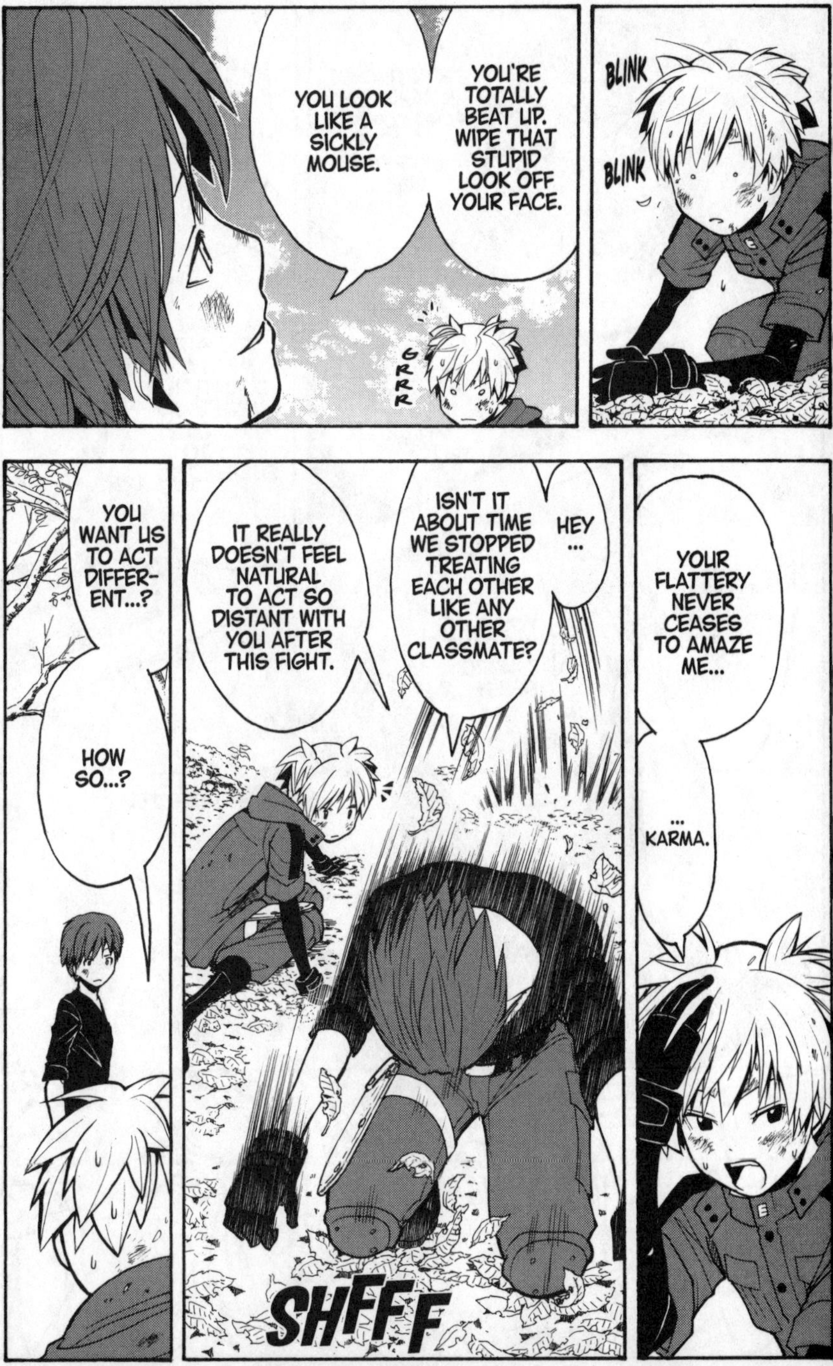
BLINK
BLINK
YOU'RE TOTALLY BEAT UP. WIPE THAT STUPID LOOK OFF YOUR FACE.
YOU LOOK LIKE A SICKLY MOUSE.
GRRR
YOUR FLATTERY NEVER CEASES TO AMAZE ME...
... KARMA.
HEY ...
ISN'T IT ABOUT TIME WE STOPPED TREATING EACH OTHER LIKE ANY OTHER CLASSMATE?
IT REALLY DOESN'T FEEL NATURAL TO ACT SO DISTANT WITH YOU AFTER THIS FIGHT.
SHFFF
YOU WANT US TO ACT DIFFER-ENT...?
HOW SO...?

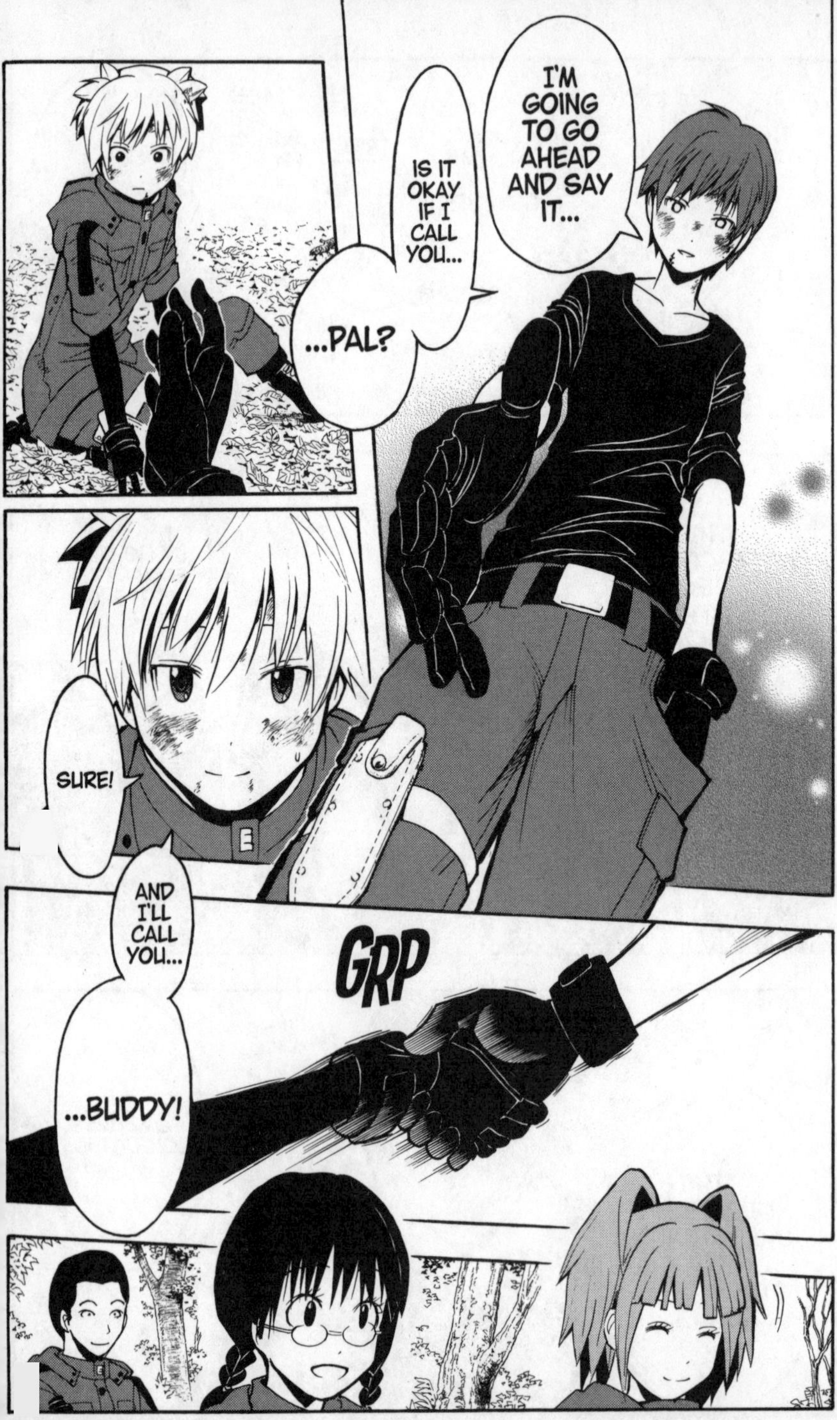
I'M GOING TO GO AHEAD AND SAY IT...
IS IT OKAY IF I CALL YOU...
...PAL?
SURE!
AND I'LL CALL YOU...
...BUDDY!
GRP

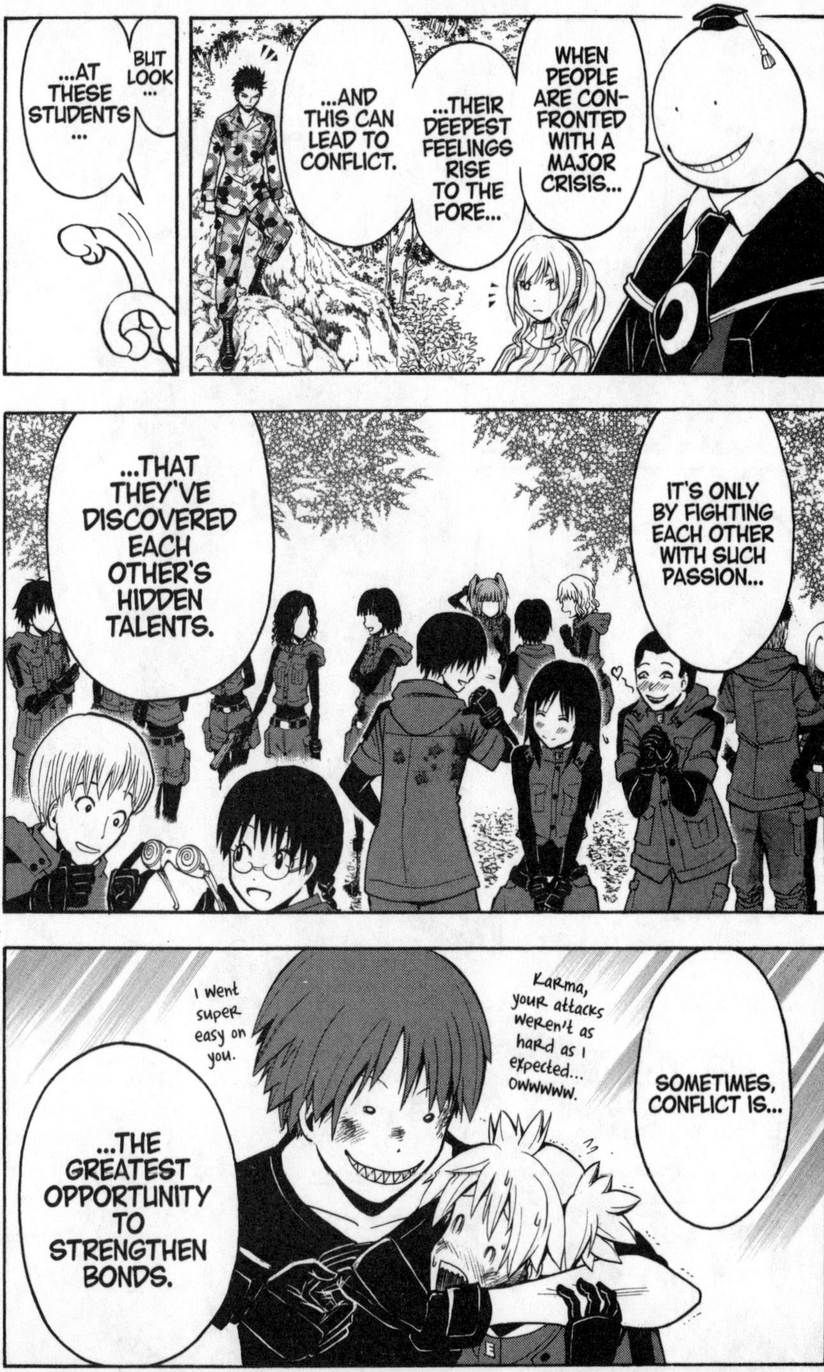
WHEN PEOPLE ARE CONFRONTED WITH A MAJOR CRISIS...
...THEIR DEEPEST FEELINGS RISE TO THE FORE...
...AND THIS CAN LEAD TO CONFLICT.
BUT LOOK...
...AT THESE STUDENTS...
IT'S ONLY BY FIGHTING EACH OTHER WITH SUCH PASSION...
...THAT THEY'VE DISCOVERED EACH OTHER'S HIDDEN TALENTS.
SOMETIMES, CONFLICT IS...
Karma, your attacks weren't as hard as I expected... OWWWWW.
I went super easy on you.
...THE GREATEST OPPORTUNITY TO STRENGTHEN BONDS.

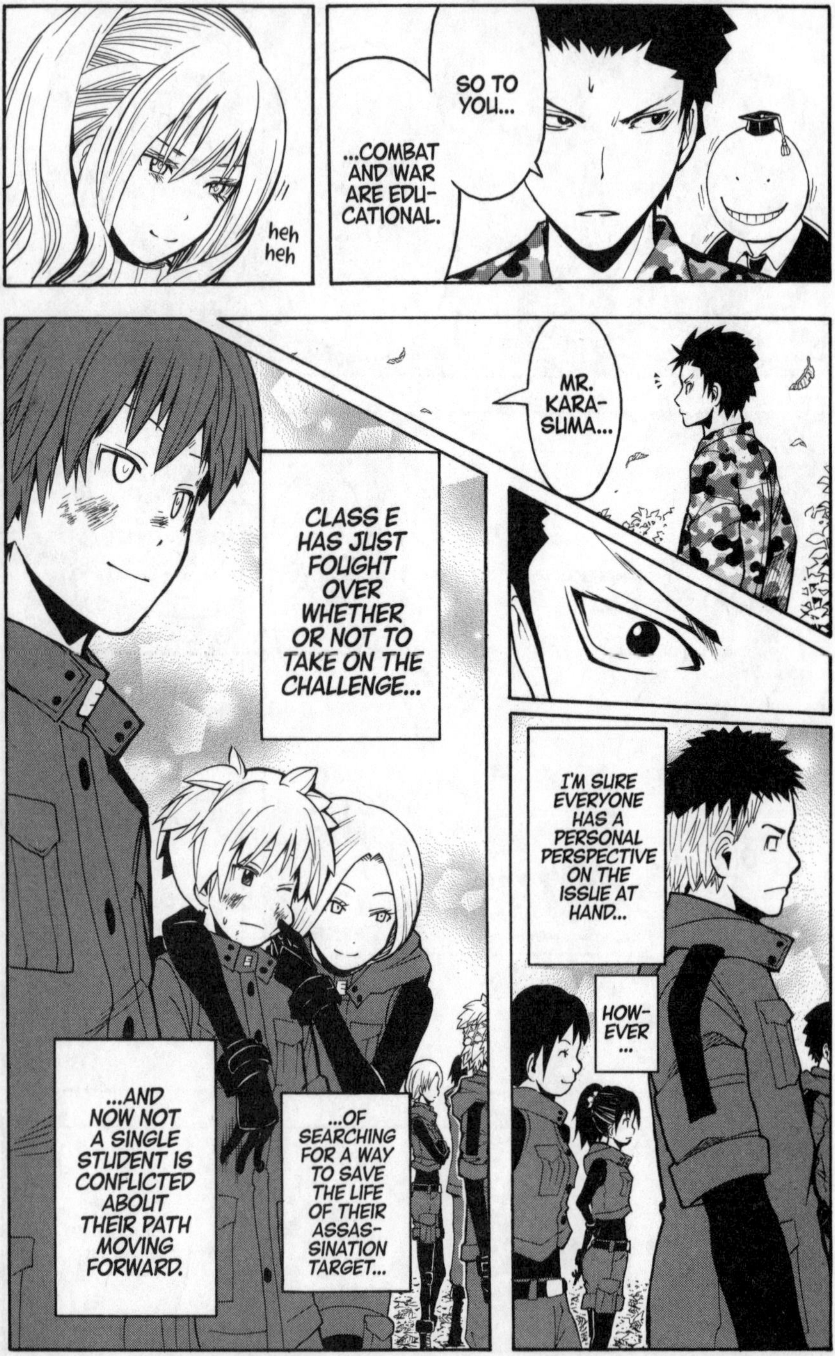

SO TO YOU...
...COMBAT AND WAR ARE EDU-CATIONAL.
heh heh
MR. KARA-SUMA...
I'M SURE EVERYONE HAS A PERSONAL PERSPECTIVE ON THE ISSUE AT HAND...
HOW-EVER...
CLASS E HAS JUST FOUGHT OVER WHETHER OR NOT TO TAKE ON THE CHALLENGE...
...OF SEARCHING FOR A WAY TO SAVE THE LIFE OF THEIR ASSAS-SINATION TARGET...
...AND NOW NOT A SINGLE STUDENT IS CONFLICTED ABOUT THEIR PATH MOVING FORWARD.

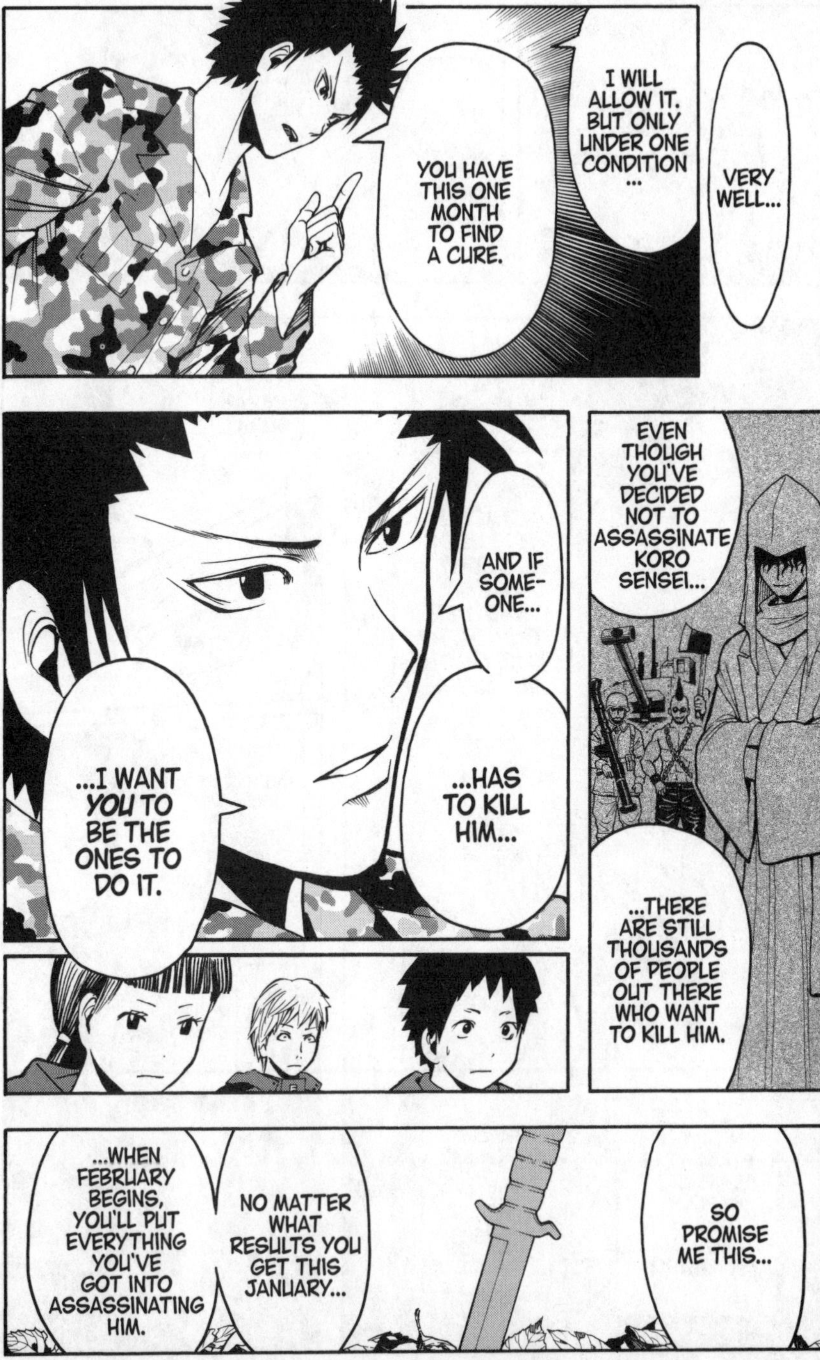
VERY WELL...
I WILL ALLOW IT. BUT ONLY UNDER ONE CONDITION...
YOU HAVE THIS ONE MONTH TO FIND A CURE.
EVEN THOUGH YOU'VE DECIDED NOT TO ASSASSINATE KORO SENSEI...
...THERE ARE STILL THOUSANDS OF PEOPLE OUT THERE WHO WANT TO KILL HIM.
AND IF SOME-ONE...
...HAS TO KILL HIM...
...I WANT *YOU* TO BE THE ONES TO DO IT.
SO PROMISE ME THIS...
NO MATTER WHAT RESULTS YOU GET THIS JANUARY...
...WHEN FEBRUARY BEGINS, YOU'LL PUT EVERYTHING YOU'VE GOT INTO ASSASSINATING HIM.

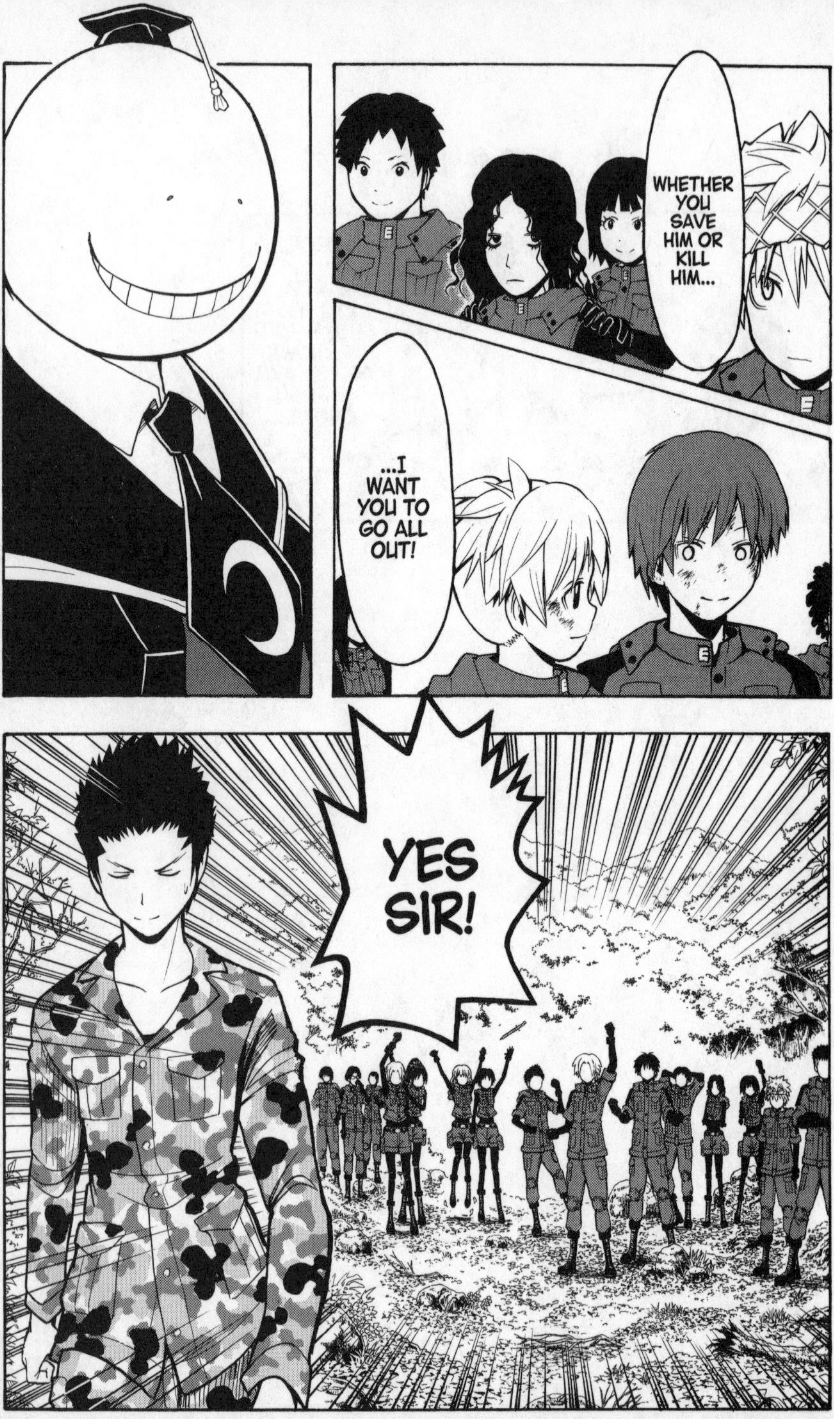
WHETHER YOU SAVE HIM OR KILL HIM...
...I WANT YOU TO GO ALL OUT!
YES SIR!

The Wise Guy

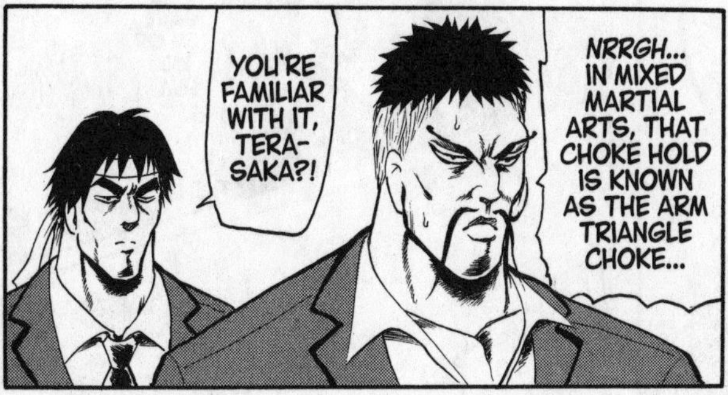
NRRGH... IN MIXED MARTIAL ARTS, THAT CHOKE HOLD IS KNOWN AS THE ARM TRIANGLE CHOKE...
YOU'RE FAMILIAR WITH IT, TERA-SAKA?!

CLASS 150 TIME FOR A RESEARCH PROJECT

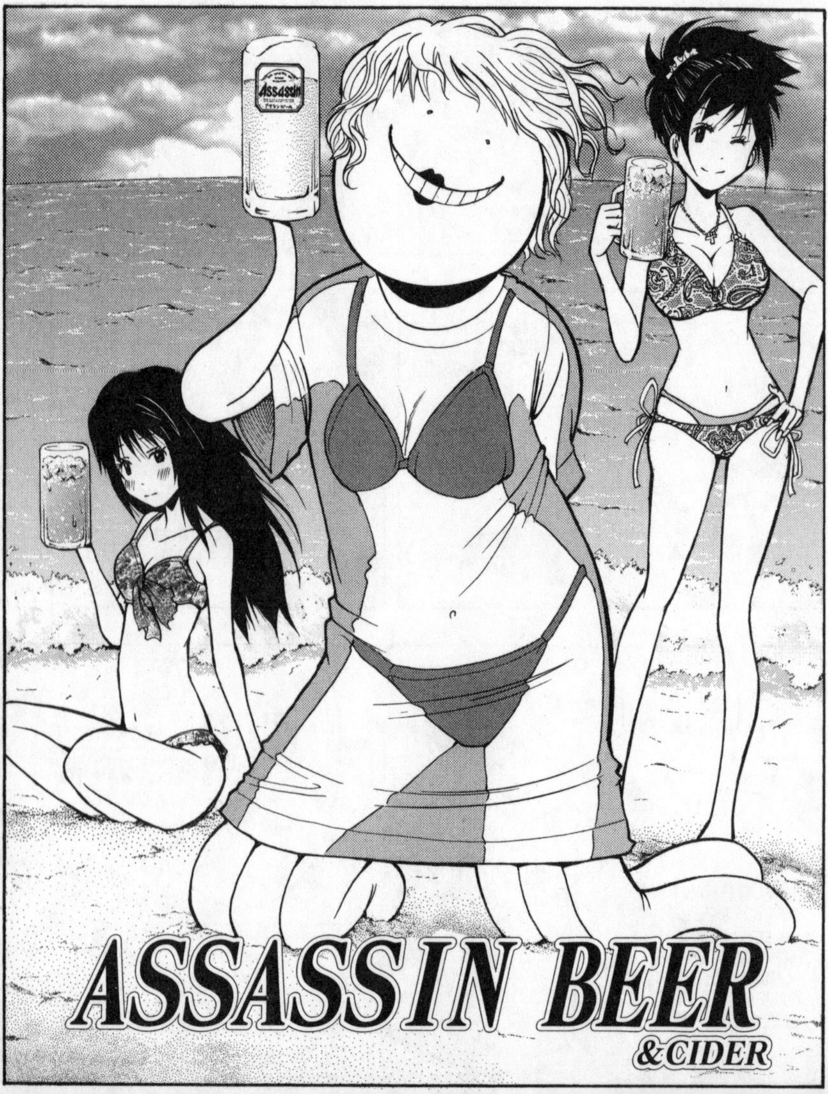
ASSASSIN BEER
&CIDER

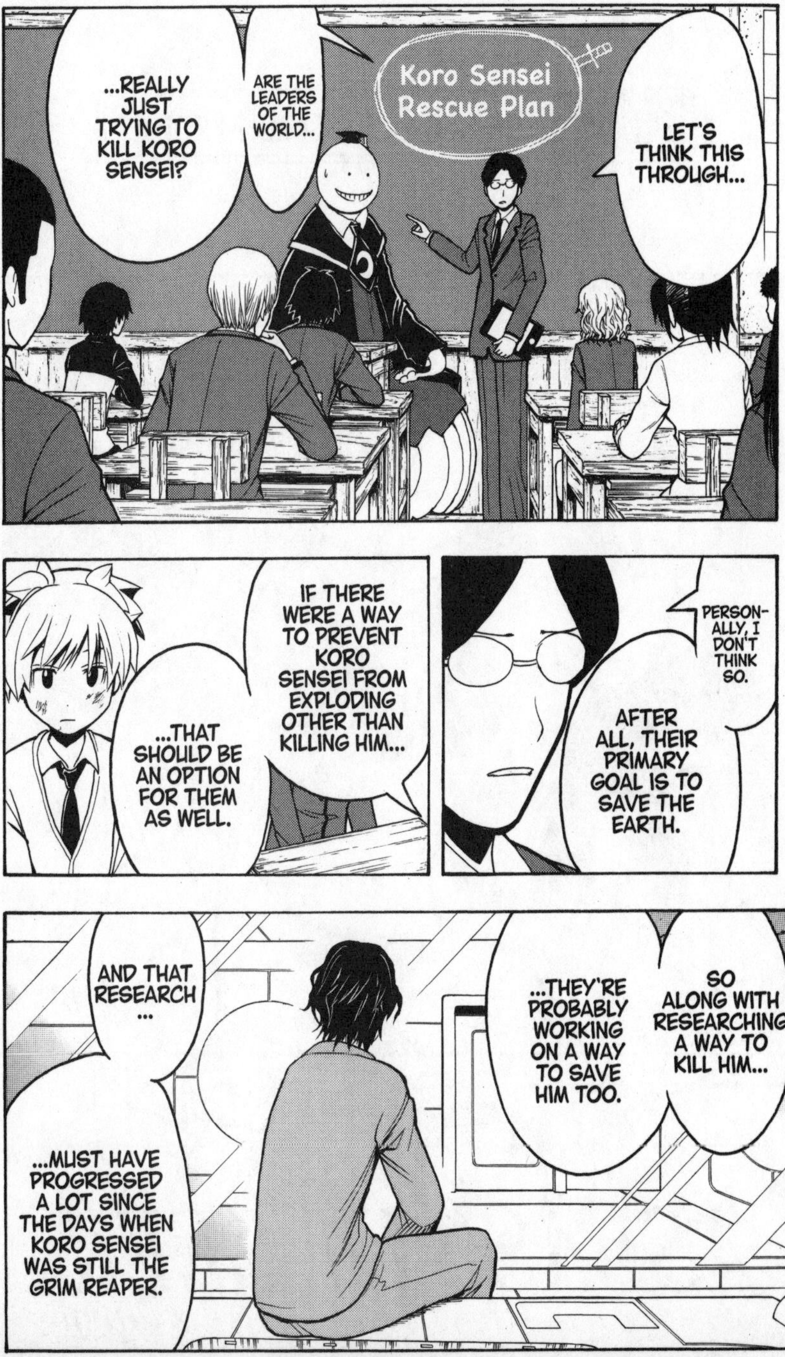
LET'S THINK THIS THROUGH...
Koro Sensei Rescue Plan
ARE THE LEADERS OF THE WORLD...
...REALLY JUST TRYING TO KILL KORO SENSEI?
PERSONALLY, I DON'T THINK SO.
AFTER ALL, THEIR PRIMARY GOAL IS TO SAVE THE EARTH.
IF THERE WERE A WAY TO PREVENT KORO SENSEI FROM EXPLODING OTHER THAN KILLING HIM...
...THAT SHOULD BE AN OPTION FOR THEM AS WELL.
SO ALONG WITH RESEARCHING A WAY TO KILL HIM...
...THEY'RE PROBABLY WORKING ON A WAY TO SAVE HIM TOO.
AND THAT RESEARCH ...
...MUST HAVE PROGRESSED A LOT SINCE THE DAYS WHEN KORO SENSEI WAS STILL THE GRIM REAPER.

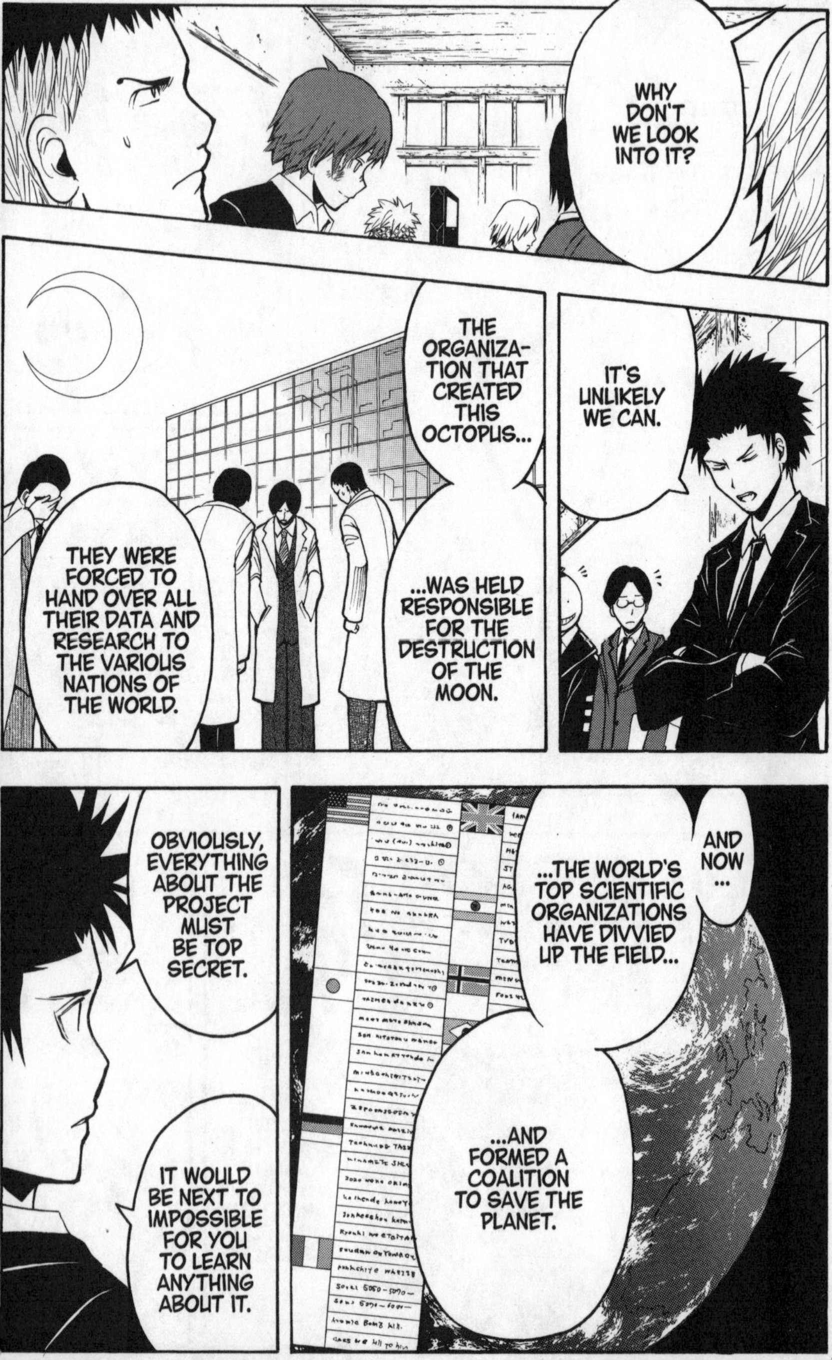
WHY DON'T WE LOOK INTO IT?
IT'S UNLIKELY WE CAN.
THE ORGANIZATION THAT CREATED THIS OCTOPUS...
...WAS HELD RESPONSIBLE FOR THE DESTRUCTION OF THE MOON.
THEY WERE FORCED TO HAND OVER ALL THEIR DATA AND RESEARCH TO THE VARIOUS NATIONS OF THE WORLD.
AND NOW...
...THE WORLD'S TOP SCIENTIFIC ORGANIZATIONS HAVE DIVVIED UP THE FIELD...
...AND FORMED A COALITION TO SAVE THE PLANET.
OBVIOUSLY, EVERYTHING ABOUT THE PROJECT MUST BE TOP SECRET.
IT WOULD BE NEXT TO IMPOSSIBLE FOR YOU TO LEARN ANYTHING ABOUT IT.

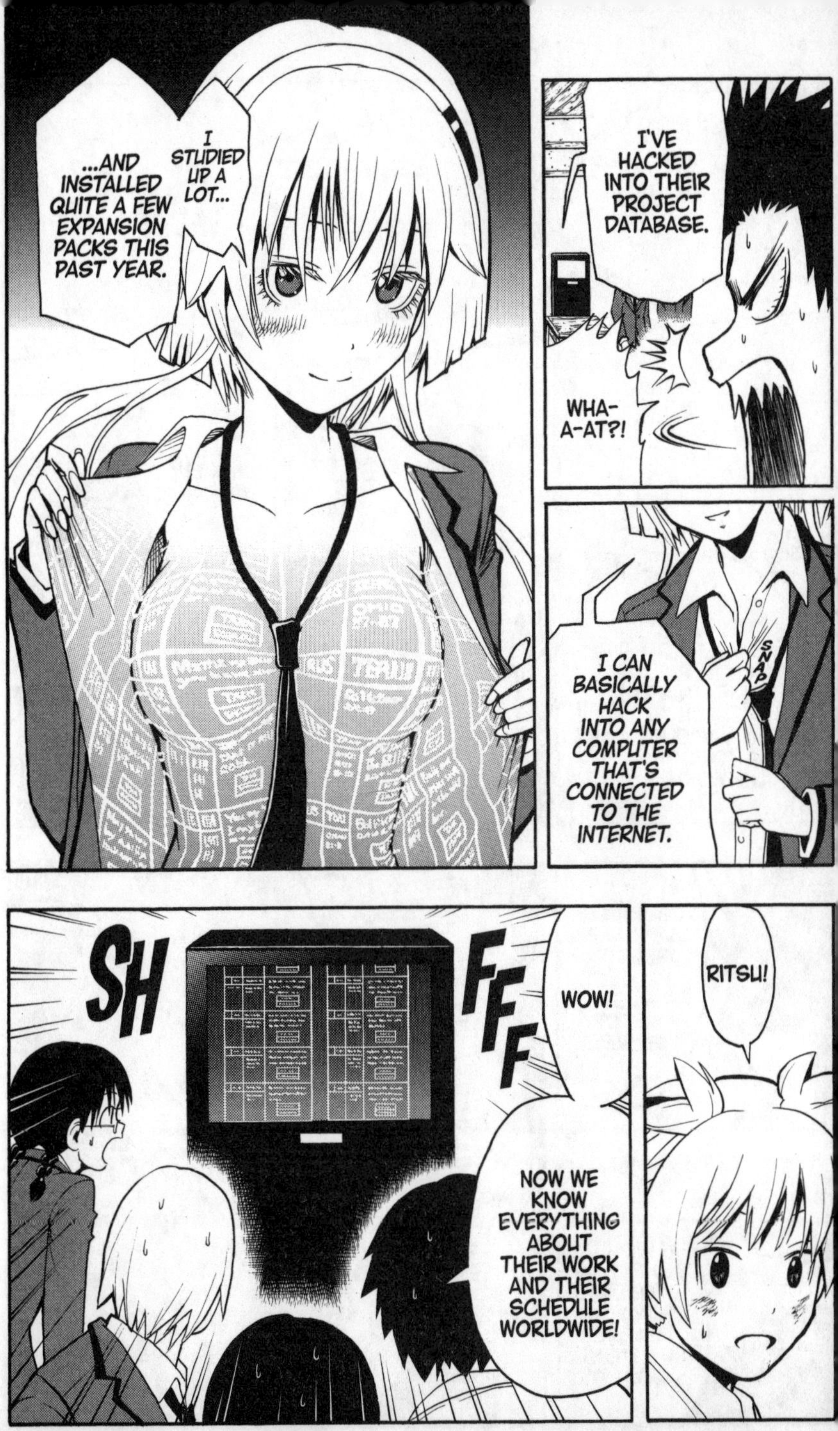
I'VE HACKED INTO THEIR PROJECT DATABASE.
WHA-A-AT?!
I CAN BASICALLY HACK INTO ANY COMPUTER THAT'S CONNECTED TO THE INTERNET.
SNAP
I STUDIED UP A LOT...
...AND INSTALLED QUITE A FEW EXPANSION PACKS THIS PAST YEAR.
RITSU!
WOW!
SH FFF
NOW WE KNOW EVERYTHING ABOUT THEIR WORK AND THEIR SCHEDULE WORLDWIDE!

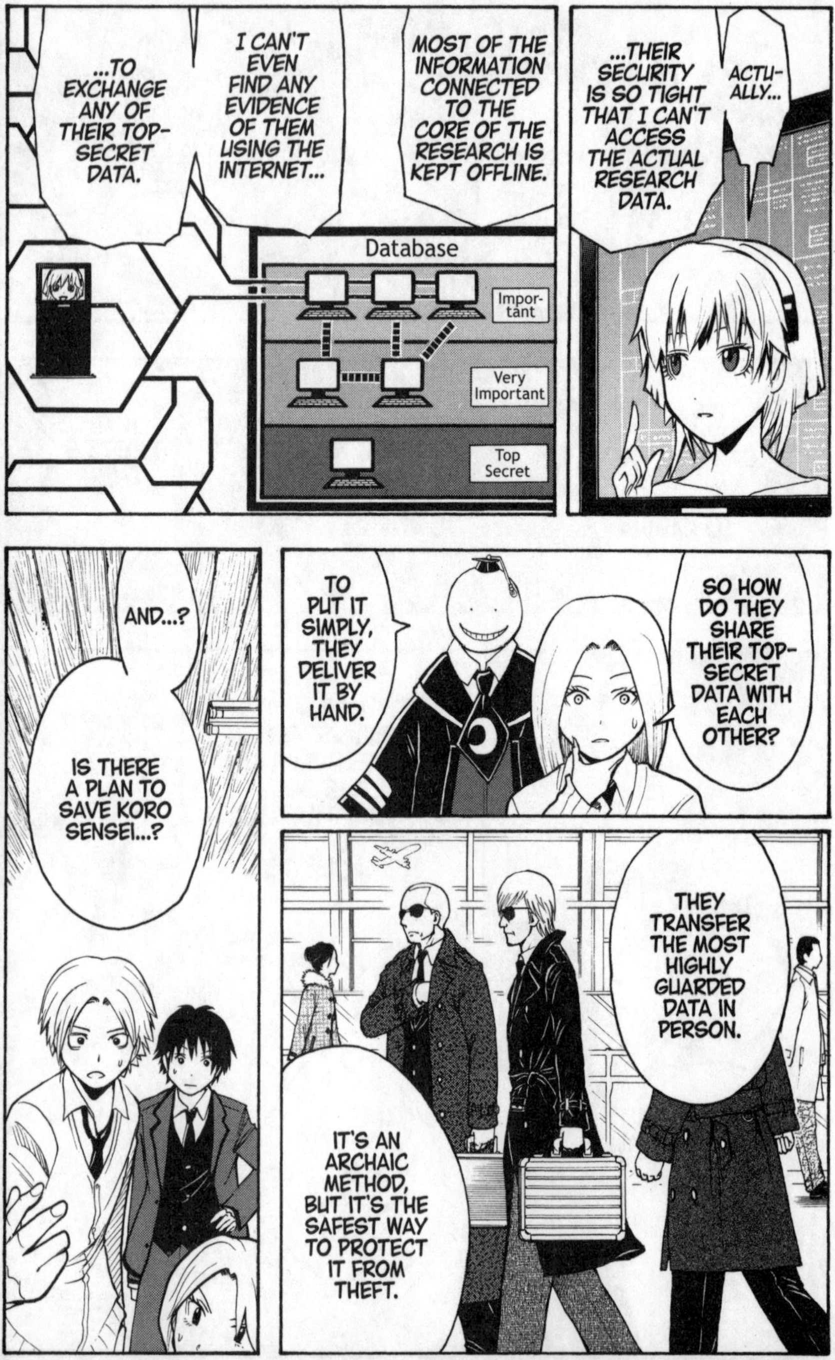
ACTU-ALLY...
...THEIR SECURITY IS SO TIGHT THAT I CAN'T ACCESS THE ACTUAL RESEARCH DATA.
MOST OF THE INFORMATION CONNECTED TO THE CORE OF THE RESEARCH IS KEPT OFFLINE.
I CAN'T EVEN FIND ANY EVIDENCE OF THEM USING THE INTERNET...
...TO EXCHANGE ANY OF THEIR TOP-SECRET DATA.
Database
Impor-tant
Very Important
Top Secret
SO HOW DO THEY SHARE THEIR TOP-SECRET DATA WITH EACH OTHER?
TO PUT IT SIMPLY, THEY DELIVER IT BY HAND.
THEY TRANSFER THE MOST HIGHLY GUARDED DATA IN PERSON.
IT'S AN ARCHAIC METHOD, BUT IT'S THE SAFEST WAY TO PROTECT IT FROM THEFT.
AND...?
IS THERE A PLAN TO SAVE KORO SENSEI...?

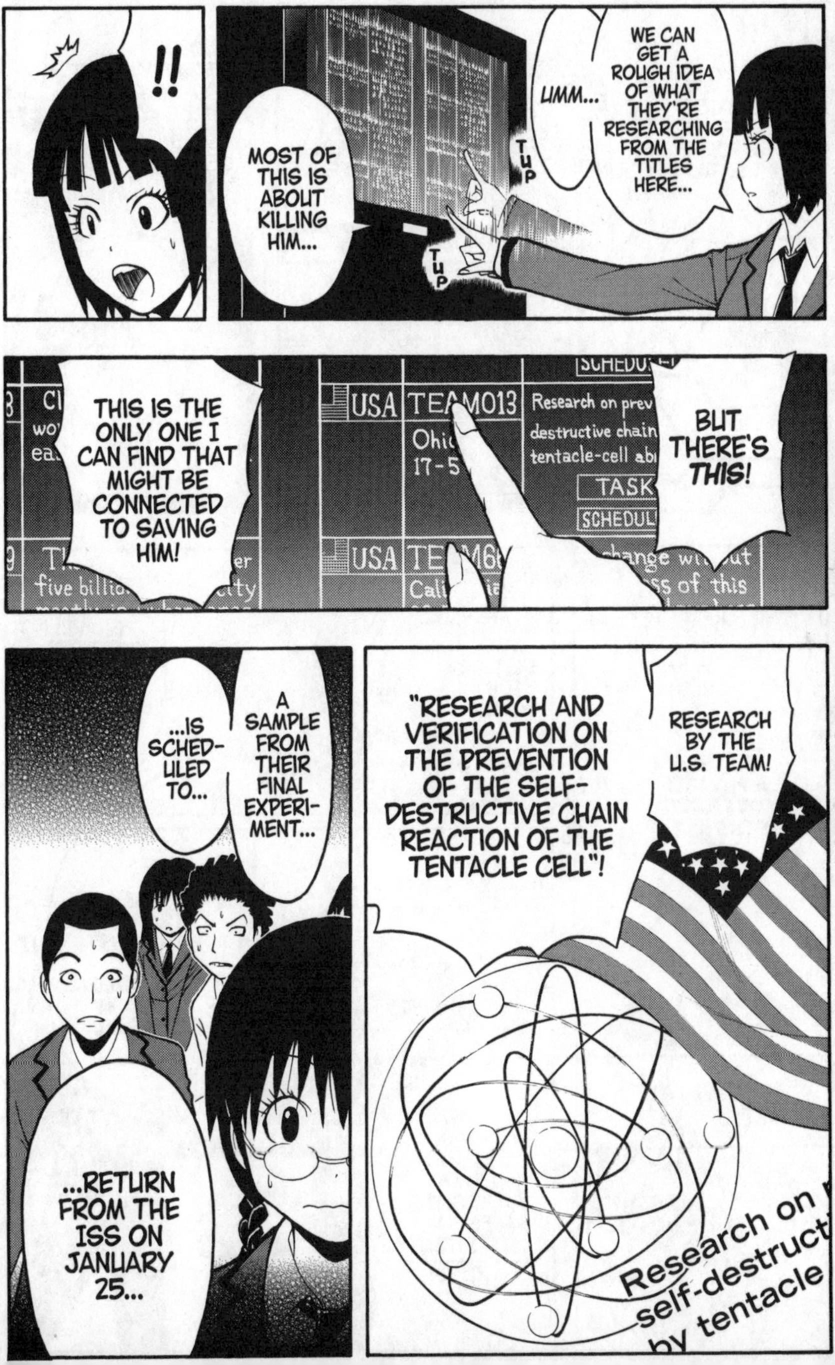
WE CAN GET A ROUGH IDEA OF WHAT THEY'RE RESEARCHING FROM THE TITLES HERE...
UMM...
TUP
MOST OF THIS IS ABOUT KILLING HIM...
TUP
!!
SCHEDUL
USA
TEAM013
Research on prev
destructive chain
tentacle-cell ab
TASK
SCHEDUL
USA
BUT THERE'S *THIS*!
THIS IS THE ONLY ONE I CAN FIND THAT MIGHT BE CONNECTED TO SAVING HIM!
RESEARCH BY THE U.S. TEAM!
"RESEARCH AND VERIFICATION ON THE PREVENTION OF THE SELF-DESTRUCTIVE CHAIN REACTION OF THE TENTACLE CELL"!
Research on
self-destruct
by tentacle
A SAMPLE FROM THEIR FINAL EXPERIMENT...
...IS SCHEDULED TO...
...RETURN FROM THE ISS ON JANUARY 25...

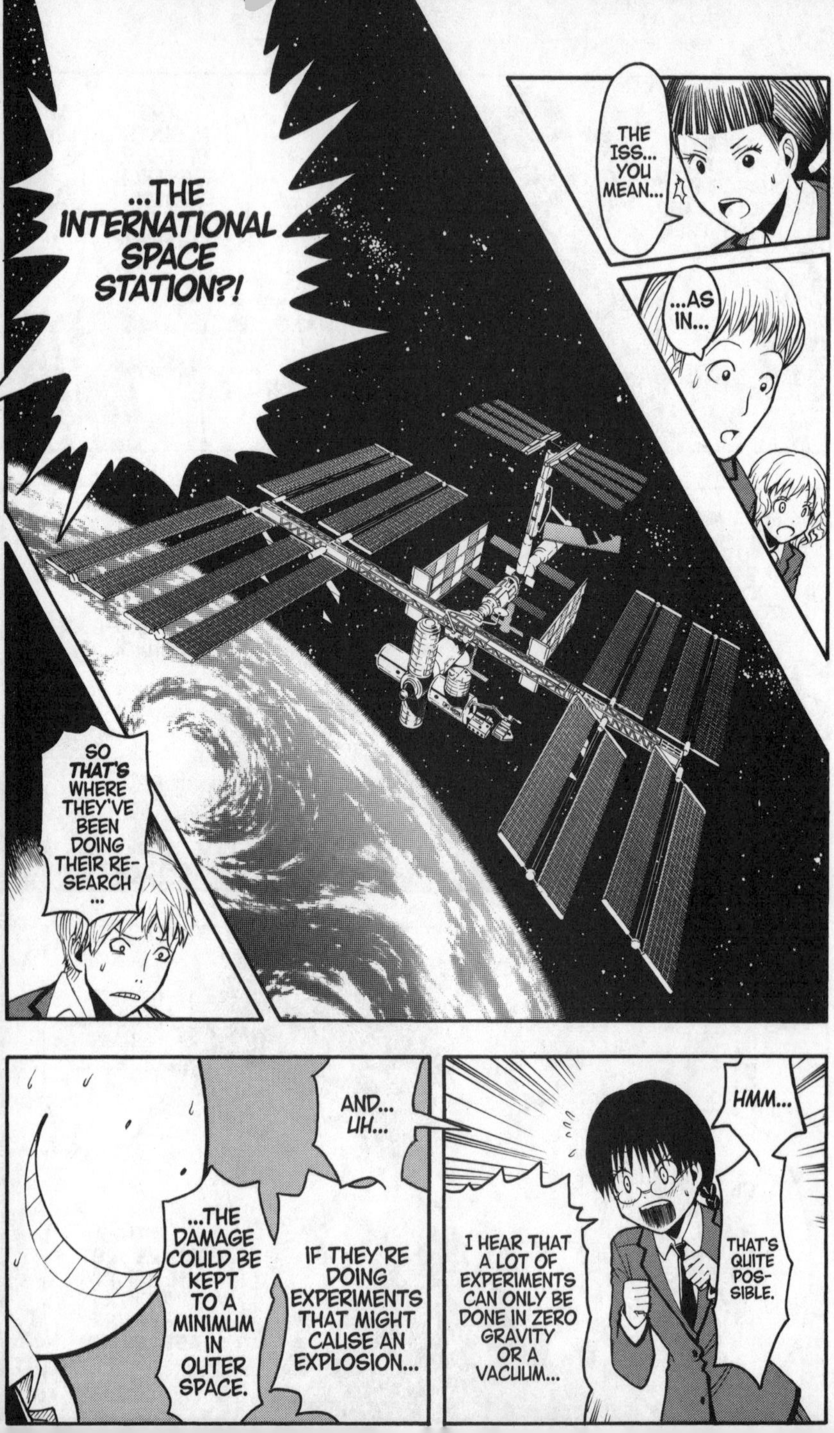
THE ISS... YOU MEAN...
...AS IN...
...THE INTERNATIONAL SPACE STATION?!
SO THAT'S WHERE THEY'VE BEEN DOING THEIR RESEARCH...
HMM...
THAT'S QUITE POSSIBLE.
I HEAR THAT A LOT OF EXPERIMENTS CAN ONLY BE DONE IN ZERO GRAVITY OR A VACUUM...
AND... UH...
IF THEY'RE DOING EXPERIMENTS THAT MIGHT CAUSE AN EXPLOSION...
...THE DAMAGE COULD BE KEPT TO A MINIMUM IN OUTER SPACE.

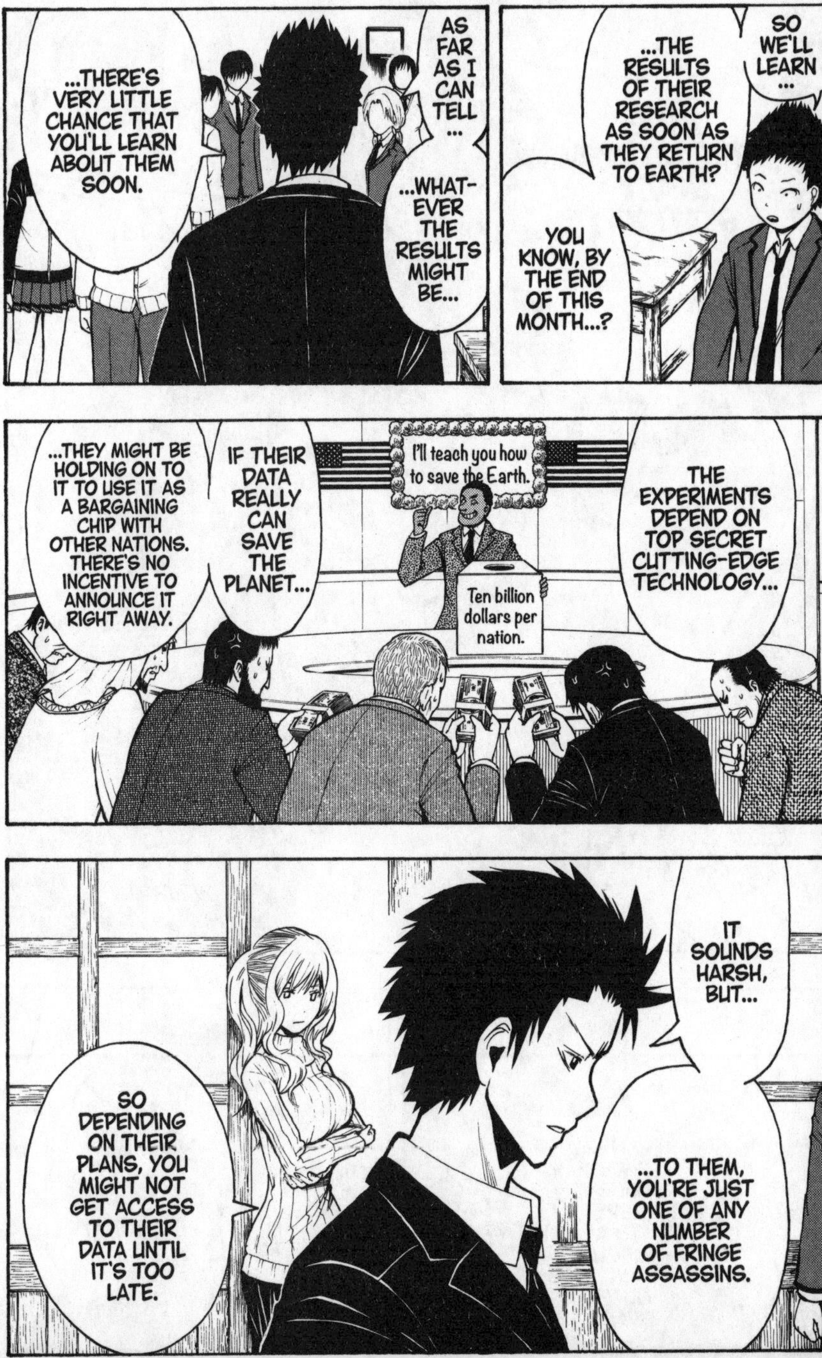
SO WE'LL LEARN ...
...THE RESULTS OF THEIR RESEARCH AS SOON AS THEY RETURN TO EARTH?
YOU KNOW, BY THE END OF THIS MONTH...?
AS FAR AS I CAN TELL ...
...WHAT-EVER THE RESULTS MIGHT BE...
...THERE'S VERY LITTLE CHANCE THAT YOU'LL LEARN ABOUT THEM SOON.
THE EXPERIMENTS DEPEND ON TOP SECRET CUTTING-EDGE TECHNOLOGY...
I'll teach you how to save the Earth.
Ten billion dollars per nation.
IF THEIR DATA REALLY CAN SAVE THE PLANET...
...THEY MIGHT BE HOLDING ON TO IT TO USE IT AS A BARGAINING CHIP WITH OTHER NATIONS. THERE'S NO INCENTIVE TO ANNOUNCE IT RIGHT AWAY.
IT SOUNDS HARSH, BUT...
...TO THEM, YOU'RE JUST ONE OF ANY NUMBER OF FRINGE ASSASSINS.
SO DEPENDING ON THEIR PLANS, YOU MIGHT NOT GET ACCESS TO THEIR DATA UNTIL IT'S TOO LATE.

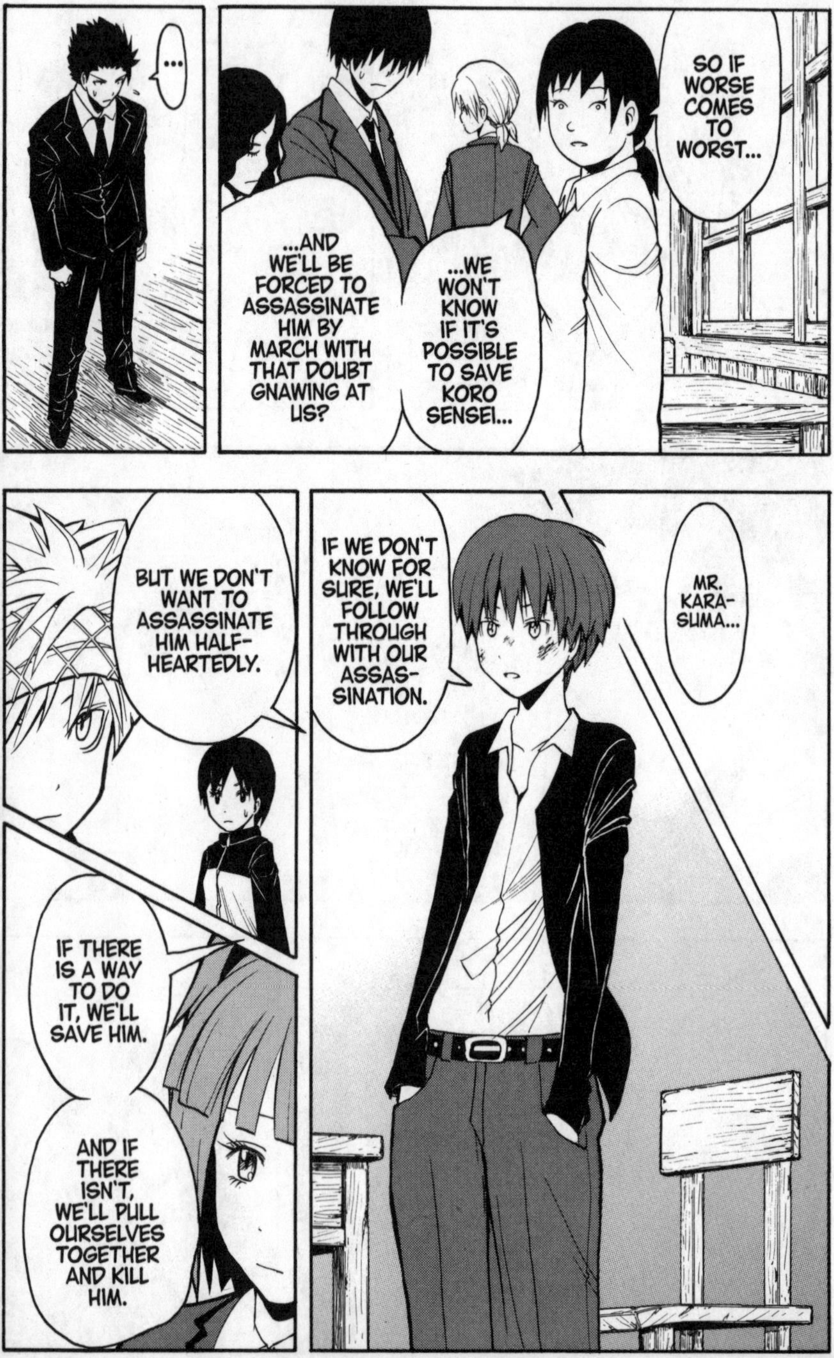
SO IF WORSE COMES TO WORST...
...WE WON'T KNOW IF IT'S POSSIBLE TO SAVE KORO SENSEI...
...AND WE'LL BE FORCED TO ASSASSINATE HIM BY MARCH WITH THAT DOUBT GNAWING AT US?
...
MR. KARASUMA...
IF WE DON'T KNOW FOR SURE, WE'LL FOLLOW THROUGH WITH OUR ASSASSINATION.
BUT WE DON'T WANT TO ASSASSINATE HIM HALF-HEARTEDLY.
IF THERE IS A WAY TO DO IT, WE'LL SAVE HIM.
AND IF THERE ISN'T, WE'LL PULL OURSELVES TOGETHER AND KILL HIM.

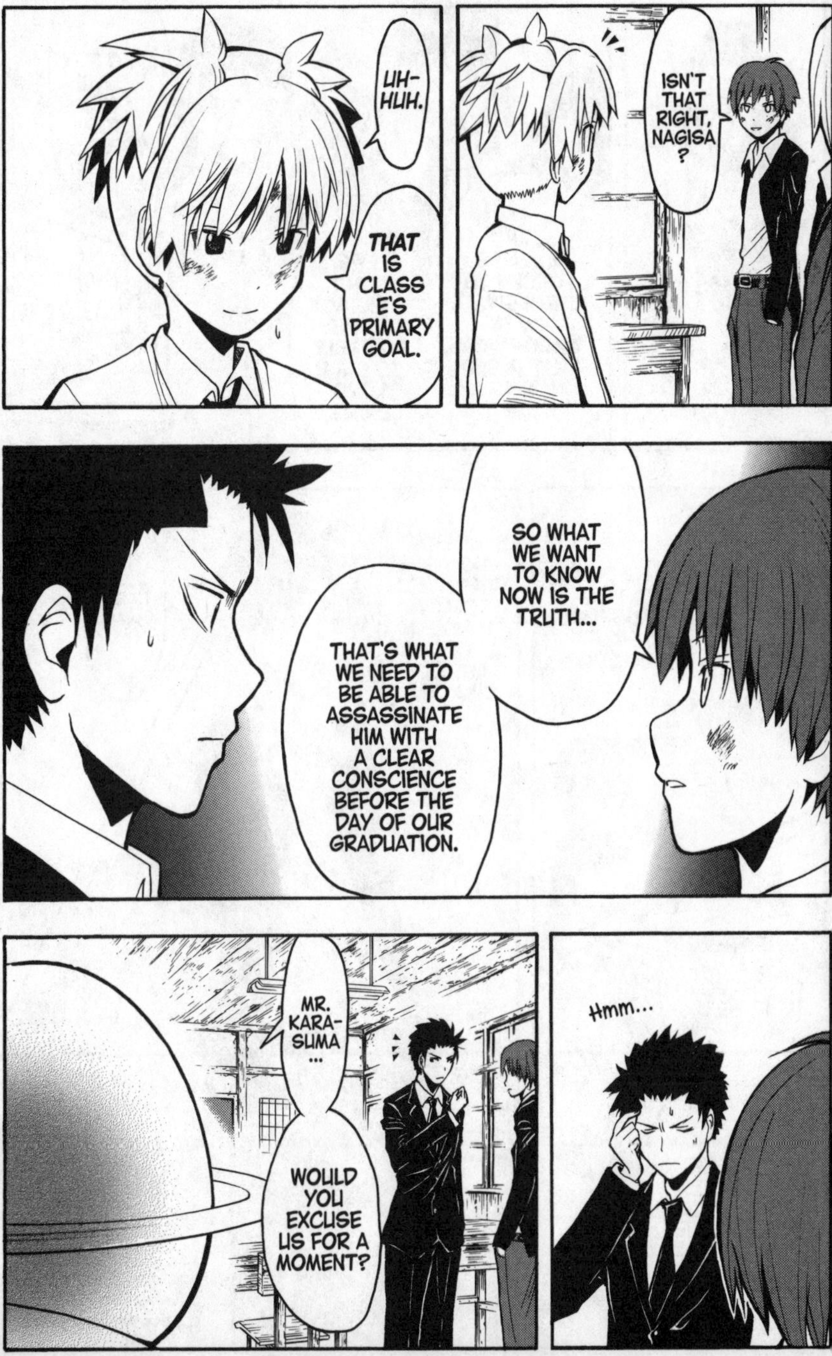
ISN'T THAT RIGHT, NAGISA?
UH-HUH.
THAT IS CLASS E'S PRIMARY GOAL.
SO WHAT WE WANT TO KNOW NOW IS THE TRUTH...
THAT'S WHAT WE NEED TO BE ABLE TO ASSASSINATE HIM WITH A CLEAR CONSCIENCE BEFORE THE DAY OF OUR GRADUATION.
Hmm...
MR. KARA-SUMA...
WOULD YOU EXCUSE US FOR A MOMENT?

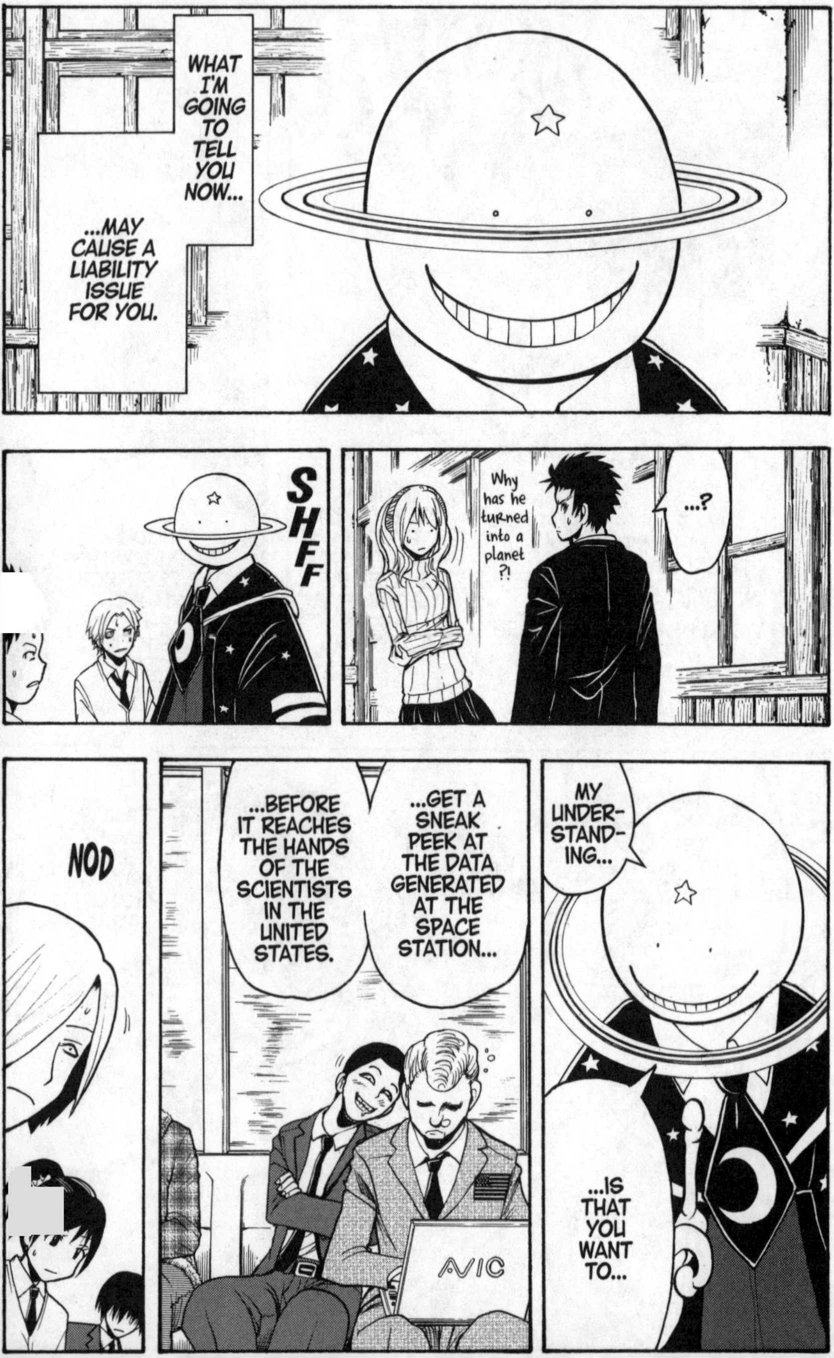
WHAT I'M GOING TO TELL YOU NOW...
...MAY CAUSE A LIABILITY ISSUE FOR YOU.
...?
Why has he turned into a planet?!
SHFF
MY UNDERSTANDING...
...IS THAT YOU WANT TO...
...GET A SNEAK PEEK AT THE DATA GENERATED AT THE SPACE STATION...
...BEFORE IT REACHES THE HANDS OF THE SCIENTISTS IN THE UNITED STATES.
NOD

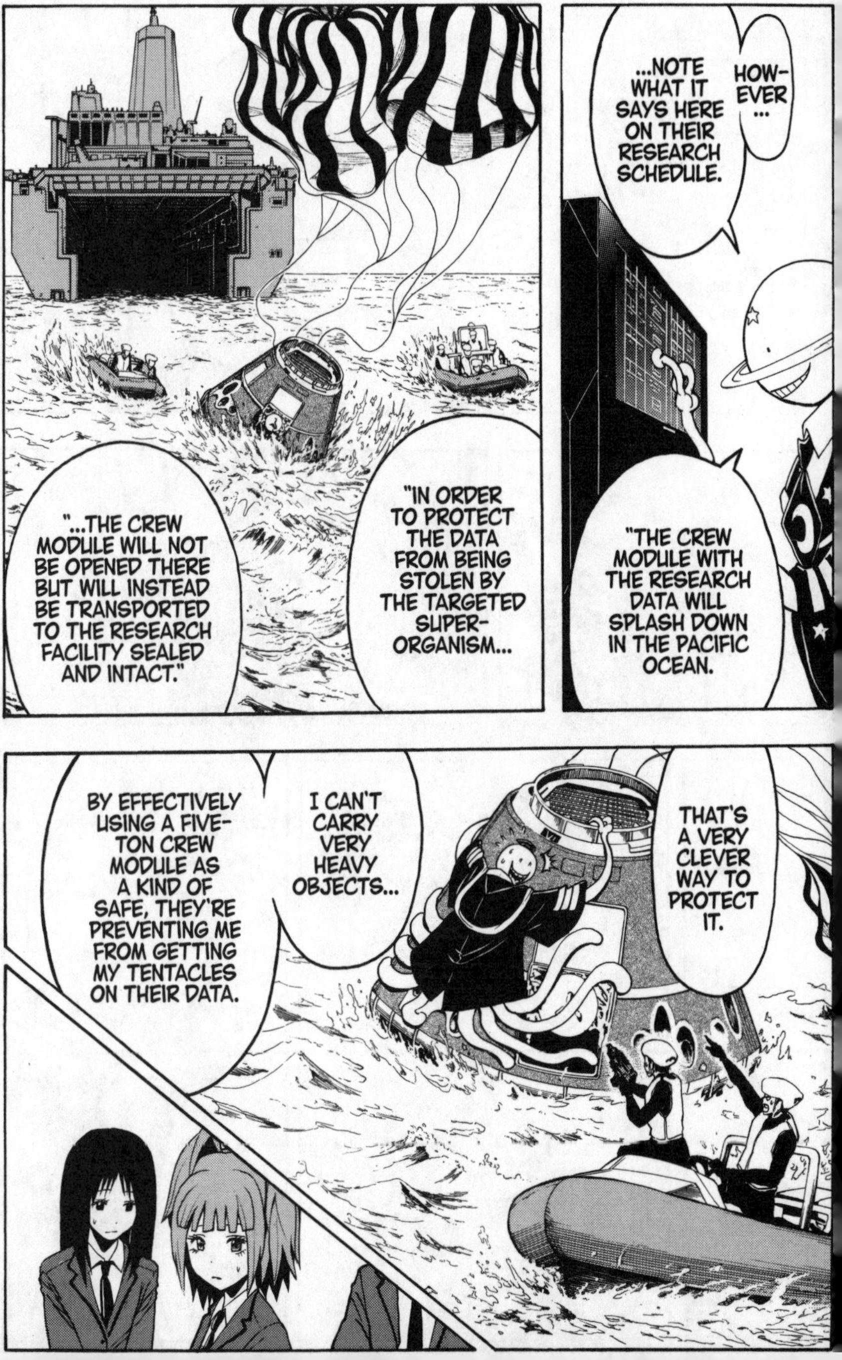
HOWEVER...
...NOTE WHAT IT SAYS HERE ON THEIR RESEARCH SCHEDULE.
"THE CREW MODULE WITH THE RESEARCH DATA WILL SPLASH DOWN IN THE PACIFIC OCEAN.
"IN ORDER TO PROTECT THE DATA FROM BEING STOLEN BY THE TARGETED SUPER-ORGANISM...
"...THE CREW MODULE WILL NOT BE OPENED THERE BUT WILL INSTEAD BE TRANSPORTED TO THE RESEARCH FACILITY SEALED AND INTACT."
THAT'S A VERY CLEVER WAY TO PROTECT IT.
I CAN'T CARRY VERY HEAVY OBJECTS...
BY EFFECTIVELY USING A FIVE-TON CREW MODULE AS A KIND OF SAFE, THEY'RE PREVENTING ME FROM GETTING MY TENTACLES ON THEIR DATA.

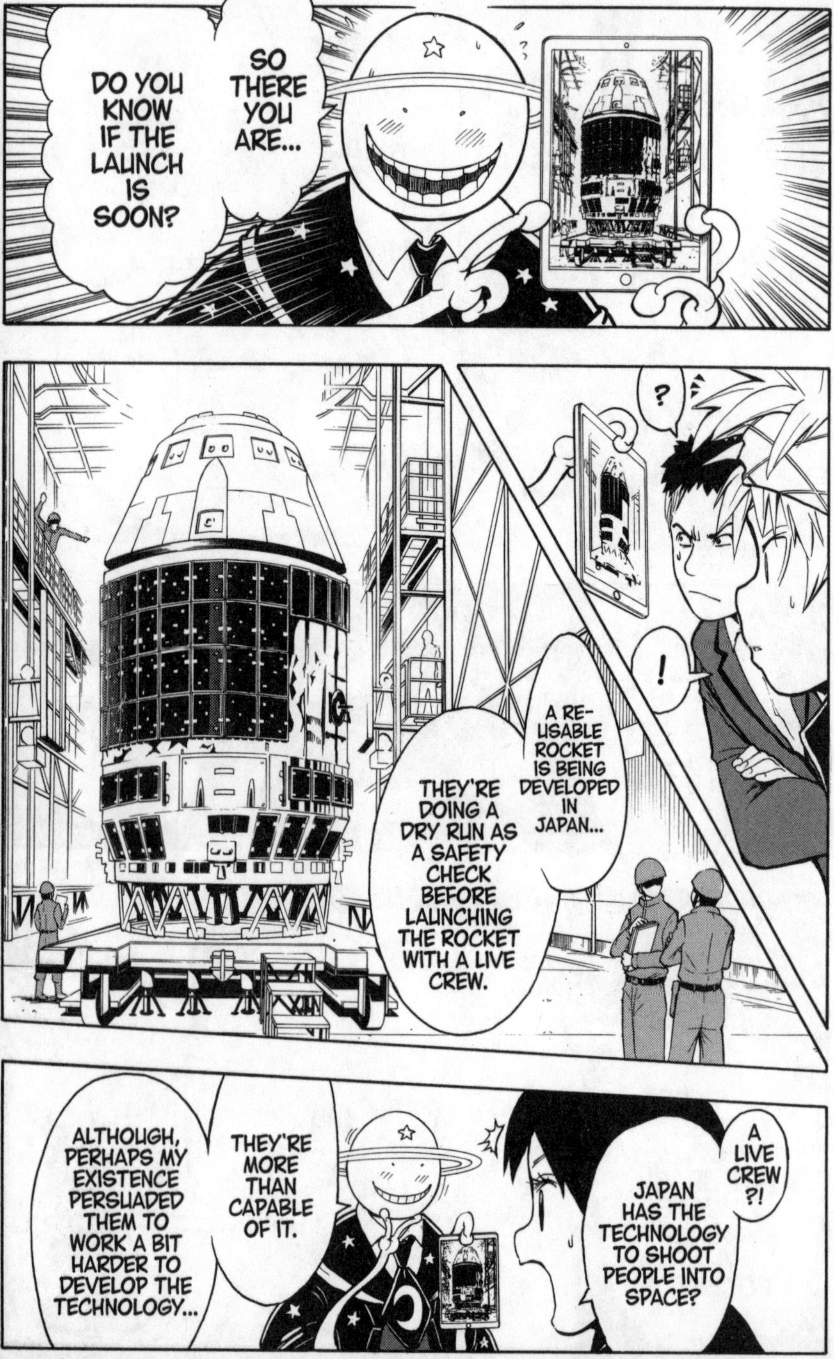
SO THERE YOU ARE...
DO YOU KNOW IF THE LAUNCH IS SOON?
?
!
A RE-USABLE ROCKET IS BEING DEVELOPED IN JAPAN...
THEY'RE DOING A DRY RUN AS A SAFETY CHECK BEFORE LAUNCHING THE ROCKET WITH A LIVE CREW.
A LIVE CREW?!
JAPAN HAS THE TECHNOLOGY TO SHOOT PEOPLE INTO SPACE?
THEY'RE MORE THAN CAPABLE OF IT.
ALTHOUGH, PERHAPS MY EXISTENCE PERSUADED THEM TO WORK A BIT HARDER TO DEVELOP THE TECHNOLOGY...

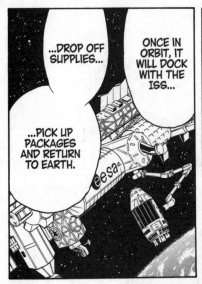

THE ROCKET WILL BE LAUNCHED WITH CRASH TEST DUMMIES EQUIPPED WITH SENSORS...
...TO RECORD ANY GLITCHES IN THE LIFE SUPPORT SYSTEM FOR LIVE ASTRONAUTS.
ONCE IN ORBIT, IT WILL DOCK WITH THE ISS...
...DROP OFF SUPPLIES...
...PICK UP PACKAGES AND RETURN TO EARTH.
THE JAPANESE ROCKET IS SCHEDULED TO ARRIVE AT THE ISS...
...THREE DAYS BEFORE THE U.S. RESEARCH TEAM DEPARTS.
SO WHAT IF...
...THERE WERE REAL PEOPLE, NOT CRASH DUMMIES, ABOARD THAT ROCKET...?

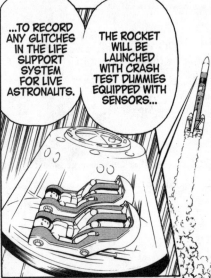

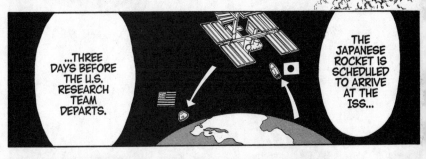

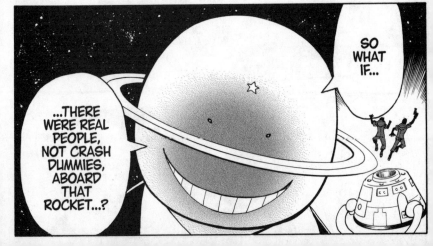

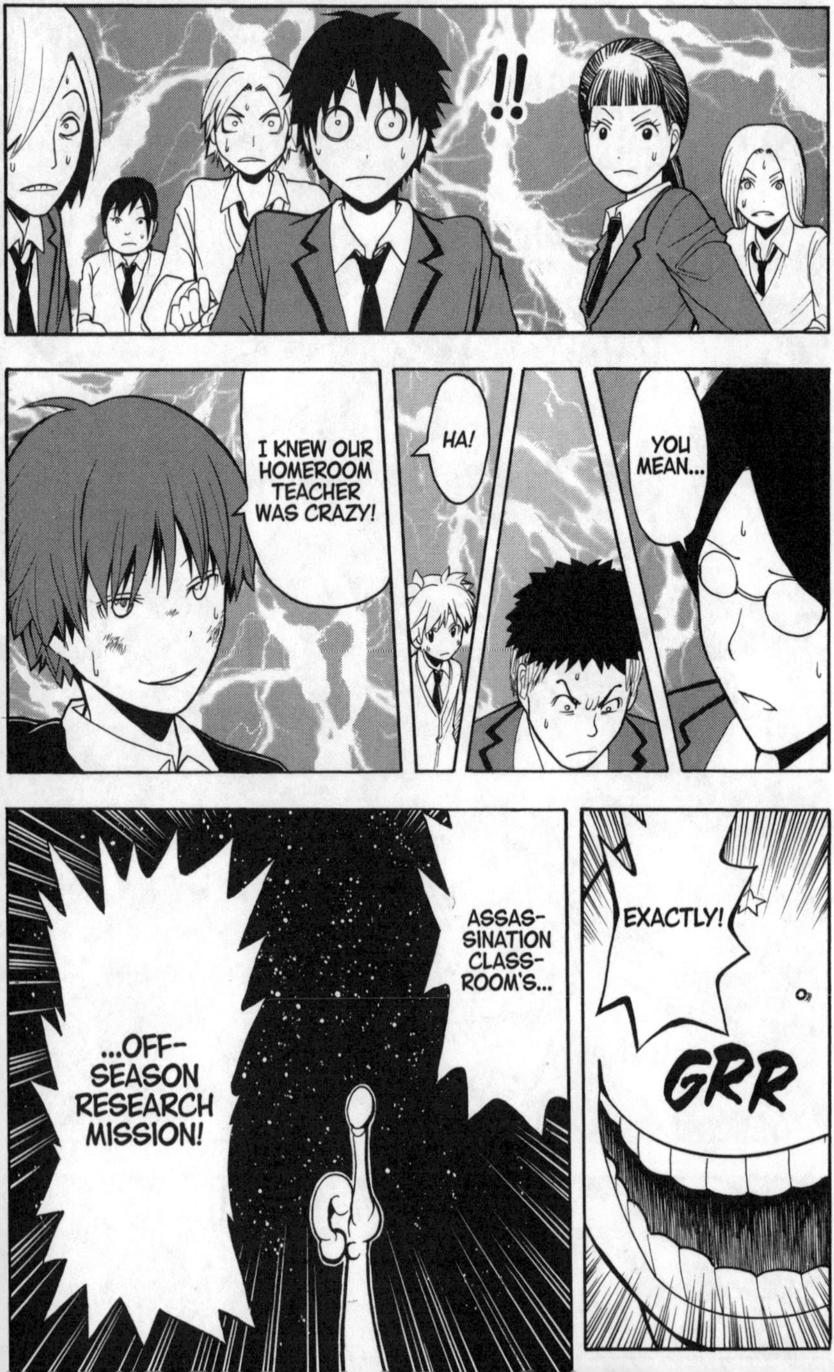
!!
YOU MEAN...
HA!
I KNEW OUR HOMEROOM TEACHER WAS CRAZY!
EXACTLY!
GRR
ASSASSINATION CLASSROOM'S...
...OFF-SEASON RESEARCH MISSION!

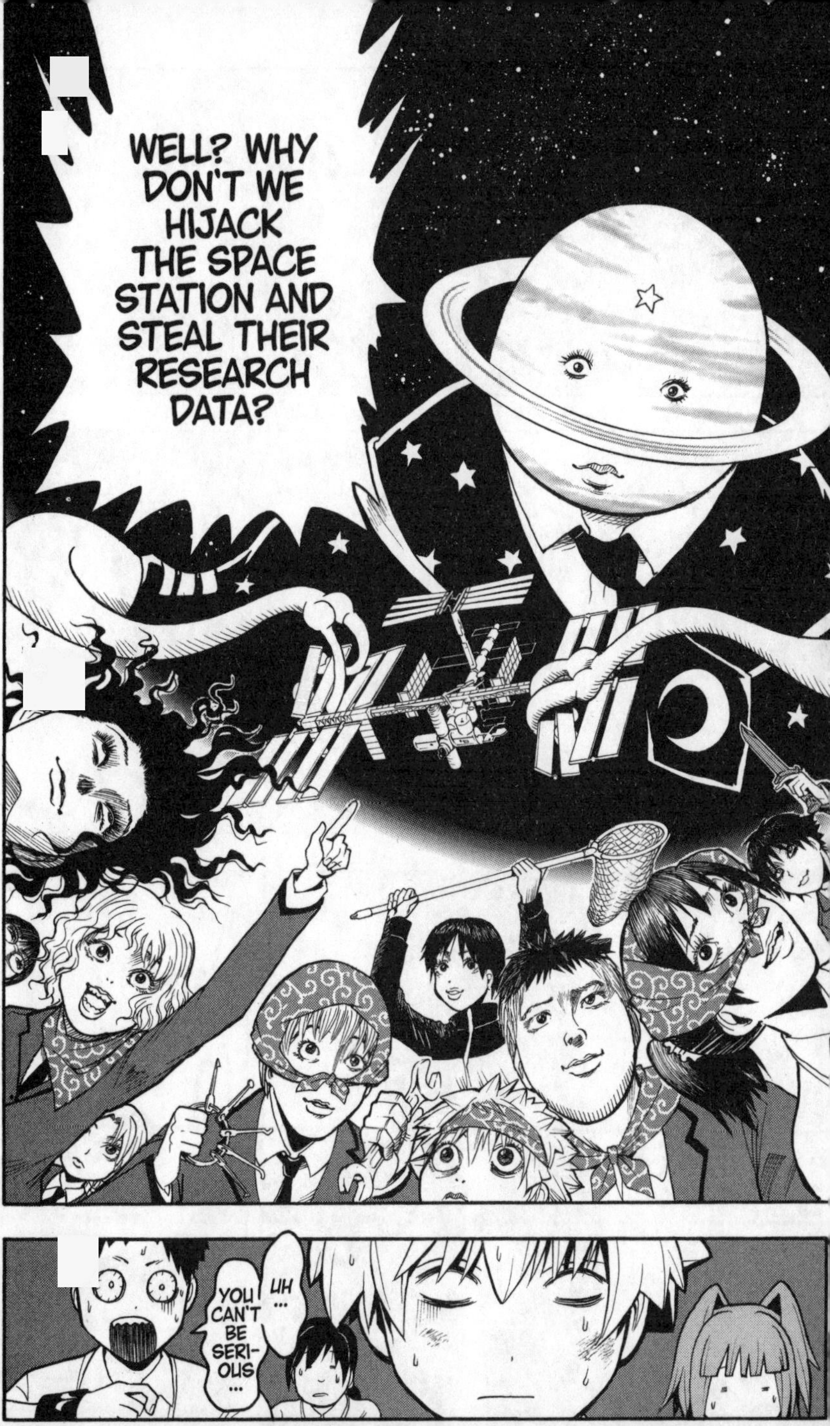
WELL? WHY DON'T WE HIJACK THE SPACE STATION AND STEAL THEIR RESEARCH DATA?
UH ...
YOU CAN'T BE SERI-OUS ...

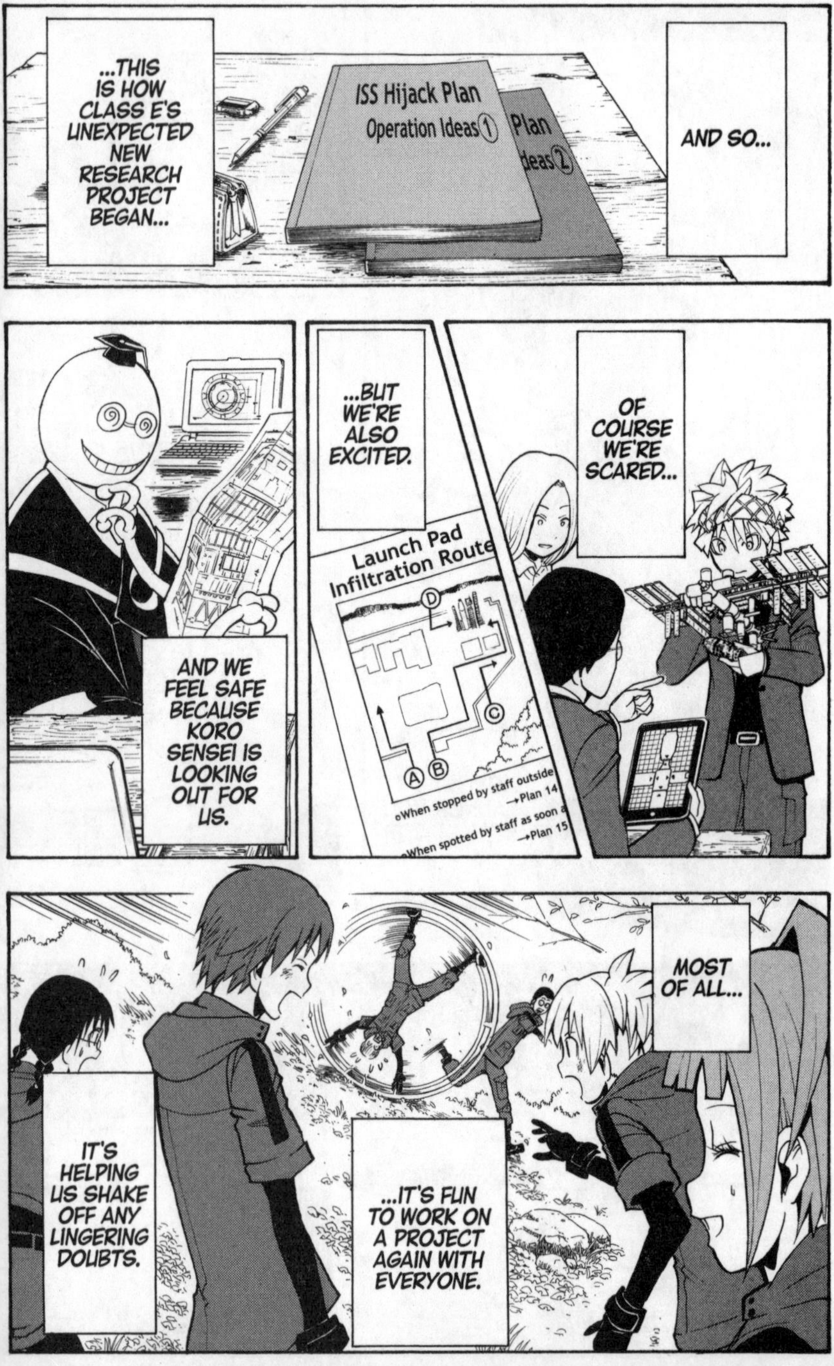
AND SO...
ISS Hijack Plan
Operation Ideas ①
...THIS IS HOW CLASS E'S UNEXPECTED NEW RESEARCH PROJECT BEGAN...
OF COURSE WE'RE SCARED...
...BUT WE'RE ALSO EXCITED.
Launch Pad Infiltration Route
Ⓐ Ⓑ Ⓒ Ⓓ
When stopped by staff outside →Plan 14
When spotted by staff as soon a →Plan 15
AND WE FEEL SAFE BECAUSE KORO SENSEI IS LOOKING OUT FOR US.
MOST OF ALL...
...IT'S FUN TO WORK ON A PROJECT AGAIN WITH EVERYONE.
IT'S HELPING US SHAKE OFF ANY LINGERING DOUBTS.

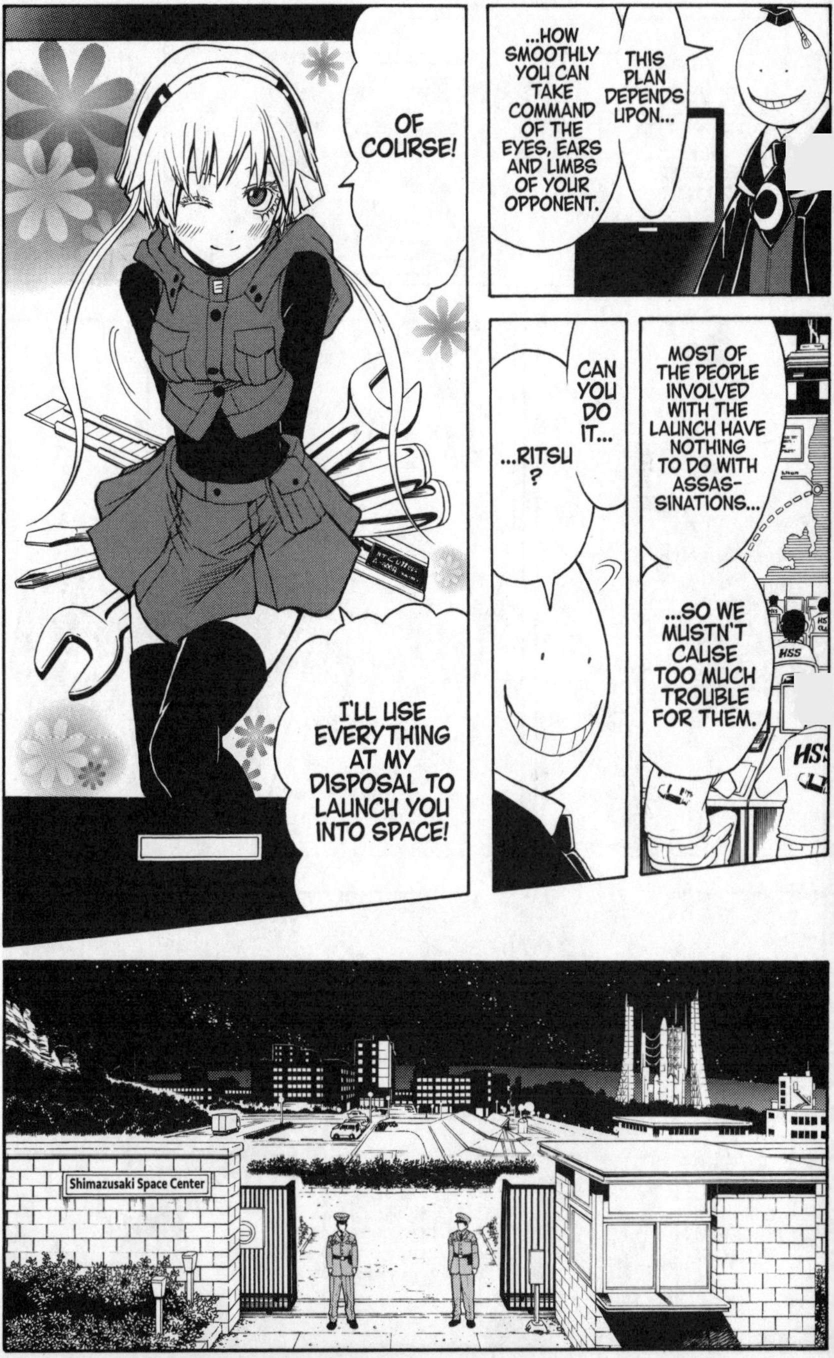
THIS PLAN DEPENDS UPON...
...HOW SMOOTHLY YOU CAN TAKE COMMAND OF THE EYES, EARS AND LIMBS OF YOUR OPPONENT.
MOST OF THE PEOPLE INVOLVED WITH THE LAUNCH HAVE NOTHING TO DO WITH ASSAS-SINATIONS...
...SO WE MUSTN'T CAUSE TOO MUCH TROUBLE FOR THEM.
CAN YOU DO IT...
...RITSU?
OF COURSE!
I'LL USE EVERYTHING AT MY DISPOSAL TO LAUNCH YOU INTO SPACE!
Shimazusaki Space Center

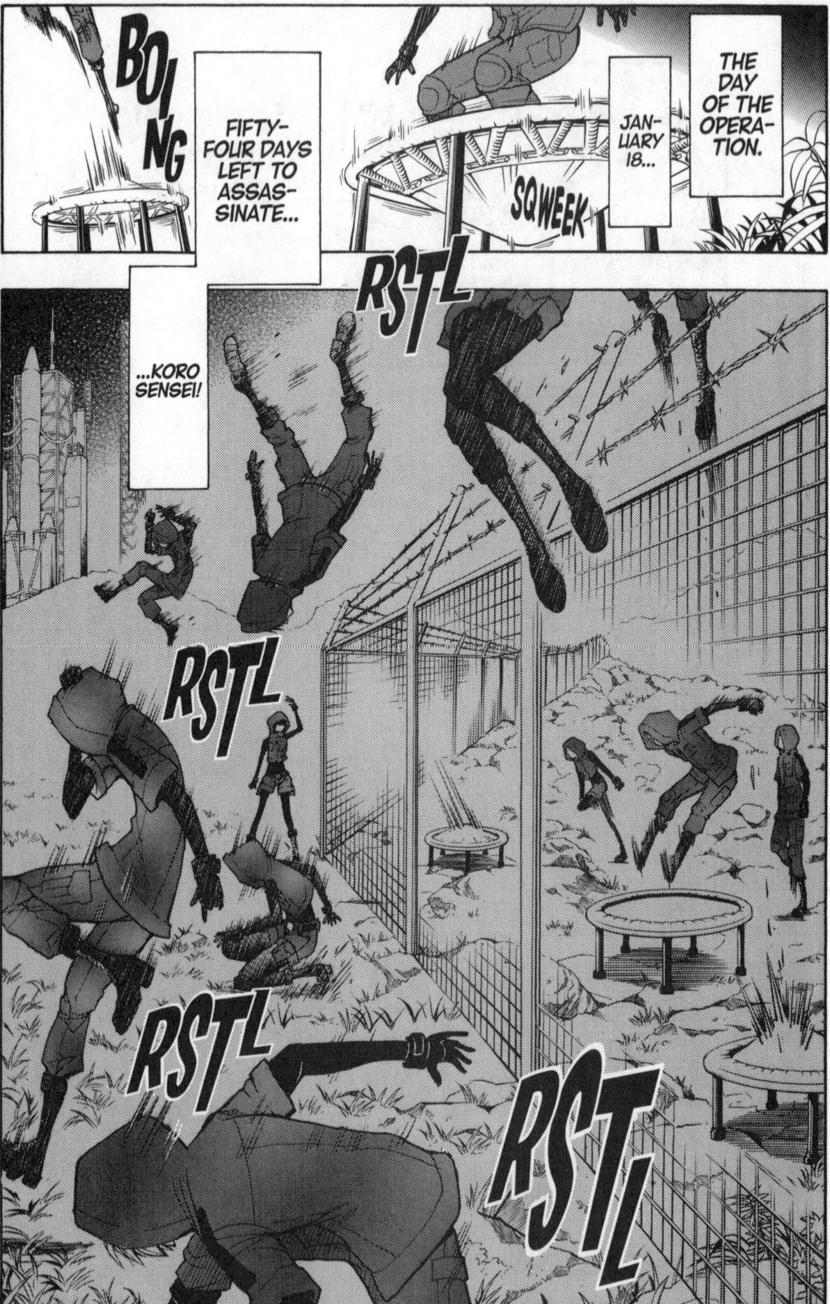
THE DAY OF THE OPERA-TION.
JAN-UARY 18...
SQWEEK
FIFTY-FOUR DAYS LEFT TO ASSAS-SINATE...
BOING
...KORO SENSEI!
RSTL
RSTL
RSTL
RSTL

Spasmodic Funnies

Darkness

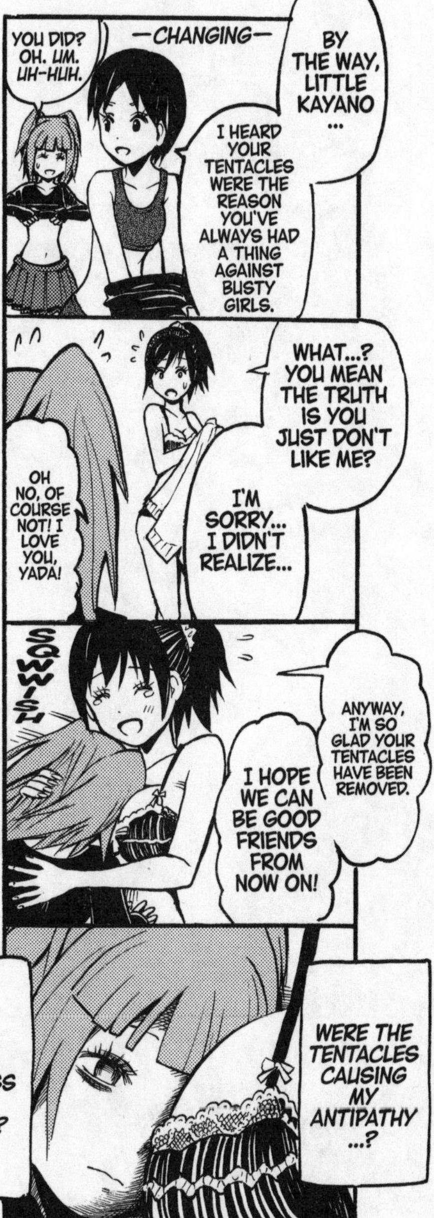

—CHANGING—
BY THE WAY, LITTLE KAYANO ...
I HEARD YOUR TENTACLES WERE THE REASON YOU'VE ALWAYS HAD A THING AGAINST BUSTY GIRLS.
YOU DID? OH. UM. UH-HUH.
WHAT...? YOU MEAN THE TRUTH IS YOU JUST DON'T LIKE ME?
I'M SORRY... I DIDN'T REALIZE...
OH NO, OF COURSE NOT! I LOVE YOU, YADA!
ANYWAY, I'M SO GLAD YOUR TENTACLES HAVE BEEN REMOVED.
I HOPE WE CAN BE GOOD FRIENDS FROM NOW ON!
SQWWISH
WERE THE TENTACLES CAUSING MY ANTIPATHY ...?
OR IS THIS A DARKNESS INSIDE OF ME...?

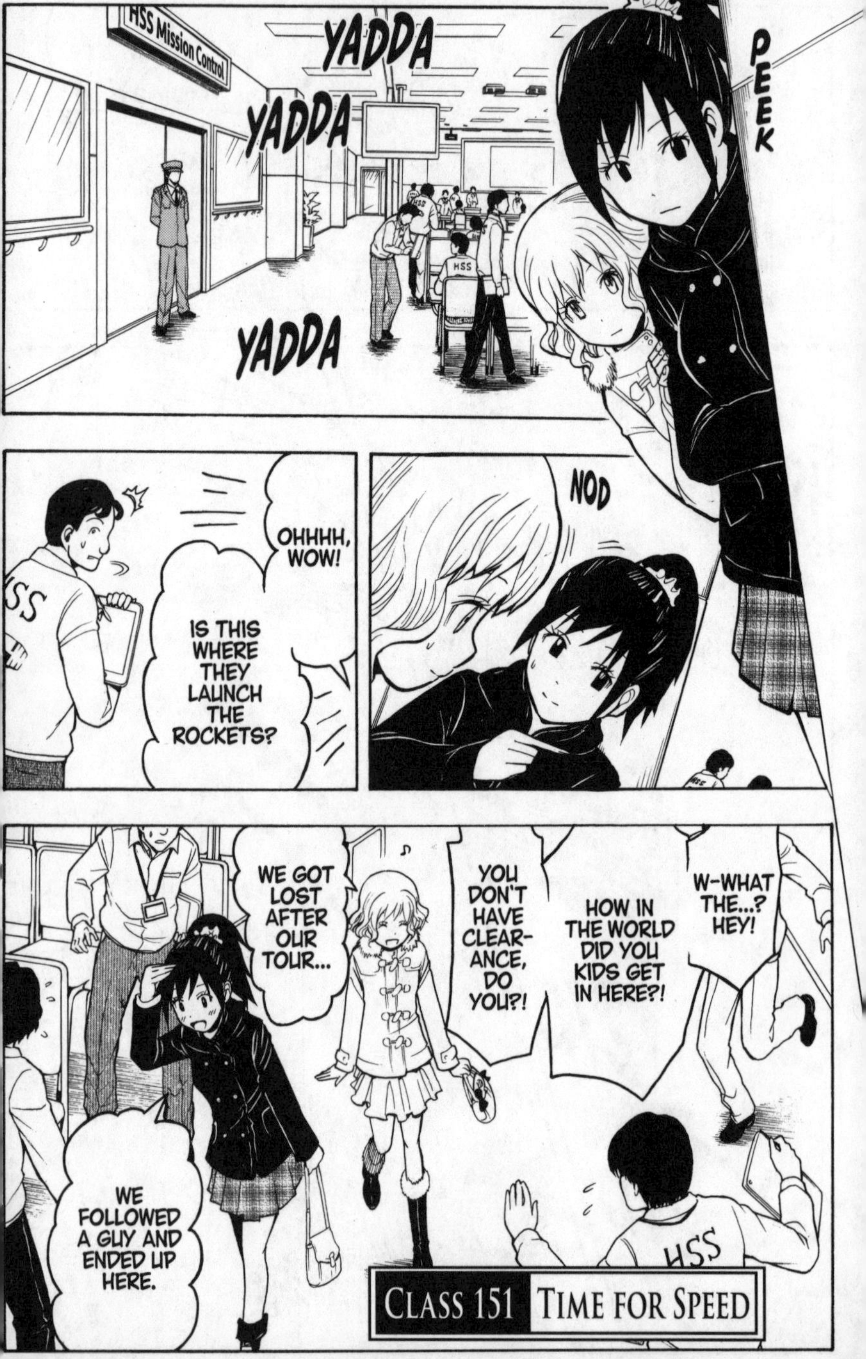
PEEK
YADDA
YADDA
YADDA
HSS Mission Control
NOD
OHHHH, WOW!
IS THIS WHERE THEY LAUNCH THE ROCKETS?
W-WHAT THE...? HEY!
HOW IN THE WORLD DID YOU KIDS GET IN HERE?!
YOU DON'T HAVE CLEARANCE, DO YOU?!
WE GOT LOST AFTER OUR TOUR...
WE FOLLOWED A GUY AND ENDED UP HERE.

CLASS 151 TIME FOR SPEED

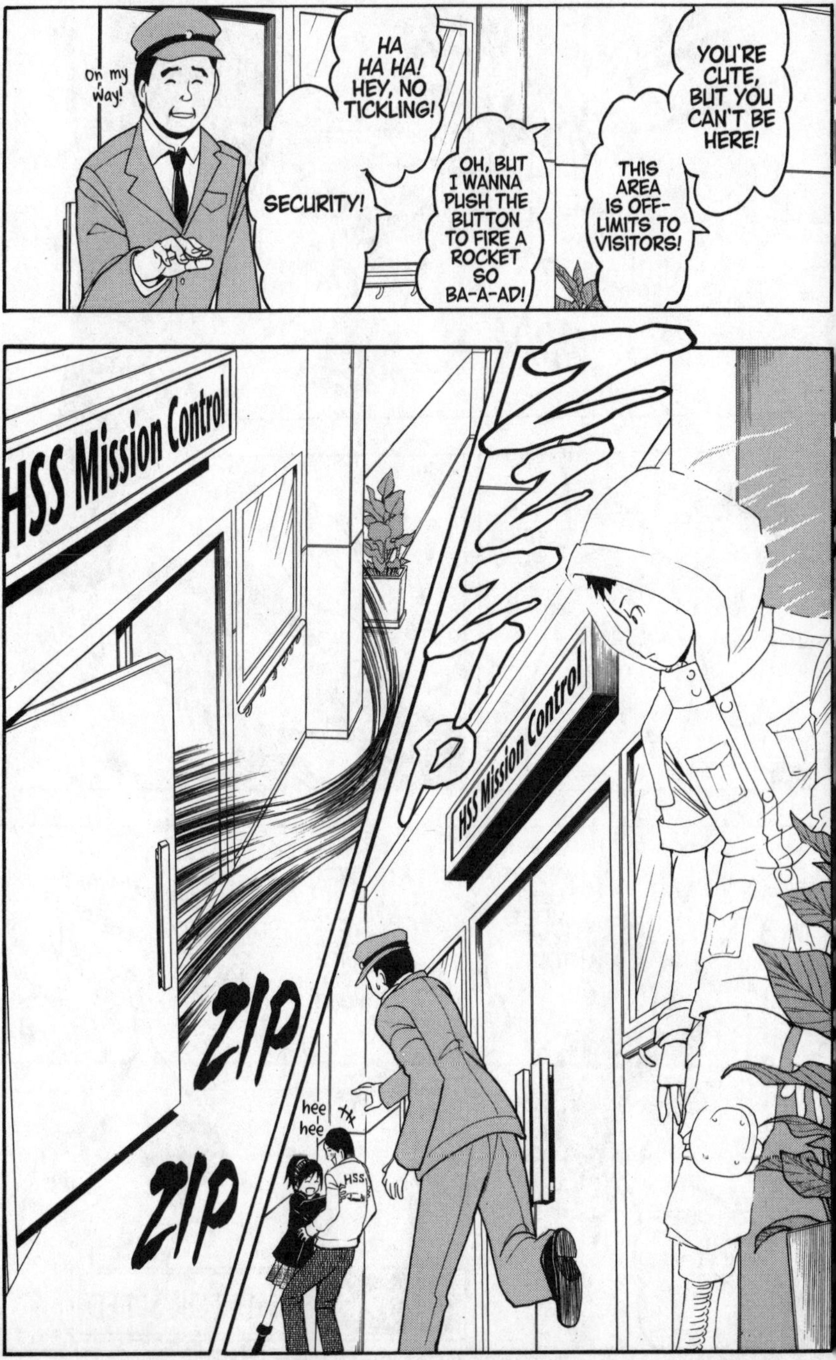
YOU'RE CUTE, BUT YOU CAN'T BE HERE!
THIS AREA IS OFF-LIMITS TO VISITORS!
HA HA HA! HEY, NO TICKLING!
OH, BUT I WANNA PUSH THE BUTTON TO FIRE A ROCKET SO BA-A-AD!
SECURITY!
On my way!
HSS Mission Control
HSS
hee hee
HSS Mission Control
ZIP
ZIP

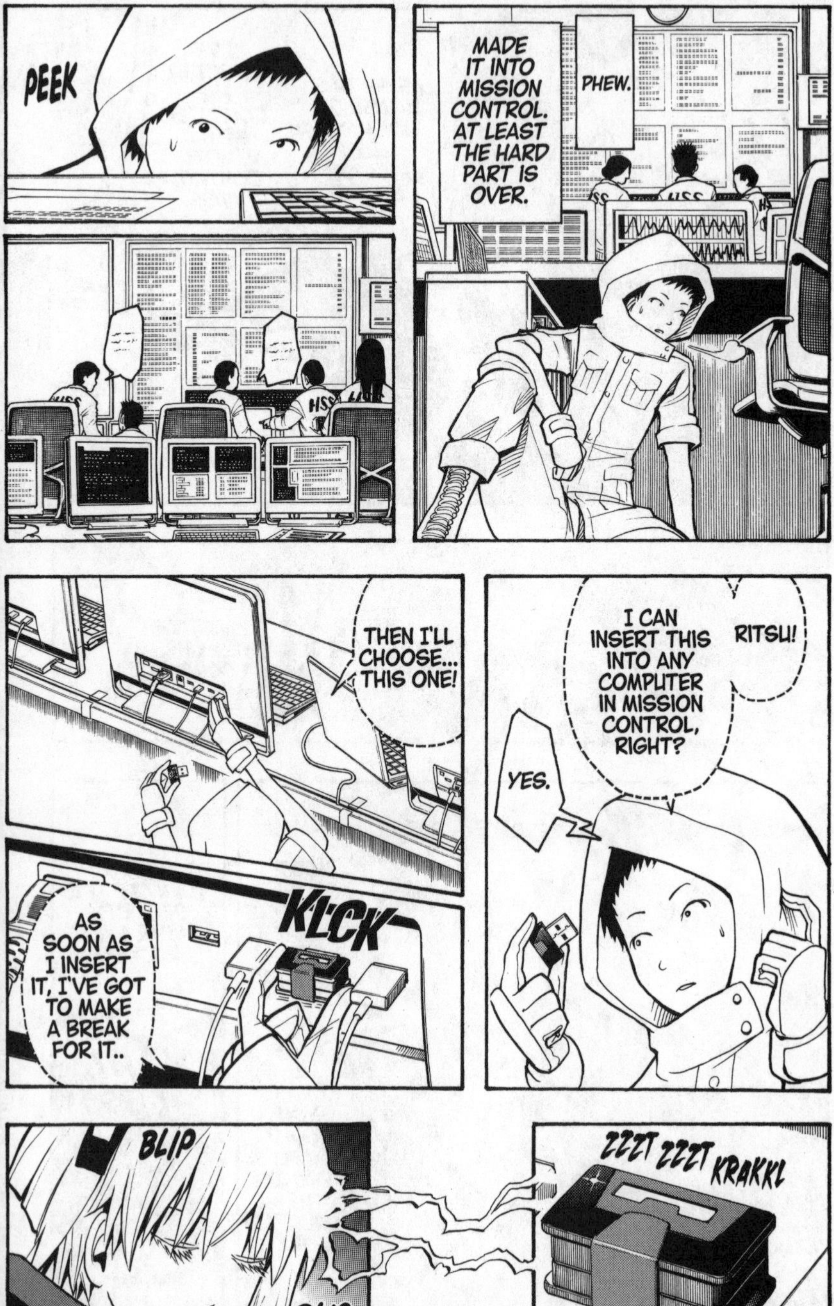
PHEW.
MADE IT INTO MISSION CONTROL. AT LEAST THE HARD PART IS OVER.
PEEK
RITSU!
I CAN INSERT THIS INTO ANY COMPUTER IN MISSION CONTROL, RIGHT?
YES.
THEN I'LL CHOOSE... THIS ONE!
KLICK
AS SOON AS I INSERT IT, I'VE GOT TO MAKE A BREAK FOR IT..
ZZZT ZZZT KRAKKL
BLIP
BLIP

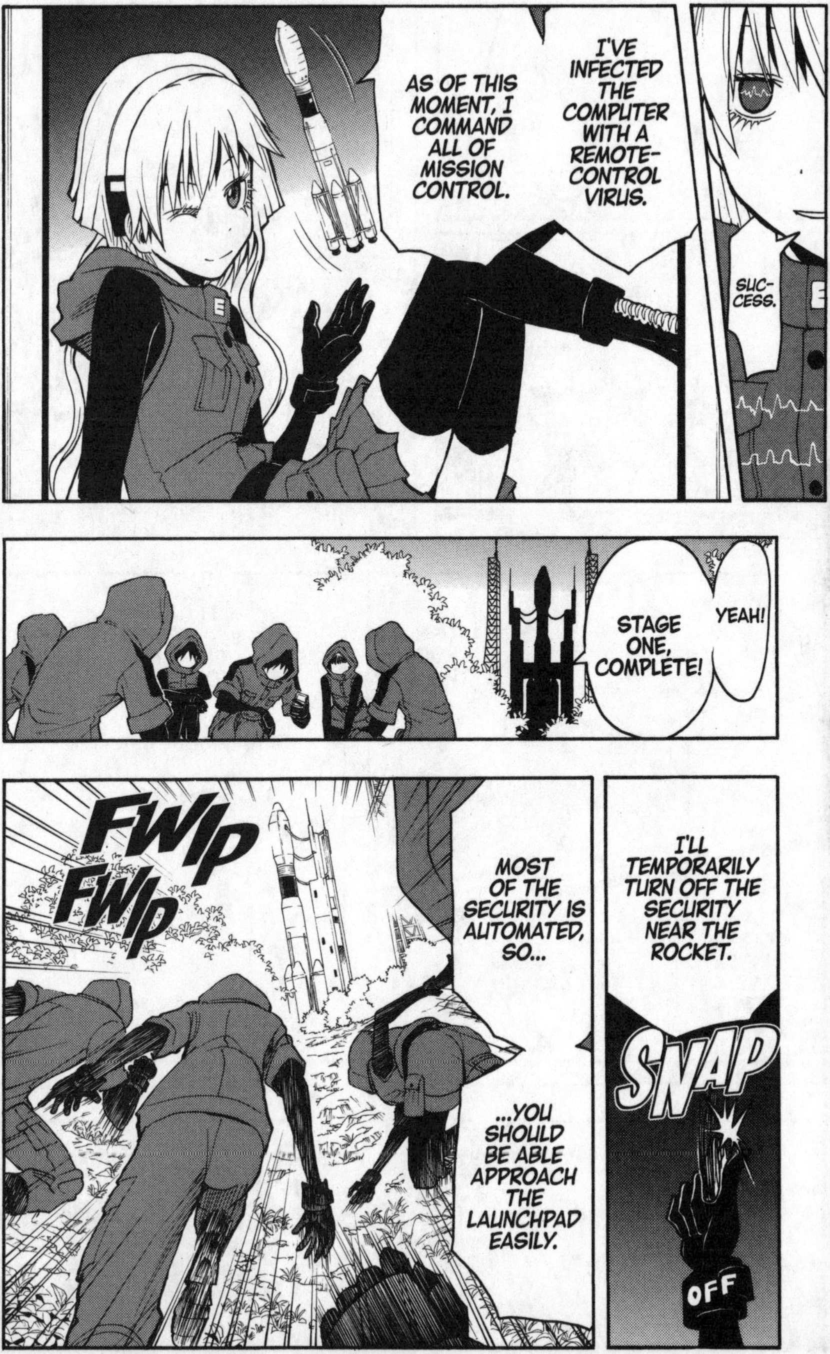
SUC-CESS.
I'VE INFECTED THE COMPUTER WITH A REMOTE-CONTROL VIRUS.
AS OF THIS MOMENT, I COMMAND ALL OF MISSION CONTROL.
YEAH!
STAGE ONE, COMPLETE!
I'LL TEMPORARILY TURN OFF THE SECURITY NEAR THE ROCKET.
SNAP
OFF
MOST OF THE SECURITY IS AUTOMATED, SO...
...YOU SHOULD BE ABLE APPROACH THE LAUNCHPAD EASILY.
FWIP FWIP

IT'S... HUGE ...!

THE BASE OF THE ROCKET IS SURROUNDED BY PERSONNEL ...

WE'LL HAVE TO HIDE TO GET PAST THEM...

YEAH.

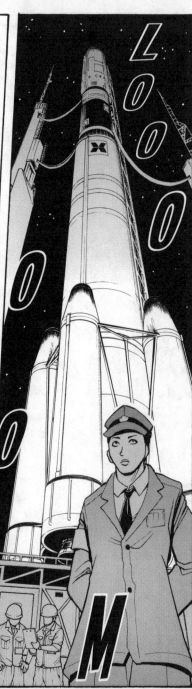

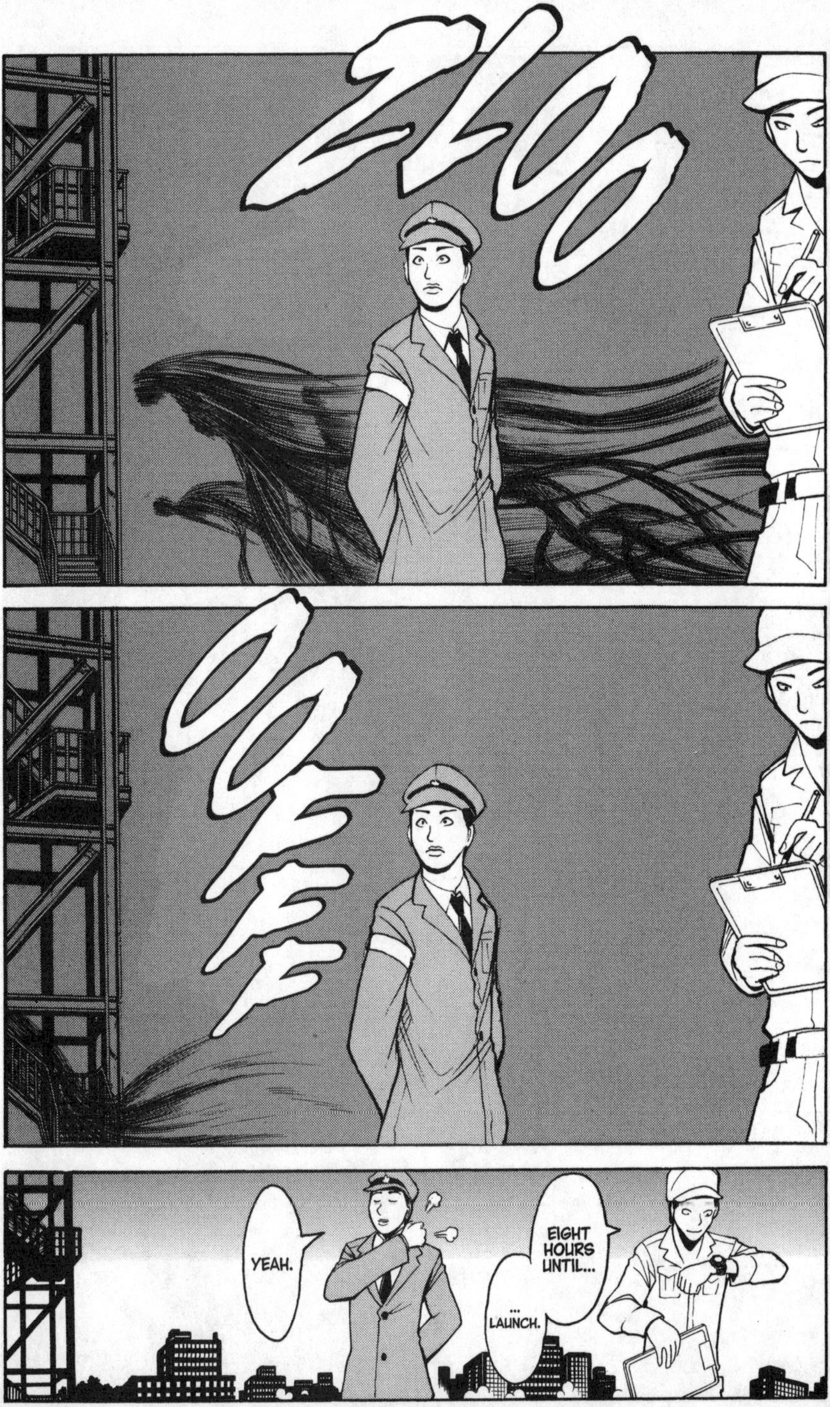
EIGHT HOURS UNTIL...
... LAUNCH.
YEAH.

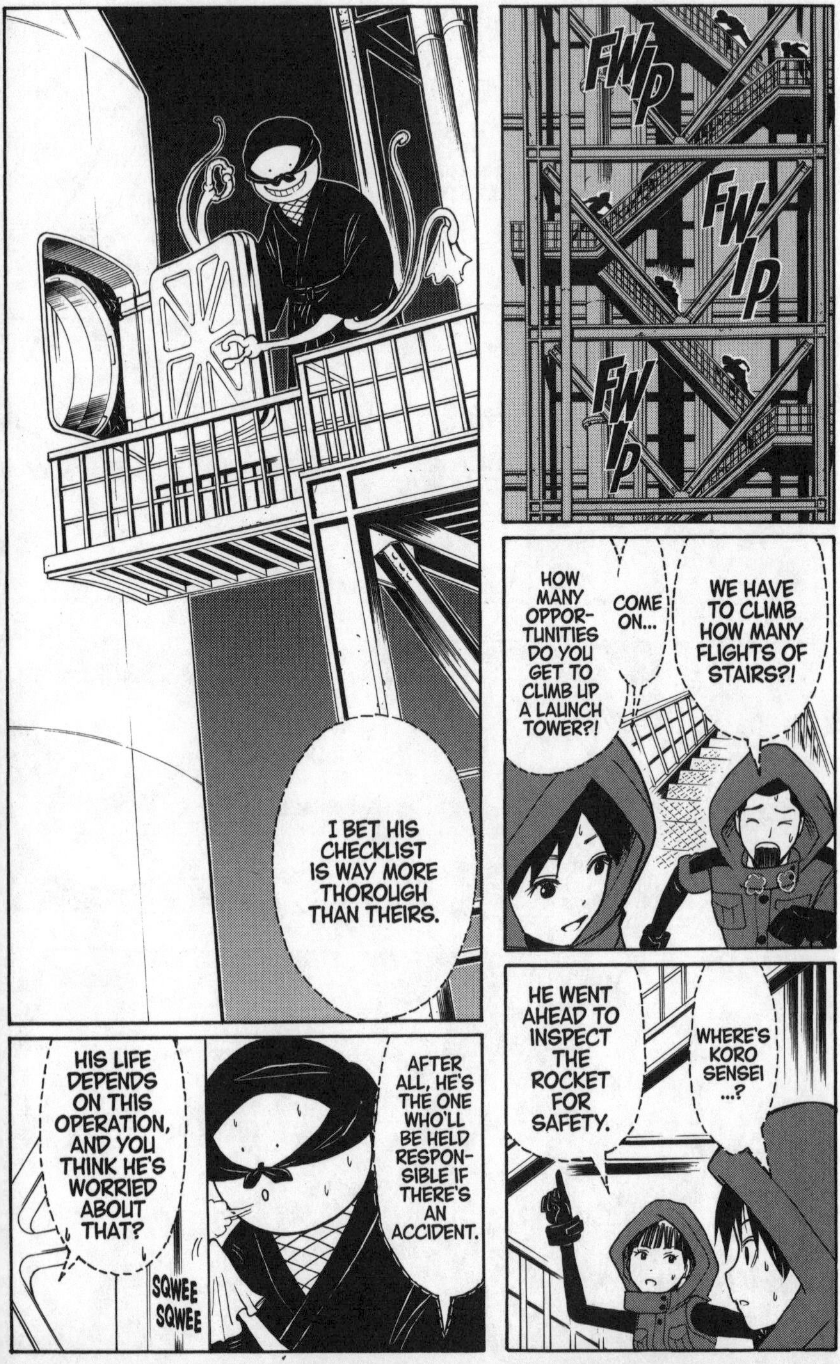
FWIP
FWIP
FWIP
WE HAVE TO CLIMB HOW MANY FLIGHTS OF STAIRS?!
COME ON...
HOW MANY OPPORTUNITIES DO YOU GET TO CLIMB UP A LAUNCH TOWER?!
WHERE'S KORO SENSEI ...?
HE WENT AHEAD TO INSPECT THE ROCKET FOR SAFETY.
I BET HIS CHECKLIST IS WAY MORE THOROUGH THAN THEIRS.
AFTER ALL, HE'S THE ONE WHO'LL BE HELD RESPONSIBLE IF THERE'S AN ACCIDENT.
SQWEE SQWEE
HIS LIFE DEPENDS ON THIS OPERATION, AND YOU THINK HE'S WORRIED ABOUT THAT?

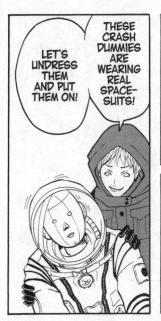

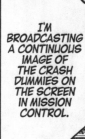

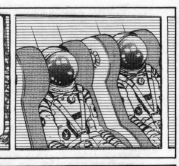

I'M BROADCASTING A CONTINUOUS IMAGE OF THE CRASH DUMMIES ON THE SCREEN IN MISSION CONTROL.
YA NK
NOW'S THE TIME TO REPLACE THEM WITH PEOPLE.
THESE CRASH DUMMIES ARE WEARING REAL SPACE-SUITS!
LET'S UNDRESS THEM AND PUT THEM ON!
NOW THEN...
ONLY TWO STUDENTS MAY RIDE THIS ROCKET INTO SPACE.
ACCORDING TO THE TESTS WE'VE ADMINISTERED, EVERY ONE OF YOU IS CAPABLE...
HANDS UP IF YOU WANT TO GO!
SH FFFF
Boys...

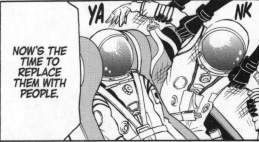

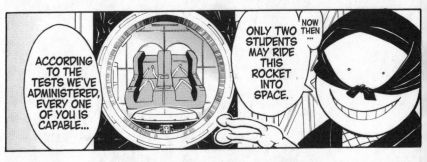

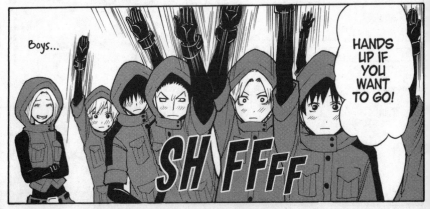

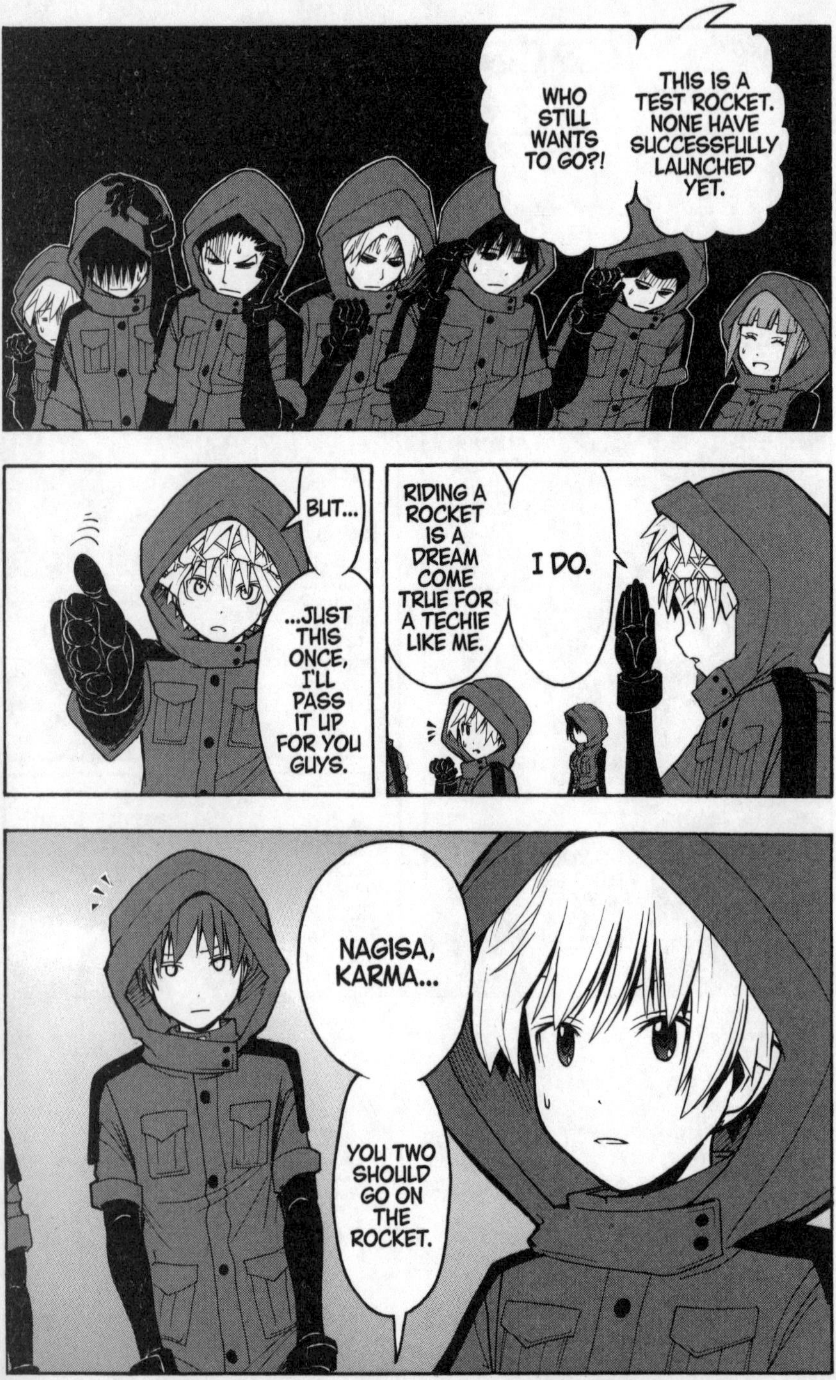
THIS IS A TEST ROCKET. NONE HAVE SUCCESSFULLY LAUNCHED YET.
WHO STILL WANTS TO GO?!
I DO.
RIDING A ROCKET IS A DREAM COME TRUE FOR A TECHIE LIKE ME.
BUT...
...JUST THIS ONCE, I'LL PASS IT UP FOR YOU GUYS.
NAGISA, KARMA...
YOU TWO SHOULD GO ON THE ROCKET.

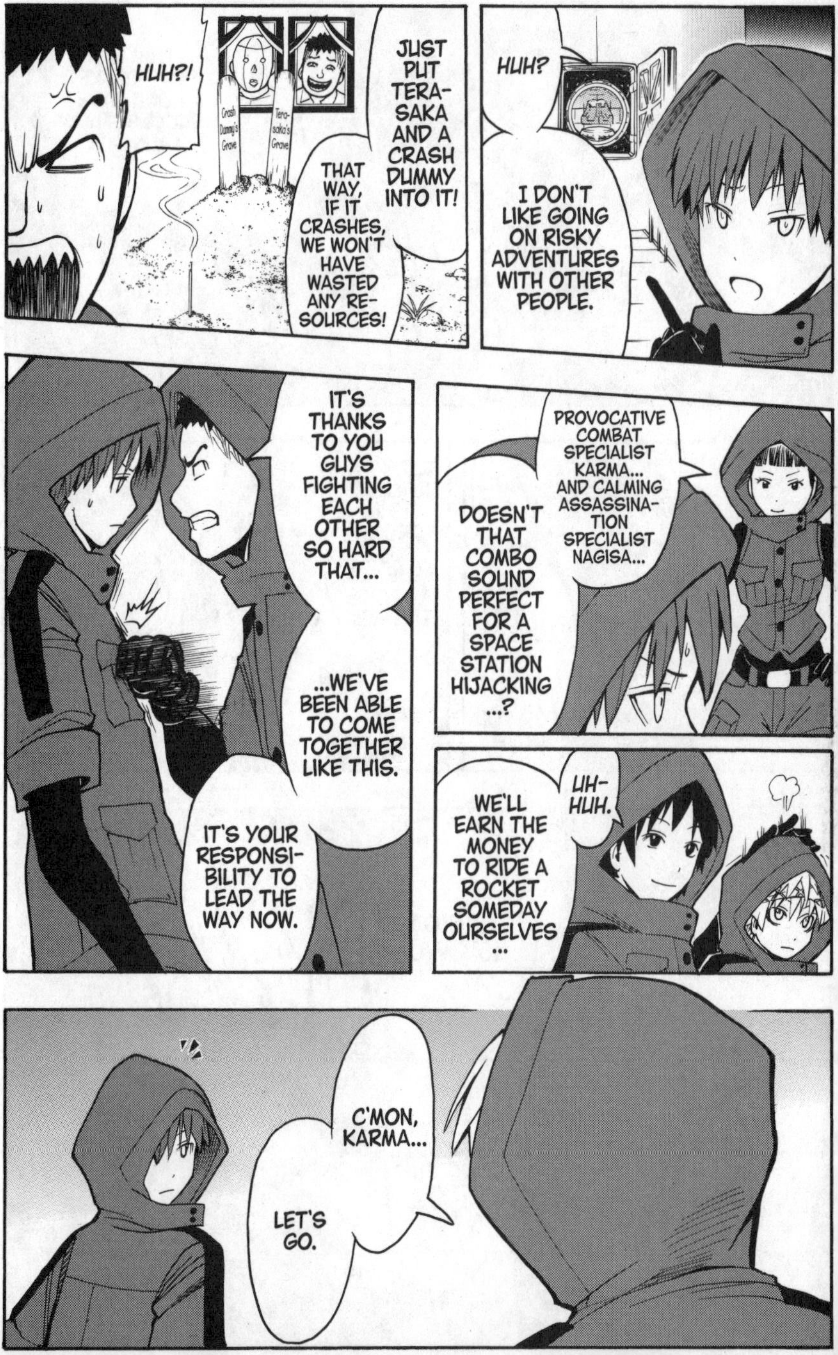
HUH?
I DON'T LIKE GOING ON RISKY ADVENTURES WITH OTHER PEOPLE.
JUST PUT TERA-SAKA AND A CRASH DUMMY INTO IT!
THAT WAY, IF IT CRASHES, WE WON'T HAVE WASTED ANY RE-SOURCES!
Tera-saka's Grave
Crash Dummy's Grave
HUH?!
PROVOCATIVE COMBAT SPECIALIST KARMA... AND CALMING ASSASSINATION SPECIALIST NAGISA...
DOESN'T THAT COMBO SOUND PERFECT FOR A SPACE STATION HIJACKING ...?
UH-HUH.
WE'LL EARN THE MONEY TO RIDE A ROCKET SOMEDAY OURSELVES ...
IT'S THANKS TO YOU GUYS FIGHTING EACH OTHER SO HARD THAT...
...WE'VE BEEN ABLE TO COME TOGETHER LIKE THIS.
IT'S YOUR RESPONSIBILITY TO LEAD THE WAY NOW.
C'MON, KARMA...
LET'S GO.

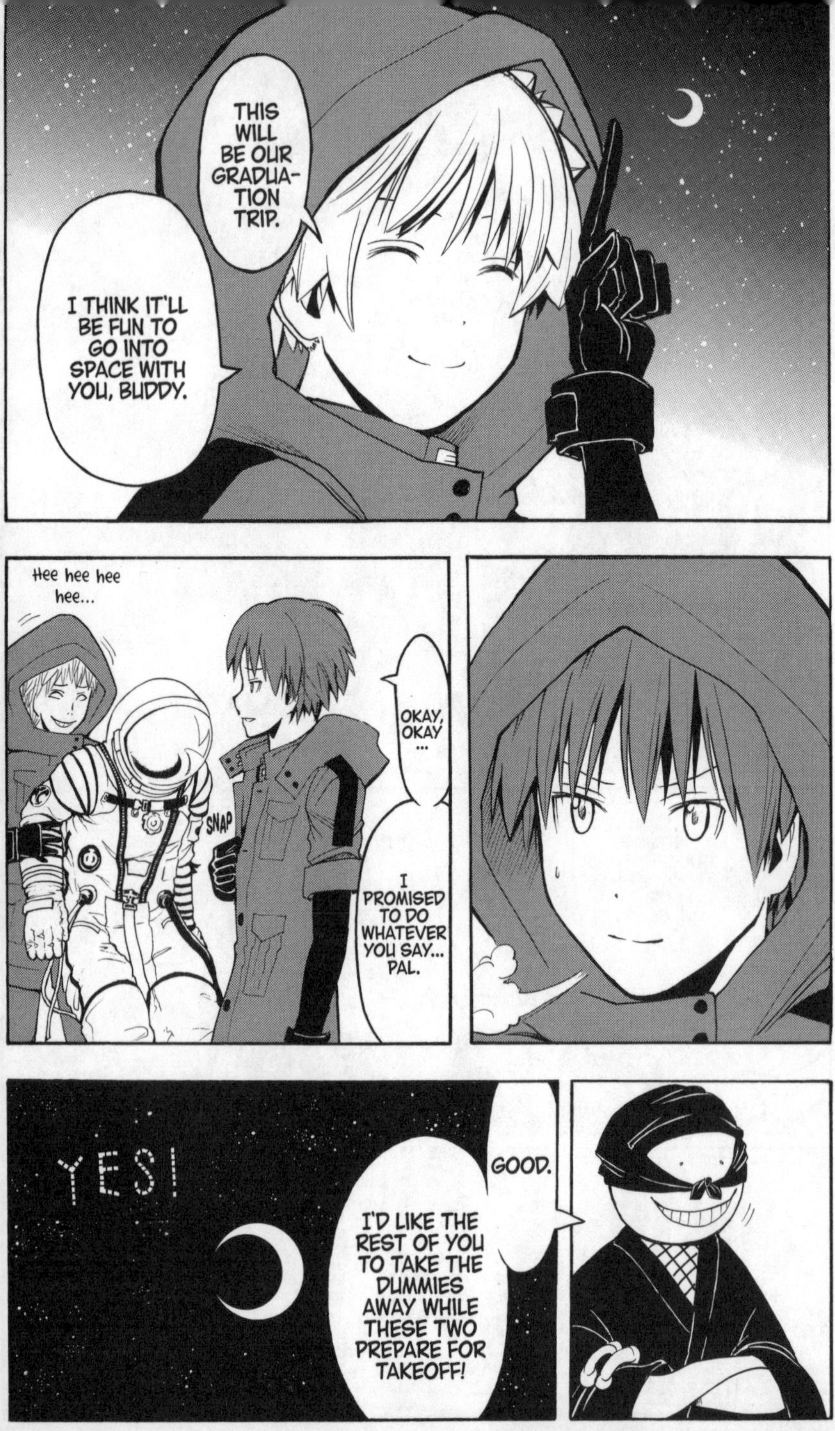
THIS WILL BE OUR GRADUATION TRIP.
I THINK IT'LL BE FUN TO GO INTO SPACE WITH YOU, BUDDY.
OKAY, OKAY ...
I PROMISED TO DO WHATEVER YOU SAY... PAL.
SNAP
Hee hee hee hee...
GOOD.
I'D LIKE THE REST OF YOU TO TAKE THE DUMMIES AWAY WHILE THESE TWO PREPARE FOR TAKEOFF!
YES!

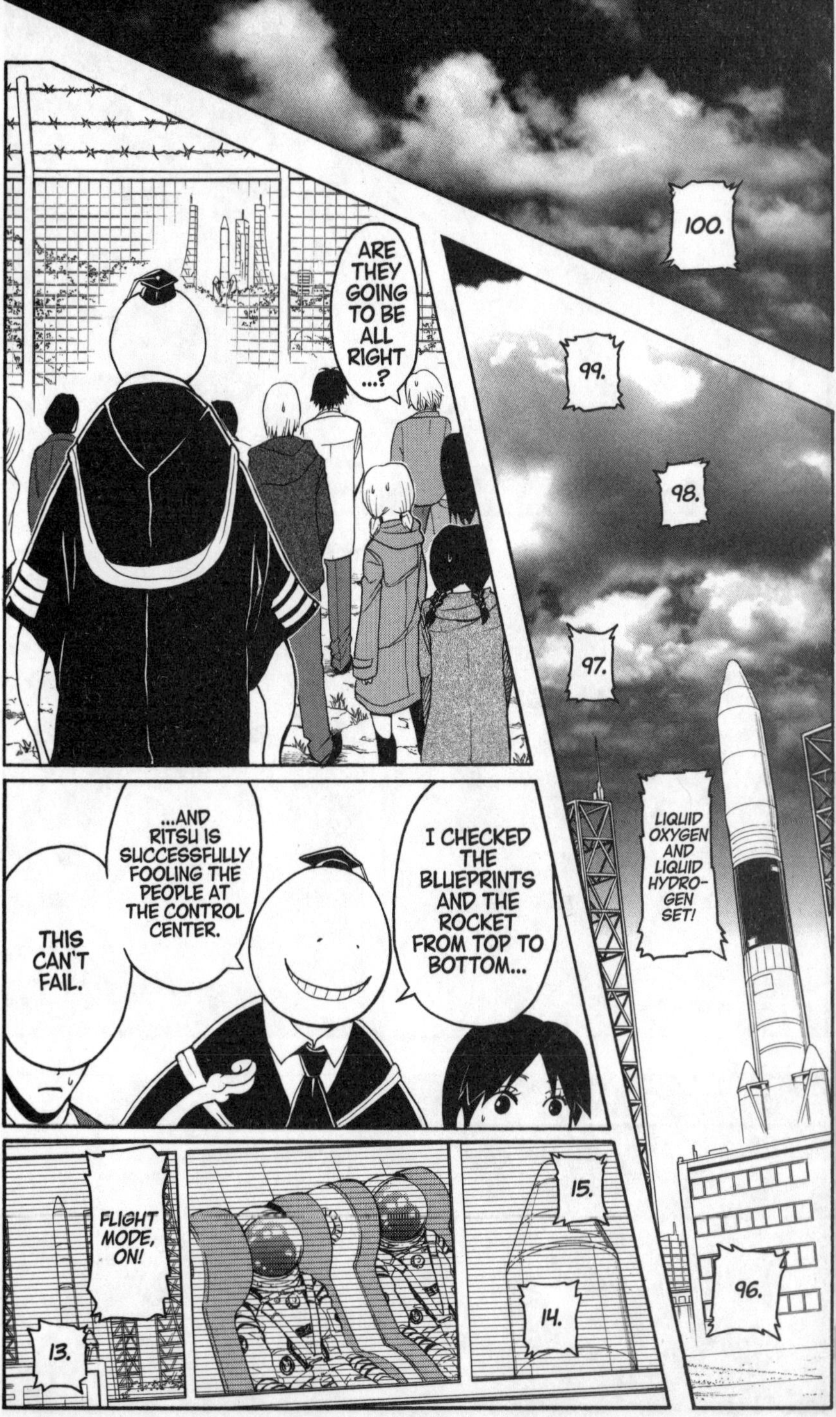
100.
99.
98.
97.
LIQUID OXYGEN AND LIQUID HYDRO-GEN SET!
96.
ARE THEY GOING TO BE ALL RIGHT ...?
I CHECKED THE BLUEPRINTS AND THE ROCKET FROM TOP TO BOTTOM...
...AND RITSU IS SUCCESSFULLY FOOLING THE PEOPLE AT THE CONTROL CENTER.
THIS CAN'T FAIL.
15.
14.
FLIGHT MODE, ON!
13.

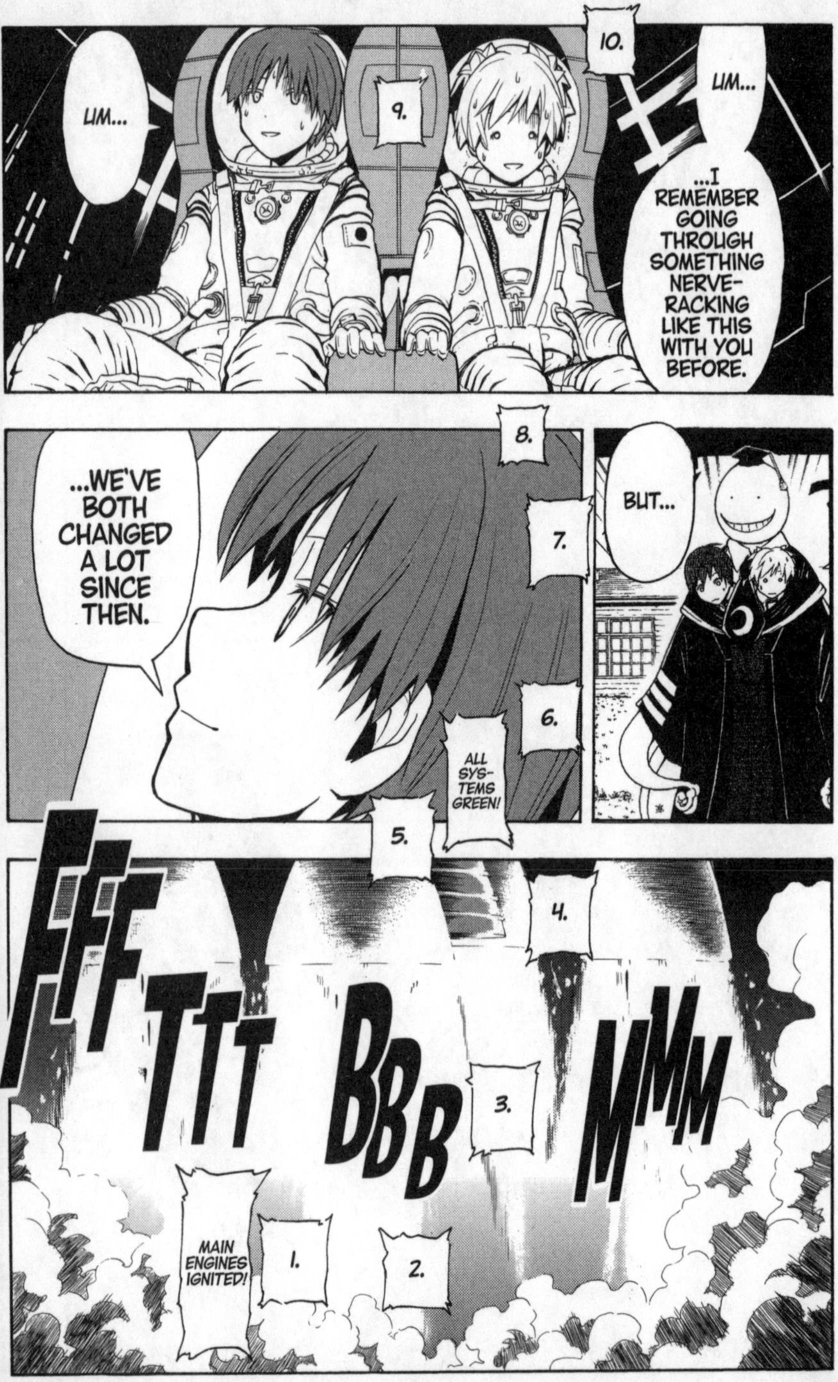
10.
UM...
...I REMEMBER GOING THROUGH SOMETHING NERVE-RACKING LIKE THIS WITH YOU BEFORE.
9.
UM...
BUT...
8.
7.
...WE'VE BOTH CHANGED A LOT SINCE THEN.
6.
ALL SYS-TEMS GREEN!
5.
4.
FFF TTT BBB MMM
3.
2.
1.
MAIN ENGINES IGNITED!

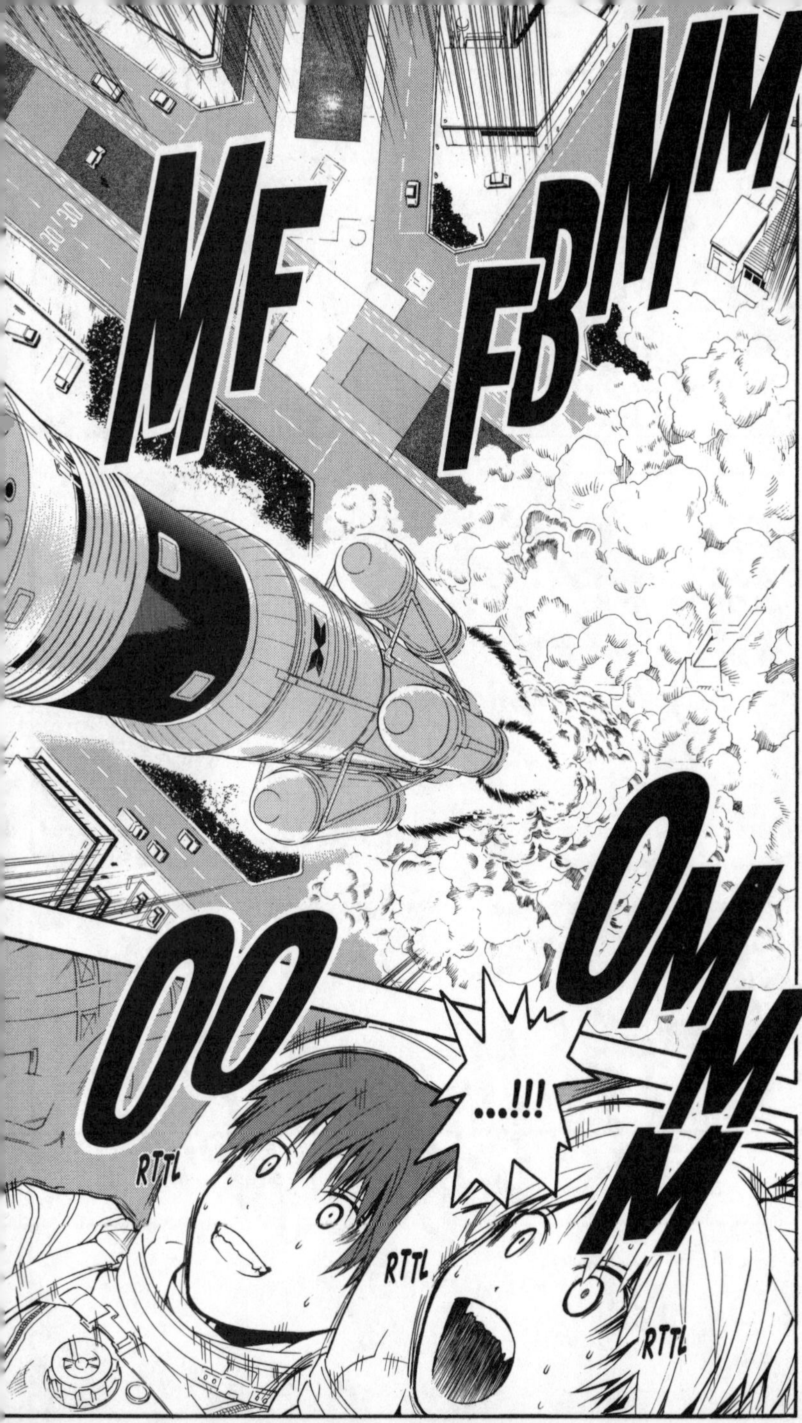
MFFBMMM
OOOMMM
...!!!
RTTL
RTTL
RTTL

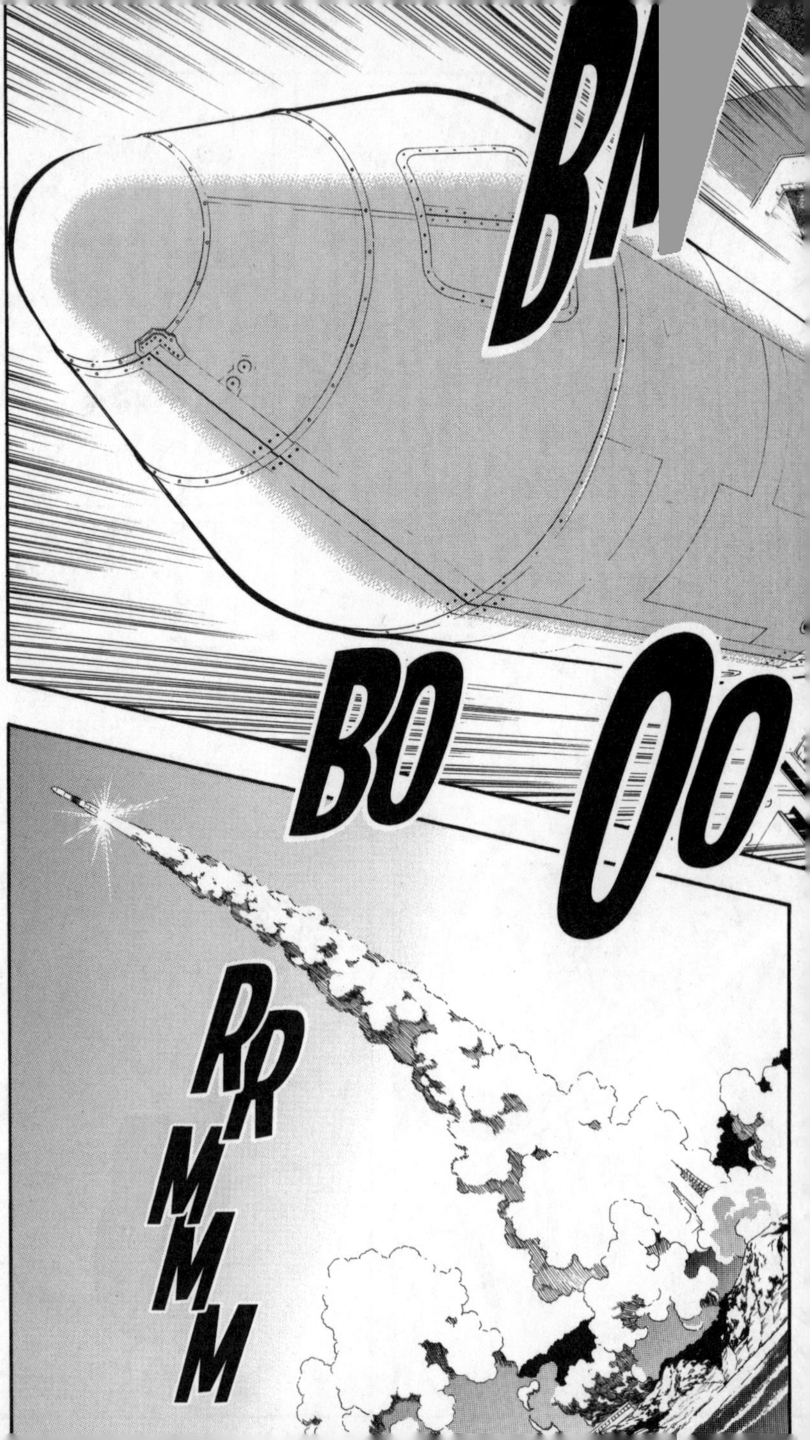
BOOO
RRMMMM

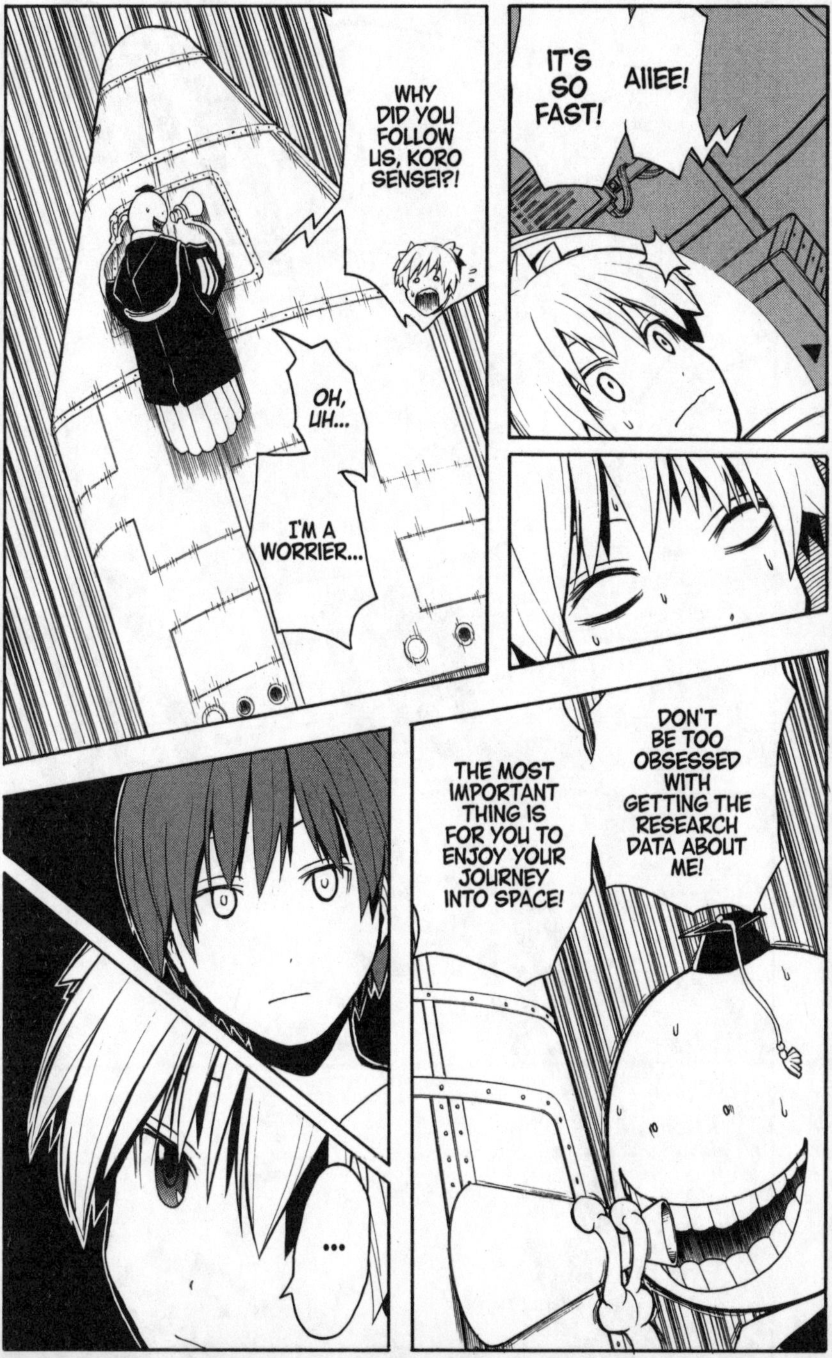
AIIEE!
IT'S SO FAST!
WHY DID YOU FOLLOW US, KORO SENSEI?!
OH, UH...
I'M A WORRIER...
DON'T BE TOO OBSESSED WITH GETTING THE RESEARCH DATA ABOUT ME!
THE MOST IMPORTANT THING IS FOR YOU TO ENJOY YOUR JOURNEY INTO SPACE!
...

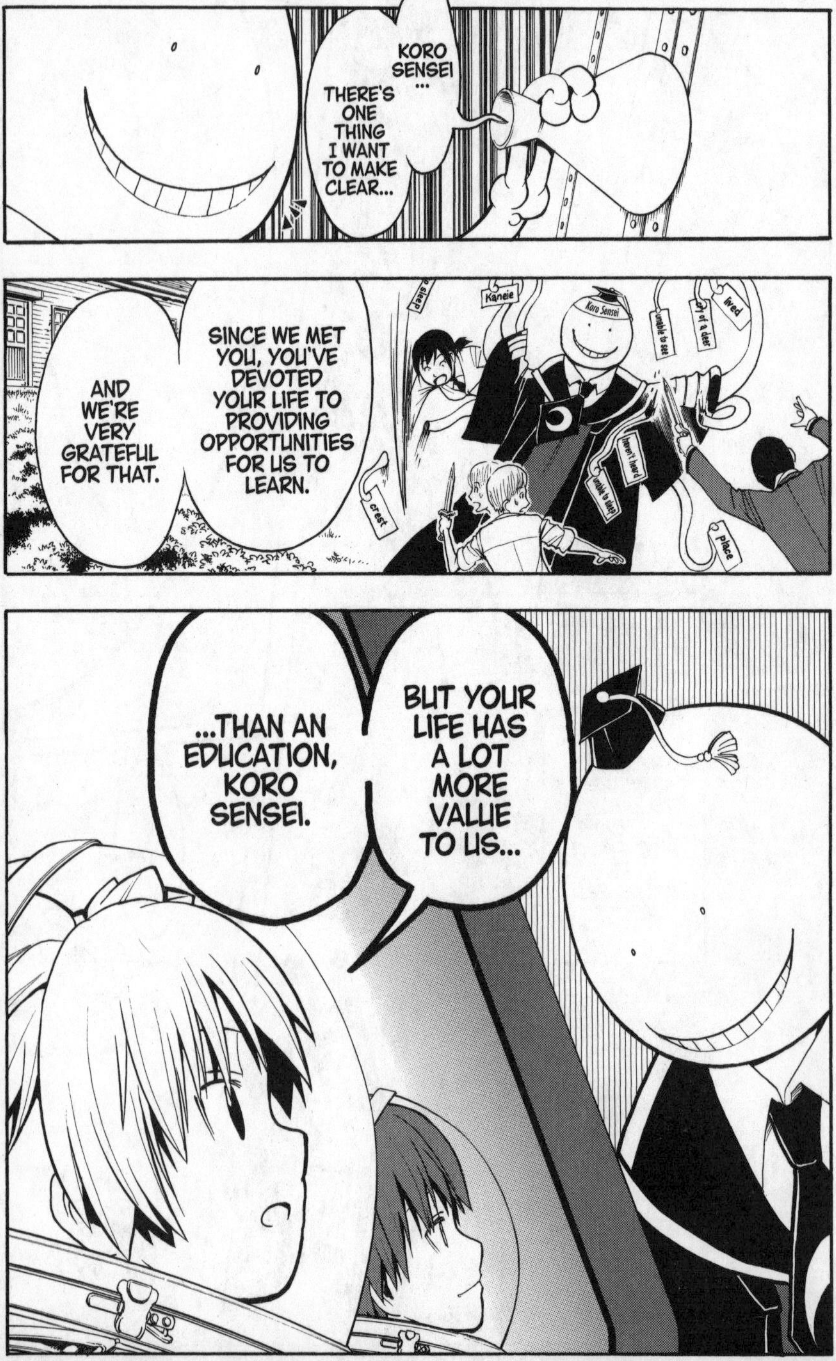
KORO SENSEI ... THERE'S ONE THING I WANT TO MAKE CLEAR...
SINCE WE MET YOU, YOU'VE DEVOTED YOUR LIFE TO PROVIDING OPPORTUNITIES FOR US TO LEARN.
AND WE'RE VERY GRATEFUL FOR THAT.
Koro Sensei
Kaneie
unable to see
haven't heard
unable to sleep
crest
place
BUT YOUR LIFE HAS A LOT MORE VALUE TO US...
...THAN AN EDUCATION, KORO SENSEI.

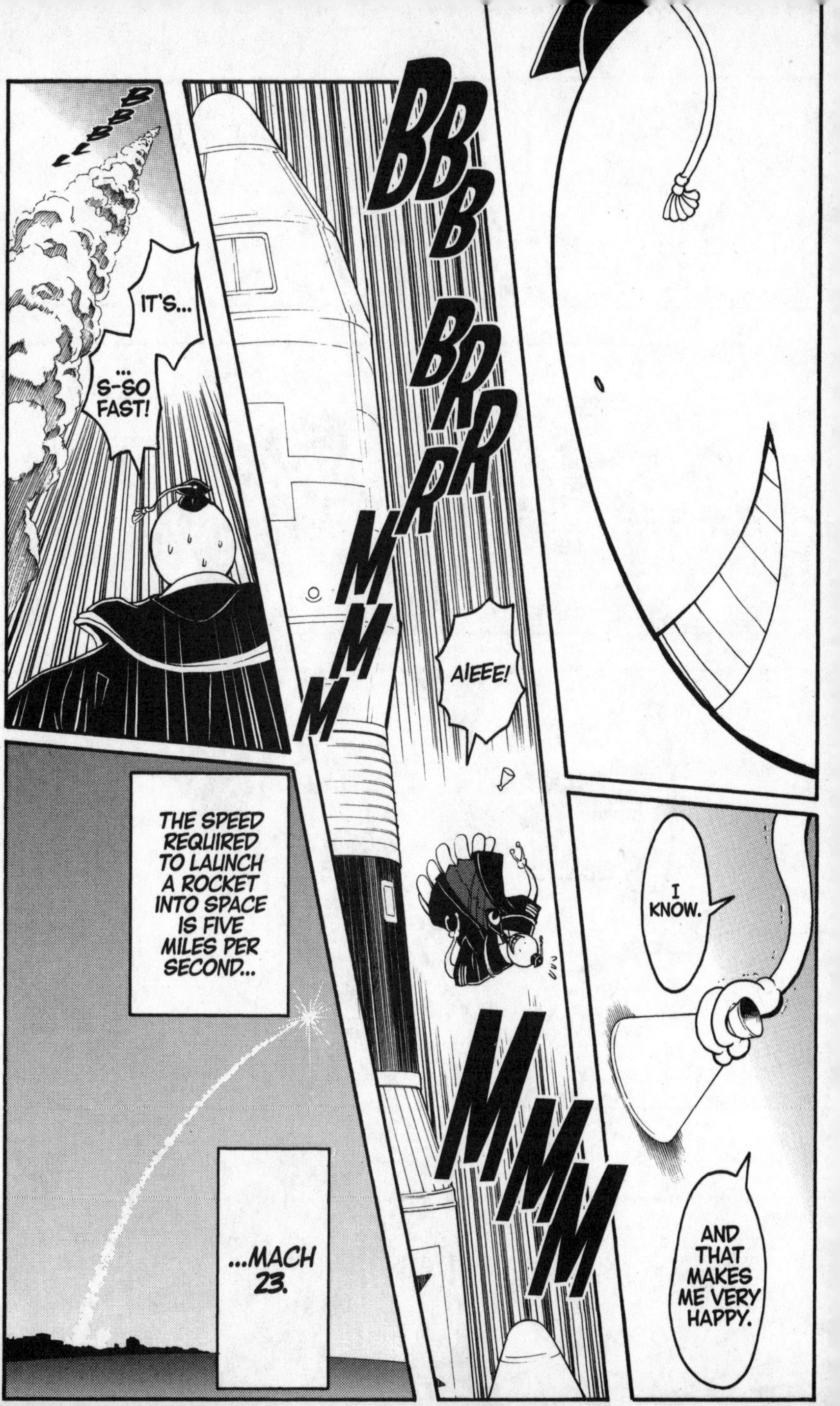
I KNOW.
AND THAT MAKES ME VERY HAPPY.
BBBBRRRRMMMMMMM
AIEEE!
BBBL
IT'S...
...S-SO FAST!
THE SPEED REQUIRED TO LAUNCH A ROCKET INTO SPACE IS FIVE MILES PER SECOND...
...MACH 23.

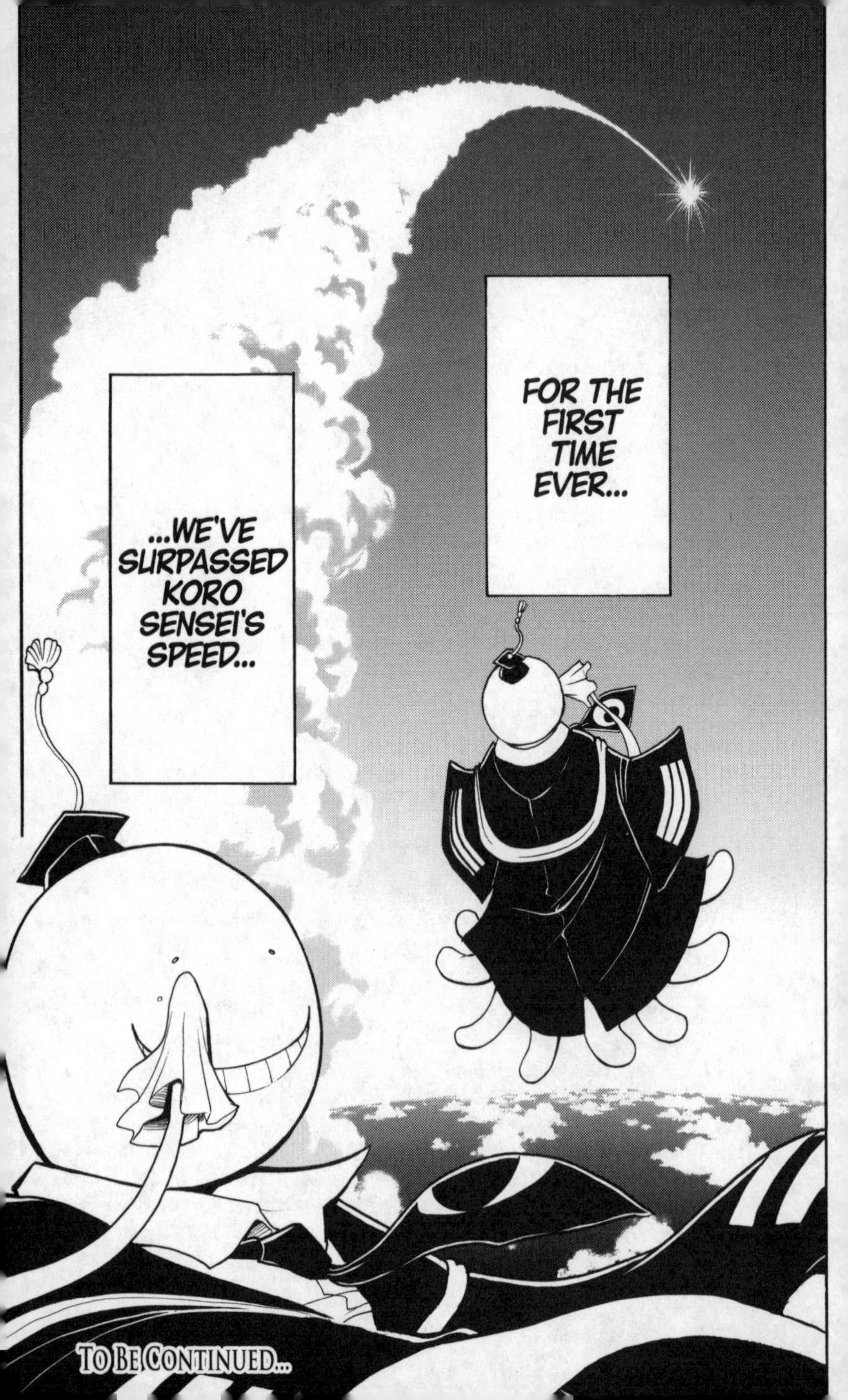
FOR THE FIRST TIME EVER...
...WE'VE SURPASSED KORO SENSEI'S SPEED...
TO BE CONTINUED...

I already have a weekly schedule for what I have to do from vol. 15 on through the final chapter, so my current work is just to create storyboards based on the list of plot points I've already written up for each week.

But that doesn't mean my work isn't cut out for me...because I continue to get ideas I want to add or notice that I've forgotten to include something essential in a chapter... So my work can still be a headache.

Sometimes I'll cut minor side stories because I don't have enough pages, and other times I'll come up with a new story I can use to wrap up the chapter in an even better way than I had originally planned.

I don't know what the best method is for working on a weekly series, but this is one way to do it.

—Yusei Matsui

Yusei Matsui was born on the last day of January in Saitama Prefecture, Japan. He has been drawing manga since elementary school. Some of his favorite manga series are *Bobobo-bo Bo-bobo*, *JoJo's Bizarre Adventure* and *Ultimate Muscle*. Matsui learned his trade working as an assistant to manga artist Yoshio Sawai, creator of *Bobobo-bo Bo-bobo*. In 2005, Matsui debuted his original manga *Neuro: Supernatural Detective* in *Weekly Shonen Jump*. In 2007, *Neuro* was adapted into an anime. In 2012, *Assassination Classroom* began serialization in *Weekly Shonen Jump*.

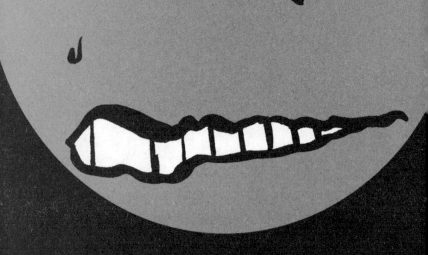

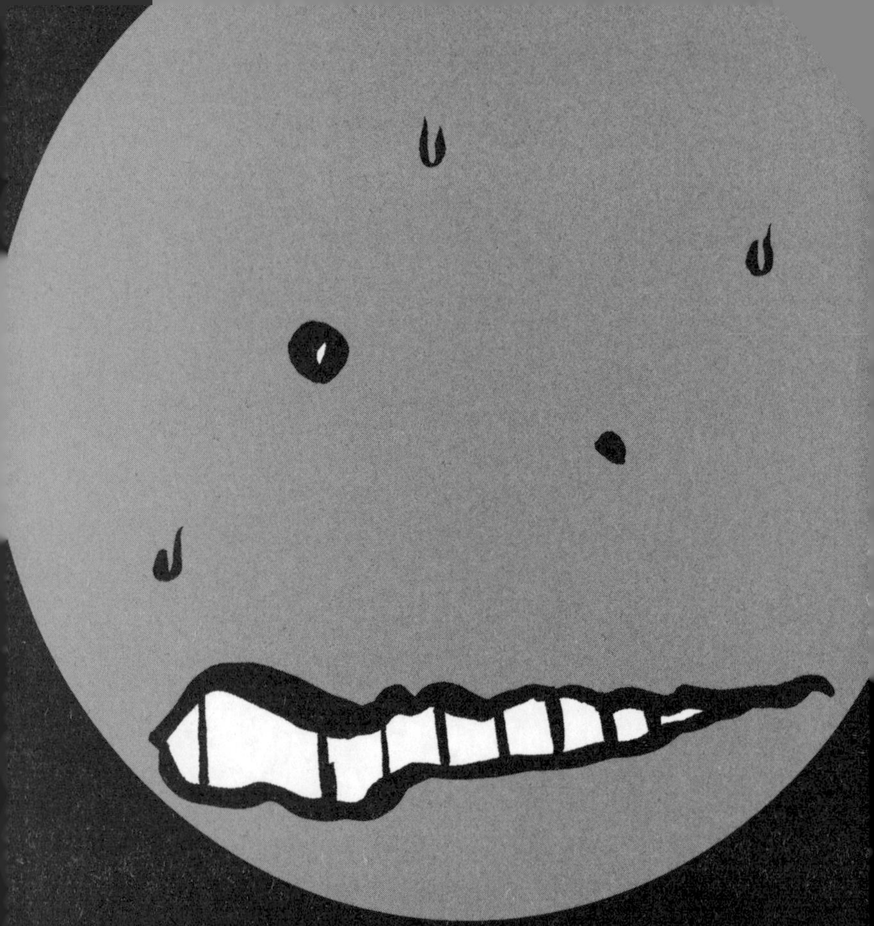

This muddy yellow color appears when Koro Sensei doesn't know what to do. Koro Sensei went into a frenzy and blurted out that this new color is called "えんじ Yellow!!"...

ASSASSINATION CLASSROOM

YUSEI MATSUI

TIME FOR A BREAKUP

A MOMENT OF TENTACLE ZEN

Are you spending too many tentacles of interest on the credit cards you're using to pay for credit-card loans or cash advances? Also...did you know that even if you've finished paying back your debt, you may still be eligible to get back those excess tentacles? Of course, there are limits to how many tentacles you can claim, so...call our offices now for a free legal consultation!

– The Offices of Koro, Attorney at Law

A S S A S S I N A T I O N
CLASSROOM

Volume 17
SHONEN JUMP Manga Edition

Story and Art by YUSEI MATSUI

Translation/Tetsuichiro Miyaki
English Adaptation/Bryant Turnage
Touch-up Art & Lettering/Stephen Dutro
Cover & Interior Design/Sam Elzway
Editor/Annette Roman

ANSATSU KYOSHITSU © 2012 by Yusei Matsui
All rights reserved.
First published in Japan in 2012 by SHUEISHA Inc., Tokyo.
English translation rights arranged by SHUEISHA Inc.

The stories, characters and incidents mentioned in this publication are entirely fictional.

Printed in the U.S.A.

Published by VIZ Media, LLC
P.O. Box 77010
San Francisco, CA 94107

10 9 8 7 6 5
First printing, August 2017
Fifth printing, May 2022

VIZ MEDIA
viz.com

SHONEN JUMP

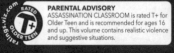

PARENTAL ADVISORY
ASSASSINATION CLASSROOM is rated T+ for Older Teen and is recommended for ages 16 and up. This volume contains realistic violence and suggestive situations.
RATED T+

Syllabus for Assassination Classroom, Vol. 18

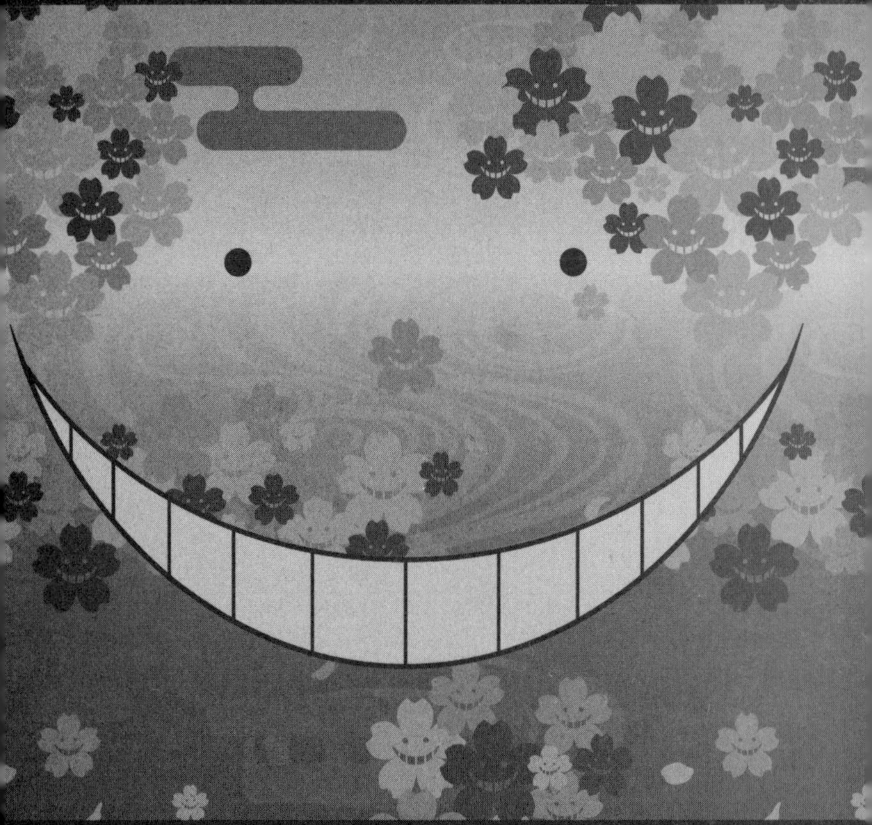

Nagisa and Karma travel to the International Space Station in hopes of learning the secret to saving Koro Sensei's life. Meanwhile, Yanagisawa and the upstart Grim Reaper II train ever harder to assassinate him. Then, when academic setbacks lower the spirits of his students, Koro Sensei comes up with an ingenious—or perhaps idiotic—way to cheer them up. Next, Valentine's Day arrives! Will any of the 3-E students or teachers find true love? And will the meddling and teasing of the others help or hinder Cupid's arrow in finding its target...?

Available Now!

THE ACTION-PACKED SUPERHERO COMEDY ABOUT ONE MAN'S AMBITION TO BE A HERO FOR FUN!

ONE-PUNCH MAN

STORY BY
ONE | ART BY
YUSUKE MURATA

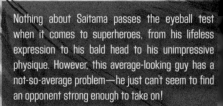

Nothing about Saitama passes the eyeball test when it comes to superheroes, from his lifeless expression to his bald head to his unimpressive physique. However, this average-looking guy has a not-so-average problem—he just can't seem to find an opponent strong enough to take on!

Can he finally find an opponent who can go toe-to-toe with him and give his life some meaning? Or is he doomed to a life of superpowered boredom?

RATED
TEEN
ratings.viz.com

SHONEN JUMP

viz media
www.viz.com

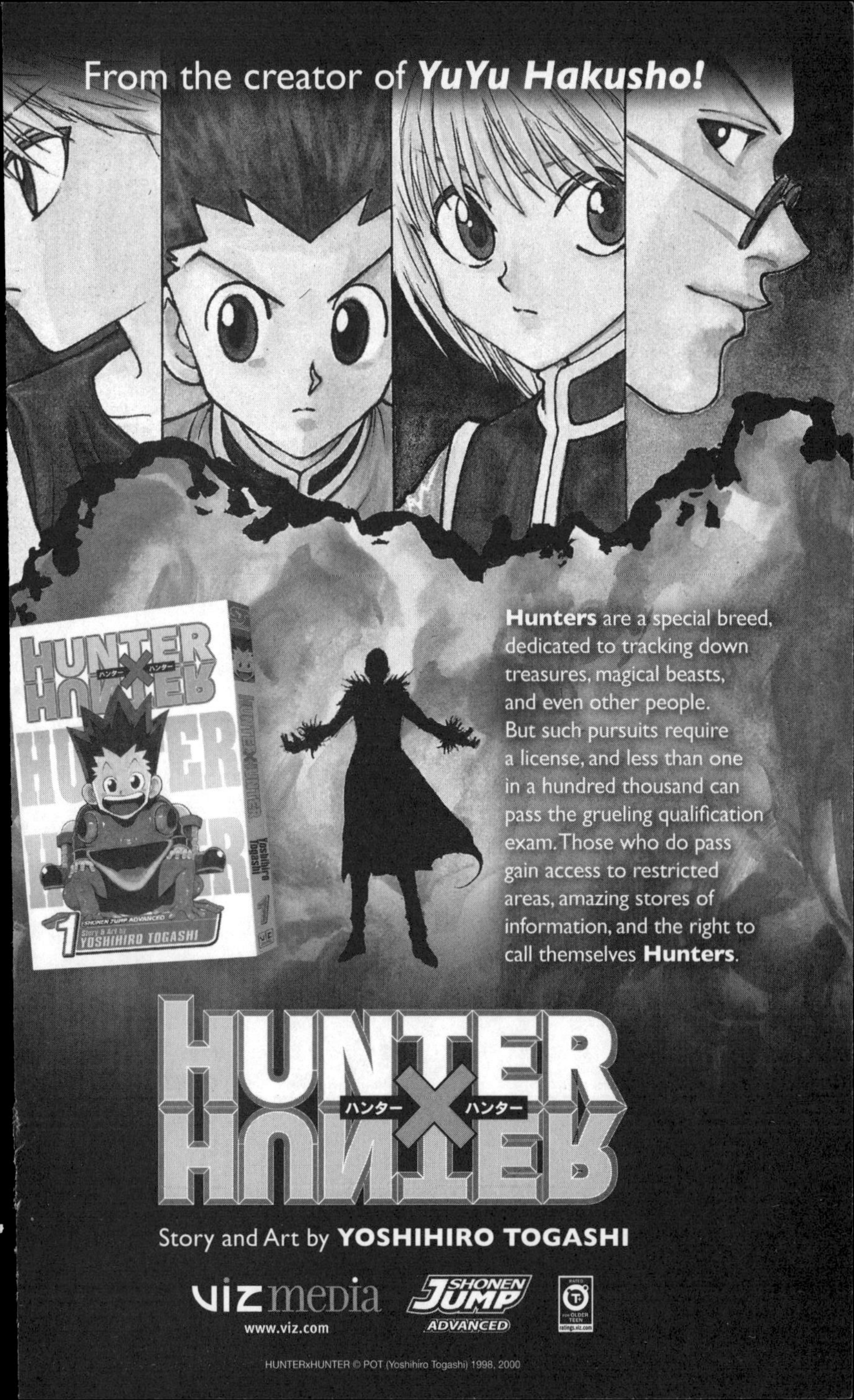
From the creator of YuYu Hakusho!
HUNTER × HUNTER
ハンター ハンター
SHONEN JUMP ADVANCED
1
Story & Art by YOSHIHIRO TOGASHI
Hunters are a special breed, dedicated to tracking down treasures, magical beasts, and even other people. But such pursuits require a license, and less than one in a hundred thousand can pass the grueling qualification exam. Those who do pass gain access to restricted areas, amazing stores of information, and the right to call themselves Hunters.
HUNTER × HUNTER
ハンター ハンター
Story and Art by YOSHIHIRO TOGASHI
viz media
www.viz.com
SHONEN JUMP ADVANCED
RATED T+ FOR OLDER TEEN
ratings.viz.com
HUNTERxHUNTER © POT (Yoshihiro Togashi) 1998, 2000

7th GAR7DEN

Awyn Gardner will do anything to protect the beautiful mistress of the equally beautiful estate gardens he lovingly tends—even enslave himself to an also beautiful demon bent on world domination! The high-pitched battle is on between powerful angels, sexy demons and innocent people to dominate a world rife with political intrigue...and to win the heart of one hapless human man!

Story & Art by
MITSU IZUMI

1

You're Reading in the Wrong Direction!!

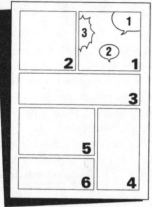

Whoops! Guess what? You're starting at the wrong end of the comic!

...It's true! In keeping with the original Japanese format, **Assassination Classroom** is meant to be read from right to left, starting in the upper-right corner.

Unlike English, which is read from left to right, Japanese is read from right to left, meaning that action, sound effects and word-balloon order are completely reversed... something which can make readers unfamiliar with Japanese feel pretty backwards themselves. For this reason, manga or Japanese comics published in the U.S. in English have sometimes been published "flopped"—that is, printed in exact reverse order, as though seen from the other side of a mirror.

By flopping pages, U.S. publishers can avoid confusing readers, but the compromise is not without its downside. For one thing, a character in a flopped manga series who once wore in the original Japanese version a T-shirt emblazoned with "M A Y" (as in "the merry month of") now wears one which reads "Y A M"! Additionally, many manga creators in Japan are themselves unhappy with the process, as some feel the mirror-imaging of their art skews their original intentions.

We are proud to bring you Yusei Matsui's **Assassination Classroom** in the original unflopped format.

For now, though, turn to the other side of the book and let the adventure begin...!

—Editor